America's Voluntary Spirit

A Book of Readings

America's Voluntary Spirit

A Book of Readings

Edited by

Brian O'Connell

Foreword by

The Honorable John W. Gardner

The Foundation Center
New York · 1983

This book is dedicated to more than
half of all Americans —

To the Givers and Volunteers

Table of Contents

The Independent Sector

JOHN W. GARDNER

In a totalitarian state, most organized activity is governmental—and the little that is not is heavily controlled or influenced by government. Almost everything is bureaucratized and subject to central goal-setting and rule-making.

In the nations that the world thinks of as democracies, there is, in contrast, a large area of activity outside of government. The United States probably outstrips all others in the size and autonomy of its nongovernmental sector. The major portion of our private sector consists of activities designed for profit; a smaller portion consists of nonprofit activities. Both profit and nonprofit segments have many dealings with government, but both recognize that their vitality depends in part on their success in holding themselves free of central bureaucratic definition of goals.

Our subject here is the nonprofit segment. It has been variously labelled the voluntary sector, the third sector or—more recently—the independent sector.

In its diversity and strength the voluntary sector is uniquely American—not in the fact of its existence, because it exists elsewhere, but in its extraordinary richness and variety. It encompasses a remarkable array of American institutions— libraries, museums, religious organizations, schools and colleges, organizations concerned with health and welfare, citizen action groups, neighborhood organizations and countless other groups such as Alcoholics Anonymous, the Urban League, the 4H Clubs, the Women's Political Caucus, the Salvation Army, and the United Way.

The Launching of Independent Sector

In recent years, interest in the voluntary sector has grown steadily. John D. Rockefeller 3rd, in the last years before his death, sought to alert others to the problems facing the sector.

In 1970, the Commission on Foundations and Private Philanthropy recommended the creation of a continuing body to concern itself with problems the Commission had addressed. Nothing came of it. In 1975, the Filer Commission recommended that a presidentially-appointed commission be formed. Again, nothing came of it.

Clearly, the institutions of the sector were deeply concerned about their future and needed some organized means of addressing their shared problems. Fortunately, excellent sponsors finally set out to fill the vacuum. In 1978, two established organizations, The Coalition of National Voluntary Organizations, familiarly known as CONVO, and the National Council on Philanthropy (NCOP), each of which represented very broad constituencies in the voluntary sector, asked Brian O'Connell to study the problem. On his recommendation, they created an Organizing Committee, which I chaired, charged with the design of a new organization encompassing virtually the whole nonprofit segment of the private sector. When the Organizing Committee submitted its report, the two sponsoring organizations voted themselves out of existence and launched Independent Sector.

The Concerns that Led to Action

It was not an unfocused concern that led to the formation of Independent Sector. Organizations in all parts of the sector shared quite explicit worries.

Private giving seemed to be eroding. At the same time, expectations for service had risen greatly; operating costs had escalated; and inflation had become an exceedingly heavy burden on a sector that is in its nature manpower-intensive. As a result of all these factors, many nonprofit institutions were in serious financial trouble.

During this same period, many nonprofits had also become increasingly dependent upon government. About 30 percent of the total revenue received by nonprofit institutions was supplied by government, and with the federal money came the federal rulebook. Never before had nonprofit agencies been more plagued with governmental regulations. It was evident that if the trend continued our voluntary institutions would become arms of the Federal government.

Nonprofit institutions were also concerned about the tax policies detrimental to private giving which had already been put into effect, as well as the even more stringent tax regulations which were being widely discussed.

For these and other reasons, nonprofit organizations and institutions had the sense of a foreshortened future. They felt that the walls were closing in.

Meeting the Needs of the Sector

The creation of the new organization was not a hasty act. For 15 months representatives of the various parts of the sector labored to design an organization that would serve *not* the whim of a few but rather the shared purposes of all who wished the sector well. The membership of the two sponsoring organizations included scores of diverse groups. The Organizing Committee was even broader in its makeup.

It was the Committee's intention to create an organization of modest size. It was *not* designed to bring order to a field whose tumultuous variety is its greatest source of creativity, nor to coordinate a sector that would break out in rebellion at the very thought of coordination. It was designed to serve the sector. The organizations of the sector are independent and intend to remain so. What we did set out to create was a "meeting ground" for the diverse institutions of the sector, a place where they could gather to discuss shared problems and plan appropriate action.

The Committee felt that one of our highest priorities was to improve public understanding of the sector, clarifying its role and function in American life. All Americans interact with voluntary or nonprofit agencies and activities regularly, though they are often unaware of this fact. They believe in the values and activities represented by the sector and if called upon, they would undoubtedly defend it ardently. Yet the thought never occurs to the public that the sector needs defending. Even people who spend their lives in the sector are not always aware of its function as a distinctive and valuable part of American life, nor do they fully understand the vigorous philanthropic activity that enables the sector to exist. It has remained too often "the invisible sector."

It also became clear to the Committee that we would have to stimulate far more research on the sector. There are libraries full of research and writings on the business sector and on government. In contrast, the body of writings on the nonprofit sector is modest indeed.

The Committee also concluded that it was essential to foster among the institutions of the sector a spirit and tradition of self-appraisal with respect to standards of performance, accessibility, and accountability. If private nonprofit institutions are to survive and retain their vitality, they must manage themselves well and serve community needs honestly and responsibly. It is important, for example, that funding organizations be accessible and accountable. Unfortunately, some nonprofit institutions are so poorly managed that they waste the money entrusted to them, and some no longer serve significant needs. There must be spirited discussion of the professed purposes and actual performance of nonprofit institutions.

Relations with Government

Finally, the Committee realized that we must address the relationship of non-profit institutions to various levels of government. There were a number of issues which had generated antagonism between these two sectors, but we had no intention of fostering an adversary relationship. Government and the voluntary sector have had important, often productive, relationships since colonial days. Government is necessary to the voluntary sector, and a vital voluntary sector is crucial to the nation's future. Our concern was to cope with the problems growing out of the relationship.

Some modes of government involvement do not significantly diminish the freedom and flexibility of the voluntary sector, while others stifle and rigidify nonprofit institutions. At the heart of the problem is the familiar conflict between the government's need for accountability and the private institution's need for independence. The tension between these two principles may never be resolved, but a compromise is possible—and essential. We must create procedures and arrangements that will effect a workable partnership.

One of the critically important problems shared by all institutions of the sector is the question of tax policy.

When people are left free to pursue all kinds of activities, as they are in this country, a surprising number will choose to serve some community purpose. The private pursuit of public purpose is an honored tradition in American life. Americans do not regard the furtherance of public purpose as a monopoly of government, and that belief has brought a great release of human energy.

Given the level of human commitment, one then needs another, more earthy ingredient—money. So it turns out that most of the activities of the nonprofit sector depend on another powerful American tradition—the tradition of private giving for public purposes. The ingredient of private giving supplies the element of freedom.

In the few foreign countries where there is any considerable private philanthropy, it is usually traceable to a few wealthy people. Only in the United States are the gifts of the wealthy simply the peak of a pyramid with a very, very broad base—a base of modest contributions made by millions of individuals. Few Americans realize how broad that base really is. In 1982, private giving totalled over $60 billion. Foundations and corporations accounted for a little more than 10 percent of that amount. The remaining 90 percent was given by individuals, roughly half of whom have incomes in the $25,000 range or less. For the most part private giving in this country is a Mississippi River of small gifts.

Government tax policy has deliberately fostered our tradition of giving. The tax deductibility of charitable gifts is a long-established means of furthering an authentically American idea—that it is a good thing for a great many people in their capacity as private citizens to contribute to charitable, religious, scientific, and educational activities of their choice. We have demonstrated that preserving a role for the private citizen in these matters encourages individual involvement and keeps alive the sense of personal caring and concern that is so essential if a mass society is to retain an element of humaneness.

The area of our national life encompassed by the charitable tax deduction lies at the very heart of our intellectual and spiritual strivings, at the very heart of our feeling about one another and about our life as a people. Traditionally, government leaders have agreed that here, if anywhere, government should keep its distance and the maximum degree of independence honored; here, if anywhere, the personal, family, and community spirit should be preserved; here, if anywhere, those elements of the human mind and spirit that wither under bureaucratization should have a place to stand free.

The policy has worked. It has permitted the emergence of great world centers of learning; it has made our museums and medical centers famous throughout the world; and it has nourished an enormous variety of neighborhood and community activities.

Have there been abuses? Of course, but they have been trivial compared to the great and lasting benefits in preserving our free society.

Attributes of the Sector

It is worth reviewing some of the characteristics of the independent sector that make it a powerfully positive force in American life. There is no point in comparing it favorably or unfavorably with other sectors of the society. Each has its function.

Perhaps the most striking feature of the sector is its relative freedom from constraints and its resulting pluralism. Within the bounds of the law, all kinds of people can pursue any idea or program they wish. Unlike government, an independent sector group need not ascertain that its idea or philosophy is supported by some large constituency, and unlike the business sector, they do not need to pursue only those ideas which will be profitable. If a handful of people want to back a new idea, they need seek no larger consensus.

Americans have always believed in pluralism—the idea that a free nation should be hospitable to many sources of initiative, many kinds of institutions, many conflicting beliefs, and many competing economic units. Our pluralism allows individuals and groups to pursue goals that they themselves formulate, and out of that pluralism has come virtually all of our creativity.

Every institution in the independent sector is not innovative, but the sector provides a hospitable environment for innovation. Ideas for doing things in a different, and possibly better, way spring up constantly. If they do not fill a need, they quickly fall by the wayside. What remains are the few ideas and innovations that have long-term value. New ideas and new ways of doing things test the validity of accepted practice and build an inventory of possible alternative solutions which can be used if circumstances change.

Government bureaucracies are simply not constructed to permit the emergence of countless new ideas, and even less suited to the winnowing out of bad ideas. An idea that is controversial, unpopular, or "strange" has little chance in either the commercial or the political marketplace. In the nonprofit sector, someone with a new idea or program may very well find the few followers necessary to help nurse it to maturity. Virtually every significant social idea of the past century in this country has been nurtured in the nonprofit sector.

The sector is the natural home of nonmajoritarian impulses, movements, and values. It comfortably harbors innovators, maverick movements, groups which feel that they must fight for their place in the sun, and critics of both liberal and conservative persuasion.

Institutions of the nonprofit sector are in a position to serve as the guardians of intellectual and artistic freedom. Both the commercial and political marketplaces are subject to leveling forces that may threaten standards of excellence. In the nonprofit sector, the fiercest champions of excellence may have their say. So may the champions of liberty and justice.

The sector preserves individual initiative and responsibility. As in the for-profit sector, there are innumerable opportunities for the resourceful—to initiate, explore, grow, cooperate, lead, make a difference. At a time in history when individuality is threatened by the impersonality of large-scale social organization, the sector's emphasis on individual initiative is a priceless counterweight.

To deal effectively with the ailments of our society today, individual initiative isn't enough, there has to be some way of linking the individual with the community. In the independent sector, such linkages are easily forged. Citizens banding together can tackle a small neighborhood problem or a great national issue.

The past century has seen a more or less steady deterioration of American communities as coherent entities with the morale and binding values that hold people together. Our sense of community has been badly battered, and every social philosopher emphasizes the need to restore it. What is at stake is the individual's sense of responsibility for something beyond the self. A spirit of concern for one's fellows is virtually impossible to sustain in a vast, impersonal, featureless society. Only in coherent human groupings (the neighborhood, the family, the community) can we keep alive our shared values and preserve the simple human awareness that we need one another. We must recreate a society that has its social and spiritual roots firmly planted in such groupings—so firmly planted that those roots cannot be ripped out by the winds of change, nor by the dehumanizing, automatizing forces of the contemporary world.

This is not to express a sentimental aversion to large-scale organization or national action. Many of the forces acting upon us can only be dealt with by large-scale organizations, national in scope, including a vigorous government. But if we intend that the overarching governmental organizations we create be our servants and not our masters, we must have vital communities.

The Great Shared Task

My observations about the positive aspects of the sector are not intended to gloss over the flaws that are evident in its institutions and organizations. Some nonprofit institutions are far gone in decay. Some are so badly managed as to make a mockery of every good intention they might have had. There is fraud, mediocrity, and silliness. In short, the human and institutional failures that afflict government and business are also present in the voluntary sector. Beyond that, it is the essence of pluralism (in the society as a whole as well as in this sector) that no particular observer will approve of everything that goes on. If you can't find a nonprofit institution that you can honestly disrespect, then something has gone wrong with our pluralism.

But these considerations are trivial compared to the attributes that make the independent sector a source of deep and positive meaning in our national life. If it were to disappear from our national life, we would be less distinctly American. The sector enhances our creativity, enlivens our communities, nurtures individual responsibility, stirs life at the grassroots, and reminds us that we were born free. Its vitality is rooted in good soil—civic pride, compassion, a philanthropic tradition, a strong problem-solving impulse, a sense of individual responsibility and, despite what cynics may say, an irrepressible commitment to the great shared task of improving our life together.

Introduction

From the earliest days of the organizing committee that created Independent Sector, we found ourselves at the disadvantage of not having at hand some of the best speeches, articles, chapters and papers that describe and define this side of American life. When we reached the stage of writing briefings and Congressional testimony, the frustration grew. It was difficult to locate descriptions, examples and statistics that backed up our passionate regard for the role and impact of this sector.

Because the need was so great, we did begin to uncover some very good resource material. We gradually found enough to realize that at every stage of this country's 300-year history, observers have been aware of the value of private philanthropy and voluntary action.

In the summer of 1980, I told John Gardner that I thought it would be useful for me to undertake a concerted search for more of the best pieces about America's third sector with an aim toward providing a book of readings for those who are writing and speaking about giving and volunteering. John's encouragement was so definite that it carried me through what has turned out to be a much larger project than envisioned. I've now been through close to 1,000 possibilities, and with almost every one, I came across other titles that should be explored. The project could be endless and deserves, at the very least, far more time than I've been able to give.

In choosing these forty-five selections, I've used the following criteria:

- Quality
- Representativeness, including different perspectives
- Long-term relevance, not dated or time limited. The articles are not necessarily timeless, but they still have relevance today.

I wanted the overall volume to provide a good overview of what this sector has meant and continues to mean to the American way of life and to be a valuable resource for speakers and writers. I was particularly determined that the book should represent a balanced view. If it turned out to be too glowing or con-gratulatory, it would not be accurate or useful. At the same time, I wanted it to be a manageable volume, rather than an all-inclusive tome.

The initial volume had about seventy-five pieces which would have made it the deadly tome I wanted to avoid. Still, the final decisions about which pieces to eliminate from the volume have been painful. There are a hundred or more that deserve to be here but aren't, and I'm afraid that includes many by good friends and associates. In the end I recognized that, at least for this first time around, I had to concentrate on an overview covering the 300 years and the vast diversity of the sector.

Some of the best writings I reviewed were too long and defied editorial cuts. Others were too scholarly for this particular volume, for example, the wonder-fully erudite examination of "Giving for a Return," by A. R. Hands, which examines the development of philanthropy in ancient Greece and Rome. One of my favorite essays, Thoreau's "Civil Disobedience," was finally left out because so much of the essay isn't immediately germaine and Thoreau's central point is reflected in other selections that are included. So it went—each decision a struggle between the value of any one selection and the need to keep the book manageable.

I have taken the liberty of editing some of the selections, but only when I felt the shorter, edited version allowed the author's intent to come ringing through.

Some readers with different perspectives may be concerned that I've left out some of their favorite pieces. Because so many good selections are not included and because the book is likely to call attention to excellent possibilities I've missed, I hope that this volume will stimulate other such anthologies, as well as more research and writing on the sector.

———————————————————

Throughout this experience, I've learned a great deal about this third part of our society. It would be impossible to summarize the major points of all the writers, but I do want to share five overall lessons.

The first is the remarkable size and pervasiveness of giving and volunteering in America. Every time I focus on this sector, I am more aware and encouraged that giving and volunteering are characteristic of our total population. We take appropriate pride in our foundations and in the growth of corporate public responsibility, but as important as these aspects of our philanthropic efforts are, they are dwarfed by the participation of individuals. Ninety percent of all giving in this country comes from individuals—85 percent through our living gifts and 5 percent through our bequests. Of our living gifts, just about half come from families with incomes under $20,000. Nine out of ten adults are regular givers, and more than half are regular volunteers. Every economic group is involved. The United States is the only country in the world where giving and volunteering are such pervasive characteristics of the total society.

The second lesson deals with the origins of our pluralism and generosity. I often hear people simplistically ascribe our participatory impulses to the Protestant ethic and English ancestry, but these are only two of many sources. Governor Winthrop's piece, "A Model of Christian Charity," makes clear that we owe a great deal to the Pilgrims and Puritans, but what we sometimes called "Christian" impulses were brought to our shores by many waves of immigrants whether they came from Sweden, Russia, China or India and whether they followed Jesus, Moses, Muhammad, or Buddha.

We also can't ascribe our tradition of voluntary action solely to religion and its lessons of goodness. The matter of pure need and mutual dependence and assistance cannot be overlooked. The Minute Men and the frontier families practiced pretty basic forms of enlightened self-interest. To portray our history of volunteering as relating solely to goodness may describe the best of our forebears, but it ignores the widespread tradition of organized neighborliness that hardship dictated and goodness tempered.

One of the most striking points in this lesson about the origins of American generosity is that we shouldn't even assume that these characteristics and traditions were imported. Robert Bremner's chapter, "Doing Good in the New World," makes clear that the Indians treated the early immigrants with far more "Christian" goodness than they practiced toward them. Bremner's descriptions of the kindly way in which the Indians greeted the intruding settlers and helped them adjust to their world dispels prior notions of imported goodness.

We came to a country where there was very little structure, and we had a chance to start all over again. For many, even the family hierarchy was absent. There were few built-in restraints imposed by centuries of laws and habits, and yet we were terribly interdependent. Daniel Boorstin's piece points out clearly that we had "communities before we had governments."

In the absence of families and controlling traditions, we demonstrated our human gregariousness by becoming, as Max Lerner describes, "a nation of joiners." These new institutions, whether they were churches, granges, fire companies or other specific organizations, became our networks for socializing and mutual activity.

It is also important to realize that we were a people determined not to be ruled, and therefore we were suspicious of central authority. We were resolved that power should be dispersed. This meant that voluntary institutions carried a large share of what governments did in other countries. Richard Lyman's piece reminds us of Burke's description of "the little platoons" that became our own way of dealing with dispersion of power and organization of mutual effort.

Several selections remind us that the words of the Declaration of Independence are not idle pronouncements. We do believe in the rights and powers of the people, and those convictions cause us to stand up and be counted on a broad array of issues.

As we experienced the benefits of so much citizen participation, including the personal satisfactions such action provides, we have become all the more committed to this kind of participatory society. Along the way, we have constantly renewed our faith in the basic intelligence and ability of people.

This list of origins of our pluralism is obviously not exhaustive, but it does make clear that our patterns and levels of giving and voluntary association have many roots. For those of us who presume some responsibility to preserve and strengthen citizen participation, it is important to understand and nurture all of them.

The third lesson involves the ease and danger of overestimating and glorifying this sector. As important as it is, we tend to give it even more credit than it deserves, and we lose our credibility as advocates for it. Pablo Eisenberg in "The Voluntary Sector: Problems and Challenges," Waldemar Nielsen in "The Third Sector: Keystone of a Caring Society," and others remind us of the sector's limitations and problems. We lose our perspective on the sector and our society when we exaggerate the importance of private philanthropy and voluntary organizations, particularly when we put them ahead of our responsibility to democratic government.

It is important to be reminded of the basic values of American society: the freedom, worth, and dignity of the individual; equal opportunity; justice; and mutual responsibility. Our largest vehicles for preserving and enhancing those basic values are:

Representative government starting with one person/one vote

The freedoms of speech and assembly

The free press

A system of justice beginning with due process and presumption of innocence

Universal public education

An active voluntary sector helps preserve and enhance these larger vehicles, but it doesn't transcend them.

The fourth lesson that has been reinforced is the importance of the independence of this sector. There are many contributions that the institutions of this sector make, including providing services and acting as vehicles through which the government fulfills some of its public responsibilities, but the largest contribution is the independence it provides for innovation and criticism.

The great movements of our society have had their origins in this independent sector. Most of those who led those efforts were viewed as unpopular, troublesome, rabble-rousing, and maybe even dangerous. One of our largest responsibilities is to keep open the freedoms which allow their successors to establish the new causes of tomorrow.

Finally, although it is important not to exaggerate the worth of voluntary effort and the giving that supports it, it is also important not to underestimate how much this participation contributes to our opportunities to be unique as individuals and as a society. Through our voluntary initiative and independent institutions, ever more Americans worship freely, study quietly, are cared for compassionately, experiment creatively, serve effectively, advocate aggressively, and contribute generously. These national traits are constantly beautiful and, hopefully, will remain beautifully constant.

Brian O'Connell
McLean, Virginia
January 20, 1983

Acknowledgements

John Gardner has been the sounding board on this effort from my initial question whether the idea made sense. For his patient advice, his patience when I didn't follow his advice, and his willingness to write the Foreword to this book, my great thanks.

I'm indebted to the many authors and publishers who granted permission to reproduce their work.

Tom Buckman, President of The Foundation Center, showed early interest in the project which was encouragement of itself, but his continuing attention and his assignment of Pat Read as editor have really pulled me along. Pat has been critical, efficient, and kind—a rare and awfully nice combination in that role.

Nancy Snyder's painstaking work in copyediting the bibliography and proofreading the manuscript numerous times was invaluable. Penny Jones provided assistance in preparing an index to a collection whose diversity and historic content defies traditional indexing approaches.

Beverly With of INDEPENDENT SECTOR has carried the administrative assignment from the start and has kept what has often been a terribly disorganized enterprise organized and flowing. She and I benefitted tremendously by the willingness of her assistant, Lori Rimby, to accept the difficult outside assignment of typing the manuscript.

Fern Portnoy and The Piton Foundation gave a small grant to INDEPENDENT SECTOR to help me secure part-time editorial assistance for several projects, and part of the gift was used for some of the research and typing costs of this undertaking. It's a lesson in grantmaking that without even that modest boost, I would not have felt free to push on with the project.

My greatest thanks by far go to Ann Brown O'Connell who searched exhaustively, read endlessly, participated enthusiastically, and bore neglect understandingly. It was not a good time for so large a side project. Without her involvement and forbearance, it could never ever have been done.

With acknowledgement and appreciation.
Brian O'Connell

America's Voluntary Spirit

Spirit

A Book of Readings

1

Our Religious Heritage

A very large part of America's attractive voluntary spirit stems from our religious heritage. The lessons are as varied as the religions of the hundreds of groups that came and still come to our shores. The common root of these varied testaments is an awareness that service beyond self is both an obligation and a joy. It is the ultimate universal truth.

Even the new religions share the belief taught by Jesus, Moses, Mohammed, and Buddha and expressed in the Bible, Old Testament, Koran, commandments, Torah, or any contemporary equivalent, that of all the virtues to be made part of each of us, the greatest is charity.

Even those who find meaning in life without religion have a grasp of these lessons. Confucius articulated this belief when he said that "goodness is God," by which he meant that God may not necessarily be a supreme being apart from us but at least is a supreme state of being within us.

The following selections represent some of the best theological references on charity and the spirit of giving.

Zedakah and the Highest Degree of Almsgiving—As Handed Down by Moses Maimonides and the Torah*

"We are duty bound to be more needful with regard to the discharge of the commandment relating to charity than with all the other precepts of the Torah, for benevolence is the characteristic of the righteous descendants of

---

*These excerpts are drawn from *The World of Moses Maimonides,* by Jacob S. Minkin (New York: Thomas Yoseloff Press, 1957), pp. 45-49.

the seed of Abraham, our father, of whom it is said, 'For I know him to the end that he command his children and his household after him that they may keep the way of the Lord, to do zedakah.'" (**Gen. 18:19**)

"Zedakah implies the fullest obligation that people owe to one another. Zedakah calls for more than mere almsgiving, because in its exercise there must be kindness, tenderness, not to shame the poor or put him to disgrace. Sacred unto the Lord is the human dignity and personality of the recipient of charity, and they must not be hurt or lowered. Moreover, of greater merit than giving to the poor, is to help him to become self-supporting." (**Sab. 63a**)

"There are eight degrees in the giving of charity, one higher than the other. The highest degree, than which there is nothing higher, is to take hold of a Jew who has been crushed and to give him a gift or a loan, or to enter into partnership with him, or to find work for him, and thus put him on his feet that he will not be dependent on his fellow-men."

Isaiah 58: 6-9 (Old Testament)

"Is not this the fast that I choose: to loose the bonds of wickedness, to undo the thongs of the yoke, to let the oppressed go free, and to break every yoke?

"Is it not to share your bread with the hungry, and bring the homeless poor into your house; when you see the naked, to cover him, and not to hide yourself from your own flesh?

Then shall your light break forth like the dawn, and your healing shall spring up speedily; your righteousness shall go before you, the glory of the Lord shall be your rear guard.

Then you shall call, and the Lord will answer; you shall cry, and he will say, Here I am."

Matthew 25: 31-46 (New Testament)

"When the Son of man comes in his glory, and all the angels with him, then he will sit on his glorious throne. Before him will be gathered all the nations, and he will separate them one from another as a shepherd separates the sheep from the goats, and he will place the sheep at his right hand, but the goats at the left. Then the King will say to those at his right hand, 'Come, O blessed of my Father, inherit the kingdom prepared for you from the foundation of the world; for I was hungry and you gave me food, I was thirsty and you gave me drink, I was a stranger and you welcomed me, I was naked and you clothed me, I was sick and you visited me, I was in prison and you came to me.' Then the righteous will answer him, 'Lord, when did we see thee hungry and feed thee, or thirst and give thee drink? And when did we see thee a stranger and welcome thee, or naked and clothe thee? And when did we see thee sick or in prison and visit thee?' And the King will answer them, 'Truly, I say to you, as you did it to one of the least of these my brethren, you did it to me.'"

II Corinthians 9: 6-7 (New Testament)

"The point is this: he who sows sparingly will also reap sparingly, and he who sows bountifully will also reap bountifully. Each one must do as he has made up his mind, not reluctantly or under compulsion, for God loves a cheerful giver."

Our well-known theological references often give the impression that these universal lessons were discovered by Western religions, when in fact some of the much older Eastern sects preached these truths long before. For example, in Hinduism, there are repeated references to sacrifice, charity, and almsgiving, such as:

"Expend in alms in God's way and the rest cast by your own hands into perdition; but do good, for God loves those who do good."

"The more that he expends for others, the more does he possess of his own; the more that he gives to others, the more does he have himself."

Perhaps the most familiar of all the theological references is the following selection from **I Corinthians 13: 1-13** (as interpreted here by Catholic Gospel).

"And I point out to you a yet more excellent way. If I should speak with the tongues of men and of angels, but do not have charity, I have become as sounding brass or a tinkling cymbal. And if I have prophecy and know all mysteries and all knowledge, and if I have all faith so as to remove mountains, yet do not have charity, I am nothing. And if I distribute all my goods to feed the poor, and if I deliver my body to be burned, yet do not have charity, it profits me nothing.

"Charity is patient, is kind; charity does not envy, is not pretentious, is not puffed up, is not ambitious, is not self-seeking, is not provoked; thinks no evil, does not rejoice over wickedness, but rejoices with the truth; bears with all things, believes all things, hopes all things, endures all things.

"Charity never fails, whereas prophecies will disappear, and tongues will cease, and knowledge will be destroyed. For we know in part and we prophesy in part; but when that which is perfect has come, that which is imperfect will be done away with. When I was a child, I spoke as a child, I felt as a child, I thought as a child. Now that I have become a man, I have put away the things of a child. We see now through a mirror in an obscure manner, but then face to face. Now I know in part, but then I shall know even as I have been known. So there abide faith, hope and charity, these three; but the greatest of these is charity."

2

Pre-Christian Philanthropy

WARREN WEAVER

WARREN WEAVER, MATHEMATICIAN, RESEARCH SCIENTIST, AND
AUTHOR, SERVED FOR 27 YEARS AS DIRECTOR OF THE
ROCKEFELLER FOUNDATION.

Philanthropy is not a modern invention. Concern for one's fellow men extends back to ancient times. A wide range of incentives leads individuals to altruistic action. The human family has presumably always contained a few prideful persons who would use almost any method to perpetuate their power and fame, but also many who aid their fellow men for religious reasons based partly on unselfish motives and partly on concern for their own salvation.

The acts through which philanthropic motivation is expressed have changed greatly since older times, reflecting alterations in social structures, in ways of thinking, and in the practical opportunities available for helping others.

Communication and transport in the modern world, for example, have profoundly influenced the range of concern of both individuals and states. No one could worry many years ago about the illness and hunger of people in a distant part of the world of which he had never heard. Centuries ago, men who asked Cain's question "Am I my brother's keeper?" necessarily thought only of close relatives and near neighbors. They could not have been disturbed about the condition of men in equatorial Africa or in Southeast Asia, for they were unaware of their existence and their needs. Even if they had known, they would have been powerless to act.

Not only recent scientific and technological advances, but other major changes in man's political, intellectual, and social life have altered the concepts and practices of philanthropy. The rise in power of the medieval church, the Reformation, the Industrial Revolution, the development of the free enterprise

Reprinted from *U.S. Philanthropic Foundations: Their History, Structure, Management, and Record*, Chapter 1, by Warren Weaver. Copyright ©1967 by the American Academy of Arts & Sciences. By permission of Harper & Row Publishers, Inc.

system in our own country, the creation of great personal fortunes—movements such as these have greatly influenced both the concepts of philanthropy and the ways in which these concepts are realized.

Unselfishness is not wholly a human invention. An article in a recent scientific journal on "The Evolution of Altruism" reported that some seventy million years ago, as is known from fossil records of Miocene times, there existed organized societies of termites and ants. Within such insect societies—bees, wasps, ants, and others—there were then, and still are, groups whose activities can in some broad sense be labeled as altruistic, with members of these groups performing specialized functions for the good of the larger society, often at individual sacrifice. For example, insects that are specialized servants of the larger group are themselves usually sexless.

There are "great difficulties in explaining, by the classical theory of natural selection, any case of behavior by which an animal promotes the advantages of other members of the species, not his direct descendants, at the expense of his own."[1] In circumstances where the gain to the group is more than double the loss to the individual, such behavior can, however, be explained.

More recently a biologist, studying the chain of life in the sea, found "support for a community theory of evolution according to which short-term advantages to individual species are sacrificed for long-term benefits for an entire living community."[2]

"Many people would be surprised to learn the extent to which animals help their own kind. Even the popular view of the wild animals of Africa as ferocious beasts, 'red in tooth and claw,' is at least partially mistaken. Throughout the animal world there is much behavior which is peaceful, cooperative and even 'altruisitic.'"[3]

Such creatures as wolves, so fierce in all legends, turn out to have been greatly maligned. The great arctic explorer V. Stefansson tried for many years to run down on this continent, in Russia, and elsewhere, an authentic case in which packs of wolves had attacked one or more humans. He found not one reliable incident.[4] Indeed, recent experience has indicated that wolves, if met with understanding and kindness, respond fully as affectionately as do domesticated dogs.[5]

It is thus interesting to observe that altruistic behavior is an invention of nature herself; that the earliest philanthropic activity occurred many millions of years before *Homo sapiens* appeared; and that nature must value such behavior, since she has seen fit to continue it over vast periods of time.

Sir Arthur Keith, in his *New Theory of Human Evolution*, has said:

> Altruism is both inborn and instinctive. The explanation of the origin of altruism which I would offer is very similar to that given by Darwin. Altruism is a vast expansion of family sympathy. Family sympathy has a diffusive

and exuberant quality; it becomes wider and wider in its influence, until it
includes all members of the primal group; it again expands when groups are
fused into tribes and again when tribes are combined to form nations. The
peoples that have survived to form the large nations of modern times are
those which are gifted with a full endowment of generous sympathy, a
quality nearly akin to altruism.[6]

Some cultures, especially those operating on slender survival margins, adopt
harsh measures in their treatment of the infirm aged, the handicapped, and the
seriously ill. But the charitable urge to help those in need is of ancient origin.
At the time of the Five Rulers in China, more than two thousand years before
Christ, it was recorded by Li Ki that oriental families recognized the needs of
the fatherless, of the old man with no wife or sons, and of the elderly woman
with no husband; and regular allowances were provided for them.

Tithing, or the giving of one-tenth of income, was not limited to the
Hebrews. It was a form of taxation for general purposes in many lands; but
among the Hebraic peoples it was "a religiously sanctioned gift to God and the
poor." Indeed, the ancient Hebrews left much evidence of their commitment to
the "blessed obligation" of *hesed*, translated in the Old Testament as "mercy",
with the corresponding word in the New Testament translated as "charity".

However, the very phrase "blessed obligation" at least in part implies that
those who are charitable will be rewarded. And the wish to propitiate the gods
played an important role in many of the earliest efforts to establish procedures
by means of which an individual could set aside a part of his wealth and could
provide that, after his death and theoretically forever, these funds would be
used to preserve his memory and ensure the peace of his soul.

Thus Harkhuf, an Egyptian nobleman who lived some twenty-three hundred
years before Christ, saw to it that his charities were recorded on his tomb, the
hieroglyphs stating that he had given these gifts because "I desired that it might
be well with me in the great god's presence."

This and comparable acts of the Pharaohs "are the earliest known efforts at
projecting private will beyond life...they constitute the most rudimentary form
of the foundation."[7]

These methods to control after death the use of wealth were available to
rulers, but the ordinary man of the ancient world was more restricted in his
opportunities. In our modern sense, the right to make a will and testament of
the total property of a man did not exist until about 500 B.C. Although there
were many more ancient exceptions in connection with mortuary and temple
service, there were nevertheless strong traditions of family inheritance. Not
only then, but to some extent even now, both custom and law affect the rights of
a spouse and those of the first-born heir.

F. Emerson Andrews, the president of the Foundation Library Center and a man who has for many years been a wise and dedicated student of foundation procedures, has emphasized the distinction between the concept of giving that resulted from Judeo-Christian influences and, on the other hand, the concept that seems to have found its first important expression with the Greeks and the early Romans.[8]

The former of these is best characterized by the word "charity." This kindly word, which, in its early Latin form *caritas* and its Greek form *charis*, meant in the first instance a high price—dearness—came to signify grace and gratitude. It was not used, in either Latin or Greek, in connection with affectionate relations between members of a family; but always referred to the good-will relation of an individual to those outside his own family. Thus in the Judeo-Christian tradition charity is a merciful giving, sanctified by the Church, and chiefly directed toward the immediate needs of the hungry, the sick, the suffering. This is the kind of unselfish direct assistance that we associate with the Good Samaritan.

Among the Greeks and Romans, however, the object of the giving was not really individual needy people, but rather the public at large. The intent was not so much to relieve suffering as to enrich life. This broader Greek concept of giving is more closely related to that of the modern philanthropic foundation than is the Judeo-Christian concept of charitable giving. Indeed, most modern foundations, and almost all the large ones, exclude gifts for personal relief. The modern foundation almost never entirely eliminates the wholly natural desire of the founder, traceable back to the earliest examples, that his donations bring esteem to him while alive and honor to his memory after he dies. But the modern foundation adds new depth and power to the Greek philosophy of giving.

One of the most notable and familiar expressions of the Greek concept of philanthropy was Plato's academy. Founded in Athens about 387 B.C., it was largely devoted to theories of ideas, to cosmogony, and to general theories of knowledge and perception. Education, in the utopian society Plato sponsored, involved heavy emphasis on music and gymnastics. Plato considered that the aim of culture was to produce gentlemen, using this word in a sense that Jefferson would have understood and approved.

Plato left this academy, along with an endowment of productive land, to a nephew, with the stipulation that it was to be administered for the benefit of Plato's student-followers. The nephew, in turn, left the foundation—for it was in effect that—to Xenocrates for use by personnel of the school. In the absence of means for setting up a permanent legal entity which could assure continuance, the plan was for each owner-director, during his life, to turn over the property to a living legal heir who could hopefully be trusted to carry on.

It is interesting to note that in Plato's great pupil Aristotle there was, as Bertrand Russell has observed "...an almost complete absence of what may be called benevolence or philanthropy. The sufferings of mankind, in so far as he is aware of them, do not move him emotionally; he holds them, intellectually, to be an evil, but there is no evidence that they cause him unhappiness except when the sufferers happen to be his friends."[9]

In the Greek tradition of broad gifts for the populace as a whole, the Athenian citizen Herodes Atticus gave a water supply to the city of Troas, a theatre to Corinth, a stadium to Delphi, aqueducts for Canusium in Italy, baths for Thermopylae. Many if not most of the other benefactions of that period were similar to his. These community-wide gifts were not "charity" in the Judeo-Christian sense. They were more closely related to what we today call philanthropy.

Pre-Christian Rome largely followed the Greek pattern of benefactions for the populace. Later, however, the Judeo-Christian type of charity did appear in many Roman municipalities, which had organizations to aid in the feeding, clothing, and educating of needy children. The division between the two concepts of giving was never absolute nor permanent.

During the closing years of the pre-Christian era, important developments in Roman custom and law liberalized the rules governing inheritance and began to furnish a dependable continuity for philanthropic activities.

In 150 B.C. Roman law further broadened the legal heir concept by declaring charitable organizations to be both "sentient reasonable beings" and also "immutable undying persons....This interpretation gave foundations immutability plus all the advantages of natural heirs save the right to receive bequests."[10] However paradoxical that ruling, it was undoubtedly important to the birth of the permanent foundation idea and, indeed, to the legal concept of a corporation.

Following these advantages gained about 150 B.C., "foundation-like" organizations—guilds, societies, and *collegia*, which were somewhat like modern fraternal organizations—grew in number and activities. Along with their financial strength, their political power increased. And because of just such political involvements, the Roman Senate, in 65 B.C., restrained the philanthropic associations. In A.D. 96, however, with the beginning of the reign of the "five good emperors," the early "foundations" recovered their good standing and their privilege of permanence. Nerva accorded the cities the right to accept and administer bequests of funds; Trajan extended this privilege to towns and Hadrian to villages; and, important indeed from our point of view, Marcus Aurelius permitted even private groups to receive bequests.

The foundation idea had been born.

Notes

1. Hans Kalmus, "The Evolution of Altruism," *New Scientist*, London, November 28, 1963, p. 550.

2. Gordon Riley of Yale University: News release 64-145 by National Science Foundation, October 5, 1964.

3. "The Compassionate Creatures," *The Sciences*, New York Academy of Sciences, Vol. 4, No. 9, February, 1965, p. 5.

4. V. Stefansson, *Adventures in Error*, Robert M. McBride & Co., New York, 1936.

5. Lois Crisler, *Arctic Wild*, Harper & Brothers, 1958.

6. Sir Arthur Keith, *New Theory of Human Evolution*, Watts & Co., London, 1949, p. 451.

7. Ernest Victor Hollis, "Evolution of the Philanthropic Foundation," *Educational Record*, American Council on Education, Washington, D.C., October, 1939, p. 576.

8. F. Emerson Andrews, *Philanthropic Giving*, Russell Sage Foundation, New York, 1950, pp. 31-35.

9. Bertrand Russell, *A History of Western Philanthropy*, Simon & Schuster, New York, 1945, p. 183.

10. Hollis, *op. cit.*, p. 577.

3

Roots of Voluntarism

ROSEMARY HIGGINS CASS AND
GORDON MANSER

ROSEMARY HIGGINS CASS AND GORDON MANSER SERVED AS
PRESIDENT AND EXECUTIVE DIRECTOR, RESPECTIVELY, OF THE
NATIONAL ASSEMBLY FOR SOCIAL POLICY AND DEVELOPMENT.

One must search far back in the history of western man for the origins of voluntary effort. From the very beginnings of human experience, as modern sociology and anthropology have evidenced, man has striven to share with as well as to destroy his fellowman. Starting with the family, the kin, and extending to the tribe and the early communities, men and women had to cooperate just to survive in the face of hostile environments, as well as of hostile strangers.

Over time efforts to "promote or advance some aspect of the common good" have taken two forms, either individual or associational. As we shall see, the pages of western history recount numberless instances of individual effort to promote the common good—frequently at great sacrifice or even risk. The impluse for these acts is to be found in the Judeo-Christian ethos of love, justice, and mercy. The millions of volunteers of every type in our society today can trace their lineage and inspiration to these devoted efforts.

Although people have banded together since the beginnings of time for many reasons, modern associational forms of voluntary effort were stimulated by the Reformation and its accompanying movement toward freedom of association, flowered with the urbanization of society during the industrial revolution, and experienced their greatest expansion during the twentieth century. These organizations exist to fulfill an incredible variety of purposes, ranging from the individual needs of their members to services to individuals and to communities.

The history of voluntary organizations which in some way or other serve others illuminates two rather contrary approaches to the solution of problems of human need which have existed down to the present day, perplexing the greatest minds of all ages. One view emanating from the Greek and Roman experi-

Reprinted from *Voluntarism at the Crossroads*, by Rosemary Higgins Cass and Gordon Manser (New York: Family Service Association of America, 1976) by permission of the publisher.

ence sought social reform as the answer to the social problems of the community. Another view, principally derived from the early Judeo-Christian heritage, believed that there was little one could do to overcome or change the particular social status in which one found oneself. One sought to alleviate the sufferings of one's fellow human beings as they passed through this "vale of tears," confident with Saint Paul that "the sufferings of this life were not worthy to be compared to the glory of the next." Thus, while the concept of mutual aid is as old as mankind itself, its evolution took two divergent paths, one very ancient which was only revived in the seventeenth and eighteenth centuries and the other which had its flowering in medieval times and is still of tremendous significance in voluntary effort today, but inadequate of itself. What is evident today is that both individual service and social reform are necessary if we are to solve the myriad social problems with which we find ourselves confronted.

In looking briefly at the chronicle of voluntary effort one is struck by the extent to which it has contributed to the development and shaping of governmental services, and conversely, the extent to which governmental services have in turn tended to shape the direction of voluntary effort. Thus, passing reference to some of the more significant public developments provides a frame of reference for better understanding of the role of voluntary effort. Similarly, the role of organized religion as a source of education, social welfare, health, and other services has been of crucial importance throughout history even as today. At no time was this more important than during the Middle Ages when the church was virtually the only organized force which perpetuated the Judeo-Christian ethic through tangible acts of service and mercy.

While Greek democracy was far removed in practice from our concept of democracy—excluding women, slaves, and the foreign-born from citizenship—some of its most renowned thinkers, such as Solon and Cleisthenes, sought both privately and through legislation to institute social reforms designed to lift up the poorer citizens and remove some of the burdens they bore. However, charity and philanthropy were not conspicuous virtues among the early Greeks, and Aristotle was constrained to commend foreign examples of benevolence in his *Politics*, while he endeavored to point out that, unless the purposes of civil and social life were carefully considered by those seeking to effect change, no amount of individual or associated action would be sufficient.

Similar to the Grecian was the Roman attitude toward the needs of the disadvantaged. While the sufferings of the poor stirred the consciences of few of the wealthy Romans, there were some with power who sought social reform. Tiberius Gracchus and his brother, Caius, were instrumental in the achievement of land reform—for which they sacrificed their lives. Tiberius had witnessed the starvation and idleness of the Roman citizens while wealthy men of the province of Tuscany profited by the labor of slaves on their vast land holdings. Curiously, the *lex frumentaria* of Caius, which gave Roman citizens the right to purchase grain from the public stores at about half price, began the demoralization of the Roman plebians. This system continued until the greater part of the Roman populace was enabled to live in idleness, dependent on what came to be a free distribution of grain at the public charge. No one of the emperors dared to change this system because the Roman citizen was a voter and would support whoever gave him bread and circuses. Perhaps, if the warnings of Aristotle had been known and listened to, the strengths of the Roman Empire would not have been dissipated and other social reforms leading to more humane conditions for all would have been introduced. Or, had Seneca, the Roman philosopher who saw man's obligation to do good to everyone, been listened to, again the course of history might have been different.[1]

What did appear on the scene and saved western civilization from disappearing entirely when the Germanic hordes began to besiege the Empire was a new philosophy of life which, in its purest form, embodied the highest concept of assistance to others. This was Christianity, whose founder had said, "This is my commandment, that you love one another as I have loved you. Greater love than this no one has, that one lay down his life for his friends" (John 15: 12-15).

Christianity had its roots in Judaism and stemmed from a tradition of help which had developed over hundreds of years. Among the Jewish people the duty of kindness to the poor, to the widows and to the fatherless was constantly shown to be pleasing to God. More than this, their notion of justice included all ethical conduct. The word for charity in Hebrew is *sedakah* or righteousness. Nowhere is the whole concept better expressed than in the oft-quoted words of Micah, "What doth the Lord require of thee, but to do justice and to love mercy and to walk humbly with thy God" (Micah 6).[2]

Many of the precepts of the Jewish tradition are spelled out in the Old Testament, particularly in the Book of Deuteronomy where Moses says, in Chapter 14, 28-29, for example:

> At the end of every three years you shall bring forth all the tithe of your produce in the same year, and lay it up within your towns; and the Levite, because he has no portion of inheritance with you, and the sojourner, the fatherless, and the widow, who are within your towns, shall come and eat and be filled....

The stories of Ruth and Naomi and the help extended to them by Boaz, and of Tobias who daily went about helping the afflicted are typical illustrations of the charity which inspired many of the ancient Jews, the same charity which enabled them to endure and to assist one another through centuries, first of domination by other nations and later of bitterest Christian persecution.

The eight degrees of charity defined by Maimonides in the Middle Ages spell out further the purpose and dignity of the Jewish concept of charity. Lowest on the scale is charity given meagerly and by a person as if forced; somewhat higher is charity contributed adequately but only after it is asked for; even better is aid given in such a manner that neither the giver nor the person assisted knows the identity of the other; and highest of all is assistance that enables a person to achieve self-support by helping him to find work or to open a business. Thus the concept of social justice has always been at the core of Jewish values. On three things the world rests, the rabbis have said: (1) the study of the Torah—the body of religious precepts and teachings, (2) prayers, and (3) acts of loving-kindness, embracing not only gifts of funds but also personal service. It is this same charity that has succeeded today in building a vast network of the finest humanitarian services ever known to exist.

One of the dominant aspects of the Christian message was its universality. No one was exempted—neither rich nor poor, man nor woman, the known sinner, the feared and often despised foreigner, the freeman nor slave. The idea of spiritual freedom which made all people brothers and sisters, the promise of another life of true happiness, the notion of sharing with one another—these revolutionary concepts were greatly appealing not just to the poor and the disenfranchised, but gradually to the wealthy and powerful, who began to accept and then themselves to promote the new message.[3]

The early Christian communities endeavored to provide help to the poor, the sick, and the afflicted. A little later came the monasteries, at first built far from the cities and thus removed from the people, and then gradually, between the fifth and the ninth centuries, coming to serve as oases of learning and help to those in need.[4] In these centuries, when the conversion of a tribal leader or king meant the conversion of all his people, the knowledge and the practice of Jesus' message of love of one another was not easily achieved. Neither warring lords, eager to consolidate their power, nor poverty-stricken peasantry struggling just to survive against the physical elements had time or inclination to do other than ignore the beggars who were everywhere, and cast out the most unfortunately ill—the lepers, those who had the plague, and the mentally ill. On the other side, church leaders, missionaries, bishops, and priests waged a continual struggle, reminding all of their common brotherhood of their duty to share with one another, to love as Christ had loved.

With the advent of Charlemagne and the birth of the Holy Roman Empire in the year 800 there began a somewhat uneasy marriage of church and state which endured for the next five centuries and brought extremes of greatness and of depravity. This year saw in the Cluniac reform a vast expansion of monasteries which were seats both of learning and of social services of every kind, and, in the spirit of St. Francis of Assisi, the beginnings of lay movements to help the poor, the sick and the old. On the other hand the Crusades, which had ostensibly been initiated to free the Holy Land from the hands of the Mohammedans, became at the hands of many unscrupulous warriors the occasion for plunder, rape, and the persecution and killing of Jews and Mohammedans. Paradoxically the same Crusades were responsible for the development of many kinds of voluntary assistance which have existed down to modern times. Though antedating the Crusades, the hospices in Jerusalem for the pilgrim and the sick spread to western Europe and groups of men, religiously inspired, formed what became known as groups of hospitalers. At the same time the privations of captivity came to the fore during this epoch and several religious orders were founded to help and to free the captive.[5] Meanwhile, at home the feudal system provided a type of rudimentary welfare in that the lord or the count considered himself responsible to provide not only protection for his people but also, in exchange for their labor, assistance in time of illness or famine.

In the aftermath of the Crusades came the great Bubonic Plague of the early fourteenth century. Already, cities had begun to wield dominant influence, to create new social and political patterns, and to reflect new associational forms. The older agrarian economy was beginning to yield to one dominated by trade and commercial enterprise, cities had begun to win their freedom from bishops and princes, and a new class of free citizens developed. Interestingly, the medieval guilds which were found in all these cities and which provided aid to members and their families were probably the first to assess their members for a type of insurance premium so as to provide for the widows and children of prematurely deceased guild members.

The plague decimated Europe's population and within a few years of its eruption was taking the life of one out of every three persons. There was no cure for it and so the ministrations of the countless religiously inspired served only to alleviate the pain of the dying and to bring spiritual comfort. The bravery of persons like Johannes Tauler in France, Catherine of Siena in Italy, Philipp Nicolai in Germany, Valerius Herberger in Poland, to name but a few, served as both example and inspiration to their fellowman.

Throughout medieval history there is little, if any, emphasis on social reform. Charity is commanded by Jesus but as interpreted it is charity to the individual. The results of the Reformation, cataclysmic in so many ways, were to affect as well the multitude of these charitable endeavors which had become part and parcel of the western experience. Foremost among these activities had been aid to the poor, which all over Europe took the form of almsgiving. Gradually the monasteries had been partially replaced by "hospitals" (*Hotels Dieu*) which ministered to the old, the sick, pregnant women, and abandoned children. But many were left to wander the countryside and it was these to whom the Church had said it was charity to give. Meanwhile, local and state governments sought to contend with the beggars, many of whom were able-bodied, and as far back as the time of Charlemagne, a statute was enacted forbidding the giving of alms to those who could be self-sustaining.

The struggle was exacerbated by the Reformation. Luther appealed to the princes of Germany to forbid begging and instead to organize in each parish a "common chest" out of which food, clothing, and money would be distributed to the needy. Similar plans for relief were set up in Switzerland, France, Austria, and Scandinavia. In this same period the forerunners of the modern social worker, the Daughters of Charity, were founded in France by St. Vincent de Paul to devote themselves to the charitable work, especially that of nursing the poor.[6]

Meanwhile in England, where all of the monasteries and convents had been secularized by Henry VIII and their properties confiscated by the state, it became necessary to devise some new method for the care of the poor, who had formerly been cared for voluntarily by groups within the Church. A series of enactments in the sixteenth century by the English Parliament culminated in the adoption of a codification known as the Poor Law of 1601. Responsibility for the poor, now recognized as governmental, rested with the local community, the parish, but was limited to persons who had been born there or had been resident for three years. Funds were provided by a general tax. Three classes of poor were distinguished: (1) the able-bodied poor who were sent to workhouses or, if they refused to work, to jails, (2) the impotent poor, those who were unable to work and who were either sent to almshouses to live or, if it were less expensive to maintain them in their homes, given food, clothing and fuel, and (3) dependent children, some of whom were placed with any person willing to keep them, or sold to the lowest bidder, or indentured to a townsperson to learn a trade, the boys until they were twenty-four years of age and the girls until they reached their twenty-first year or were married.

With some modifications these laws prevailed in England until well into the nineteenth century, when in the wave of the Industrial Revolution various social reform movements for better health, better working conditions, and housing and prison reform culminated in a number of pieces of legislation making more humane the conditions for all of the poor and the disadvantaged. Important too in this era was the creation in London in 1869 of the Society for Organizing Charitable Relief and Repressing Mendicity, shortly to be known as the Charity Organization Society, which coordinated the activities of private and public charities. Its format soon provided a model for similar groups in other cities in Europe and the United States. Operating on the philosophy first put into practice by the Reverend Thomas Chalmers, a Scottish minister, of helping the poor to help themselves, and emphasizing an individualistic approach as well as seeking to find a solution to the cause of the problems of the poor, the Charity Organization Society laid the early foundations for what we today call "case-work."[7]

What is noteworthy of the period in history from the Protestant Reformation to the present day is the ever-increasing necessity for the involvement of government in the solution of the problems of health, social welfare, education, housing, and working conditions. Starting with the vacuum precipitated when the Christian Church was displaced in its efforts to care for the needs of the people, fostered by Lutheran teachings about work and the separation of church and state; impelled by the unification of nations; and further carried along by the tumultous changes in the aftermath of the Industrial Revolution, the scientific advances, and the concomitant population increases—governments, at first most reluctantly, came to recognize the responsibility, which they alone could meet, for providing for their citizenry what the citizens alone could not provide for themselves.

But where is voluntary effort in all this? Were it not for the crusading efforts of many individuals in the eighteenth and nineteenth centuries, much of the European reform movement, ultimately translated into new private groups and into legislation, would never have eventuated. This was equally true in the United States, where the somewhat feeble beginnings of voluntary effort can be traced to pre-Revolutionary days. Though the Colonies felt Dutch and French influences, it was the English influence which predominated, and many of the now basically governmental patterns familiar at home were incorporated into the early colonial treatment of the poor, the aged, the ill, and the abandoned. In principle, the Colonies adapted the Elizabethan Poor Law, with two major adjustments, to the New World. Where in England the poor were more often assigned to almshouses, in the Colonies it was customary to provide "outdoor relief," that is, relief in kind—food, clothes, and fuel. In England legacies and endowments made possible the support of many poor in hospitals, asylums, and orphanages but such private charity did not exist in the Colonies. However, colonial churches were active in providing help, albeit only to members of their own congregation. A singular exception was Pennsylvania, which so long as it remained under Quaker influence, was an example of humane treatment to all within its boundaries, as was also early Catholic Maryland.

The sad fact remains that there was little of true charity or benevolence in the voluntary or legislated activities of the American colonists in the seventeenth and eighteenth centuries. As Carter has noted,

> ...A biding belief in the depravity of the unfortunate had been imported to the North American colonies by the most pious and energetic of the early settlers. Everything they found here confirmed their outlook. The new land was a place of opportunity beyond all precedent, a milch cow incapable of running dry. There seemed to be no excuse for an American who failed to exercise his free, individual initiative in acquisition of personal property. In exchange for resourceful toil, he could have anything he was determined to get, and the God of his fathers, as interpreted by Calvinism, or a variant, would bless him forever.[8]

The poor tax was therefore resented, the poor were despised and degraded and frequently cruelly treated. Yet it must be remembered that the life of many of the colonists was one of great privation. Many lived in remote settlements, in constant fear of the recurrent attacks of the Indians. Mutual aid was one thing but there was little place for the unfortunate, especially if it appeared that the misfortune was of one's own making. Nevertheless, as the cities along the coast began to flourish, there arose a host of civic and charitable activities.

In this period the work of Benjamin Franklin stands out. Inspired by the writings of the famous preacher, Cotton Mather, Franklin went beyond him in believing that men should show their gratitude to God "by the only means in their power, promoting the happiness of his other children." Among his achievements were the part he played in the establishment of a free library, the Pennsylvania Hospital, and the Academy, which later became the University of Pennsylvania. He founded a volunteer fire department and developed plans for cleaning and lighting the streets of Philadelphia. He emphasized the importance of self-help but also the need to band together in projects for the general welfare.[9]

The new nation, an experiment in democracy, also found itself an experiment involving a variety of social problems. While its earliest tasks seemed to be to deal with poverty and ill health, others very soon appeared on the scene. There were the blind, the deaf, the mentally ill. Then, beginning in the 1840s, came wave upon wave of immigrants, most with a language barrier, all with different cultural expectations and perceptions. They needed places in which to live, work, and worship, as well as education to fit into this new society, and many other special services. Ethnic societies, many of them religiously inspired, were set up to help the immigrant to become assimilated. The earliest settlement houses provided a unique service to these sometimes bewildered persons and at the same time awakened the sensibilities of many of the well-to-do to the plight of the poor. A conspicuous example of voluntary effort was provided by the Jewish communities, which provided a wide range of services to meet recognized needs—relief societies, orphan homes, clinics and hospitals, institutions of the aged, and others.

The nineteenth century, which saw the abolition of slavery, the wrenching effect of the Civil War, the rise of industry and the birth of labor unions, saw also the birth of many voluntary social service organizations, the establishment of many private schools and colleges, a vast expansion of health services and hospitals (a number of which had earlier been part of the almshouses), and the initiation of special institutions such as the Perkins Institute for the Blind in Watertown, Massachusetts; the Asylum for the Deaf in Hartford, Connecticut; and the Germantown (Pennsylvania) School for the Mentally Deficient. Similarly, the organization of the United States Sanitary Commission in 1861, financed by private means, to "combat filth and disease" in Union army camps during the Civil War laid the groundwork for organizing state departments of public health.[10] Many of the persons responsible for the establishment of such agencies had borrowed techniques already developed in England and on the Continent. Thus came the first American YMCA in 1851, the efforts at prison reform inspired by the work of the American Red Cross impelled by the work of Jean Henri Dunant, the Swiss banker, to name but a few.

These voluntary groups sprang up for a variety of reasons: reaction to the admittedly inadequate governmental care of the poor, desire to aid special groups in the population, the effective propagandizing of the social reformers, and the desire of many religious groups to provide for the needs of their own within the doctrine and structure of their church.[11] The desire for the exchange of information and a forum to discuss mutual problems led to the organization in 1873 of the National Conference on Social Welfare, while the Charity Organization Society movement, another offshoot from English tradition, beginning in Buffalo in 1877, represented in part an effort to bring local agencies into closer working relationships. These proved to be the forerunners of the present health and welfare councils and the councils of social agencies.

During the first half of the twentieth century an enormous proliferation of every type of voluntary organization imaginable appeared on the scene—local, regional, and national. To cite but one example from the health field: its concern with education, research, and treatment of specific diseases led in this period to the creation of at least seventy-five national disease-oriented agencies.[12] The country's borders stretched from one ocean to the other and there was a diversity of its religious and ethnic groups for every possible interest and need—recreational and sports groups, choral societies, farmers' co-ops, men's service organizations, homes for the aged, professional societies, mental health facilities, youth-serving organizations, and myriad others.

But the efforts of voluntary organizations and local and state governments to cope with the problems of the poor, the unemployed, the aged, and the chronically ill became increasingly inadequate to meet the mounting demands. The federal government, which philosophically had up to this point denied its responsibility in these areas, was forced by the Great Depression of the early 1930s to a complete reversal of its thinking and an acceptance not only of its obligation to provide for relief of economic distress but also of the right of needy persons to assistance without a loss of respect for their dignity and worth as human beings.[13] Various forms of emergency relief were enacted, and the first permanent Social Security legislation was passed in 1935. Amendments to the legislation in intervening years have extended coverage to greater numbers of persons and the institution of Medicare in the 1960s has provided a renewed sense of security for the growing percentage of older persons for whom the cost of health care has reached astronomical proportions.

President Johnson's "Antipoverty Program" of the 1960s saw the inauguration of many innovative programs which involved persons at the local level in solving, with governmental and nongovernmental funds, and, through governmental and nongovernmental agencies, some of the persistent problems that have been, over the generations, afflicting American life. That this program was not more successful was attributable to a number of complex factors beyond the scope of this limited survey by including such endemic human failings as political machinations, malfeasance, and the failure of too many Americans to look beyond the costs in tax dollars to the ultimate benefit that this would bring to the nation as a whole. The alternative offered, "revenue sharing," has meant the abandonment of many human services programs begun in the sixties.

Ironically, in the depths of the Depression, it was because the many voluntary organizations and local and state governments were inadequate to fund and man the programs needed to sustain the massive numbers of unemployed that the federal government finally took a hand. Today, nearly fifty years later and with a nation twice as large, where resources of voluntary groups are more strained than ever, and where many a state and city is on the verge of bankruptcy, the federal government is turning back to these agencies and jurisdictions some of the very responsibilities it had assumed. There appears to be a lack of recognition that many problems are national in scope, transcending state and local boundaries. Whether such a policy is justified or realistic at this time must be left to history.

Our society has fallen heir to a social philosophy rooted in Aristotle and Aquinas, furthered by the writings of Locke and Mills, and given a practical reality in the Constitution and its interpretation by our Founding Fathers and by major decisions of the United States Supreme Court, particularly those of the twentieth century in the area of social jurisprudence. Unwittingly, the religious thinkers of the Protestant Reformation, with their concepts of governmental responsibility, set the stage as well for the reform efforts made during the eighteenth and nineteenth centuries when the Industrial Revolution turned upside down the still predominantly agrarian societies of the western world.

The enlivening principle which has kindled efforts in social reform has been the Judeo-Christian concept of love of one's neighbor. Without it social reform is stunted and cut off at its roots, having only self-interest as its motivating force; and when altruism is no longer apparent, as perhaps in the aftermath of the first exciting days of the Antipoverty Program, it dies. The idea of one common humanity, of the basic dignity and worth of all persons without exception, has been the inspiration for countless legions to give of themselves in service to others.[14]

Notes

1. For an interesting historical discussion of the early development of charity and philanthropy, cf. Edward Grubb, "Philanthropy," *Encyclopedia of Religion and Ethics*, Vol. 9, pp. 837-840.

2. Louis Finkelstein, J. Elliott Ross, and William Adams Brown, *The Religions of Democracy* (New York: The Devin Adair Company, 1941), pp. 17-18. See also Edward Grubb, *op. cit*.

3. The development of the social teachings of the Christian churches is extraordinarily illuminated in the work by Ernst Troeltsch, *The Social Teaching of the Christian Churches*, Vols. I and II, trans. by Olive Wyon (New York: The Macmillan Company, 1931).

4. *Ibid.*, Vol. I, pp. 162-164.

5. Heinz Vonhoff, *People Who Care, An Illustrated History of Human Compassion* (Philadelphia: Fortress Press, 1971), pp. 44-47.

6. Walter A. Friedlander, *Introductions to Social Welfare* (Englewood Cliffs, N.J.: Prentice-Hall, 1968), pp. 10-13.

7. *Ibid.*, pp. 16-37, especially pp. 22-23 and 32-37.

8. Richard Carter, *The Gentle Legions* (New York: Doubleday and Company, Inc., 1961), p. 31.

9. Robert H. Bremner, "Private Philanthropy and Public Needs, Historical Perspective" (unpublished manuscript, Ohio State University, Department of History), pp. 12-13.

10. Walter H. Trattner, *From Poor Law to Welfare State* (New York: Free Press, 1974), pp. 68-71.

11. Gordon Manser, "Voluntary Organization for Social Welfare," *Encyclopedia of Social Work*, 15th ed., p. 824.

12. *Ibid.*, p. 825.

13. Walter A. Friedlander, *op. cit.*, p. 120.

14. Cf. Richard M. Titmuss, *The Gift Relationship: From Human Blood to Social Policy* (New York: Pantheon Books, 1971).

4

Altruism: Self-Sacrifice for Others

LEWIS THOMAS

LEWIS THOMAS, A PHYSICIAN AND DEAN OF THE MEMORIAL
SLOAN-KETTERING CANCER CENTER, WON THE NATIONAL BOOK
AWARD IN 1974 FOR THE MEDUSA AND THE SNAIL.

Altruism has always been one of biology's deep mysteries. Why should any animal, off on its own, specified and labeled by all sorts of signals as its individual self, choose to give up its life in aid of another being? Nature, long viewed as a wild, chaotic battlefield swarming with more than 10 million different species, comprising unnumbered billions of competing selves locked in endless combat, offers only one sure measure of success: survival. Survival, in the cool economics of biology, means simply the persistence of one's own genes in the generations to follow.

At first glance, it seems an unnatural act, a violation of nature, to give away one's life, or even one's possessions, to another. And yet, in the face of improbability, examples of altruism abound. When a worker bee, patrolling the frontiers of the hive, senses the nearness of an intruder, its attack is pure, unqualified suicide; the bee's sting is barbed, and in the act of pulling away, the insect is fatally injured. Among other varieties of social insects, such as ants and higher termites, there are castes of soldiers for whom self-sacrifice is an everyday chore.

It is easy to dismiss the problem by saying that altruism is the wrong technical term for behavior of this kind. The word is a human word, strung together to describe an unusual aspect of human behavior, and we should not be using it for

Reprinted from *The Saturday Evening Post* (May/June, 1982). From the forthcoming book, *Late Night Thoughts on Listening to Mahler's Ninth Symphony,* by Lewis Thomas, to be published by Viking Penguin Inc. Reprinted by permission of Viking Penguin Inc.

the behavior of tiny machines, mindless automata. A honeybee has no connection to creatures like us, no brain for figuring out the future, no way of predicting the inevitable outcome of that sting.

But the mind of a single bee, not to mention the 50,000 or so connected minds of a whole hive, is not so easy to dismiss. A bee can tell the time of day, calculate the geometry of the sun's position, argue with other bees about the best location for the next swarm, even anticipate the movements of a Princeton biologist who is shifting a dish of sugar further and further from the hive. Bees do a lot of close observing of other bees: maybe they know what follows stinging and do it anyway.

Altruism is not restricted to the social insects, in any case. Birds risk their lives, and sometimes lose them, in efforts to distract the attention of predators from the nest. Among baboons, zebras, moose, wildebeests and wild dogs there are always stubborn, doomed guardians, prepared to be done in first in order to buy time for the herd to escape.

It is genetically determined behavior, no doubt about it. Animals have genes for altruism, and those genes have been selected in the evolution of many creatures because of the advantage they confer for the continuing survival of the species. It is, looked at in this way, not the emotion-laden problem that we feel when we try to put ourselves in the animal's place; it is just another plain fact of life, perhaps not as hard a fact as some others, something rather nice, in fact, to think about.

J. B. S. Haldane, the eminent British geneticist, summarized the chilly arithmetic of the problem by announcing, "I would give up my life for two brothers or eight cousins." This calculates the requirement for ultimate self-interest: the preservation and survival of an individual's complement of genes. Biologists—Trivers, Hamilton and others—have constructed mathematical models to account nicely for the altruistic behavior of social insects, quantifying the profit for the genes of a defending bee in the act of tearing its abdomen apart. The hive is filled with siblings, ready to carry the *persona* of the dying bee through all the hive's succeeding generations. Altruism is based on kinship: by preserving kin, one preserves one's self. In a sense.

Haldane's prediction has the sound of a beginning sequence: two brothers, eight (presumably) first cousins and then another series of much larger numbers of more distant relations. Where does the influence tail off? At what point does the sharing of the putative altruist's genes become so diluted as to be meaningless? Would the line on a graph charting altruism plummet to zero soon after those eight cousins, or is it a long, gradual slope? When the combat marine throws himself belly-down on the live grenade in order to preserve the rest of his platoon, is this the same sort of altruism, or is this an act without any technically biological meaning? Surely the marine's genes will be blown away forever; the statistical likelihood of having two brothers or eight cousins in that platoon is vanishingly small. And yet there he is, belly-down as if by instinct, and the same kind of event has been recorded often enough in wartime to make it seem a natural human act, normal enough, though rare, to warrant the stocking of medals by the armed services.

At what point do our genetic ties to each other become so remote that we feel no instinctual urge to help? I can imagine an argument about this, with two sides, but it would be a highly speculative discussion, not by any means pointless but still impossible to settle one way or the other. One side might assert with total justification that altruistic behavior among human beings has nothing at all to do with genetics, that there is no such thing as a gene for self-sacrifice, not even a gene for helpfulness or concern or even affection. These are attributes, they would say, that must be learned from society, acquired by cultures, taught by example. The other side could maintain with equal justification, since the facts are not known, precisely the opposite position: we get along together in human society because we are genetically designed to be social animals, and we are obliged by instructions from our genes to be useful to each other. This side would argue further that when we behave badly, killing or maiming or snatching, we are acting on misleading information learned from the wrong kinds of society we put together; if our cultures were not deformed, we would be better company, paying attention to what our genes are telling us.

For the purposes of this essay, I take the side of the sociobiologists, who contend that human behavior is genetically controlled, because I wish to carry their side of the argument a certain distance afield, beyond the human realm. I have no difficulty in imagining a close enough resemblance among the genes of all human beings, of all races and geographical origins, to warrant a biological mandate for each of us to do whatever we can to keep the rest of the species alive. I maintain, despite the moment's evidence against the claim, that we are born and grow up with a fondness for each other and that we have genes for that. We can be talked out of that fondness, for the genetic message is like a distant music and some of us are hard of hearing. Societies are noisy affairs, drowning out the sound of ourselves and our connection. Hard of hearing, we go to war. Stone deaf, we make thermonuclear missiles. Nonetheless, the music is there, waiting for more listeners.

But the matter does not end with our species. If we are to take seriously the notion that the sharing of similiar genes imposes a responsibility on the sharers to sustain each other, and if I am right in guessing that even very distant cousins carry at least traces of this responsibility and will act on it whenever they can, then the whole world becomes something to be concerned about on solidly scientific, reductionist, genetic grounds. For we have cousins more than we can count, and they are all over the place, run by genes so similar to ours that the differences are minor technicalities. All of us—men, women, children, fish, sea grass, sandworms, dolphins, hamsters and soil bacteria, everything alive on the planet — roll ourselves along through all our generations by replicating DNA and RNA, and although the alignments of nucleotides within these molecules are different in different species, the molecules themselves are fundamentally the same substance.

This is, in fact, the way it should be. If cousins are defined by common descent, the human family is only one small and very recent additon to a much larger family in a tree extending back at least 3.5 billion years. Our common ancestor was a single cell from which all subsequent cells derived, most likely a cell resembling one of today's bacteria in today's soil. For almost three-fourths of the earth's existence, cells of that first kind were the only life there was. It was less than a billion years ago that cells like ours appeared in the first marine invertebrates, and these were somehow pieced together by the joining up and fusion of the earlier primitive cells, retaining the same bloodlines. Some of the joiners, bacteria that had learned how to use oxygen, are with us still, part of our flesh, lodged inside the cells of all animals, all plants, moving us from place to place and doing our breathing for us. Now there's a set of cousins!

Even if I try to discount the other genetic similarities linking human beings to all other creatures by common descent, the existence of these beings in my cells is enough, in itself, to relate me to the chestnut tree in my backyard and to the squirrel in that tree.

There ought to be a mathematics for connections like this before anyone claims any kinship function, but the numbers are too big. At the same time, even if we wanted to, we cannot think the sense of obligation away. It is there, maybe in our genes for the recognition of cousins or, if not, because we have learned about the matter. Altruism, in its biological sense, is required of us. We have an enormous family to look after, or perhaps that assumes too much, making us sound like official gardeners and zoo keepers for the planet, responsibilities for which we are probably not yet grown-up enough. We need new technical terms for concern, respect, affection, substitutes of altruism. But at least we can acknowledge the family ties and, with them, obligations. If we do it wrong, scattering pollutants, clouding the atmosphere with too much carbon dioxide, extinguishing the thin carapace of ozone, burning up the forests, dropping the bombs, rampaging at large through nature as though we owned the place, there will be a lot of paying back to do and, at the end, nothing to pay back with.

5

Without Volunteers,
A Lost Civilization

ERMA BOMBECK

ERMA BOMBECK, A SYNDICATED COLUMNIST AND AUTHOR OF
SEVERAL BOOKS, HAS WRITTEN FREQUENTLY ABOUT GIVING AND
VOLUNTEERING.

I had a dream the other night that every volunteer in this country, disillusioned with the lack of compassion, had set sail for another country.

As I stood smiling on the pier, I shouted, "Good-bye, creamed chicken. Good-bye, phone committees. So long, Disease-of-the-Month. No more saving old egg cartons. No more getting out the vote. Au revoir, playground duty, bake sales and three-hour meetings.

As the boat got smaller and they could no longer hear my shouts, I reflected, "Serves them right. A bunch of yes people. All they had to do was to put their tongue firmly against the roof of their mouth and make an O sound. Nnnnnnn-nooooo. Nnnnnnnnnnnnnnnooooooooo. Nnoo! No! It would certainly have spared them a lot grief. Oh well, who needs them!"

The hospital was quiet as I passed it. Rooms were void of books, flowers and voices. The children's wing held no clowns...no laughter. The reception desk was vacant.

The Home for the Aged was like a tomb. The blind listened for a voice that never came. The infirm were imprisoned by wheels on a chair that never moved. Food grew cold on trays that would never reach the mouths of the hungry.

All the social agencies had closed their doors, unable to implement their programs of scouting, recreation, drug control, Big Sisters, Big Brothers, YW, YM, the retarded, the crippled, the lonely, and the abandoned.

The health agencies had a sign in the window, "Cures for cancer, muscular dystrophy, birth defects, multiple sclerosis, emphysema, sickle cell anemia, kidney disorders, heart diseases, etc., have been cancelled due to lack of interest.

Reprinted from *At Wit's End,* by Erma Bombeck. ©1975 Field Enterprises, Inc. Courtesy of Field Newspaper Syndicate.

The schools were strangely quiet with no field trips, no volunteer aids on the playground or in the classrooms...as were the colleges where scholarships and financial support were no more.

The flowers on church altars withered and died. Children in day nurseries lifted their arms but there was no one to hold them in love. Alcoholics cried out in despair, but no one answered, and the poor had no recourse for health care or legal aid.

But the saddest part of the journey was the symphony hall which was dark and would remain that way. So were the museums that had been built and stocked by volunteers with the art treasures of our times.

I fought in my sleep to regain a glimpse of the ship of volunteers just one more time. It was to be my last glimpse of civilization...as we were meant to be.

6

A Model of
Christian Charity

JOHN WINTHROP

JOHN WINTHROP WAS THE FIRST GOVERNOR OF MASSACHUSETTS.
THE FOLLOWING SERMON WAS DELIVERED TO HIS COMPANION
PURITANS ON THE SHIP ARBELLA ON THE WAY TO AMERICA
IN 1630.

God Almighty in His most holy and wise providence hath so disposed of the condition of mankind as in all times some must be rich, some poor; some high and eminent in power and dignity, others mean in subjection.

The reason hereof:

First, to hold conformity with the rest of His works, being delighted to show forth the glory of His wisdom in the variety and difference of the creatures and the glory of His power, in ordering all these differences for the preservation and good of the whole, and the glory of His greatness: that as it is the glory of princes to have many officers, so this great King will have many stewards, counting Himself more honored in dispensing his gifts to man by man than if he did it by His own immediate hand.

Secondly, that He might have the more occasion to manifest the work of his Spirit: first, upon the wicked in moderating and restraining them, so that the rich and mighty should not eat up the poor, nor the poor and despised rise up against their superiors and shake off their yoke; secondly, in the regenerate, in exercising His graces in them—as in the great ones, their love, mercy, gentleness, temperance, etc., in the poor and inferior sort, their faith, patience, obedience, etc.

Thirdly, that every man might have need of other, and from hence they might be all knit more nearly together in the bond of brotherly affection. From hence it appears plainly that no man is made more honorable than another or more wealthy, etc., out of any particular and singular respect to himself, but for the glory of his creator and the common good of the creature, man. Therefore God still reserves the property of these gifts to Himself (*Ezek. 16: 17*). He there calls wealth His gold and His silver, etc. (*Prov. 3: 9*). He claims their service as His due: "Honor the Lord with thy riches." All men being thus (by divine providence) ranked into two sorts, rich and poor, under the first are comprehended all such as are able to live comfortably by their own means duly improved, and all others are poor, according to the former distribution.

There are two rules whereby we are to walk, one towards another: justice and mercy. These are always distinguished in their act and in their object, yet may they both concur in the same subject in each respect: as sometimes there may be an occasion of showing mercy to a rich man in some sudden danger of distress, and also doing of mere justice to a poor man in regard of some particular contract.

There is likewise a double law by which we are regulated in our conversation, one towards another: in both the former respects, the law of nature and the law of grace, or the moral law or the law of the Gospel—to omit the rule of justice as not properly belonging to this purpose, otherwise than it may fall into consideration in some particular cases. By the first of these laws, man, as he was enabled so, withal [is] commanded to love his neighbor as himself; upon this ground stand all the precepts of the moral law, which concerns our dealings with men. To apply this to the works of mercy, this law requires two things: first, that every man afford his help to another in every want or distress; secondly, that he perform this out of the same affection which makes him careful of his own good according to that of our savior (*Matt. 7: 12*): "Whatsoever ye would that men should do to you." This was practiced by Abraham and Lot in entertaining the angels and the old man of Gibea.

The law of grace or the Gospel hath some difference from the former, as in these respects: first, the law of nature was given to man in the estate of innocency, this of the Gospel in the estate of regeneracy. Secondly, the former propounds one man to another as the same flesh and image of God, this as a brother in Christ also, and in the communion of the same spirit, and so teacheth us to put a difference between Christians and others. "Do good to all, especially to the household of faith." Upon this ground the Israelites were to put a difference between the brethren of such as were strangers though not of the Canaanites. Thirdly, the law of nature could give no rules for dealing with enemies, for all are to be considered as friends in the estate of innocency; but the Gospel commands love to an enemy. Proof: "If thine enemy hunger, feed him; love your enemies, do good to them that hate you" (*Matt. 5: 44*).

This law of the Gospel propounds likewise a difference of seasons and occasions. There is a time when a Christian must sell all and give to the poor as they did in the apostles' times; there is a time also when a Christian, though they give not all yet, must give beyond their ability, as they of Macedonia (*II Cor. 8*). Likewise, community of perils calls for extraordinary liberality, and so doth community in some special service for the church. Lastly, when there is no other means whereby our Christian brother may be relieved in this distress, we must help him beyond our ability, rather than tempt God in putting him upon help by miraculous or extraordinary means....

1. For the persons, we are a company professing ourselves fellow members of Christ, in which respect only, though we were absent from each other many miles, and had our employments as far distant, yet we ought to account ourselves knit together by this bond of love, and live in the exercise of it, if we would have comfort of our being in Christ. This was notorious in the practice of the Christians in former times, as is testified of the Waldenses from the mouth of one of the adversaries, Aeneas Sylvius: *Mutuo solent amare pene antequam norint*— they used to love any of their own religion even before they were acquainted with them.

2. For the work we have in hand, it is by mutual consent, through a special overruling providence and a more than an ordinary approbation of the churches of Christ, to seek out a place of cohabitation and consortship, under a due form of government both civil and ecclesiastical. In such cases as this, the care of the public must oversway all private respects by which not only conscience but mere civil policy doth bind us; for it is a true rule that particular estates cannot subsist in the ruin of the public.

3. The end is to improve our lives to do more service to the Lord, the comfort and increase of the body of Christ whereof we are members, that ourselves and posterity may be the better preserved from the common corruptions of this evil world, to serve the Lord and work out our salvation under the power and purity of His holy ordinances.

4. For the means whereby this must be effected, they are twofold: a conformity with the work and the end we aim at; these we see are extraordinary, therefore we must not content our-

selves with usual ordinary means. Whatsoever we did or ought
to have done when we lived in England, the same must we do,
and more also where we go. That which the most in their
churches maintain as truth in profession only, we must bring
into familiar and constant practice: as in this duty of love we
must love brotherly without dissimulation, we must love one
another with a pure heart fervently, we must bear one another's burdens, we must not look only on our own things but
also on the things of our brethren. Neither must we think that
the Lord will bear with such failings at our hands as He doth
from those among whom we have lived...

Thus stands the cause between God and us: we are entered into covenant with
Him for this work; we have taken out a commission, the Lord hath given us
leave to draw our own articles. We have professed to enterprise these actions
upon these and these ends; we have hereupon besought Him of favor and
blessing. Now if the Lord shall please to hear us and bring us in peace to the
place we desire, then hath He ratified this covenant and sealed our Commission, [and] will expect a strict performance of the articles contained in it. But if
we shall neglect the observation of these articles which are the ends we have
propounded, and dissembling with our God, shall fall to embrace this present
world and prosecute our carnal intentions, seeking great things for ourselves
and our posterity, the Lord will surely break out in wrath against us, be re-
venged of such a perjured people, and make us know the price of the breach of
such a covenant.

Now the only way to avoid this shipwreck and to provide for our posterity is
to follow the counsel of Micah: to do justly, to love mercy, to walk humbly with
our God. For this end, we must be knit together in this work as one man. We
must entertain each other in brotherly affection; we must be willing to abridge
ourselves of our superfluities, for the supply of others' necessities; we must
uphold a familiar commerce together in all meekness, gentleness, patience and
liberality. We must delight in each other, make other's conditions our own,
rejoice together, mourn together, labor and suffer together: always having before our eyes our commission and community in the work, our community as
members of the same body. So shall we keep the unity of the spirit in the bond
of peace, the Lord will be our God and delight to dwell among us, as His own
people, and will command a blessing upon us in all our ways, so that we shall
see much more of His wisdom, power, goodness, and truth than formerly we
have been acquainted with. We shall find that the God of Israel is among us,
when ten of us shall be able to resist a thousand of our enemies, when He shall

make us a praise and glory, that men shall say of succeeding plantations: "The Lord make it like that of New England." For we must consider that we shall be as a city upon a hill, the eyes of all people are upon us. So that if we shall deal falsely with our God in this work we have undertaken, and so cause Him to withdraw His present help from us, we shall be made a story and a by-word through the world: we shall shame the faces of many of God's worthy servants, and cause their prayers to be turned into curses upon us, till we be consumed out of the good land whither we are going.

And to shut up this discourse with that exhortation of Moses, that faithful servant of the Lord, in his last farewell to Israel (Deut. 30): Beloved, there is now set before us life and good, death and evil, in that we are commanded this day to love the Lord our God, and to love one another, to walk in His ways and to keep His commandments and His ordinance and His laws and the articles of our covenant with Him, that we may live and be multiplied, and that the Lord our God may bless us in the land whither we go to possess it: but if our hearts shall turn away so that we will not obey, but shall be seduced and worship...other gods, our pleasures and profits, and serve them, it is propounded unto us this day, we shall surely perish out of the good land whither we pass over this vast sea to possess it.

Therefore, let us choose life,
that we, and our seed,
may live; by obeying His
voice and cleaving to Him,
for He is our life and
our prosperity.

7

Doing Good in the New World

ROBERT BREMNER

ROBERT BREMNER, PROFESSOR OF HISTORY AT OHIO STATE
UNIVERSITY, ALSO WROTE **THE PUBLIC GOOD: PHILANTHROPY
AND WELFARE IN THE CIVIL WAR ERA** AND PREPARED ONE OF
THE BASIC PAPERS FOR THE COMMISSION ON PRIVATE
PHILANTHROPY AND PUBLIC NEEDS.

*If any man ask, Why it is so necessary to
do good? I must say, it sounds not like
the question of a good man.*
Cotton Mather

The earliest American philanthropists, as far as European records go, were
those gentle Indians of the Bahama Islands who greeted Columbus at his first
landfall in the New World. In view of the cruelty and exploitation these natives
were to suffer at the hands of white men there is something ominous in Columbus' report that they were "ingenuous and free" with all they had, gave away
anything that was asked of them, and bestowed each gift "with as much love as if
their hearts went with it."

From other Indians pioneer white settlers obtained a wealth of practical
assistance in the difficult task of adjusting to life in an alien land. The names of
most of these benefactors are forgotten, but one at least is familiar to every
schoolboy. Squanto, who had once been kidnapped by an Englishman and
carried off to be sold into slavery, escaped from bondage and returned to New
England. There, during the starving time at Plymouth in the winter of 1620-21,
Squanto proved "a special instrument sent of God" for the good of the enfeebled, bewildered Pilgrims. He taught them, in the words of William Brad-

Reprinted from *American Philanthropy*, Chapter 1, by Robert Bremner (Chicago: University of
Chicago Press, 1960) by permission of the publisher.

ford, "how to set their corn, where to take fish, and to procure other commodities, and was also their pilot to bring them to unknown places for their profit, and never left them till he died." Sad to relate, Squanto used his connections with the Pilgrims to extort gifts for himself from other Indians, and so his hands, like those of some other eminent philanthropists, were not entirely clean. On his deathbed he asked the governor "to pray for him that he might go to the Englishman's God in Heaven, and bequeathed sundry of his things to sundry of his English friends as remembrances of his love..."

Philanthropy is philanthropy wherever and by whomever practiced. When we speak of American philanthropy, however, we usually have in mind an imported product rather than an indigenous growth. Our systems and principles of benevolence, both public and private, originated in Europe before the colonization of America began. They were brought to this country by Europeans, and their subsequent development was influenced by European experience and theory. For many years our philanthropic institutions sought and received support from abroad; and until quite recently those institutions were copies of European models. All we can lay claim to on the score of uniqueness is that philanthropy *in* America took such firm root and grew so prodigiously that it early assumed a stature and significance all its own.

To understand why this happened we must remember, first, that the age of colonization coincided with one of the great periods of European philanthropy. The seventeenth century saw the launching of heroic missionary enterprises, a revival of interest in charitable works, the development in England of a system of tax-supported poor relief, and the organization of a host of associations for specialized philanthropic purposes. America inspired some of these undertakings and benefited directly or indirectly from nearly all of them, for the discovery of the New World affected the conscience as well as the cupidity of the Old. Almost every effort at colonization had, or claimed to have, a philanthropic motivation: there were natives to be converted to Christianity, poor men to be provided with land and work, and a wilderness to be supplied with the institutions of civilization. It is not too much to say that many Europeans regarded the American continent mainly as a vastly expanded field for the exercise of benevolence.

The real founders of American philanthropy, however, were men and women who crossed the Atlantic to establish communities that would be *better* than, instead of like or different from, the ones they had known at home. The Puritan leader, John Winthrop (1588-1649) forthrightly stated their purpose in the lay sermon, "A Model of Christian Charity," which he preached on the ship *Arbella* to "the great company of religious people" voyaging from old to New England in the year 1630. Winthrop used "Charity" as a synonym for love rather than in the modern sense of aid to the poor; and the "Model" he proposed was not a new scheme of benevolence but a code of conduct for a company of Christians who had entered into a convenant with God. The Puritans' God permitted no breach of contract but demanded strict performance of each article in the convenant. Therefore, as Winthrop said, "In this duty of love we must love brotherly without dissimulation, we must love one another with a pure heart fervently, we must bear one another's burdens, we must not look only on our own things but also on the things of our brethren. Neither must we think that the Lord will bear with such failings at our hands as He doth from those among whom we have lived..."

Like later philanthropists, Winthrop justified disparities in wealth and condition as divinely ordained. He had no wish to tamper with God's design, and he did not hesitate to distinguish between "the great ones," "high and eminent in power and dignity," and "the poor and inferior sort" of men. Winthrop looked upon such distinctions as necessary for the good and preservation of society. He was convinced, however, that no man was made richer or more honorable than his neighbor for his own sake, but only "for the glory of his creator and the common good of the creature man." The poor must not rise up against their superiors; neither should the rich and mighty be allowed to eat up the poor. Differences in condition existed, not to separate and alienate men from one another, but to make them have more need of each other, and to bind them closer together "in the bond of brotherly affection." And those differences, important and essential though Winthrop believed them to be, seemed less significant to him than "our community as members of the same body." "We must be knit together in this work as one man," he said. "We must delight in each other, make others' conditions our own, rejoice together, mourn together, labor and suffer together..." The common objective—"to improve our lives to do more service to the Lord"—must never be lost sight of, and "the care of the public" must take precedence over all private interests.

Winthrop's vision of community united and exalted by religious dedication was not to be realized even in Puritan New England. The mean and despised were not content to remain in the state to which God had assigned them; the powerful showed little disposition to forego opportunities to profit at the expense of the weak; and neither rich nor poor was willing to remain for long under the rule of divinely commissioned magistrates. Competition, individualism, and self-interest proved too strong to be suppressed, and what Roger Williams, in a letter to Winthrop's son, called "the common trinity of the world—Profit, Preferment, Pleasure"—soon made their appearance. Even so, Winthrop's ideal was never entirely foresaken. The forces of disunity, although they could not be held down, did not quite prevail; and, not only in the colonial period, but in later eras as well, Americans continued to feel under a special obligation to bring the duty of neighborly and brotherly love, everywhere professed, into "familiar and constant practice."

Half a century after Winthrop and the Puritans started to build their city upon a hill in New England, William Penn (1644-1718) began his holy experiment in Pennsylvania. Although Penn founded the colony as a refuge for Quakers and members of other persecuted sects, the idea of withdrawing from or renouncing the world had no place in his plans. "True Godliness," he said, "don't turn men out of the World, but enables them to live better in it, and excites their Endeavors to Mend it." To Penn and the Quakers there was no conflict between efforts to live better in the world and endeavors to improve it. The two were inseparably bound together, and the one was the means of achieving the other. Living better in the world meant following the urge of moderation, or, more specifically, observing diligence (the middle path between drudgery and idleness) and frugality (as opposed to the extremes of miserliness and extravagance) in one's daily affairs. Mending the world was to be accomplished by employing the rewards of diligence and frugality for benevolent and humanitarian purposes—not casually and incidentally, but wholeheartedly—as the major business of life.

A good deal of the hostility the Quakers encountered arose from the fact that they regarded the conduct of daily life as much, if not more, a part of religious observance than formal worship. But the Quaker outlook, radical in its belief in separation of church and state and in its insistence upon the individual's right of freedom of conscience, was conservative in its attitude toward social organization. Penn, no less than Winthrop, deemed class distinctions an essential part of the divine order. God has not placed men "on the level," he said, but has arranged them in descending orders of subordination and dependency; due respect for these God-ordained differences required "Obedience to Superiors, Love to Equals, ...*Help* and *Countenance* to Inferiors."

Assumptions of social superiority and inferiority, however, were typical of seventeenth-century thought rather than peculiar to the Quakers. Penn himself emphasized the responsibilities rather than the privileges that went with rank. He took the doctrine of stewardship both seriously and literally, believing that men were indebted to God not only for their wealth but for their very being, and accountable to Him for the way they spent their lives as well as their fortunes. His concept of stewardship was free of the condescension with which it is so often associated because, in his case, the doctrine of stewardship was joined to an equally serious and literal belief in the brotherhood of man. Penn was, after all, one of "The People called Friends," and, like other Quakers, he rejected the Calvinistic notion of the Elect. Whatever the differences in material conditions among men, all men were children of God, carriers of His seed, and spiritually equal in His sight.

Penn anticipated Benjamin Franklin in admiration for industry, thrift, and the other economic virtues that are now attributed to the middle class. Practical man that he was, Penn certainly had an appreciation for the value of money, but he believed that God gave men wealth to use rather than to love or hoard. Of all the vices, avarice struck him as worst. The spectacle of men, already comfortably fixed, who scrambled by day and plotted by night to increase their wealth moved him to scorn. "They are running up and down," he commented, "as if it were to save the life of a condemned innocent." Their conduct, personally disgraceful, was socially ruinous; for the reason the poor had too little was that the rich, already possessing too much, were striving to pile up even more.

Next to avarice Penn abhorred waste, display, and the pursuit of pleasure. Here again Penn's puritanical attitude expressed his social conscience: if all the money wasted on luxury and extravagance were put to public use, the wants of the poor would be well satisfied. To be sure, mortal man required diversion; but (or so Penn said), "The best recreation is to do good." There will be time enough for making merry "when the pale faces are more commiserated, the pinched bellies relieved and naked backs clothed, when the famished poor, the distressed widow, and the helpless orphan...are provided for."

Penn's writings, personal influence, and deeds left indelible influence on Quakerdom and, through his followers, on nearly all subsequent humanitarian movements. Penn was, however, an Englishman. He visited America only twice, at widely separated intervals, and his total stay in this country amounted to no longer than four years. It is not Penn, therefore, but a native Yankee, the grandson of two of the founders of Massachusetts, who must be considered the chief exponent of do-goodism in colonial America.

Cotton Mather (1663-1728), unfortunately better remembered today for his part in the witchcraft trials than for his benevolent activities, is one of the commanding figures in the history of American philanthropy. The son of a president of Harvard, and himself one of the founders of Yale, Mather was the most prolific and conspicuously learned writer of the colonial period. Of the approximately four hundred and fifty works he is known to have published, one of the least pretentious, *Bonifacius*, or, as it is usually known, *Essays To Do Good* (1710), enjoyed the greatest and longest popularity. In it Mather proposed that men and women, acting either as individuals or as members of voluntary associations, should engage in "a perpetual endeavor to do good in the world." Such advice, coming from a son of the Puritans, was hardly novel. It was the method Mather outlined rather than the objective that was new. And it was this individualistic, voluntary method—taken not from the Quakers, whom Mather disliked, but from the German Pietists, especially August Hermann Francke of Halle—that was destined to characterize American philanthropy for many years to come.

In the passage quoted at the head of this chapter, Mather disposed in summary fashion of one of the persistent objections to the gospel and practice of doing good. It is interesting, however, to consider why Mather himself thought it so necessary to do good. He regarded the performance of good works as an obligation owed to God rather than as a means of salvation; yet, as a constant expounder of the doctrine of stewardship, he had no doubt that God would punish the unfaithful steward. Moreover, as he was frank enough to admit and bold enough to proclaim, doing good was a reward in itself. To help the unfortunate was an honor, a privilege, "an incomparable pleasure." Not content to let he case rest here, Mather cited an entire catalogue of worldly advantages including long life and business success he thought would surely accrue to the benevolent. Besides, as Mather took pain to point out, doing good was sound policy, a mild but effective instrument of social control. Pious example, moral leadership, voluntary effort, and private charity were the means by which competing and conflicting interests in society might be brought into harmony.

To Mather charity emphatically did begin at home; for he believed that each man must start his career of doing good by correcting whatever was amiss in his own heart and life. Yet for all the emphasis on personal reform, Mather's was a social gospel. Keep a list of the needy in your neighborhood, he urged his readers; be on the lookout for persons who may require help, and seize each opportunity to be useful with "rapturous assiduity." Always bear in mind that "charity to the *souls* of men" is the highest form of benevolence. Send preachers, Bibles, and other books of piety to heathens at home and abroad; support the church, and keep a watchful eye on the spiritual health of the community. Very often, he said, the poor need "admonitions of piety" quite as much as alms. "Cannot you contrive to mingle a spiritual charity with your temporal bounty?"

Mather's own charitable gifts were sufficient to make him a one-man relief and aid society. But Mather's real contribution to the practice of philanthropy lay in his recognition of the need for enlisting the support of others in benevolent enterprises. He was a tireless promoter of associations for distributing tracts, supporting missions, relieving needy clergymen, and building churches in poor communities. At the same time, in sermons and private conversations, he called the attention of the rich to the needs, physical as well as spiritual, of the poor. From personal experience he learned that the recompense of the charitable was multiplication of occasions to be serviceable. "Those who devote themselves to good devices," he drily observed, "usually find a wonderful increase of their opportunities." In a beautiful simile he likened a good deed to "a stone falling into a pool—one circle and service will produce another, till they extend—who can tell how far?"

Despite, or as Mather would have said, because of his sincere concern for the poor, he advocated extreme care in the bestowal of alms. "Let us try to do good with as much application of mind as wicked men employ in doing evil," was his motto. Giving wisely was therefore an even greater obligation than giving generously; and withholding alms from the undeserving as needful and essentially benevolent as bestowing them on the deserving. In a famous and widely approved sermon delivered in 1698 Mather told the good people of Boston: "Instead of exhorting you to augment your charity, I will rather utter an exhortation...that you may not *abuse* your charity by misapplying it." He was disturbed by the increase of idleness and fearful that an excess of benevolence might nourish and confirm the idle in their evil ways. "The poor that can't work are objects for your liberality," he said. "But the poor that *can* work and *won't*, the best liberality to them is to *make* them." The thing to do was to cure them of their idleness: "Find 'em work; set 'em to work; keep 'em to work. Then, as much of your bounty to them as you please."

The most famous tribute to the *Essays To Do Good* came from an unlikely source. In youth—actually boyhood—Benjamin Franklin (1706-90) had been an enemy of the Mathers, and the pseudonym adopted in his earliest published work, Silence Dogood, was an unkind thrust at Cotton Mather. In old age, however, Franklin advised Samuel Mather, Cotton's son, that the *Essays* had influenced his conduct throughout life. "I have always set a greater value on the character of a *doer of good*, than on any other kind of reputation," he wrote, "and if I have been...a useful citizen, the public owes the advantage of it to that book."

Franklin did not acknowledge and possibly was not aware of the influence Quakerism exerted on his character and career. Nevertheless there was much in his approach to life that bore witness to his prolonged association with the Friends. He did not learn the virtues of discretion, moderation, and attention to his business from his first master, his brother James; in these, as in so many other arts, Franklin was self-taught. Yet he presumably derived something, if only concern for reputability, from the example of solid Quaker businessmen for whom he worked as a young man and whose patronage he solicited when he entered business for himself. At any rate it was a happy circumstance that Franklin, with his Puritan background and avowed indebtedness to Mather, should have carried out his highly successful experiments in useful living in the city founded by William Penn.

In addition to numerous similarities, there was significant difference between Franklin's views and those of Penn and Mather. Penn demanded that money, instead of being hoarded or spent on impious luxuries, should be used for comforting the poor. Mather dreamed of a city in which each house would have an alms-box bearing the message *"Think* on the Poor." Franklin, however, conceived of a society in which there would be no poor and little need for relief or charity. He sprang from a different class and addressed himself to a different audience than Penn or Mather. Far from forgetting his humble origin, he traded on it throughout life. In the successive volumes of *Poor Richard's Almanack* Franklin spoke to "leather-aproned" folk as a man of their own sort. As he preached it, the gospel of industry, frugality, and sobriety was worldly wisdom rather than spiritual discipline. Contrary to what is sometimes assumed, Franklin did not advise his readers to seek riches or tell them how to gain wealth. If he had really wanted to do so, with his knowledge of the world, he could have offered more practical suggestions than maxims of self-help. It was the road to independence, not the "Way to Wealth" that Franklin pointed out. "Be *industrious* and *free; be frugal* and *free,"* he counseled—free among other things of dependency upon the uncertain charity of the world.

In conducting his own affairs Franklin observed the maxims of the *Almanack*, if not to the letter, closely enough to become financially independent at a relatively early age. At forty-two he sold his printing house and devoted most of the rest of his life to serving the public. Long before quitting business, however, he had begun to practice what he so often preached to others: "Leisure is Time of doing something useful." It goes without saying that Franklin used his leisure to advance his own knowledge and reputation; but he employed it as earnestly for social as for self-improvement. Although the fact is well known, it is worth recalling that instead of patenting and seeking profit from his inventions, Franklin willingly gave the products of his ingenuity to the world. He introduced a secular spirit into the do-good gospel and shifted the emphasis from pious works and personal charity to efforts to further the general welfare. To Franklin, God was "the Great Benefactor." His religion consisted in the belief that men should show their gratitude to God "by the only means in their power, promoting the happiness of His other children."

Franklin was above all a man of the eighteenth century and it is not wise to insist too strongly on the modernity of his approach to social problems. In much that he did or suggested, however, it is possible to recognize principles that later came to be recognized as characteristic both of enlightened public policy and of constructive philanthropy. Preventing poverty always impressed him as a more sensible course than relieving it. In calling for repeal of the poor laws on the ground that public provision for the needy had an even greater tendency than almsgiving to pauperize the poor, Franklin went beyond Mather, who had warned of the abuses of private charity, and foreshadowed the scientific philanthropists and reformers of the nineteenth century. "I am for doing good to the poor," he wrote "but I differ in opinion about the means. I think the best way of doing good to the poor is, not making them easy *in* poverty, but leading or driving them out of it." In practice Franklin relied on leading rather than driving, on persuasion and encouragement rather than coercion. Unlike some later advocates of individualism, however, Franklin was not content merely to exhort the poor to become self-supporting. He was ever mindful of the need for widening opportunities for self-help, and throughout life he strove, as he put it, "to promote the happiness of mankind" by working for the establishment of conditions in which men would be able to take care of themselves.

Franklin's philanthropic activities, although varied, followed a consistent pattern. Starting in 1727 with the Junto, a club for the mutual improvement of its members, and the library (1731) which was the Junto's first offshoot, Franklin proceeded to organize or assist in organizing a host of civic projects. He founded a volunteer fire company, developed schemes for paving, cleaning, and lighting the streets of Philadelphia, and sponsored a plan for policing the city. His political talents were never better displayed than in his ability to unite public and private support behind municipal improvements. He played a leading part in the establishment of both the Pennsylvania Hospital (1751) and the academy which became the University of Pennsylvania. Funds provided in his will made possible the founding, more than a century after his death, of a technical institute in Boston. His interest in "improving the common Stock of Knowledge" led to the formation in 1743 of the American Philosophical Society, the first and for many years the foremost American institution for promoting research in natural and social sciences.

Franklin demonstrated that the sovereign remedy of self-help, so often prescribed for individuals, could be applied with equally beneficial results to society. He did not invent the principle of improving social conditions through voluntary associations, but more than any American before him he showed the availability, usefulness, and appropriateness of that method to American conditions. The voluntary method, as Franklin's success with it suggested, and as later events were to prove, was precisely suited to the inclinations of his countrymen.

8

Bonifacius—
Essays to Do Good

COTTON MATHER

COTTON MATHER WAS A PREACHER, EDUCATOR, BENEFACTOR,
AND ONE OF THE MOST PROLIFIC WRITERS OF THE COLONIAL
PERIOD. ALTHOUGH **BONIFACIUS—ESSAYS TO DO GOOD** WAS
PROBABLY HIS MOST POPULAR PIECE, MATHER WAS ALSO
RESPONSIBLE FOR OVER 450 OTHER WORKS INCLUDING AN
ECCLESIASTICAL HISTORY OF AMERICA, **MAGNALIA CHRISTI
AMERICANA.**

Methinks, this excellent zeal should be carried into our Neighborhood. Neighbors! you stand related unto one another. And you should be full of devices that all the neighbors may have cause to be glad of your being in the neighborhood. We read: "The righteous is more excellent than his neighbor." But we shall scarce own him so, except he be more excellent *as* a neighbor. He must excel in the duties of good neighborhood. Let that man be better than his neighbor who labors to be a better neighbor, to do most good unto his neighbor.

And here first: the poor people that lie wounded must have wine and oil poured into their wounds. It was a charming stroke in the character which a modern prince had given to him: "To be in distress is to deserve his favor." O good neighbor, put on that princely, that more than royal quality! See who in the neighborhood may deserve thy favor. We are told: "This is pure religion and undefiled" (a jewel that neither is counterfeit nor has any flaws in it), "to visit the fatherless and widows in their affliction." The orphans and widows, and so all the children of affliction in the neighborhood, must be visited and relieved with all agreeable kindness.

Neighbors—be concerned that the orphans and widows in your neighborhood may be well provided for. They meet with grievous difficulties, with unknown temptations. While their next relatives were yet living, they were,

Originally published in 1710, the essays were later reprinted in many volumes. This version is reprinted from *The American Puritans: This World and the Next*, edited by Perry Miller (Garden City, New York: Anchor Books, 1956).

perhaps, but meanly provided for. What must they now be in their more solitary condition? Their condition should be considered, and the result of the consideration should be: "I delivered the orphan that had no helper, and I caused the heart of the widow to sing for joy."

By consequence, all the afflicted in the neighborhood are to be thought upon. Sirs, would it be too much for you at least once in a week to think: "What neighbor is reduced into pinching and painful poverty? Or in any degree impoverished with heavy losses?" Think: "What neighbor is heartbroken with sad bereavements, bereaved of desirable relatives?" And think: "What neighbor has a soul buffeted and hurried with violent assaults of the wicked one?" But then think: "What shall be done for such neighbors?"

First: you will pity them. The evangelical precept is: "Have compassion one of another—be pitiful." It was of old, and ever will be, the just expectation: "To him that is afflicted, pity should be shown." And let our pity to them flame out in our prayer for them. It were a very lovely practice for you, in the daily prayer of your closet every evening, to think: "What miserable object have I seen today that I may do well now to mention for the mercies of the Lord?"

But this is not all. 'Tis possible, 'tis probable, you may do well to visit them: and when you visit them, comfort them. Carry them some good word which may raise a gladness in an heart stooping with heaviness.

And lastly: give them all the assistances that may answer their occasions. Assist them with advice to them, assist them with address to others for them. And if it be needful, bestow your alms upon them: "Deal thy bread to the hungry; bring to thy house the poor that are cast out; when thou seest the naked, cover him." At least Nazianzen's charity, I pray: *Si nihil habes, da lacrymulam*—"if you have nothing else to bestow upon the miserable, bestow a tear or two upon their miseries." This little is better than nothing...

In moving for the devices of good neighborhood, a principal motion which I have to make is that you consult the spiritual interests of your neighborhood as well as the temporal. Be concerned lest the deceitfulness of sin undo any of the neighbors. If there be any idle persons among them, I beseech you, cure them of their idleness. Don't nourish 'em and harden 'em in that, but find employment for them. Find 'em work; set 'em to work; keep 'em to work. Then, as much of your other bounty to them as you please.

If any children in the neighborhood are under no education don't allow 'em to continue so. Let care be taken that they may be better educated, and be taught to read, and be taught their catechism and the truths and way of their only savior.

One more: if any in the neighborhood are taking to bad courses—lovingly and faithfully admonish them. If any in the neighborhood are enemies to their own welfare or families—prudently dispense your admonitions unto them. If there are any prayerless families, never leave off entreating and exhorting them till you have persuaded them to set up the worship of God. If there be any service of God or of His people to which anyone may need to be excited, give him a tender excitation. Whatever snare you see anyone in, be so kind as to tell him of his danger to be ensnared, and save him from it. By putting of good books into the hands of your neighbors, and gaining of them a promise to read the books—who can tell what good you may do unto them! It is possible you may in this way, with ingenuity and with efficacy, administer those reproofs which you may owe unto such neighbors as are to be reproved for their miscarriages. The books will balk nothing that is to be said on the subjects that you would have the neighbors advised upon.

Finally: if there be any base houses, which threaten debauch and poison and confound the neighborhood, let your charity to your neighbors make you do all you can for the suppression of them.

That my proposal to do good in the neighborhood and as a neighbor may be more fully formed and followed, I will conclude it with minding you that a world of self denial is to be exercised in the execution of it. You must be armed against selfishness, all selfish and squinting intentions in your generous resolutions. You shall see how my demands will grow upon you.

First: you must not think of making the good you do a pouring of water into a pump to draw out something for yourselves. This might be the meaning of our savior's direction: "Lend, hoping for nothing again." To lend a thing, properly is to hope that we shall receive it again. But this probably refers to the EpavlouA, or collation usual among the ancients, whereof we find many monuments and mentions in antiquity. If any man by burnings or shipwrecks or other disasters had lost his estate, his friends did use to lend him considerable sums of money, to be repaid not at a certain day but when he should find himself able to repay it without inconvenience. Now, they were so cunning that they would rarely lend upon such disasters unto any but such as they had hope would recover out of their present impoverishment, and not only repay them their money but also requite their kindness, if ever there should be need of it. The thing required by our savior is: "Do good unto such as you are never like to be the better for."

But then, there is yet an higher thing to be demanded. That is: "Do good unto those neighbors who have done hurt unto you." So says our savior: "Love your enemies; bless them that curse you; do good to them that hate you, and pray for them which despitefully use you and persecute you." Yea, if an injury have been done you, improve it as a provocation to do a benefit unto him who did the injury. This is noble! It will bring marvelous consolations! Another method might make you even with your forward neighbors: this will set you above them all. It were nobly done if, in the close of the day when you are alone before the Lord, you make a particular prayer for the pardon and prosperity of any person from whom you may have suffered any abuse in the day. And it would be nobly done if, at last calling over the catalogue of such as have been abusive to you, you maybe able to say (the only intention that can justify your doing anything like to keeping a catalogue of them!): "There is not one of these but I have done him, or watched to do him, a kindness." Among the Jews themselves there were the Hasideans, one of whose institutions it was to make this daily prayer unto God: *Remitte et condona omnibus qui vexant nos* ("Forgive all who trouble and harass us"). Christians— go beyond them! Yea, Justin Martyr tell us, in primitive times they did so: "Praying for their enemies."

But I won't stop here. There is yet an higher thing to be demanded. That is: do good unto those neighbors who will speak ill of you after you have done it. So says our savior: "Ye shall be the children of the highest: he is kind unto the unthankful and unto the evil." You will every day find, I can tell you, monsters of ingratitude. Yea, if you distinguish any person with doing for him something more than you have done for others, it will be well if that very person do not at some time or other hurt you wonderfully. Oh! the wisdom of divine providence in ordering this thing! Sirs, it is that you may do good on a divine principle: good merely for the sake of good! "Lord, increase our faith!"

And God forbid that a Christian faith should not come up to a Jewish! There is a memorable passage in the Jewish records. There was a gentleman of whose bounty many people every day received reliefs and succors. One day he asked: "Well, what do our people say today?" They told him: "Why, the people partook of your kindnesses and services, and then they blessed you very fervently." "Did they so?" said he, "Then I shall have no great reward for this day." Another day he asked: "Well, and what say our people now?" They told him: "Alas, good sir, the people enjoyed your kindnesses today, and when all was done, they did nothing but rail at you." "Indeed!" said he, "Now for this day I am sure that God will give me a good and great reward."

Though vile constructions and harsh invectives be never so much the present reward of doing the best offices for the neighborhood, yet, my dear Boniface, be victorious over all discouragements. "Thy work shall be well rewarded," saith the Lord.

If your opportunities to do good reach no further, yet I will offer you a consolation, which one has elegantly thus expressed: "He that praises God only on a ten-stringed instrument, with his authority extending but unto his family and his example but unto his neighborhood, may have as thankful an heart here, and as high a place in the celestial choir hereafter, as the greatest monarch that praiseth God upon a ten-thousand-stringed instrument, upon the loud sounding organ having as many millions of pipes as there be people under him."

9

Man the Reformer

RALPH WALDO EMERSON

RALPH WALDO EMERSON IS BEST REMEMBERED AS ONE OF
AMERICA'S FOREMOST POETS, ESSAYISTS, AND PHILOSOPHERS. HE
WAS ALSO AN EARLY AND FREQUENT COMMENTATOR ON
PHILANTHROPY AND VOLUNTARY ACTION. IN THIS FINAL SECTION
OF THIS LECTURE, EMERSON PRESENTS ONE OF HIS MOST
COMPELLING CALLS FOR PEOPLE TO AFFIRM THEIR FAITH IN MAN
THROUGH THE FORCEFUL PURSUIT OF REFORM.

What is a man born for but to be a Reformer, a Re-maker of what man has made; a renouncer of lies; a restorer of truth and good, imitating that great Nature which embosoms us all, and which sleeps no moment on an old past, but every hour repairs herself, yielding us every morning a new day, and with every pulsation a new life? Let him renounce everything which is not true to him, and put all his practices back on their first thoughts, and do nothing for which he has not the whole world for his reason. If there are inconveniences, and what is called ruin in the way, because we have so enervated and maimed ourselves, yet it would be like dying of perfumes to sink in the effort to reattach the deeds of every day to the holy and mysterious recesses of life.

The power, which is at once spring and regulator in all efforts of reform, is faith in Man, the conviction that there is an infinite worthiness in him which will appear at the call of worth, and that all particular reforms are the removing of some impediment. Is it not the highest duty that man should be honored in us? I ought not to allow any man, because he has broad lands, to feel that he is rich in my presence. I ought to make him feel that I can do without his riches, that I cannot be bought,— neither by comfort, neither by pride,—and though I be utterly penniless, and receiving bread from him, that he is the poor man beside me. And if, at the same

Excerpted from "Man the Reformer" as it appeared in *The Collected Works of Ralph Waldo Emerson*, Volume I: Nature, Addresses, and Lectures, edited by Robert E. Spiller and Alfred R. Ferguson (Cambridge, Mass.: Belknap Press of Harvard University Press, 1971). The essay was originally published in 1841.

time, a woman or a child discovers a sentiment of piety, or a juster way of thinking than mine, I ought to confess it by my respect and obedience, though it go to alter my whole way of life.

The Americans have many virtues, but they have not Faith and Hope. I know no two words whose meaning is more lost sight of. We use these words as if they were as obsolete as Selah and Amen. And yet they have the broadest meaning and the most cogent application to Boston in this year. The Americans have no faith. They rely on the power of a dollar; they are deaf to sentiment. They think you may talk the north wind down as easily as raise society; and no class more faithless than the scholars or intellectual men. Now if I talk with a sincere wise man and my friend, with a poet, with a conscientious youth who is still under the dominion of his own wild thoughts, and not yet harnessed in the team of society to drag with us all the ruts of custom, I see at once how paltry is all this generation of unbelievers, and what a house of cards their institutions are, and I see what one brave man, what one great thought executed might effect. I see that the reason of the distrust of the practical man in all theory, is his inability to perceive the means whereby we work. Look, he says, at the tools with which this world of yours is to be built. As we cannot make a planet, with atmosphere, rivers, and forests, by means of the best carpenters' or engineers' tools, with chemist's laboratory and smith's forge to boot,—so neither can we ever construct that heavenly society you prate of, out of foolish, sick, selfish men and women, such as we know them to be. But the believer not only beholds his heaven to be possible, but already to begin to exist,—not by the men or materials the statesman uses, but by men transfigured and raised above themselves by the power of principles. To principles something else is possible that transcends all the power of expedients.

Every great and commanding moment in the annals of the world is the triumph of some enthusiasm. The victories of the Arabs after Mahomet, who, in a few years, from a small and mean beginning, established a larger empire than that of Rome, is an example. They did they knew not what. The naked Derar, horsed on an idea, was found an overmatch for a troop of Roman cavalry. The women fought like men, and conquered the Roman men. They were miserably equipped, miserably fed. They were Temperance troops. There was neither brandy nor flesh needed to feed them. They conquered Asia, and Africa, and Spain, on barley. The Caliph Omar's walking stick struck more terror into those who saw it, than another man's sword. His diet was barley bread; his sauce was salt; and oftentimes by way of abstinence he ate his bread without salt. His drink was water. His palace was built of mud; and when he left Medina to go to the conquest of Jerusalem, he rode on a red camel, with a wooden platter hanging at his saddle, with a bottle of water and two sacks, one holding barley, and the other dried fruits.

But there will dawn ere long on our modes of living, a nobler morning than that Arabian faith, in the sentiment of love. This is the one remedy for all ills, the panacea of nature. We must be lovers, and instantly the impossible becomes possible. Our age and history, for these thousand years, has not been the history of kindness, but of selfishness. Our distrust is very expensive. The money we spend for courts and prisons is very ill laid out. We make by distrust the thief, and burglar, and incendiary, and by our court and jail we keep him so. An acceptance of the sentiment of love throughout Christendom for a season, would bring the felon and the outcast to our side in tears, with the devotion of his faculties to our service. See this wide society of laboring men and women. We allow ourselves to be served by them, we live apart from them, and meet them without a salute in the streets. We do not greet their talents, nor rejoice in their good fortune, nor foster their hopes, nor in the assembly of the people vote for what is dear to them. Thus we enact the part of the selfish noble and king from the foundation of the world. See, this tree always bears one fruit. In every household, the peace of a pair is poisoned by the malice, slyness, indolence, and alienation of domestics. Let any two matrons meet, and observe how soon their conversation turns on the troubles from their "help," as our phrase is. In every knot of laborers, the rich man does not feel himself among his friends,—and at the polls he finds them arrayed in a mass in distinct opposition to him. We complain that the politics of masses of the people are so often controlled by designing men, and led in opposition to manifest justice and the common weal, and to their own interest. But the people do not wish to be represented or ruled by the ignorant and base. They only vote for these because they were asked with the voice and semblance of kindness. They will not vote for them long. They inevitably prefer wit and probity. To use an Egyptian metaphor, it is not their will for any long time "to raise the nails of wild beasts, and to depress the heads of the sacred birds." Let our affection flow out to our fellows; it would operate in a day the greatest of all revolutions. It is better to work on institutions by the sun than by the wind. The state must consider the poor man, and all voices must speak for him. Every child that is born must have a just chance for his bread. Let the amelioration of our laws of property proceed from the concession of the rich, not from the grasping of the poor. Let us begin by habitual imparting. Let us understand that the equitable rule is, that no one should take more than his share, let him be ever so rich. Let me feel that I am to be a lover. I am to see to it that the world is the better for me, and to find my reward in the act. Love would put a new face on this weary old world in which we dwell as pagans and enemies too long, and it would warm the heart to see how fast the vain diplomacy of statesmen, the impotence of armies, and navies, and lines of defence, would be superseded by this unarmed child. Love will creep where it cannot go, will accomplish that by imperceptible methods,—being its own lever, fulcrum, and power,—which force could never achieve. Have you not seen in the woods, in a late autumn morning, a poor fungus or mushroom,—a plant without any solidity, nay, that seemed nothing but a soft mush or jelly,—by its constant, total, and inconceivably gentle pushing, manage to break its way up through the frosty ground, and actually to lift a hard crust on its head? It is the symbol of the power of kindness. The virtue of this principle in human society in application to great interests is obsolete and forgotten. Once or twice in history it has been tried in illustrious instances, with signal success. This great, overgrown, dead Christendom of ours still keeps alive at least the name of a lover of mankind. But one day all men will be lovers; and every calamity will be dissolved in the universal sunshine.

Will you suffer me to add one trait more to this portrait of man the reformer? The finished man should have a great prospective prudence, that he may perform the high office of mediator between the spiritual and the actual world. An Arabian poet describes his hero by saying,

> *"Sunshine was he*
> *In the winter day;*
> *And in the midsummer*
> *Coolness and shade".*

He who would help himself and others, should not be a subject of irregular and interrupted impulses of virtue, but a continent, persisting, immovable person,— such as we have seen a few scattered up and down in time for the blessing of the world; men who have in the gravity of their nature a quality which answers to the fly-wheel in a mill, which distributes the motion equably over all the wheels, and hinders it from falling unequally and suddenly in destructive shocks. It is better that joy should be spread over all the day in the form of strength, than that it should be concentrated into ecstasies, full of danger and followed by reactions. There is a sublime prudence, which is the very highest that we know of man, which, believing in a vast future,—sure of more to come than is yet seen,—postpones always the present hour to the whole life; postpones always talent to genius, and special results to character. As the merchant gladly takes money from his income to add to his capital, so is the great man very willing to lose particular powers and talents, so that he gain in the elevation of his life. The opening of the spiritual senses disposes men ever to greater sacrifices, to leave their signal talents, their best means and skill of procuring a present success, their power and their fame,—to cast all things behind, in the insatiable thirst for divine communications. A purer fame, a greater power rewards the sacrifice. It is the conversion of our harvest into seed. Is there not somewhat sublime in the act of the farmer, who casts into the ground the finest ears of his grain? The time will come when we too shall hold nothing back, but shall eagerly convert more than we now possess into means and powers, when we shall be willing to sow the sun and the moon for seeds.

10

Of The Use Which the Americans Make Of Public Associations In Civil Life

ALEXIS DE TOCQUEVILLE

ALEXIS CHARLES HENRI CLEREL DE TOCQUEVILLE WAS A FRENCH
STATESMAN AND PHILOSOPHER WHO IS BEST KNOWN TODAY FOR
HIS OBSERVATIONS OF THE AMERICAN REPUBLICAN SYSTEM. THE
IMPRESSIONS OF THE AMERICAN IMPULSE TO ORGANIZE WHICH
TOCQUEVILLE FORMED DURING HIS TRAVELS THROUGH THE
UNITED STATES IN 1831 ARE STILL READ AND QUOTED
FREQUENTLY TODAY.

I do not propose to speak of those political associations by the aid of which men
endeavor to defend themselves against the despotic action of a majority or
against the aggressions of regal power. That subject I have already treated. If
each citizen did not learn, in proportion as he individually becomes more feeble
and consequently more incapable of preserving his freedom single-handed, to
combine with his fellow citizens for the purpose of defending it, it is clear that
tyranny would unavoidably increase together with equality.

Only those associations that are formed in civil life without reference to
political objects are here referred to. The political associations that exist in the
United States are only a single feature in the midst of the immense assemblage
of associations in that country. Americans of all ages, all conditions, and all
dispositions constantly form associations. They have not only commercial and
manufacturing companies, in which all take part, but associations of a thousand
other kinds, religious, moral, serious, futile, general or restricted, enormous or

Democracy in America was originally published in 1835. This selection is reprinted from Volume II,
Book II, Chapter V in the edition published by Borzoi Books of Alfred A. Knopf, Inc., New York, 1976
(translated by Henry Reeve; revised by Francis Bowen; edited by Phillips Bradley). Copyright ©1945,
renewed 1973, Alfred A. Knopf, Inc. Reprinted by permission of Alfred A. Knopf, Inc.

diminutive. The Americans make associations to give entertainments, to found seminaries, to build inns, to construct churches, to diffuse books, to send missionaries to the antipodes; in this manner they found hospitals, prisons, and schools. If it is proposed to inculcate some truth or to foster some feeling by the encouragement of a great example, they form a society. Wherever at the head of some new undertaking you see the government in France, or a man of rank in England, in the United States you will be sure to find an association.

I met with several kinds of associations in America of which I confess I had no previous notion; and I have often admired the extreme skill with which the inhabitants of the United States succeed in proposing a common object for the exertions of a great many men and in inducing them voluntarily to pursue it.

I have since traveled over England, from which the Americans have taken some of their laws and many of their customs; and it seemed to me that the principle of association was by no means so constantly or adroitly used in that country. The English often perform great things singly, whereas the Americans form associations for the smallest undertakings. It is evident that the former people consider association as a powerful means of action, but the latter seem to regard it as the only means they have of acting.

Thus, the most democratic country on the face of the earth is that in which men have, in our time, carried to the highest perfection the art of pursuing in common the object of their common desires and have applied this new science to the greatest number of purposes. Is this the result of accident, or is there in reality any necessary connection between the principle of association and that of equality?

Aristocratic communities always contain, among a multitude of persons who by themselves are powerless, a small number of powerful and wealthy citizens, each of whom can achieve great undertakings single-handed. In aristocratic societies men do not need to combine in order to act, because they are strongly held together. Every wealthy and powerful citizen constitutes the head of a permanent and compulsory association, composed of all those who are dependent upon him or whom he makes subservient to the execution of his designs.

Among democratic nations, on the contrary, all the citizens are independent and feeble; they can do hardly anything by themselves, and none of them can oblige his fellow men to lend him their assistance. They all, therefore, become powerless if they do not learn voluntarily to help one another. If men living in democratic countries had no right and no inclination to associate for political purposes, their independence would be in great jeopardy, but they might long preserve their wealth and their cultivation: whereas if they never acquired the habit of forming associations in ordinary life, civilization itself would be endangered. A people among whom individuals lost the power of achieving great things single-handed, without acquiring the means of producing them by united exertions, would soon relapse into barbarism.

Unhappily, the same social condition that renders associations so necessary to democratic nations renders their formation more difficult among those nations than among all others. When several members of an aristocracy agree to combine, they easily succeed in doing so; as each of them brings great strength to the partnership, the number of its members may be very limited; and when the members of an association are limited in number, they may easily become mutually acquainted, understand each other, and establish fixed regulations. The same opportunities do not occur among democratic nations, where the associated members must always be very numerous for their association to have any power.

I am aware that many of my countrymen are not in the least embarrassed by this difficulty. They contend that the more enfeebled and incompetent the citizens become, the more able and active the government ought to be rendered in order that society at large may execute what individuals can no longer accomplish. They believe this answers the whole difficulty, but I think they are mistaken.

A government might perform the part of some of the largest American companies, and several states, members of the Union, have already attempted it; but what political power could ever carry on the vast multitude of lesser undertakings which the American citizens perform every day, with the assistance of the principle of association? It is easy to foresee that the time is drawing near when man will be less and less able to produce, by himself alone, the commonest necessaries of life. The task of the governing power will therefore perpetually increase, and its very efforts will extend it every day. The more it stands in the place of associations, the more will individuals, losing the notion of combining together, require its assistance: these are causes and effects that unceasingly create each other. Will the administration of the country ultimately assume the management of all the manufactures which no single citizen is able to carry on? And if a time at length arrives when, in consequence of the extreme subdivision of landed property, the soil is split into an infinite number of parcels, so that it can be cultivated only by companies of tillers, will it be necessary that the head of the government should leave the helm of state to follow the plow? The morals and the intelligence of a democratic people would be as much endangered as its business and manufactures if the government ever wholly usurped the place of private companies.

Feelings and opinions are recruited, the heart is enlarged, and the human mind is developed only by the reciprocal influence of men upon one another. I have shown that these influences are almost null in democratic countries; they must therefore be artificially created, and this can only be accomplished by associations.

When the members of an aristocratic community adopt a new opinion or conceive a new sentiment, they give it a station, as it were, beside themselves, upon the lofty platform where they stand; and opinions or sentiments so conspicuous to the eyes of the multitude are easily introduced into the minds or hearts of all around. In democratic countries the governing power alone is naturally in a condition to act in this matter, but it is easy to see that its action is always inadequate, and often dangerous. A government can no more be competent to keep alive and to renew the circulation of opinions and feelings among a great people than to manage all the speculations of productive industry. No sooner does a government attempt to go beyond its political sphere and to enter upon this new track than it exercises, even unintentionally, an insupportable tyranny; for a government can only dictate strict rules, the opinions which it favors are rigidly enforced, and it is never easy to discriminate between its advice and its commands. Worse still will be the case if the government really believes itself interested in preventing all circulation of ideas; it will then stand motionless and oppressed by the heaviness of voluntary torpor. Governments, therefore, should not be the only active powers; associations ought, in democratic nations, to stand in lieu of those powerful private individuals whom the equality of conditions has swept away.

As soon as several of the inhabitants of the United States have taken up an opinion or a feeling which they wish to promote in the world, they look out for mutual assistance; and as soon as they have found one another out, they combine. From that moment they are no longer isolated men, but a power seen from afar, whose actions serve for an example and whose language is listened to. The first time I heard in the United States that a hundred thousand men had bound themselves publicly to abstain from spirituous liquors, it appeared to me more like a joke than a serious engagement, and I did not at once perceive why these temperate citizens could not content themselves with drinking water by their own firesides. I at last understood that these hundred thousand Americans, alarmed by the progress of drunkenness around them, had made up their minds to patronize temperance. They acted in just the same way as a man of high rank who should dress very plainly in order to inspire the humbler orders with a contempt of luxury. It is probable that if these hundred thousand men had lived in France, each of them would singly have memorialized the government to watch the public houses all over the kingdom.

Nothing, in my opinion, is more deserving of our attention than the intellectual and moral associations of America. The political and industrial associations of that country strike us forcibly; but the others elude our observation, or if we discover them, we understand them imperfectly because we have hardly ever seen anything of the kind. It must be acknowledged, however, that they are as necessary to the American people as the former, and perhaps more so. In democratic countries the science of associations is the mother science; the progress of all the rest depends upon the progress it has made.

Among the laws that rule human societies there is one which seems to be more precise and clear than all others. If men are to remain civilized or to become so, the art of associating together must grow and improve in the same ratio in which the equality of conditions is increased.

11

True and False Philanthropy

MCGUFFEY'S READER

WILLIAM HOLMES MCGUFFEY, AN EDUCATOR AND PREACHER,
HAD A PROFOUND EFFECT ON AMERICAN EDUCATION,
PARTICULARLY IN THE AREAS OF TEACHER TRAINING AND
CURRICULUM MATERIALS.

Mr. Fantom: I despise a narrow field. O for the reign of universal benevolence! I want to make all mankind good and happy.

Mr. Goodman: Dear me! Sure that must be a wholesale sort of a job: had you not better try your hand at a *town* or *neighborhood* first?

Mr. Fantom: Sir, I have a plan in my head for relieving the miseries of the *whole world*. Every thing is bad as it now stands. I would alter all the laws, and put an end to all the wars in the world. I would put an end to all punishments; I would not leave a single prisoner on the face of the globe. *This* is what I call doing things on a grand scale.

Mr. Goodman: A scale with a vengeance! As to releasing the prisoners, however, I do not much like that, as it would be liberating a few rogues at the expense of all honest men; but as to the rest of your plan, if all countries would be so good as to turn *Christians*, it might be helped on a good deal. There would be still misery enough left indeed; because God intended this world should be earth and not heaven. But, sir, among all your changes, you must destroy human corruption, before you can make the world quite as perfect as you pretend.

Mr. Fantom: *Your* project would rivet the chains which *mine* is designed to *break*.

Mr. Goodman: Sir, I have no projects. Projects are, in general, the offspring of restlessness, vanity, and idleness. I am too busy for projects, too contented for theories, and I hope, have too much honesty and humility for a

Reprinted from William H. McGuffey's *Newly Revised Eclectic Reader* (1844), pp. 50-53.

philosopher. The utmost extent of my ambition at present is, to redress the wrongs of a poor apprentice, who has been cruelly used by his master: indeed, I have another little scheme, which is to prosecute a fellow, who has suffered a poor wretch in the poorhouse, of which he has the care, to perish through neglect, and you must assist me.

Mr. Fantom: Let the town do that. You must not apply to me for the redress of such petty grievances. I own that the wrongs of the Poles and South Americans so fill my mind, as to leave me no time to attend to the petty sorrows of poorhouses, and apprentices. It is provinces, empires, continents, that the benevolence of the philosopher embraces; every one can do a little paltry good to his next neighbor.

Mr. Goodman: Every one *can*, but I do not see that every one *does*. If they would indeed, your business would be ready done to your hands, and your grand ocean of benevolence would be filled with the drops, which private charity would throw into it. I am glad, however, you are such a friend to the prisoners, because I am just now getting a little subscription, to set free your poor old friend Tom Saunders, a very honest brother mechanic, who first got into debt, and then into jail, through no fault of his own, but merely through the pressure of the times. A number of us have given a trifle every week towards maintaining his young family since he has been in prison; but we think we shall do much more service to Saunders, and indeed in the end, lighten our own expense, by paying down, at once, a little sum, to release him, and put him in the way of maintaining his family again. We have made up all the money except five dollars. I am already promised four, and you have nothing to do but to give me the fifth. And so, for a single dollar, without any of the trouble we have had in arranging the matter, you will, at once, have the pleasure of helping to save a worthy family from starving, of redeeming an old friend from jail, and of putting a little of your boasted benevolence into action. Realize! Mr. Fantom: There is nothing like realizing.

Mr. Fantom: Why, hark ye, Mr. Goodman, do not think I value a dollar; no sir, I despise money; it is trash, it is dirt, and beneath the regard of a wise man. It is one of the unfeeling inventions of artificial society. Sir, I could talk to you half a day on the abuse of riches, and my own contempt of money.

Mr. Goodman: O pray do not give yourself that trouble. It will be a much easier way of proving your sincerity, just to put your hand in your pocket, and give me a dollar without saying a word about it: and then to you, who value time so much, and money so little, it will cut the matter short. But come now, (for I see you will give nothing), I should be mighty glad to know what is the sort of good you do yourselves, since you always object to what is done by others.

Mr. Fantom: Sir, the object of a true philosopher is, to diffuse light and knowledge. I wish to see the whole world enlightened.

Mr. Goodman: Well, Mr. Fantom, you are a wonderful man, to keep up such a stock of benevolence, at so small an expense; to love mankind so dearly, and yet *avoid* all opportunities of doing them *good;* to have such a noble zeal for the *millions,* and to feel so little compassion for the units; to long to free *empires* and enlighten *kingdoms,* and deny instruction to your own *village* and comfort to your own *family.* Surely, none but a *philosopher* could indulge so much *philanthropy* and so much *frugality* at the same time. But come, do assist me in a partition I am making in our poorhouse, between the *old,* whom I want to have better *fed,* and the *young,* whom I want to have more *worked.*

Mr. Fantom: Sir, my mind is so engrossed with the partition of Poland, that I cannot bring it down to an object of such insignificance. I despise the man, whose benevolence is swallowed up in the narrow concerns of his own family, or village, or country.

Mr. Goodman: Well, now I have a notion, that it is as well to do one's own duty, as the duty of *another* man; and that to do good at *home,* is as well as to do good abroad. For *my* part, I had as lief help *Tom Saunders* to freedom, as a *Pole* or a *South American,* though I should be very glad to help *them too.* But one must begin to love somewhere; and I think it is as natural to love one's own family, and to do good in one's own neighborhood, as to any body else. And if every man in every family, village, and county did the same, why then all the schemes would be met, and the end of one village or town where I was doing good, would be the beginning of another village where somebody else was doing good; so my schemes would jut into my neighbor's; his projects would unite with those of some other local reformer; and all would fit with a sort of dovetail exactness.

Mr. Fantom: Sir, a man of large views will be on the watch for great occasions to prove his benevolence.

Mr. Goodman: Yes, sir; but if they are so distant that he cannot reach them, or so vast that he cannot grasp them, he may let a thousand little, snug, kind, good actions slip through his fingers in the meanwhile: and so, between the great thing that he *cannot* do, and the little ones that he *will not* do, life passes, and *nothing* will be done.

12

Raising Money

BOOKER T. WASHINGTON

BOOKER T. WASHINGTON, EDUCATOR, WRITER, LECTURER, AND
EARLY CIVIL RIGHTS LEADER, FOUNDED THE TUSKEGEE
INSTITUTE IN 1881 AND SERVED AS ITS PRINCIPAL UNTIL HIS
DEATH IN 1915.

When we opened our boarding department, we provided rooms in the attic of Porter Hall, our first building, for a number of girls. But the number of students, of both sexes, continued to increase. We could find rooms outside the school grounds for many of the young men, but the girls we did not care to expose in this way. Very soon the problem of providing more rooms for the girls, as well as a larger boarding department for all the students, grew serious. As a result, we finally decided to undertake the construction of a still larger building—a building that would contain rooms for the girls and boarding accommodations for all.

After having had a preliminary sketch of the needed building made, we found that it would cost about ten thousand dollars. We had no money whatever with which to begin; still we decided to give the needed building a name. We knew we could name it, even though we were in doubt about our ability to secure the means for its construction. We decided to call the proposed building Alabama Hall, in honour of the state in which we were labouring. Again Miss Davidson began making efforts to enlist the interest and help of the coloured and white people in and near Tuskegee. They responded willingly, in proportion to their means. The students, as in the case of our first building, Porter Hall, began digging out the dirt in order to allow the laying of the foundations.

When we seemed at the end of our resources, so far as securing money was concerned, something occurred which showed the greatness of General Armstrong—something which proved how far he was above the ordinary individual. When we were in the midst of great anxiety as to where and how we

Originally published in *Up from Slavery: An Autobiography,* Chapter XII, by Booker T. Washington (1901). This version is reprinted from the edition published by Doubleday Publishing Co., Inc., Garden City, New York, in 1963.

were to get funds for the new building, I received a telegram from General Armstrong asking me if I could spend a month travelling with him through the North, and asking me, if I could do so, to come to Hampton at once. Of course I accepted General Armstrong's invitation, and went to Hampton immediately. On arriving there I found that the General had decided to take a quartette of singers through the North, and hold meetings for a month in important cities, at which meetings he and I were to speak. Imagine my surprise when the General told me, further, that these meetings were to be held, not in the interests of Hampton but in the interests of Tuskegee, and that the Hampton Institute was to be responsible for all the expenses.

Although he never told me so in so many words, I found out that General Armstrong took this method of introducing me to the people of the North, as well as for the sake of securing some immediate funds to be used in the erection of Alabama Hall. A weak and narrow man would have reasoned that all the money which came to Tuskegee in this way would be just so much taken from the Hampton Institute; but none of these selfish or short-sighted feelings ever entered the breast of General Armstrong. He knew that the people in the North who gave money gave it for the purpose of helping the whole cause of Negro civilization, and not merely for the advancement of any one school. The General knew, too, that the way to strengthen Hampton was to make it a center of unselfish power in the working out of the whole Southern problem.

In regard to the addresses which I was to make in the North, I recall just one piece of advice which the General gave me. He said: "Give them an idea for every word." I think it would be hard to improve upon this advice; and it might be made to apply to all public speaking. From that time to the present I have always tried to keep his advice in mind.

Meetings were held in New York, Brooklyn, Boston, Philadelphia, and other large cities, and at all of these meetings General Armstrong pleaded, together with myself, for help, not for Hampton, but for Tuskegee. At these meetings an especial effort was made to secure help for the building of Alabama Hall, as well as to introduce the school to the attention of the general public. In both these respects the meetings proved successful.

After that kindly introduction I began going North alone to secure funds. During the last fifteen years I have been compelled to spend a large proportion of my time away from the school, in an effort to secure money to provide for the growing needs of the institution. In my efforts to get funds I have had some experiences that may be of interest to my readers. Time and time again I have been asked, by people who are trying to secure money for philanthropic purposes, what rule or rules I followed to secure the interest and help of people who were able to contribute money to worthy objects. As far as the science of what is called begging can be reduced to rules, I would say that I have had but two rules. First, always to do my whole duty regarding making our work known to individuals and organizations; and second, not to worry about the results. This second rule has been the hardest for me to live up to. When bills are on the eve of falling due, with not a dollar in hand with which to meet them, it is pretty difficult to learn not to worry, although I think I am learning more and more each year that all worry simply consumes, and to no purpose, just so much physical and mental strength that might otherwise be given to effective work. After considerable experience in coming into contact with wealthy and noted men, I have observed that those who have accomplished the greatest results are those who "keep under the body"; are those who never grow excited or lose self-control, but are always calm, self-possessed, patient, and polite. I think that President William McKinley is the best example of a man of this class that I have ever seen.

In order to be successful in any kind of undertaking, I think the main thing is for one to grow to the point where he completely forgets himself; that is, to lose himself in a great cause. In proportion as one loses himself in this way, in the same degree does he get the highest happiness out of his work.

My experience in getting money for Tuskegee has taught me to have no patience with those people who are always condemning the rich because they are rich, and because they do not give more to objects of charity. In the first place, those who are guilty of such sweeping criticisms do not know how many people would be made poor, and how much suffering would result, if wealthy people were to part all at once with any large proportion of their wealth in a way to disorganize and cripple great business enterprises. Then very few persons have any idea of the large number of applications for help that rich people are constantly being flooded with. I know wealthy people who receive as many as twenty calls a day for help. More than once, when I have gone into the offices of rich men, I have found half a dozen persons waiting to see them, and all come for the same purpose, that of securing money. And all these calls in person, to say nothing of the applications received through the mails. Very few people have any idea of the amount of money given away by persons who never permit their names to be known. I have often heard persons condemned for not giving away money, who, to my own knowledge, were giving away thousands of dollars every year so quietly that the world knew nothing about it.

As an example of this, there are two ladies in New York, whose names rarely appear in print, but who, in a quiet way, have given us the means with which to erect three large and important buildings during the last eight years. Besides the gift of these buildings, they have made other generous donations to the school. And they not only help Tuskegee, but they are constantly seeking opportunities to help other worthy causes.

Although it has been my privilege to be the medium through which a good many hundred thousand dollars have been received for the work at Tuskegee, I have always avoided what the world calls "begging." I often tell people that I have never "begged" any money, and that I am not a "beggar." My experience and observation have convinced me that persistent asking outright for money from the rich does not, as a rule, secure help. I have usually proceeded on the principle that persons who possess sense enough to earn money have sense enough to know how to give it away, and that the mere making known of the facts regarding Tuskegee, and especially the facts regarding the work of the graduates, has been more effective than outright begging. I think that the presentation of facts, on a high, dignified plane, is all the begging that most rich people care for.

While the work of going from door to door and from office to office is hard, disagreeable, and costly in bodily strength, yet it has some compensations. Such work gives one a rare opportunity to study human nature. It also has its compensations in giving one an opportunity to meet some of the best people in the world—to be more correct, I think I should say *the best* people in the world. When one takes a broad survey of the country, he will find that the most useful and influential people in it are those who take the deepest interest in institutions that exist for the purpose of making the world better.

At one time, when I was in Boston, I called at the door of a rather wealthy lady, and was admitted to the vestibule and sent up my card. While I was waiting for an answer, her husband came in, and asked me in the most abrupt manner what I wanted. When I tried to explain the object of my call, he became still more ungentlemanly in his words and manner; and finally grew so excited that I left the house without waiting for a reply from the lady. A few blocks from that house I called to see a gentleman who received me in the most cordial manner. He wrote me his check for a generous sum, and then, before I had had an opportunity to thank him, said: "I am so grateful to you, Mr. Washington, for giving me the opportunity to help a good cause. It is a privilege to have a share in it. We in Boston are constantly indebted to you for doing *our* work." My experience in securing money convinces me that the first type of man is growing more rare all the time, and that the latter type is increasing; that is, that, more and more, rich people are coming to regard men and women who apply to them for help for worthy objects, not as beggars, but as agents for doing their work.

In the city of Boston I have rarely called upon an individual for funds that I have not been thanked for calling, usually before I could get an opportunity to thank the donor for the money. In that city the donors seem to feel, in a large degree, that an honour is being conferred upon them in their being permitted to give. Nowhere else have I met with, in so large a measure, this fine and Christlike spirit as in the city of Boston, although there are many notable instances of it outside that city. I repeat my belief that the world is growing in the direction of giving. I repeat that the main rule by which I have been guided in collecting money is to do my full duty in regard to giving people who have money an opportunity to help.

In the early years of the Tuskegee school I walked the streets or travelled country roads in the North for days and days without receiving a dollar. Often it has happened, when during the week I had been disappointed in not getting a cent from the very individuals from whom I most expected help, and when I was almost broken down and discouraged, that generous help has come from someone who I had had little idea would give at all.

I recall that on one occasion I obtained information that led me to believe that a gentleman who lived about two miles out in the country from Stamford, Conn., might become interested in our efforts at Tuskegee if our conditions and needs were presented to him. On an unusually cold and stormy day I walked the two miles to see him. After some difficulty I succeeded in securing an interview with him. He listened with some degree of interest to what I had to say, but did not give me anything. I could not help having the feeling that, in a measure, the three hours that I had spent in seeing him had been thrown away. Still, I had followed my usual rule of doing my duty. If I had not seen him, I should have felt unhappy over neglect of duty.

Two years after this visit a letter came to Tuskegee from this man, which read like this: "Enclosed I send you a New York draft for ten thousand dollars, to be used in furtherance of your work. I had placed this sum in my will for your school, but deem it wiser to give it to you while I live. I recall with pleasure your visit to me two years ago."

I can hardly imagine any occurrence which could have given me more genuine satisfaction than the receipt of this draft. It was by far the largest single donation which up to that time the school had ever received. It came at a time when an unusually long period had passed since we had received any money. We were in great distress because of lack of funds, and the nervous strain was tremendous. It is difficult for me to think of any situation that is more trying on the nerves than that of conducting a large institution, with heavy financial obligations to meet, without knowing where the money is to come from to meet these obligations from month to month.

In our case I felt a double responsibility, and this made the anxiety all the more intense. If the institution had been officered by white persons, and had failed, it would have injured the cause of Negro education; but I knew that the failure of our institution, officered by Negroes, would not only mean the loss of a school, but would cause people, in a large degree, to lose faith in the ability of the entire race. The receipt of this draft for ten thousand dollars, under all these circumstances, partially lifted a burden that had been pressing down upon me for days.

From the beginning of our work to the present I have always had the feeling, and lose no opportunity to impress our teachers with the same idea, that the school will always be supported in proportion as the inside of the institution is kept clean and pure and wholesome.

The first time I ever saw the late Collis P. Huntington, the great railroad man, he gave me two dollars for our school. The last time I saw him, which was a few months before he died, he gave me fifty thousand dollars toward our endowment fund. Between these two gifts there were others of generous proportions which came every year from both Mr. and Mrs. Huntington.

Some people may say that it was Tuskegee's good luck that brought to us this gift of fifty thousand dollars. No, it was not luck. It was hard work. Nothing ever comes to one, that is worth having, except as a result of hard work. When Mr. Huntington gave me the first two dollars, I did not blame him for not giving me more, but made up my mind that I was going to convince him by tangible results that we were worthy of larger gifts. For a dozen years I made a strong effort to convince Mr. Huntington of the value of our work. I noted that just in proportion as the usefulness of the school grew, his donations increased. Never did I meet an individual who took a more kindly and sympathetic interest in our school than did Mr. Huntington. He not only gave money to us, but took time in which to advise me, as a father would a son, about the general conduct of the school.

More than once I have found myself in some pretty tight places while collecting money in the North. The following incident I have never related but once before, for the reason that I feared that people would not believe it. One morning I found myself in Providence, Rhode Island, without a cent of money with which to buy breakfast. In crossing the street to see a lady from whom I hoped to get some money, I found a bright new twenty-five-cent piece in the middle of the street-car track. I not only had this twenty-five cents for my breakfast, but within a few minutes I had a donation from the lady on whom I had started to call.

At one of our Commencements I was bold enough to invite the Rev. E. Winchester Donald, D.D., rector of Trinity Church, Boston, to preach the Commencement sermon. As we then had no room large enough to accommodate all who would be present, the place of meeting was under a large, improvised arbour, built partly of brush and partly of rough boards. Soon after Dr. Donald had begun speaking, the rain came down in torrents, and he had to stop, while some one held an umbrella over him.

The boldness of what I had done never dawned upon me until I saw the picture made by the rector of Trinity Church standing before that large audience under an old umbrella, waiting for the rain to cease so that he could go on with his address.

It was not very long before the rain ceased and Dr. Donald finished his sermon; and an excellent sermon it was, too, in spite of the weather. After he had gone to his room, and had gotten the wet threads of his clothes dry, Dr. Donald ventured the remark that a large chapel at Tuskegee would not be out of place. The next day a letter came from two ladies who were then travelling in Italy, saying that they had decided to give us the money for such a chapel as we needed.

A short time ago we received twenty thousand dollars from Mr. Andrew Carnegie, to be used for the purpose of erecting a new library building. Our first library and reading-room were in a corner of a shanty, and the whole thing occupied a space about five by twelve feet. It required ten years of work before I was able to secure Mr. Carnegie's interest and help. The first time I saw him, ten years ago, he seemed to take but little interest in our school, but I was determined to show him that we were worthy of his help. After ten years of hard work I wrote him a letter reading as follows:

December 15, 1900

Mr. Andrew Carnegie
5 W. Fifty-First St.
New York.

Dear Sir:

Complying with the request which you made of me when I saw you at your residence a few days ago, I now submit in writing an appeal for a library building for our institution.

We have 1100 students, 86 officers and instructors, together with their families, and about 200 coloured people living near the school, all of whom would make use of the library building.

We have over 12,000 books, periodicals, etc., gifts from our friends, but we have no suitable place for them, and we have no suitable reading-room.

Our graduates go to work in every section of the South, and whatever knowledge might be obtained in the library would serve to assist in the elevation of the whole Negro race.

Such a building as we need could be erected for about $20,000. All of the work for the building, such as brickmaking, brick-masonry, carpentry, blacksmithing, etc., would be done by the students. The money which you would give would not only supply the building, but the erection of the building would give a large number of students an opportunity to learn the building trades, and the students would use the money paid to them to keep themselves in school. I do not believe that a similar amount of money often could be made to go so far in uplifting a whole race.

If you wish further information, I shall be glad to furnish it.

Yours truly,

Booker T. Washington, Principal

The next mail brought back the following reply:

"I will be very glad to pay the bills for the library building as they are incurred, to the extent of twenty thousand dollars, and I am glad of this opportunity to show the interest I have in your noble work."

I have found that strict business methods go a long way in securing the interest of rich people. It has been my constant aim at Tuskegee to carry out, in our financial and other operations, such business methods as would be approved of by any New York banking house.

I have spoken of several large gifts to the school; but by far the greater proportion of the money that has built up the institution has come in the form of small donations from persons of moderate means. It is upon these small gifts, which carry with them the interest of hundreds of donors, that any philanthropic work must depend largely for its support. In my efforts to get money I have often been surprised at the patience and deep interest of the ministers, who are besieged on every hand and at all hours of the day for help. If no other consideration had convinced me of the value of the Christian life, the Christlike work which the Church of all denominations in America has done during the last thirty-five years for the elevation of the black man would have made me a Christian. In a large degree it has been the pennies, the nickels, and the dimes which have come from the Sunday-schools, the Christian Endeavour societies, and the missionary societies, as well as from the Church proper, that have helped to elevate the Negro at so rapid a rate.

This speaking of small gifts reminds me to say that very few Tuskegee graduates fail to send us an annual contribution. These contributions range from twenty-five cents up to ten dollars.

Soon after beginning our third year's work we were surprised to receive money from three special sources, and up to the present time we have continued to receive help from them. First, the State Legislature of Alabama increased its annual appropriation from two thousand dollars to three thousand dollars; I might add that still later it increased this sum to four thousand five hundred dollars a year. The effort to secure this increase was led by the Hon. M. F. Foster, the member of the Legislature from Tuskegee. Second, we received one thousand dollars from the John F. Slater Fund. Our work seemed to please the trustees of this Fund, as they soon began increasing their annual grant. This has been added to from time to time until at present we receive eleven thousand dollars annually from this Fund. The other help to which I have referred came in the shape of an allowance from the Peabody Fund. This was at first five hundred dollars, but it has since been increased to fifteen hundred dollars.

The effort to secure help from the Slater and Peabody Funds brought me into contact with two rare men—men who have had much to do in shaping the policy for the education of the Negro. I refer to the Hon. J. L. M. Curry, of Washington, who is the general agent for these two funds, and Mr. Morris K. Jesup, of New York. Dr. Curry is a native of the South, an ex-Confederate soldier, yet I do not believe there is any man in the country who is more deeply interested in the highest welfare of the Negro than Dr. Curry, or one who is more free from race prejudice. He enjoys the unique distinction of possessing to an equal degree the confidence of the black man and the Southern white man. I shall never forget the first time I met him. It was in Richmond, Va., where he was then living. I had heard much about him. When I first went into his presence, trembling because of my youth and inexperience, he took me by the hand so cordially, and spoke such encouraging words, and gave me such helpful advice regarding the proper course to pursue, that I came to know him then, as I have known him ever since, as a high example of one who is constantly and unselfishly at work for the betterment of humanity.

Mr. Morris K. Jesup, the treasurer of the Slater Fund, I refer to because I know of no man of wealth and large and complicated business responsibilities who gives not only money but his time and thought to the subject of the proper method of elevating the Negro to the extent that is true of Mr. Jesup. It is very largely through his effort and influence that during the last few years the subject of industrial education has assumed the importance that it has, and been placed on its present footing.

13

Charitable Effort

JANE ADDAMS

JANE ADDAMS, WRITER, ACTIVIST, AND PIONEER OF CHILD LABOR
REFORM, FOUNDED HULL HOUSE IN 1889. SHE WON THE NOBEL
PEACE PRIZE (WITH NICHOLAS MURRAY BUTLER) IN 1931 FOR HER
ROLE AS PRESIDENT OF THE WOMEN'S INTERNATIONAL LEAGUE
FOR PEACE AND FREEDOM.

All those hints and glimpses of a larger and more satisfying democracy, which literature and our own hopes supply, have a tendency to slip away from us and to leave us sadly unguided and perplexed when we attempt to act upon them.

Our conceptions of morality, as all our other ideas, pass through a course of development; the difficulty comes in adjusting our conduct, which has become hardened into customs and habits, to these changing moral conceptions. When this adjustment is not made, we suffer from the strain and indecision of believing one hypothesis and acting upon another.

Probably there is no relation in life which our democracy is changing more rapidly than the charitable relation—that relation which obtains between benefactor and beneficiary; at the same time there is no point of contact in our modern experience which reveals so clearly the lack of that equality which democracy implies. We have reached the moment when democracy has made such inroads upon this relationship, that the complacency of the old-fashioned charitable man is gone forever; while, at the same time, the very need and existence of charity, denies us the consolation and freedom which democracy will at last give.

It is quite obvious that the ethics of none of us are clearly defined, and we are continually obliged to act in circles of habit, based upon convictions which we no longer hold. Thus our estimate of the effect of environment and social conditions has doubtless shifted faster than our methods of administrating charity have changed. Formerly when it was believed that poverty was syn-

Excerpted from Chapter II of *Democracy and Social Ethics*, by Jane Addams, originally published in 1902. This material is drawn from the edition edited by Anne Firor Scott and published by The Belknap Press of Harvard University Press, Cambridge, Massachusetts, in 1964, by permission of the publisher.

onymous with vice and laziness, and that the prosperous man was the righteous man charity was administered harshly with a good conscience; for the charitable agent really blamed the individual for his poverty, and the very fact of his own superior prosperity gave him a certain consciousness of superior morality. We have learned since that time to measure by other standards, and have ceased to accord to the money-earning capacity exclusive respect; while it is still rewarded out of all proportion to any other, its possession is by no means assumed to imply the possession of the highest moral qualities. We have learned to judge men by their social virtues as well as by their business capacity, by their devotion to intellectual and disinterested aims, and by their public spirit, and we naturally resent being obliged to judge poor people so solely upon the industrial side. Our democratic instinct instantly takes alarm. It is largely in this modern tendency to judge all men by one democratic standard, while the old charitable attitude commonly allowed the use of two standards, that much of the difficulty adheres. We know that unceasing bodily toil becomes wearing and brutalizing, and our position is totally untenable if we judge large numbers of our fellows solely upon their success in maintaining it.

A very little familiarity with the poor districts of any city is sufficient to show how primitive and genuine are the neighborly relations. There is the greatest willingness to lend or borrow anything, and all the residents of the given tenement know the most intimate family affairs of all the others. The fact that the economic condition of all alike is on a most precarious level makes the ready outflow of sympathy and material assistance the most natural thing in the world. There are numberless instances of self-sacrifice quite unknown in the circles where greater economic advantages make that kind of intimate knowledge of one's neighbors impossible. An Irish family in which the man has lost his place, and the woman is struggling to eke out the scanty savings by day's work, will take in the widow and her five children who have been turned into the street, without a moment's reflection upon the physical discomforts involved. The most maligned landlady who lives in the house with her tenants is usually ready to lend a scuttle full of coal to one of them who may be out of work, or to share her supper. A woman for whom the writer had long tried in vain to find work failed to appear at the appointed time when employment was secured at last. Upon investigation it transpired that a neighbor further down the street was taken ill, that the children ran for the family friend, who went of course, saying simply when reasons for her non-appearance were demanded, "It broke me heart to leave the place, but what could I do?" A woman whose husband was sent up to the city prison for the maximum term, just three months before the birth of her child, found herself penniless at the end of that time, having gradually sold her supply of household furniture. She took refuge with a friend whom she supposed to be living in three rooms in another part of town. When she arrived, however, she discovered that her friend's husband had been out of work so long that they had been reduced to living in one room. The friend, however, took her in, and the friend's husband was obliged to sleep upon a bench in the park every night for a week, which he did uncomplainingly if not cheerfully. Fortunately it was summer, "and it only rained one night." The writer could not discover from the young mother that she had any special claim upon the "friend" beyond the fact that they had formerly worked together in the same factory. The husband she had never seen until the night of her arrival, when he at once went forth in search of a midwife who would consent to come upon his promise of future payment.

The evolutionists tell us that the instinct to pity, the impulse to aid his fellow, served man at a very early period, as a rude rule of right and wrong. There is no doubt that this rude rule still holds among many people with whom charitable agencies are brought into contact, and that their ideas of right and wrong are quite honestly outraged by the methods of these agencies. When they see the delay and caution with which relief is given, it does not appear to them a conscientious scruple, but as the cold and calculating action of a selfish man. It is not the aid that they are accustomed to receive from their neighbors, and they do not understand why the impulse which drives people to "be good to the poor" should be so severely supervised. The feel, remotely, that the charity visitor is moved by motives that are alien and unreal. They may be superior motives, but they are different, and they are "agin nature."

Even those of us who feel most sorely the need of more order in altruistic effort and see the end to be desired, find something distasteful in the juxtaposition of the words "organized" and "charity." We say in defence that we are striving to turn this emotion into a motive, that pity is capricious, and not to be depended on; that we mean to give it the dignity of conscious duty. But at bottom we distrust a little a scheme which substitutes a theory of social conduct for the natural promptings of the heart, even although we appreciate the complexity of the situation. The poor man who has fallen into distress, when he first asks aid, instinctively expects tenderness, consideration, and forgiveness. If it is the first time, it has taken him long to make up his mind to take the step. He comes somewhat bruised and battered, and instead of being met with warmth of heart and sympathy, he is at once chilled by an investigation and an intimation that he ought to work. He does not recognize the disciplinary aspect of the situation.

The first impulse of our charity visitor is to be somewhat severe with her shiftless family for spending money on pleasures and indulging their children out of all proportion to their means. The poor family which receives beans and coal from the county, and pays for a bicycle on the installment plan, is not unknown to any of us. But as the growth of juvenile crime becomes gradually understood, and as the danger of giving no legitimate and organized pleasure to the child becomes clearer, we remember that primitive man had games long before he cared for a house or regular meals.

There are certain boys in many city neighborhoods who form themselves into little gangs with a leader who is somewhat more intrepid than the rest. Their favorite performance is to break into an untenanted house, to knock off the faucets, and cut the lead pipe, which they sell to the nearest junk dealer. With the money thus procured they buy beer and drink it in little free-booter's groups sitting in the alley. From beginning to end they have the excitement of knowing that they may be seen and caught by the "coppers," and are at times quite breathless with suspense. It is not the least unlike, in motive and execution, the practice of country boys who go forth in squads to set traps for rabbits or to round up a coon.

It is characterized by a pure spirit for adventure, and the vicious training really begins when they are arrested, or when an older boy undertakes to guide them into further excitements. From the very beginning the most enticing and exciting experiences which they have seen have been connected with crime. The policeman embodies all the majesty of successful law and established government in his brass buttons and dazzlingly equipped patrol wagon.

The boy who has been arrested comes back more or less a hero with a tale to tell of the interior recesses of the mysterious police station. The earliest public excitement the child remembers is divided between the rattling fire engines, "the time there was a fire in the next block," and all the tense interest of the patrol wagon "the time the drunkest lady in our street was arrested."

In the first year of their settlement the Hull-House residents took fifty kindergarten children to Lincoln Park, only to be grieved by their apathetic interest in trees and flowers. As they came back with an omnibus full of tired and sleepy children, they were surprised to find them galvanized into sudden life because a patrol wagon rattled by. Their eager little heads popped out of the windows full of questioning: "Was it a man or a woman?" "How many policemen inside?" and eager little tongues began to tell experiences of arrests which baby eyes had witnessed.

The excitement of a chase, the chances of competition, and the love of a fight are all centered in the outward display of crime. The parent who receives charitable aid and yet provides pleasure for his child, and is willing to indulge him in his play, is blindly doing one of the wisest things possible; and no one is more eager for playgrounds and vacation schools than the conscientious charity visitor.

A certain charity visitor is peculiarly appealed to by the weakness and pathos of forlorn old age. She is responsible for the well-being of perhaps a dozen old women to whom she sustains a sincerely affectionate and almost filial relation. Some of them learn to take her benefactions quite as if they came from their own relatives, grumbling at all she does, and scolding her with a family freedom. One of these poor old women was injured in a fire years ago. She has but the fragment of a hand left, and is grievously crippled in her feet. Through years of pain she had become addicted to opium, and when she first came under the visitor's care, was only held from the poorhouse by the awful thought that she would there perish without her drug. Five years of tender care have done wonders for her. She lives in two neat little rooms, where with her thumb and two fingers she makes innumerable quilts, which she sells and gives away with the greatest delight. Her opium is regulated to a set amount taken each day, and she has been drawn away from much drinking. She is a voracious reader, and has her head full of strange tales made up from books and her own imagination. At one time it seemed impossible to do anything for her in Chicago, and she was kept for two years in a suburb, where the family of the charity visitor lived, and where she was nursed through several hazardous illnesses. She now lives a better life than she did, but she is still far from being a model old woman. The neighbors are constantly shocked by the fact that she is supported and comforted by a "charity lady," while at the same time she occasionally "rushes the growler," scolding at the boys lest they jar her in her tottering walk. The care of her has broken through even that second standard, which the neighborhood had learned to recognize as the standard of charitable societies, that only the "worthy poor" are to be helped; that temperance and thrift are the virtues which receive the plums of benevolence. The old lady herself is conscious of this criticism. Indeed, irate neighbors tell her to her face that she doesn't in the least deserve what she gets. In order to disarm them, and at the same time to explain what would otherwise seem loving-kindness so colossal as to be abnormal, she tells them that during her sojourn in the suburb she discovered an awful family secret—a horrible scandal connected with the long-suffering charity visitor; that it is in order to prevent the divulgence of this that she constantly receives her ministrations. Some of her perplexed neighbors accept this explanation as simple and offering a solution of this vexed problem. Doubtless many of them have a glimpse of the real state of affairs, of the love and patience which ministers to need irrespective of worth. But the standard is too high for most of them, and it sometimes seems unfortunate to break down the second standard, which holds that people who "rush the growler," are not worthy of charity, and that there is a certain justice attained when they go to the poorhouse. It is certainly dangerous to break down the lower, unless the higher is made clear.

Just when our affection becomes large enough to care for the unworthy among the poor as we would care for the unworthy among our own kin, is certainly a perplexing question. To say that it should never be so, is a comment upon our democratic relations to them which few of us would be willing to make.

Of what use is all this striving perplexity? Has the experience any value? It is certainly genuine, for it induces an occasional charity visitor to live in a tenement house as simply as the other tenants do. It drives others to give up visiting the poor altogether, because, they claim, it is quite impossible unless the individual becomes a member of a sisterhood, which requires, as some of the Roman Catholic sisterhoods do, that the member first take the vows of obedience and poverty, so that she can have nothing to give save as it is first given to her, and thus she is not harassed by a constant attempt at adjustment.

Both the tenement-house resident and the sister assume to have put themselves upon the industrial level of their neighbors, although they have left out the most awful element of poverty, that of imminent fear of starvation and a neglected old age.

The young charity visitor who goes from a family living upon a most precarious industrial level to her own home in a prosperous part of the city, if she is sensitive at all, is never free from perplexities which our growing democracy forces upon her.

We sometimes say that our charity is too scientific, but we would doubtless be much more correct in our estimate if we said that it is not scientific enough. We dislike the entire arrangement of cards alphabetically classified according to streets and names of families, with the unrelated and meaningless details attached to them. Our feeling of revolt is probably not unlike that which afflicted the students of botany and geology in the middle of the last century, when flowers were tabulated in alphabetical order, when geology was taught by colored charts and thin books. No doubt the students, wearied to death, many times said that it was all too scientific, and were much perplexed and worried when they found traces of structure and physiology which their so-called scientific principles were totally unable to account for. But all this happened before science had become evolutionary and scientific at all, before it had a principle of life from within. The very indications and discoveries which formerly perplexed, later illumined and made the study absorbing and vital.

We are singularly slow to apply this evolutionary principle to human affairs in general, although it is fast being applied to the education of children. We are at last learning to follow the development of the child; to expect certain traits under certain conditions; to adapt methods and matter to his growing mind. No "advanced educator" can allow himself to be so absorbed in the question of what a child ought to be as to exclude the discovery of what he is. But in our charitable efforts we think much more of what a man ought to be than of what he is or of what he may become; and we ruthlessly force our conventions and standards upon him, with a sternness which we would consider stupid indeed did an educator use it in forcing his mature intellectual convictions upon an undeveloped mind.

Let us take the example of a timid child, who cries when he is put to bed because he is afraid of the dark. The "soft-hearted" parent stays with him, simply because he is sorry for him and wants to comfort him. The scientifically trained parent stays with him, because he realizes that the child is in a stage of development in which his imagination has the best of him, and in which it is impossible to reason him out of a belief in ghosts. These two parents, wide apart in point of view, after all act much alike, and both very differently from the pseudo-scientific parent, who acts from dogmatic conviction and is sure he is right. He talks of developing his child's self-respect and good sense, and leaves him to cry himself to sleep, demanding powers of self-control and development which the child does not possess. There is no doubt that our development of charity methods has reached this pseudo-scientific and stilted stage. We have learned to condemn unthinking, ill-regulated kind-heartedness, and we take great pride in mere repression much as the stern parent tells the visitor below how admirably he is rearing the child, who is hysterically crying upstairs and laying the foundation for future nervous disorders. The pseudo-scientific spirit, or rather, the undeveloped stage of our philanthropy, is perhaps most clearly revealed in our tendency to lay constant stress on negative action. "Don't give;" "don't break down self-respect," we are constantly told. We distrust the human impulse as well as the teachings of our own experience, and in their stead substitute dogmatic rules for conduct. We forget that the accumulation of knowledge and the holding of convictions must finally result in the application of that knowledge and those convictions to life itself; that the necessity for activity and a pull upon the sympathies is so severe, that all the knowledge in the possession of the visitor is constantly applied, and she has a reasonable chance for an ultimate intellectual comprehension. Indeed, part of the perplexity in the administration of charity comes from the fact that the type of person drawn to it is the one who insists that her convictions shall not be unrelated to action. Her moral concepts constantly tend to float away from her, unless they have a basis in the concrete relation of life. She is confronted with the task of reducing her scruples to action, and of converging many wills so as to unite the strength of all of them into one accomplishment, the value of which no one can foresee.

On the other hand, the young woman who has succeeded in expressing her social compunction through charitable effort finds that the wider social activity, and the contact with the larger experience, not only increases her sense of social obligation but at the same time recasts her social ideals. She is chagrined to discover that in the actual task of reducing her social scruples to action, her humble beneficiaries are far in advance of her, not in charity or singleness of purpose, but in self-sacrificing action. She reaches the old-time virtue of humility by a social process, not in the old way, as the man who sits by the side of the road and puts dust upon his head, calling himself a contrite sinner, but she gets the dust upon her head because she has stumbled and fallen in the road through her efforts to push forward the mass, to march with her fellows. She has socilized her virtues not only through a social aim but by a social process.

The Hebrew prophet made three requirements from those who would join the great forward-moving procession led by Jehovah. "To love mercy" and at the same time "to do justly" is the difficult task; to fulfil the first requirement alone is to fall into the error of indiscriminate giving with all its disastrous results; to fulfil the second solely is to obtain the stern policy of withholding, and it results in such a dreary lack of sympathy and understanding that the establishment of justice is impossible. It may be that the combination of the two can never be attained save as we fulfil still the third requirement—"to walk humbly with God," which may mean to walk for many dreary miles beside the lowliest of His creatures, not even in that peace of mind which the company of the humble is popularly supposed to afford, but rather with the pangs and throes to which the poor human understanding is subjected whenever it attempts to comprehend the meaning of life.

14

The Joiners

MAX LERNER

MAX LERNER IS A NOTED EDUCATOR, ECONOMIST, AND WRITER
ON MANY ASPECTS OF AMERICAN SOCIETY. HIS MANY OTHER
PUBLICATIONS INCLUDE TOCQUEVILLE AND AMERICAN
CIVILIZATION (1969).

A standard cliche about American society is that the Americans are "joiners" and "belongers." The derisive attack on the symbol of Sinclair Lewis's Babbitt, who belonged to the Elks, Boosters, and a network of other service clubs and lodges, became a stereotype of American social criticism. It is true that the associative impulse is strong in American life: no other civilization can show as many secret fraternal orders, businessmen's "service clubs," trade and occupational associations, social clubs, garden clubs, women's clubs, church clubs, theater groups, political and reform associations, veterans' groups, ethnic societies, and other clusterings of trivial or substantial importance.

When the intellectuals speak scornfully of Americans as "joiners" they usually forget to include themselves: there are more academic organizations in the United States than in the whole of Europe. They have in mind a middle-class American who may be a Shriner or an Elk, a Rotarian, a Legionnaire, a member of a country club or outing club, and at least a dozen other organizations. In the Warner studies of "Yankee City" (Newburyport) which had 17,000 people, there were over 800 associations, about 350 of them more or less permanent. Taking some random figures in the mid-1950s for illustration, the fraternal orders included in the past at least twenty million members; there were about 100,000 women's clubs; there were two million young people who belonged to the rural and small-town "4-H" clubs. At least 100 million Americans were estimated to belong to some kind of national organization.

Max Weber, the German sociologist, visited America in 1905 and spoke of these "voluntary associations" as bridging the transition between the closed hierarchical society of the Old World and the fragmented individualism of the

Reprinted from *America as a Civilization*, Vol. I: The Basic Frame, Chapter II (New York: Simon & Schuster, 1967). Copyright © 1957 by Max Lerner. Reprinted by permission of Simon & Schuster, a Division of the Gulf & Western Corporation.

New World, and he saw how crucial a social function these groupings perform in American life. After World War II the students of German society, looking back at the Nazi experience, thought they could trace a connection between the lesser role of such voluntary groups in Germany and the rise of totalitarianism. Their assumption was that when the associative impulse is balked, it may express itself in a more destructive way.

Certainly one of the drives behind "joining" is the integrative impulse of forming ties with like-minded people and thus finding status in the community. Americans join associations for a number of motives: to "get ahead," to "meet people" and "make contacts," to "get something done," to learn something, to fill their lives. These drives shed some light on the human situation in America. Constantly mobile, Americans need continuities to enable them easily to meet people, make friends, eat and drink with them, call them by their first names. The clubs and lodges help fill the need. They are at once a way of breaking up "cliques" and "sets" and at the same time forming new ones. They are a means for measuring social distance, narrowing it for those who break in and are included, lengthening it for those who are excluded. For a newcomer in a community it is hard to break the shell of the tight local social groups unless he comes with a recognized stamp from a national organization or makes his way into a local one. Once in it, he joins with the others in a critical surveillance of the next newcomer. This is a way of solving the need in any society both for clannishness and for social flexibility.

In the midst of constant change and turbulence, even in a mass society, the American feels alone. In a society of hierarchy, loneliness is more tolerable because each member knows his position in the hierarchy—lower than some, higher than others, but always known. In a mobile, nonhierarchical society like the American, social position does not have the same meaning as in a vertical scheme of deference and authority. A man's status in the community is a matter of making horizontal connections, which give him his place in what would otherwise be a void. It is this social placing of an American—in church, lodge, service or women's club, eating club, Community Fund drive, veterans' group, country club, political party—that defines his social personality. Through it he gets the sense of effectiveness he does not have as a minor part of the machine process of the corporate organization. Here he can make his way as a person, by his qualities of geniality and friendliness, his ability to talk at a meeting or run it or work in a committee, his organizing capacities, his ardor, his public spirit. Here also he stretches himself, as he rarely does on the job, by working with others for common nonprofit ends.

Thus Americans achieve a sense of collective expression which belies the outward atomism of American life. "Not to belong to a *we* makes you lonesome," says the adolescent girl in Carson McCullers' *The Member of the Wed-*

ding. "When you say *we,* I'm not included, and it's not fair." Since there is little emphasis in America on some mystical community of religion, there is a greater hunger to belong to a "we." This was less true in the earlier history of the nation. The American rarely thought of himself as "lonely" until the twentieth century. Before that time the dominant note in his thinking was that he was a self-sufficient individual. But he is no longer sufficient unto himself. He gets a certain degree of shared experience from his job at the factory or office, and from his trade-union, but he needs a good deal more from personal relations outside his job life. Margaret Mead notes that at their first meeting Americans are distant and ill at ease, but at their second they act like old friends. It is because they have had a shared experience, no matter how slight, which removes their inhibitions and makes them feel expansive because of it. Karen Horney, coming from Germany to America, was compelled to change her whole theory about the neurotic personality when she found how different were the inner sources of conflict in America from those in Germany, and how much of a role loneliness played in American conflicts.

It is a striking fact that friendships in America, especially male friendships, are not as deep as in other cultures. The American male suspects that there is something sissified about a devoted and demonstrative friendship, except between a man and woman, and then it must pass over into love, or perhaps just into sex. In their clubs and associations, however, at first in school clubs and college fraternities and later in secret lodges or women's clubs, Americans find a level of friendship that does not lay them open to the charge of being sentimental. In his clubs a man is not ashamed to call another man "brother," although outside of the lodge, the trade-union, and the church the term "brother" is used sardonically in American speech.

It is the hunger for shared experience that makes the American fear solitude as he does. More than a century ago Emerson spoke of the polar needs of "society and solitude." The days in which Americans pushed into the wilderness to find solitude are largely over. Many of them still leave the crowded cities for "the country," but their search is not so much for solitude as for greater living space and smaller and more compassable groups. Lewis Mumford has made a plea for housing arrangements that will assure each member of the family a room of his own to which he can retreat when the need for solitude comes upon him, to rediscover the shape of his personality. But for many Americans solitude is still too frightening, whether because they dare not face the dilemma of their own personality or because they recognize themselves more easily by reference to their association with others.

There are many ways of dividing American associations into broad types, none wholly satisfactory. The best one can do is to point out some dramatic contrasts between them. There are the occupational and economic groups at one end of the spectrum, geared to self-interest, and the crusading and cultural ones at the other. There are the patriotic societies of the "Old Americans" and the newer ethnic societies of minority groups. There are broadly inclusive associations (political parties, trade unions, *ad hoc* reform groups) at one end, and at the other there are highly personal groups that run all the way from high-school cliques to the adult eating clubs and the "country-club set." There are, as Warner has put it, "secular" organizations and "sacred" ones, matter-of-fact ones and highly ritualistic ones.

Some of these are more saturated with symbolism than others, yet all of them in one way or another deal in symbols and take their appeal from them. The symbolic complexity of American life is largely expressed in these clubs, lodges, and associations, which fulfill to the hilt what Durkheim long ago laid down as the essence of religious groupings—"collective representation." The degree of ritual varies, being very high in the case of Masonic lodges and church groups and less so in the case of *ad hoc* reform groups. Yet the symbolism and the ritual are present, explicitly or implicitly, in all of them.

Behind the urge toward "joining" is the sense of the mysterious and exotic. To belong to a secret order and be initiated into its rites, to be a part of a "Temple" with a fancy Oriental name, to parade in the streets of Los Angeles, Chicago, or New York dressed in an Arab fez and burnoose, to have high-sounding titles of potentates of various ranks in a hierarchy: all this has appeal in a nonhierarchical society from which much of the secrecy and mystery of life has been squeezed out. The fraternal groups flourish best in the small towns of the Middle West: the drearier the cultural wasteland of the small town, the greater the appeal of the exotic. Americans have an ambivalent attitude toward secrecy: they want everything out in the open, yet they delight in the secrecy of fraternal groups, as Tom Sawyer's gang of boys in Mark Twain's books did, and as the cellar clubs and the boys' gangs in the big-city slums still do. Much of the appeal of the Ku Klux Klan lies in this mysterious flim-flammery, at once sadistic and grimly prankish. In many ways the American male of adult years is an arrested small boy, playing with dollars and power as he did once with toys or in gangs, and matching the violence of his recreation to the intensity of his loneliness.

This is especially clear in the veterans' groups, like the American Legion or the Veterans of Foreign Wars, which banded together not only for bonuses and other lobbying purposes but through a nostalgia for the ultimate shared experience of killing and facing death. Under the form of vigilant patriotism they are an effort to recapture the adventure of youth and death in a life that seems humdrum by contrast with the memories of war and derring-do. Since they have the self-assurance of being patriots and hunters of subversives, they come to feel that they have earned a license for license. Their political views take on something of the same cast as their prankishness at conventions, and there is a peculiar irony in the spectacle of drunken and boisterous middle-aged men whose leaders deliver solemn speeches about saving the nation. Curiously, some of the men who are pursued by these Hounds of God got themselves into trouble originally by reason of the same proclivity to become joiners, sponsoring a series of liberal and Leftist letterheads through a mixed impulse of gregariousness and reformist action.

For many American women, the women's club fills the emotional void of middle age, helping in the fight against loneliness and boredom. For others it means a chance to act as culture surrogates for their husbands, who are too busy to keep up with the trends in literature, the arts, or the community services. Americans have learned to take the clubwomen with a kindly bantering acceptance, much as in the Helen Hokinson caricatures. The jokes about the ladies' club lecture circuits cannot conceal a measure of pride on the part of a new nation in having wives with leisure enough to spend on veneer, like garden clubs, reading and discussion clubs, parent-teacher associations, and child-study clubs. In every American community the lecture forums, Little Theater groups, concerts and symphonies and poetry readings are in the custody of little groups of devoted people—men as well as women—who combine the sense of community service with a feeling of membership in a cultural elite.

These cultural groups are part of the array of *ad hoc* organizations which Americans form for every conceivable purpose. Some of them are meddlers and priers, seeking to impose their will upon the society by hunting other Americans down and boycotting and censoring their activities; others are formed to combat them with equal militancy. There are vigilante groups and civil liberties groups; there are radical, conservative, liberal, reactionary, and crackpot groups. Each of the three great religious communities—Protestant, Catholic and Jewish—has its own welfare, charity, social, recreational, social work, and reformist clubs. In fact, the Negroes as well as the newer minority ethnic groups have a more intense participation in associational life than the "old Americans": it is their way of retaining their cohesiveness and morale in the face of the pressures of the majority culture. Cutting across the religious and ethnic divisions are Community Chest drives, hospital societies, private schools, settlement house and welfare groups, and groups built around every conceivable hobby. They go back in their impulse to the idea of self-help, and many of them combine the pressure group with self-interest and "do goodism." To some degree they embody the fanatical energy drive that has transformed the face of American life.

It is through these associations that Americans avoid the excesses both of state worship and of complete individualism. It is in them, and not in the geographical locality, that the sense of community comes closest to being achieved. Through them also the idea of neighborhood has been re-created in America: for in most American cities the neighbors next door, who may be fellow tenants or fellow houseowners, have little else in common. The real common interests are shared by people working in the same industry or profession, sending their children to the same school, belonging to the same welfare organization or club, fighting for the same causes. Sometimes this involves "sets" and "cliques" which form from the encrustation of shared experience; sometimes it involves common membership in leisure-and-recreation groups whose chief tie is an interchange of taste and experience. But through the sum of these ways the American manages to achieve a functional set of social relations with like-minded people, the core of which is not propinquity of place but community of interests, vocations, preferences, and tastes.

The propensity to join is not new in America. It goes back to the ladies' reading clubs and other cultural groups which spread on the moving frontier and softened some of its rigors, and which were the forerunners of the parent-teacher associations and the civic and forum groups of today. The jungle of voluntary associations was already dense enough for De Tocqueville to note that "in no country in the world has the principle of association been...more unsparingly applied to a multitude of different objects than in America." The permissiveness of the state, the openness of an open society, the newness of the surroundings, the need for interweaving people from diverse ethnic groups— or, conversely, of their huddling together inside the ethnic tent until they could be assimilated—all these shaping forces were present from the start. What came later was the breaking up of the rural and small-town life of America and the massing in impersonal cities, bringing a dislocation that strengthened the impulse to join like-minded people.

Yet here again one runs a danger in generalizing about Americans as a nation. There are phases of class and status that must be taken into account. There has been a tendency to believe that because Babbitt was a joiner all joiners and belongers must therefore be Babbitts and must come from the middle classes. But the studies show a different picture. Warner found in Newburyport a direct correlation between the height of the class level and the propensity to join associations. Using his own six class categories (two uppers, two middles, and two lowers), he found that 72 percent of the people in the upper classes belonged to associations, 64 percent in the upper middle, 49 percent in the lower middle, and 39 percent and 22 percent in the two lowers respectively.

Moreover, each of the classes tended to join different kinds of groups, for somewhat different purposes, and each of them had a different "style" of behavior within them. The elites used the associations chiefly as instruments for the strategic manipulation of the life of the community—through their control of the country clubs, the eating and discussion clubs, the civic associations, the fund-raising drives. Even when they belonged to such middle-class groups as the women's clubs or the businessmen's service clubs, they brought with them a prestige which enabled them to run the show, and sometimes they used their social power as a form of blackmail in extracting larger civic contributions from the parvenu groups. The middle classes used the associations largely as a way of improving their social status and for training themselves in articulateness and leadership. For the lower classes the emphasis was mainly upon church activities. Actually, the figures for their participation in club life would be even lower if it were not for the fact that a large proportion were in the minority ethnic groups and belonged therefore to their ethnic societies. The lower-class "old American" has very few associational ties.

An added word as to why the "low-status" people (as a number of studies have shown) belong to relatively few associations: partly it is because the nature of their work leaves them less time, partly because they lack the needed money for membership, partly because their interests and perspectives are more limited. With more limited life chances there is a corresponding shrinkage of participation in community experience through the associations. In fact, the Lunds found in their *Middletown* studies that the low-income and low-status groups made few visits except in their immediate neighborhood, formed few ties outside it, and had few friendships: their contacts of a more intimate sort were with their "own kin." Thus the low-status groups in America tend to become isolated, and their isolation is all the greater because they are part of a culture in which everybody else "belongs." I have spoken of the differences in class style. One of the striking differences is that the club activities of the lower and middle classes tend to be more symbolic, emotional, and ritualistic: those of the upper classes are more rationalist, with greater emphasis on speeches and discussions.

There are certain common elements, however, in the whole range of associational life. Members are expected to be "active." They belong to committees, take part in campaigns, try to get publicity for their activities in the local press, lay a good deal of stress on fund raising (especially in the case of women's groups), and engage in a kind of gift exchange by a reciprocity of contributions which Warner compares to the potlatches of some of the American Indian tribes. A good deal of American humor has concerned itself with club life, including Robert Benchley's classic film on *The Treasurer's Report*. But club and committee work has also meant a training in democratic forms and procedures and an instrument for integrating the community.

Some commentators have guessed that Americans are intense joiners because they need some way of alleviating the tensions and anxieties that arise in their competitive living—which would account for the large number of philanthropic, service, and reformist organizations. Certainly the ritual of the fraternal associations may be an answer to the humdrum character of the daily tasks, and the sense of brotherliness and of service may be a way of allaying the accumulated hostilities and guilt feelings. E. D. Chapple, using an anthropological approach to the theory of associations, suggests that a person who has suffered a serious disturbance may get relocated either by some form of ritual (the *rites of passage* mentioned above) or by changes in his "tangent relations," which he achieves by activity in clubs and associations. This is a technical and roundabout way of saying that the American propensity to join meets a need of the personality and mediates disturbances within that personality, and that keeping busy in association work is one way of meeting, avoiding, or channeling tensions within oneself. Yet this seems a negative and partial approach. Like other human beings, Americans don't do things just to avoid trouble or allay guilt. In a deeper and more affirmative sense the joining impulse is part of the expansion of personality, even while it may often help to create some of the insecurities it seeks to allay.

This jibes with what I said above about class differences in community participation. If joining were only an answer to inner tensions, then the low-status groups would be fully as active as the middle classes, or even more so: yet they are much less active. Their lesser activity derives from their lesser income, lesser education, narrower perspectives and life chances. The urge to associate is thus linked with the expansion of perspective and personality, at least in the intermediate stage, since there is plenty of evidence that a highly developed personality tends in the end to seek solitude. But solitude is different from isolation. Another bit of evidence is found in the trend toward suburban living. The theory has been that the impersonality of the big city breeds associations. Yet recent experience shows that when people move from the mass city to the more compassable suburb, their participation in club and association life increases deeply. Again this indicates that the American is a joiner because he feels the freedom to expand, to fill out a personality-on-the-make, and he has an inner need to find outer symbols of the fact that he belongs to his culture and has not been left behind by it.

The clubs and associations which he joins do not, however, simplify his life but make it more crowded and complex. The demands on his time and participation multiply. The "new leisure," which is in itself the product of mechanization and the shorter working week, is getting filled in with the beehive activities of common ventures. Keeping up with club work has become one of the new imperatives of middle-class life. What makes it worse for a small group is that the range of leadership is a constricted one, and the most difficult tasks fall upon a few. America has become overorganized and association-saturated. Yet it may be worth the cost since the associations serve as filaments to tie people together in a community of interests less accidental and casual than it may seem.

Such filaments reach across the continent, so that periodically Americans gather in "conventions" of every sort, which serve formally as legislative bodies but actually as ways of tightening the ties of interest by face-to-face encounters. It may be a convention of a political party or of a trade-union or trade association, sales representatives of a big national corporation, scientists or scholars, church groups or women's clubs, Shriners or Elks or Legionnaires. In the case of a big national organization as many as 100,000 people may descend upon the convention city to stay for a week, although usually it means only a few hundred or a few thousand. They outdo one another in antics and pranks; they swarm over the hotels, sustaining the hotel industry, bars, night clubs, and call girls. In the case of conventions called by big corporations or trade associations, the purpose is to build morale and give a personal touch to an otherwise impersonal organization. The dominant note is that of "greeterism," in which the managers and inside groups seek to make the "visiting firemen" feel at home.

But changes have come over American conventions, as over the whole institution of "joining." The "service clubs" such as Kiwanis and Rotarians—a combination of Big Brother, Good Neighbor, and Greeter—are regarded with some amusement even among their own circles. The world of Babbitt exists in perfect form only in the pages of Sinclair Lewis and the "Americana" items enshrined in the faded issues of Mencken's *American Mercury*. Even in the conventions, as Raoul Denney has pointed out, the "greeters" are becoming "meeters"; and the techniques of "participating" sessions, in which work experiences are exchanged, have reached the trade association and corporate meetings.

Yet with all this sobering current of change, Americans as joiners have not wholly lost the *elan* which has made their associational impulse a cross between promotion, interchange of ideas, and the exorcising of loneliness through modern saturnalia.

15

Philanthropy

HENRY DAVID THOREAU

HENRY DAVID THOREAU OF WALDEN POND WROTE EXTENSIVELY
ON VOLUNTARY ACTION, INCLUDING HIS IMPORTANT PIECE "CIVIL
DISOBEDIENCE."

I confess that I have hitherto indulged very little in philanthropic enterprises. I have made some sacrifices to a sense of duty, and among others have sacrificed this pleasure also. There are those who have used all their arts to persuade me to undertake the support of some poor family in the town; and if I had nothing to do,— for the devil finds employment for the idle,—I might try my hand at some such pastime as that. However, when I have thought to indulge myself in this respect, and lay their Heaven under an obligation by maintaining certain poor persons in all respects as comfortably as I maintain myself, and have even ventured so far as to make them the offer, they have one and all unhesitatingly preferred to remain poor. While my townsmen and women are devoted in so many ways to the good of their fellows, I trust that one at least may be spared to other and less humane pursuits. You must have a genius for charity as well as for any thing else. As for Doing-good, that is one of the professions which are full. Moreover, I have tried it fairly, and, strange as it may seem, am satisfied that it does not agree with my constitution. Probably I should not consciously and deliberately forsake my particular calling to do the good which society demands of me, to save the universe from annihilation; and I believe that a like but infinitely greater steadfastness elsewhere is all that now preserves it. But I would not stand between any man and his genius; and to him who does this work, which I decline, with his whole heart and soul and life, I would say, Persevere, even if the world call it doing evil, as it is mostly likely they will.

I am far from supposing that my case is a peculiar one; no doubt many of my readers would make a similar defence. At doing something,—I will not engage that my neighbors shall pronounce it good,—I do not hesitate to say that I

Excerpted from *Walden*, Chapter I, "Economy," by Henry David Thoreau (Columbus, Ohio: Charles E. Merrill Co., 1969) by permission of the publisher. *Walden* was originally published in 1854.

should be a capital fellow to hire; but what that is, it is for my employer to find out. What *good* I do, in the common sense of that word, must be aside from my main path, and for the most part wholly unintended. Men say, practically, Begin where you are and such as you are, without aiming mainly to become of more worth, and with kindness aforethought to go about doing good. If I were to preach at all in this strain, I should say rather, Set about being good. As if the sun should stop when he had kindled his fires up to the splendor of a moon or a star of the sixth magnitude, and go about like a Robin Goodfellow, peeping in at every cottage window, inspiring lunatics, and tainting meats, and making darkness visible, instead of steadily increasing his genial heat and beneficence till he is of such brightness that no mortal can look him in the face, and then, and in the mean while too, going about the world in his own orbit, doing it good, or rather, as a truer philosophy has discovered, the world going about him getting good. When Phaeton, wishing to prove his heavenly birth by his beneficence, had the sun's chariot but one day, and drove out of the beaten track, he burned several blocks of houses in the lower streets of heaven, and scorched the surface of the earth, and dried up every spring, and made the great desert of Sahara, till at length Jupiter hurled him headlong to the earth with a thunderbolt, and the sun, through grief at his death, did not shine for a year.

There is no odor so bad as that which arises from goodness tainted. It is human, it is divine, carrion. If I knew for a certainty that a man was coming to my house with the conscious design of doing me good, I should run for my life, as from that dry and parching wind of the African deserts called the simoom, which fills the mouth and nose and ears and eyes with dust till you are suffocated, for fear that I should get some of his good done to me,—some of its virus mingled with my blood. No,—in this case I would rather suffer evil the natural way. A man is not a good *man* to me because he will feed me if I should be starving, or warm me if I should be freezing, or pull me out of a ditch if I should ever fall into one. I can find you a Newfoundland dog that will do as much. Philanthropy is not love for one's fellow-man in the broadest sense. Howard was no doubt an exceedingly kind and worthy man in his way, and has his reward; but, comparatively speaking, what are a hundred Howards to *us*, if their philanthropy do not help *us* in our best estate, when we are most worthy to be helped? I never heard of a philanthropic meeting in which it was sincerely proposed to do any good to me, or the like of me.

The Jesuits were quite balked by those Indians who, being burned at the stake, suggested new modes of torture to their tormentors. Being superior to physical suffering, it sometimes chances that they were superior to any consolation which the missionaries could offer; and the law to do as you would be done by fell with less persuasiveness on the ears of those, who, for their part, did not care how they were done by, who loved their enemies after a new fashion, and came very near freely forgiving them all they did.

Be sure that you give the poor the aid they most need, though it be your example which leaves them far behind. If you give money, spend yourself with it, and do not merely abandon it to them. We make curious mistakes sometimes. Often the poor man is not so cold and hungry as he is dirty and ragged and gross. It is partly his taste, and not merely his misfortune. If you give him money, he will perhaps buy more rags with it. I was wont to pity the clumsy Irish laborers who cut ice on the pond, in such mean and ragged clothes, while I shivered in my more tidy and somewhat more fashionable garments, till, one bitter cold day, one who had slipped into the water came to my house to warm him, and I saw him strip off three pairs of pants and two pairs of stockings ere he got down to the skin, though they were dirty and ragged enough, it is true, and that he could afford to refuse the *extra* garments which I offered him, he had so many *intra* ones. This ducking was the very thing he needed. Then I began to pity myself, and I saw that it would be a greater charity to bestow on me a flannel shirt than a whole slop-shop on him. There are a thousand hacking at the branches of evil to one who is striking at the root, and it may be that he who bestows the largest amount of time and money on the needy is doing the most by his mode of life to produce that misery which he strives in vain to relieve. It is the pious slave-breeder devoting the proceeds of every tenth slave to buy a Sunday's liberty for the rest. Some show their kindness to the poor by employing them in their kitchens. Would they not be kinder if they employed themselves there? You boast of spending a tenth part of your income in charity; may be you should spend the nine tenths so, and done with it. Society recovers only a tenth part of the property then. Is this owing to the generosity of him in whose possession it is found, or to the remissness of the officers of justice?

Philanthropy is almost the only virtue which is sufficiently appreciated by mankind. Nay, it is greatly overrated; and it is our selfishness which overrates it. A robust poor man, one sunny day here in Concord, praised a fellow-townsman to me, because, as he said, he was kind to the poor; meaning himself. The kind uncles and aunts of the race are more esteemed than its true spiritual fathers and mothers. I once heard a reverend lecturer on England, a man of learning and intelligence, after enumerating her scientific, literary, and political worthies, Shakespeare, Bacon, Crowell, Milton, Newton, and others, speak next of her Christian heroes, whom, as if his profession required it of him, he elevated to a place far above all the rest, as the greatest of the great. They were Penn, Howard, and Mrs. Fry. Every one must feel the falsehood and cant of this. The last were not England's best men and women; only, perhaps, her best philanthropists.

I would not subtract any thing from the praise that is due to philanthropy, but merely demand justice for all who by their lives and works are a blessing to mankind. I do not value chiefly a man's uprightness and benevolence, which are, as it were, his stem and leaves. Those plants of whose greenness withered we make herb tea for the sick, serve but a humble use, and are most employed by quacks. I want the flower and fruit of a man; that some fragrance be wafted over from him to me, and some ripeness flavor our intercourse. His goodness must not be a partial and transitory act, but a constant superfluity, which costs him nothing and of which he is unconscious. This is a charity that hides a multitude of sins. The philanthropist too often surrounds mankind with the remembrance of his own cast-off griefs as an atmosphere, and calls it sympathy. We should impart our courage, and not our despair, our health and ease, and not our disease, and take care that this does not spread by contagion. From what southern plains comes up the voice of wailing? Under what latitudes reside the heathen to whom we would send light? Who is that intemperate and brutal man whom we would redeem? If any thing ail a man, so that he does not perform his functions, if he have a pain in his bowels even,—for that is the seat of sympathy,—he forthwith sets about reforming—the world. Being a microcosm himself, he discovers, and it is a true discovery, and he is the man to make it,—that the world has been eating green apples; to his eyes, in fact, the globe itself is a great green apple, which there is danger awful to think of that the children of men will nibble before it is ripe; and straightway his drastic philanthropy seeks out the Esquimaux and the Patagonian, and embraces the populous Indian and Chinese villages; and thus, by a few years of philanthropic activity, the powers in the mean while using him for their own ends, no doubt, he cures himself of his dyspepsia, the globe acquires a faint blush on one or both of its cheeks, as if it were beginning to be ripe, and life loses its crudity and is once more sweet and wholesome to live. I never dreamed of any enormity greater than I have committed. I never knew, and never shall know, a worse man than myself.

I believe that what so saddens the reformer is not his sympathy with his fellows in distress, but, though he be the holiest son of God, is his private ail. Let this be righted, let the spring come to him, the morning rise over his couch, and he will forsake his generous companions without apology. My excuse for not lecturing against the use of tobacco is, that I never chewed it; that is a penalty which reformed tobacco-chewers have to pay; though there are things enough I have chewed, which I could lecture against. If you should ever be betrayed into any of these philanthropies, do not let your left hand know what your right hand does, for it is not worth knowing. Rescue the drowning and tie your shoe-strings. Take your time, and set about some free labor.

Our manners have been corrupted by communication with the saints. Our hymn-books resound with a melodious cursing of God and enduring him forever. One would say that even the prophets and redeemers had rather consoled the fears than confirmed the hope of man. There is nowhere recorded a simple and irrespressible satisfaction with the gift of life, any memorable praise of God. All health and success does me good, however far off and withdrawn it may appear; all disease and failure helps to make me sad and does me evil, however much sympathy it may have with me or I with it. If, then, we would indeed restore mankind by truly Indian, botanic, magnetic, or natural means, let us first be as simple and well as Nature ourselves, dispel the clouds which hang over our own brows, and take up a little life into our pores. Do not stay to be an overseer of the poor; but endeavor to become one of the worthies of the world.

I read in the Gulistan, Flower Garden, of Sheik Sadi of Shiraz, that "They asked a wise man, saying; Of the many celebrated trees which the Most High God has created lofty an umbrageous, they call none azad, or free, excepting the cypress, which bears no fruit; what mystery is there in this? He replied; Each has its appropriate produce, and appointed season, during the continuance of which it is fresh and blooming, and during their absence dry and withered; to neither of which states is the cypress exposed, being always flourishing; and of this nature are the azads, or religious independents. — Fix not thy heart on that which is transitory; for the Dijlah, or Tigris, will continue to flow through Bagdad after the race of caliphs is extinct: if thy hand has plenty, be liberal as the date tree; but if it affords nothing to give away, be an azad, or free man, like the cypress."

16

The Gospel of Wealth

ANDREW CARNEGIE

ANDREW CARNEGIE, A SUCCESSFUL CAPITALIST AND
PHILANTHROPIST, ESTABLISHED MANY PHILANTHROPIC
INSTITUTIONS, INCLUDING THE CARNEGIE CORPORATION OF NEW
YORK, ONE OF THE NATION'S LARGEST AND MOST INFLUENTIAL
PRIVATE FOUNDATIONS.

Part I: The Problem of the Administration of Wealth

The problem of our age is the proper administration of wealth, that the ties of brotherhood may still bind together the rich and poor in harmonious relationship. The conditions of human life have not only been changed, but revolutionized, within the past few hundred years. In former days there was little difference between the dwelling, dress, food, and environment of the chief and those of his retainers. The Indians are to-day where civilized man then was. When visiting the Sioux, I was led to the wigwam of the chief. It was like the others in external appearance, and even within the difference was trifling between it and those of the poorest of his braves. The contrast between the palace of the millionaire and the cottage of the laborer with us to-day measures the change which has come with civilization. This change, however, is not to be deplored, but welcomed as highly beneficial. It is well, nay, essential, for the progress of the race that the houses of some should be homes for all that is highest and best in literature and the arts, and for all the refinements of civilization, rather than that none should be so. Much better this great irregularity than universal squalor. Without wealth there can be no Maecenas. The "good old times" were not good old times. Neither master nor servant was as well situated then as to-day. A relapse to old conditions would be disastrous to both—not the least so to him who serves—and would sweep away civilization

Reprinted from *The Gospel of Wealth: And Other Timely Essays*, by Andrew Carnegie (New York: The Century Co., 1900). The essay was originally published in five parts under the title "Wealth" in *North American Review* June, 1889: 653-664 and December, 1889: 682-698.

with it. But whether the change be for good or ill, it is upon us, beyond our power to alter, and, therefore, to be accepted and made the best of. It is a waste of time to criticize the inevitable.

It is easy to see how the change has come. One illustration will serve for almost every phase of the cause. In the manufacture of products we have the whole story. It applies to all combinations of the human industry, as stimulated and enlarged by the inventions of this scientific age. Formerly, articles were manufactured at the domestic hearth, or in small shops which formed part of the household. The master and his apprentices worked side by side, the latter living with the master, and therefore subject to the same conditions. When these apprentices rose to be masters, there was little or no change in their mode of life, and they, in turn, educated succeeding apprentices in the same routine. There was, substantially, social equality, and even political equality, for those engaged in industrial pursuits had then little or no voice in the State.

The inevitable result of such a mode of manufacture was crude articles at high prices. To-day the world obtains commodities of excellent quality at prices which even the preceding generation would have deemed incredible. In the commercial world similar causes have produced similar results, and the race is benefited thereby. The poor enjoy what the rich could not before afford. What were the luxuries have become the necessaries of life. The laborer has now more comforts than the farmer had a few generations ago. The farmer has more luxuries than the landlord had, and is more richly clad and better housed. The landlord has books and pictures rarer and appointments more artistic than the king could then obtain.

The price we pay for this salutary change is, no doubt, great. We assemble thousands of operatives in the factory, and in the mine, of whom the employer can know little or nothing, and to whom he is little better than a myth. All intercourse between them is at an end. Rigid castes are formed, and, as usual, mutual ignorance breeds mutual distrust. Each caste is without sympathy with the other, and ready to credit anything disparaging in regard to it. Under the law of competition, the employer of thousands is forced into the strictest econo- mies, among which the rates paid to labor figure prominently, and often there is friction between the employer and the employed, between capital and labor, between rich and poor. Human society loses homogeneity.

The price which society pays for the law of competition, like the price it pays for cheap comforts and luxuries, is also great; but the advantages of this law are also greater still than its cost—for it is to this law that we owe our wonderful material development, which brings improved conditions in its train. But, whether the law be benign or not, we must say of it, as we say of the change in the conditions of men to which we have referred: It is here; we cannot evade it;

no substitutes for it have been found; and while the law may be sometimes hard for the individual, it is best for the race, because it insures the survival of the fittest in every department. We accept and welcome, therefore, as conditions to which we must accommodate ourselves, great inequality of environment; the concentration of business, industrial and commercial, in the hands of a few; and the law of competition between these, as being not only beneficial, but essential to the future progress of the race. Having accepted these, it follows that there must be great scope for the exercise of special ability in the merchant and in the manufacturer who has to conduct affairs upon a great scale. That this talent for organization and management is rare among men is proved by the fact that it invariably secures enormous rewards for its possessor, no matter where or under what laws or conditions. The experienced in affairs always rate the man whose services can be obtained as a partner as not only the first consideration, but such as render the question of his capital scarcely worth considering: for able men soon create capital; in the hands of those without the special talent required, capital soon takes wings. Such men become interested in firms or corporations using millions; and, estimating only simple interest to be made upon the capital invested, it is inevitable that their income must exceed their expenditure and that they must, therefore, accumulate wealth. Nor is there any middle ground which such men can occupy, because the great manufacturing or commercial concern which does not earn at least interest upon its capital soon becomes bankrupt. It must either go forward or fall behind; to stand still is impossible. It is a condition essential to its successful operation that it should be thus far profitable, and even that, in addition to interest on capital, it should make profit. It is a law, as certain as any of the others named, that men possessed of this peculiar talent for affairs, under the free play of economic forces must, of necessity, soon be in receipt of more revenue than can be judiciously expended upon themselves; and this law is as beneficial for the race as the others.

Objections to the foundations upon which society is based are not in order, because the condition of the race is better with these than it has been with any other which has been tried. Of the effect of any new substitutes proposed we cannot be sure. The Socialist or Anarchist who seeks to overturn present conditions is to be regarded as attacking the foundation upon which civilization itself rests, for civilization took its start from the day when the capable, industrious workman said to his incompetent and lazy fellow, "If thou dost not sow, thou shalt not reap," and thus ended primitive Communism by separating the drones from the bees. One who studies this subject will soon be brought face to face with the conclusion that upon the sacredness of property civilization itself depends—the right of the laborer to his hundred dollars in the savings-bank, and equally the legal right of the millionaire to his millions. Every man must be allowed "to sit under his own vine and fig-tree, with none to make afraid," if human society is to advance, or even to remain so far advanced as it is. To those who propose to substitute Communism for this intense Individualism, the answer therefore is: The race has tried that. All progress from the barbarous day to the present time has resulted from its displacement. Not evil, but good, has come to the race from the accumulation of wealth by those who have had the ability and energy to produce it. But even if we admit for a moment that it might be better for the race to discard its present foundation, Individualism,— that it is a nobler ideal that man should labor, not for himself alone, but in and for a brotherhood of his fellows, and share with them all in common, realizing Swedenborg's idea of heaven, where, as he says, the angels derive their happiness, not from laboring for self, but for each other,—even admit all this, and a sufficient answer is, This is not evolution, but revolution. It necessitates the changing of human nature itself—a work of eons, even if it were good to change it, which we cannot know.

It is not practicable in our day or in our age. Even if desirable theoretically, it belongs to another and long-succeeding sociological stratum. Our duty is with what is practicable now—with the next step possible in our day and generation. It is criminal to waste our energies in endeavoring to uproot, when all we can profitably accomplish is to bend the universal tree of humanity a little in the direction most favorable to the production of good fruit under existing circumstances. We might as well urge the destruction of the highest existing type of man because he failed to reach our ideal as to favor the destruction of Individualism, Private Property, the Law of Accumulation of Wealth, and the Law of Competition; for these are the highest result of human experience, the soil in which society, so far, has produced the best fruit. Unequally or unjustly, perhaps, as these laws sometimes operate, and imperfect as they appear to the Idealist, they are, nevertheless, like the highest type of man, the best and most valuable of all that humanity has yet accomplished.

We start, then, with a condition of affairs under which the best interests of the race are promoted, but which inevitably gives wealth to the few. Thus far, accepting conditions as they exist, the situation can be surveyed and pronounced good. The question then arises,—and if the foregoing be correct, it is the only question with which we have to deal,—What is the proper mode of administering wealth after the laws upon which civilization is founded have thrown it into the hands of the few? And it is of this great question that I believe I offer the true solution. It will be understood that fortunes are here spoken of, not moderate sums saved by many years of effort, the returns from which are required for the comfortable maintenance and education of families. This is not wealth, but only competence, which it should be the aim of all to acquire, and which it is for the best interests of society should be acquired.

There are but three modes in which surplus wealth can be disposed of. It can be left to the families of the decedents; or it can be bequeathed for public purposes; or, finally, it can be administered by its possessors during their lives. Under the first and second modes most of the wealth of the world that has reached the few has hitherto been applied. Let us in turn consider each of these modes. The first is the most injudicious. In monarchical countries, the estates and the greatest portion of the wealth are left to the first son, that the vanity of the parent may be gratified by the thought that his name and title are to descend unimpaired to succeeding generations. The condition of this class in Europe to-day teaches the failure of such hopes or ambitions. The successors have become impoverished through their follies, or from the fall in the value of land. Even in Great Britain the strict law of entail has been found inadequate to maintain an hereditary class. Its soil is rapidly passing into the hands of the stranger. Under republican institutions the division of property among the children is much fairer; but the question which forces itself upon thoughtful men in all lands is, Why should men leave great fortunes to their children? If this is done from affection, is it not misguided affection? Observation teaches that, generally speaking, it is not well for the children that they should be so burdened. Neither is it well for the State. Beyond providing for the wife and daughters moderate sources of income, and very moderate allowances indeed, if any, for the sons, men may well hesitate; for it is no longer questionable that great sums bequeathed often work more for the injury than for the good of the recipients. Wise men will soon conclude that, for the best interests of the members of their families, and of the State, such bequests are an improper use of their means.

It is not suggested that men who have failed to educate their sons to earn a livelihood shall cast them adrift in poverty. If any man has seen fit to rear his sons with a view to their living idle lives, or, what is highly commendable, has instilled in them the sentiment that they are in a position to labor for public ends without reference to pecuniary considerations, then, of course, the duty of the parent is to see that such are provided for in moderation. There are instances of millionaires' sons unspoiled by wealth, who, being rich, still perform great services to the community. Such are the very salt of the earth, as valuable as, unfortunately, they are rare. It is not the exception, however, but the rule, that men must regard; and, looking at the usual result of enormous sums conferred upon legatees, the thoughtful man must shortly say, "I would as soon leave to my son a curse as the almighty dollar," and admit to himself that it is not the welfare of the children, but family pride, which inspires these legacies.

As to the second mode, that of leaving wealth at death for public uses, it may be said that this is only a means for the disposal of wealth, provided a man is content to wait until he is dead before he becomes of much good in the world. Knowledge of the results of legacies bequeathed is not calculated to inspire the brightest hopes of much posthumous good being accomplished by them. The cases are not few in which the real object sought by the testator is not attained, nor are they few in which his real wishes are thwarted. In many cases the bequests are so used as to become only monuments of his folly. It is well to remember that it requires the exercise of not less ability than that which acquires it, to use wealth so as to be really beneficial to the community. Besides this, it may fairly be said that no man is to be extolled for doing what he cannot help doing, nor is he to be thanked by the community to which he only leaves wealth at death. Men who leave vast sums in this way may fairly be thought men who would not have left it at all had they been able to take it with them. The memories of such cannot be held in grateful remembrance, for there is no grace in their gifts. It is not to be wondered at that such bequests seem so generally to lack the blessing.

The growing disposition to tax more and more heavily large estates left at death is a cheering indication of the growth of a salutary change in public opinion. The State of Pennsylvania now takes—subject to some exceptions— one tenth of the property left by its citizens. The budget presented in the British Parliament the other day proposes to increase the death duties; and most significant of all, the new tax is to be a graduated one. Of all forms of taxation this seems the wisest. Men who continue hoarding great sums all their lives, the proper use of which for public ends would work good to the community from which it chiefly came, should be made to feel that the community, in the form of the State, cannot thus be deprived of its proper share. By taxing estates heavily at death the State marks its condemnation of the selfish millionaire's unworthy life.

It is desirable that nations should get much further in this direction. Indeed, it is difficult to set bounds to the share of a rich man's estate which should go at his death to the public through the agency of the State, and by all means such taxes should be graduated, beginning at nothing upon moderate sums to dependants, and increasing rapidly as the amounts swell, until of the millionaire's hoard, as of Shylock's, at least:

> The other half
> Comes to the privy coffer of the State.

This policy would work powerfully to induce the rich man to attend to the administration of wealth during his life, which is the end that society should always have in view, as being by far the most fruitful for the people. Nor need it be feared that this policy would sap the root of enterprise and render men less anxious to accumulate, for, to the class whose ambition it is to leave great fortunes and be talked about after their death, it will attract even more attention, and, indeed, be a somewhat nobler ambition, to have enormous sums paid over to the State from their fortunes.

There remains, then, only one mode of using great fortunes; but in this we have the true antidote for the temporary unequal distribution of wealth, the reconciliation of the rich and the poor—a reign of harmony, another ideal, differing, indeed, from that of the Communist in requiring only the further evolution of existing conditions, not the total overthrow of our civilization. It is founded upon the present most intense Individualism, and the race is prepared to put it in practice by degrees whenever it pleases. Under its sway we shall have an ideal State, in which the surplus wealth of the few will become, in the best sense, the property of the many, because administered for the common good; and this wealth, passing through the hands of the few, can be made a much more potent force for the elevation of our race than if distributed in small sums to the people themselves. Even the poorest can be made to see this, and to agree that great sums gathered by some of their fellow-citizens and spent for public purposes, from which the masses reap the principal benefit, are more valuable to them than if scattered among themselves in trifling amounts throughout the course of many years.

If we consider the results which flow from the Cooper Institute, for instance, to the best portion of the race in New York not possessed of means, and compare these with those which would have ensued for the good of the masses from an equal sum distributed by Mr. Cooper in his lifetime in the form of wages, which is the highest form of distribution, being for work done and not for charity, we can form some estimate of the possibilities for the improvement of the race which lie embedded in the present law of the accumulation of wealth. Much of this sum, if distributed in small quantities among the people, would have been wasted in the indulgence of appetite, some of it in excess, and it may be doubted whether even the part put to the best use, that of adding to the comforts of the home, would have yielded results for the race, as a race, at all comparable to those which are flowing and are to flow from the Cooper Institute from generation to generation. Let the advocate of violent or radical change ponder well this thought.

We might even go so far as to take another instance—that of Mr. Tilden's bequest of five millions of dollars for a free library in the city of New York; but in referring to this one cannot help saying involuntarily: How much better if Mr. Tilden had devoted the last years of his own life to the proper administration of this immense sum; in which case neither legal contest nor any other cause of delay could have interfered with his aims. But let us assume that Mr. Tilden's millions finally become the means of giving to this city a noble public library, where the treasures of the world contained in books will be open to all forever, without money and without price. Considering the good of that part of the race which congregates in and around Manhattan Island, would its permanent benefit have been better promoted had these millions been allowed to circulate in small sums through the hands of the masses? Even the most strenuous advocate of communism must entertain a doubt upon this subject. Most of those who think will probably entertain no doubt whatever.

Poor and restricted are our opportunities in this life, narrow our horizon, our best work most imperfect; but rich men should be thankful for one inestimable boon. They have it in their power during their lives to busy themselves in organizing benefactions from which the masses of their fellow's will derive lasting advantage, and thus dignify their own lives. The highest life is probably to be reached, not by such imitation of the life of Christ as Count Tolstoi gives us, but while animated by Christ's spirit, by recognizing the changed conditions of this age, and adopting modes of expressing this spirit suitable to the changed conditions under which we live, still laboring for the good of our fellows, which was the essence of his life and teaching, but laboring in a different manner.

This, then, is held to be the duty of the man of wealth: To set an example of modest, unostentatious living, shunning display or extravagance; to provide moderately for the legitimate wants of those dependent upon him; and, after doing so, to consider all surplus revenues which come to him simply as trust funds, which he is called upon to administer, and strictly bound as a matter of duty to administer in the manner which, in his judgment, is best calculated to produce the most beneficial results for the community—the man of wealth thus becoming the mere trustee and agent for his poorer brethren, bringing to their service his superior wisdom, experience, and ability to administer, doing for them better than they would or could do for themselves.

We are met here with the difficulty of determining what are moderate sums to leave to members of the family; what is modest, unostentatious living; what is the test of extravagance. There must be different standards for different conditions. The answer is that it is as impossible to name exact amounts or actions as it is to define good manners, good taste, or the rules of propriety; but, nevertheless, these are verities, well known, although indefinable. Public sentiment is quick to know and to feel what offends these. So in the case of wealth. The rule in regard to good taste in the dress of men or women applies here. Whatever makes one conspicuous offends the canon. If any family be chiefly known for display, for extravagance in home, table, or equipage, for enormous sums ostentatiously spent in any form upon itself—if these be its chief distinctions, we have no difficulty in estimating its nature or culture. So likewise in regard to the use or abuse of its surplus wealth, or to generous, free handed cooperation in good public uses, or to unabated efforts to accumulate and hoard to the last, or whether they administer or bequeath. The verdict rests with the best and most enlightened public sentiment. The community will surely judge, and its judgments will not often be wrong.

The best uses to which surplus wealth can be put have already been indicated. Those who would administer wisely must, indeed, be wise; for one of the serious obstacles to the improvement of our race is indiscriminate charity. It were better for mankind that the millions of the rich were thrown into the sea than so spent as to encourage the slothful, the drunken, the unworthy. Of every thousand dollars spent in so-called charity to-day, it is probable that nine hundred and fifty dollars is unwisely spent—so spent, indeed, as to produce the very evils which it hopes to mitigate or cure. A well-known writer of philosophic books admitted the other day that he had given a quarter of a dollar to a man who approached him as he was coming to visit the house of his friend. He knew nothing of the habits of this beggar, knew not the use that would be made of this money, although he had every reason to suspect that it would be spent improperly. This man professed to be a disciple of Herbert Spencer; yet the quarter-dollar given that night will probably work more injury than all the money will do good which its thoughtless donor will ever be able to give in true charity. He only gratified his own feelings, saved himself from annoyance—and this was probably one of the most selfish and very worst actions of his life, for in all respects he is most worthy.

In bestowing charity, the main consideration should be to help those who will help themselves; to provide part of the means by which those who desire to improve may do so; to give those who desire to rise the aids by which they may rise; to assist, but rarely or never to do all. Neither the individual nor the race is improved by almsgiving. Those worthy of assistance, except in rare cases, seldom require assistance. The really valuable men of the race never do, except in case of accident or sudden change. Every one has, of course, cases of individuals brought to his own knowledge where temporary assistance can do genuine good, and these he will not overlook. But the amount which can be wisely given by the individual for individuals is necessarily limited by his lack of knowledge of the circumstances connected with each. He is the only true reformer who is as careful and as anxious not to aid the unworthy as he is to aid the worthy, and, perhaps, even more so, for in almsgiving more injury is probably done by rewarding vice than by relieving virtue.

The rich man is thus almost restricted to following the examples of Peter Cooper, Enoch Pratt of Baltimore, Mr. Pratt of Brooklyn, Senator Stanford, and others, who know that the best means of benefiting the community is to place within its reach the ladders upon which the aspiring can rise—free libraries, parks, and means of recreation, by which men are helped in body and mind; works of art, certain to give pleasure and improve the public taste; and public institutions of various kinds, which will improve the general condition of the people; in this manner returning their surplus wealth to the mass of their fellows in the forms best calculated to do them lasting good.

Thus is the problem of rich and poor to be solved. The laws of accumulation will be left free, the laws of distribution free. Individualism will continue, but the millionaire will be but a trustee for the poor, intrusted for a season with a great part of the increased wealth of the community, but administering it for the community far better than it could or would have done for itself. The best minds will thus have reached a stage in the development of the race in which it is clearly seen that there is no mode of disposing of surplus wealth creditable to thoughtful and earnest men into whose hands it flows, save by using it year by year for the general good. This day already dawns. Men may die without incurring the pity of their fellows, still sharers in great business enterprises from which their capital cannot be or has not been withdrawn, and which is left chiefly at death for public uses; yet the day is not far distant when the man who dies leaving behind him millions of available wealth, which was free for him to administer during life, will pass away "unwept, unhonored, and unsung," no matter to what uses he leaves the dross which he cannot take with him. Of such as these the public verdict will then be: "The man who dies thus rich dies disgraced."

Such, in my opinion, is the true gospel concerning wealth, obedience to which is destined some day to solve the problem of the rich and the poor, and to bring "Peace on earth, among men good will."

Part II: The Best Fields For Philanthropy

This part of the essay was actually written after Carnegie had received many responses to the original "Gospel." Most of Part II was an identification and elaboration of seven "best uses to which a millionaire can devote the surplus of which he should regard himself as only the trustee."

The seven were: 1. The founding of a university; 2. Free libraries; 3. Founding or extension of hospitals, medical colleges, laboratories and other institutions connected with the alleviation of human suffering, and especially with the prevention rather than the cure of human suffering; 4. Public parks; 5. Providing halls suitable for meetings of all kinds, and for concerts of elevating music; 6. Public swimming baths; and 7. One's own church and churches in poor neighborhoods.

After outlining these seven, Carnegie went on to say:

Many other avenues for the wise expenditure of surplus wealth might be indicated. I enumerate but a few—a very few—of the many fields which are open, and only those in which great or considerable sums can be judiciously used. It is not the privilege, however, of millionaires alone to work for or aid measures which are certain to benefit the community. Every one who has but a small surplus can give at least a part of their time, which is usually as important as funds, and often more so.

It is not expected, neither is it desirable, that there should be general concurrence as to the best possible use of surplus wealth. For different men and different localities there are different uses. What commends itself most highly to the judgment of the administrator is the best use for him, for his heart should be in the work. It is as important in administering wealth as it is in any other branch of a man's work that he should be enthusiastically devoted to it and feel that in the field selected his work lies.

Besides this, there is room and need for all kinds of wise benefactions for the common weal. The man who builds a university, library, or laboratory performs no more useful work than he who elects to devote himself and his surplus means to the adornment of a park, the gathering together of a collection of pictures for the public, or the building of a memorial arch. These are all true laborers in the vineyard. The only point required by the gospel of wealth is that the surplus which accrues from time to time in the hands of a man should be administered by him in his own lifetime for that purpose which is seen by him, as trustee, to be best for the good of the people. To leave at death what he cannot take away, and place upon others the burden of the work which it was his own duty to perform, is to do nothing worthy. This requires no sacrifice, or any sense of duty to his fellows.

Time was when the words concerning the rich man entering the kingdom of heaven were regarded as a hard saying. To-day, when all questions are probed to the bottom and the standards of faith receive the most liberal interpretations, the startling verse has been relegated to the rear, to await the next kindly revision as one of those things which cannot be quite understood, but which, meanwhile, it is carefully to be noted, are not to be understood literally. But is it so very improbable that the next stage of thought is to restore the doctrine in all its pristine purity and force, as being in perfect harmony with sound ideas upon the subject of wealth and poverty, the rich and the poor, and the contrasts everywhere seen and deplored? In Christ's day, it is evident, reformers were against the wealthy. It is none the less evident that we are fast recurring to that position to-day; and there will be nothing to surprise the student of sociological development if society should soon approve the text which has caused so much anxiety: "It is easier for a camel to enter the eye of a needle than for a rich man to enter the kindgom of heaven." Even if the needle were the small casement at the gates, the words betoken serious difficulty for the rich. It will be but a step for the theologian from the doctrine that he who dies rich dies disgraced, to that which brings upon the man punishment or deprivation hereafter.

The gospel of wealth but echoes Christ's words. It calls upon the millionaire to sell all that he hath and give it in the highest and best form to the poor by administering his estate himself for the good of his fellows, before he is called upon to lie down and rest upon the bosom of Mother Earth. So doing, he will approach his end no longer the ignoble hoarder of useless millions; poor, very poor indeed, in money, but rich, very rich, twenty times a millionaire still, in the affection, gratitude, and admiration of his fellow-men, and—sweeter far— soothed and sustained by the still, small voice within, which, whispering, tells him that, because he has lived, perhaps one small part of the great world has been bettered just a little. This much is sure: against such riches as these no bar will be found at the gates of Paradise.

17

The Difficult Art
of Giving

JOHN D. ROCKEFELLER

JOHN D. ROCKEFELLER WAS ONE OF THE NATION'S LEADING
PHILANTHROPISTS WHO IS PERHAPS BEST REMEMBERED FOR THE
FOUR PRESTIGIOUS CHARITABLE CORPORATIONS HE CREATED: THE
ROCKEFELLER FOUNDATION, THE ROCKEFELLER INSTITUTE FOR
MEDICAL RESEARCH, THE LAURA SPELMAN ROCKEFELLER
MEMORIAL, AND THE GENERAL EDUCATION BOARD.

It is, no doubt, easy to write platitudes and generalities about the joys of giving, and the duty that one owes to one's fellow men, and to put together again all the familiar phrases that have served for generations whenever the subject has been taken up.

I can hardly hope to succeed in starting any new interest in this great subject when gifted writers have so often failed. Yet I confess I find much more interest in it at this time than in rambling on, as I have been doing, about the affairs of business and trade. It is most difficult, however, to dwell upon a very practical and businesslike side of benefactions generally, without seeming to ignore, or at least to fail to appreciate fully, the spirit of giving which has its source in the heart, and which, of course, makes it all worth-while.

In this country we have come to the period when we can well afford to ask the ablest men to devote more of their time, thought, and money to the public well-being. I am not so presumptuous as to attempt to define exactly what this betterment work should consist of. Every man will do that for himself, and his own conclusion will be final for himself. It is well, I think, that no narrow or preconceived plan should be set down as the best.

This piece represents substantial excerpts from the third article in Rockefeller's series, "Some Random Reminiscences of Men and Events," which appeared in *The World's Work* in 1907 and 1908. The article was later renamed "The Difficult Art of Giving" and was published often as a separate piece.

I am sure it is a mistake to assume that the possession of money in great abundance necessarily brings happiness. The very rich are just like all the rest of us; and if they get pleasure from the possession of money, it comes from their ability to do things which give satisfaction to someone besides themselves.

Limitations of the Rich

The mere expenditure of money for things, so I am told by those who profess to know, soon palls upon one. The novelty of being able to purchase anything one wants soon passes, because what people most seek cannot be bought with money. These rich men we read about in the newspapers cannot get personal returns beyond a well-defined limit for their expenditure. They cannot gratify the pleasures of the palate beyond very moderate bounds, since they cannot purchase a good digestion; they cannot lavish very much money on fine raiment for themselves or their families without suffering from public ridicule; and in their homes they cannot go much beyond the comforts of the less wealthy without involving them in more pain than pleasure. As I study wealthy men, I can see but one way in which they can secure a real equivalent for money spent, and that is to cultivate a taste for giving where the money may produce an effect which will be a lasting gratification; and I would respectfully present this as a Christmas thought, even though crudely expressed, to the so-called "money-kings," great and small.

A man of business may often most properly consider that he does his share in building up a property which gives steady work for few or many people; and his contribution consists in giving to his employees good working conditions, new opportunities, and a strong stimulus to good work. Just so long as he has the welfare of his employees in his mind and follows his convictions, no one can help honoring such a man. It would be the narrowest sort of view to take, and I think the meanest, to consider that good works consist chiefly in the outright giving of money.

The Best Philanthropy

The best philanthropy, the help that does the most good and the least harm, the help that nourishes civilization at its very root, that most widely disseminates health, righteousness, and happiness, is not what is usually called charity. It is, in my judgment, the investment of effort or time or money, carefully considered with relation to the power of employing people at a remunerative wage, to expand and develop the resources at hand, and to give opportunity for progress and healthful labor where it did not exist before. No mere money-giving is comparable to this in its lasting and beneficial results.

If, as I am accustomed to think, this statement is a correct one, how vast indeed is the philanthropic field! It may be urged that the daily vocation of life is one thing, and the work of philanthropy quite another. I have no sympathy with this notion. The man who plans to do all his giving on Sunday is a poor prop for the institutions of the country.

The excuse for referring so often to the busy man of affairs is that his help is most needed. I know of men who have followed out this large plan of developing work, not as a temporary matter, but as a permanent principle. These men have taken up doubtful enterprises and carried them through to success often at great risk, and in the face of great scepticism, not as a matter only of personal profit, but in the larger spirit of general uplift.

Disinterested Service: The Road to Success

If I were to give advice to a young man starting out in life, I should say to him: If you aim for a large, broad-gauged success, do not begin your business career, whether you sell your labor or are an independent producer, with the idea of getting from the world by hook or crook all you can. In the choice of your profession or your business employment, let your first thought be: Where can I fit in so that I may be most effective in the work of the world? Where can I lend a hand in a way most effectively to advance the general interests? Enter life in such a spirit, choose your vocation in that way, and you have taken the first step on the highest road to a large success. Investigation will show that the great fortunes which have been made in this country, and the same is probably true of other lands, have come to men who have performed great and far-reaching economic services—men who, with great faith in the future of their country, have done most for the development of its resources. The man will be most successful who confers the greatest service on the world. Commercial enterprises that are needed by the public will pay. Commercial enterprises that are not needed fail, and ought to fail.

On the other hand, the one thing which such a business philosopher would be most careful to avoid in his investments of time and effort or money, is the unnecessary duplication of existing industries. He would regard all money spent in increasing needless competition as wasted, and worse. The man who puts up a second factory when the factory in existence will supply the public demand adequately and cheaply is wasting the national wealth and destroying the national prosperity, taking the bread from the laborer and unnecessarily introducing heartache and misery into the world.

Probably the greatest single obstacle to the progress and happiness of the American people lies in the willingness of so many men to invest their time and money in multiplying competitive industries instead of opening up new fields and putting their money into lines of industry and development that are needed. It requires a better type of mind to seek out and to support or to create the new than to follow the worn paths of accepted success; but here is the great chance in our still rapidly developing country. The penalty of a selfish attempt to make the world confer a living without contributing to the progress or happiness of mankind is generally a failure to the individual. The pity is that when he goes down he inflicts heartache and misery also on others who are in no way responsible.

The Generosity of Service

Probably the most generous people in the world are the very poor, who assume each other's burdens in the crises which come so often to the hard pressed. The mother in the tenement falls ill and the neighbor in the next room assumes her burdens. The father loses his work, and neighbors supply food to his children from their own scanty store. How often one hears of cases where the orphans are taken over and brought up by the poor friend whose benefaction means great additional hardship! This sort of genuine service makes the most princely gift from superabundance look insignificant indeed. The Jews have had for centuries a precept that one-tenth of a man's possessions must be devoted to good works, but even this measure of giving is but a rough yardstick to go by. To give a tenth of one's income is wellnigh an impossibility to some, while to others it means a miserable pittance. If the spirit is there, the matter of proportion is soon lost sight of. It is only the spirit of giving that counts, and the very poor give without any self-consciousness. But I fear that I am dealing with generalities again.

The education of children in my early days may have been straightlaced, yet I have always been thankful that the custom was quite general to teach young people to give systematically of money that they themselves had earned. It is a good thing to lead children to realize early the importance of their obligations to others but, I confess, it is increasingly difficult; for what were luxuries then have become commonplaces now. It should be a greater pleasure and satisfaction to give money for a good cause than to earn it, and I have always indulged the hope that during my life I should be able to help establish efficiency in giving so that wealth may be of greater use to the present and future generations.

Perhaps just here lies the difference between the gifts of money and service. The poor meet promptly the misfortunes which confront the home circle and household of the neighbor. The giver of money, if his contribution is to be valuable, must add service in the way of study, and he must help to attack and improve underlying conditions. Not being so pressed by the racking necessities, it is he that should be better able to attack the subject from a more scientific standpoint; but the final analysis is the same: his money is a feeble offering without the study behind it which will make its expenditure effective.

Great hospitals conducted by noble and unselfish men and women are doing wonderful work; but no less important are the achievements in research that reveal hitherto unknown facts about diseases and provide the remedies by which many of them can be relieved or even stamped out.

To help the sick and distressed appeals to the kindhearted always, but to help the investigator who is striving successfully to attack the causes which bring about sickness and distress does not so strongly attract the giver of money. The first appeals to the sentiments overpoweringly, but the second has the head to deal with. Yet I am sure we are making wonderful advances in this field of scientific giving. All over the world the need of dealing with the questions of philanthropy with something beyond the impulses of emotion is evident, and everywhere help is being given to those heroic men and women who are devoting themselves to the practical and essentially scientific tasks. It is a good and inspiring thing to recall occasionally the heroism, for example, of the men who risked and sacrificed their lives to discover the facts about yellow fever, a sacrifice for which untold generations will bless them; and this same spirit has animated the professions of medicine and surgery.

The Fundamental Thing in All Help

If the people can be educated to help themselves, we strike at the root of many of the evils of the world. This is the fundamental thing and it is worth saying even if it has been said so often that its truth is lost sight of in its constant repetition.

The only thing which is of lasting benefit to a man is that which he does for himself. Money which comes to him without effort on his part is so seldom a benefit and often a curse. That is the principal objection to speculation—it is not because more lose than gain, though that is true—but it is because those who gain are apt to receive more injury from their success than they would have received from failure. And so with regard to money or other things which are given by one person to another. It is only in the exceptional case that the receiver is really benefited. But, if we can help people to help themselves, then there is a permanent blessing conferred.

Men who are studying the problem of disease tell us that it is becoming more and more evident that the forces which conquer sickness are within the body itself, and that it is only when these are reduced below the normal that disease can get a foothold. The way to ward off disease, therefore, is to tone up the body generally; and, when disease has secured a foothold, the way to combat it is to help these natural resisting agencies which are in the body already. In the same way the failures which a man makes in his life are due almost always to some defect in his personality, some weakness of body, or mind, or character, will, or temperament. The only way to overcome these failings is to build up his personality from within him, that he may overcome the weakness which was the cause of the failure. It is only those efforts the man himself puts forth that can really help him.

We all desire to see the widest possible distribution of the blessings of life. Many crude plans have been suggested, some of which utterly ignore the essential facts of human nature, and if carried out would perhaps drag our whole civilization down into hopeless misery. It is my belief that the principal cause for the economic differences between people is their difference in personality, and that it is only as we can assist in the wider distribution of those qualities which go to make up a strong personality that we can assist in the wider distribution of wealth. Under normal conditions the man who is strong in body, in mind, in character, and in will need never suffer want. But these qualities can never be developed in a man unless by his own efforts, and the most that any other can do for him is, as I have said, to help him to help himself.

We must always remember that there is not enough money for the work of human uplift and that there never can be. How vitally important it is, therefore, that the expenditure should go as far as possible and be used with the greatest intelligence!

I have been frank to say that I believe in the spirit of combination and cooperation when properly and fairly conducted in the world of commercial affairs, on the principle that it helps to reduce waste; and waste is a dissipation of power. I sincerely hope and thoroughly believe that this same principle will eventually prevail in the art of giving as it does in business. It is not merely the tendency of the times developed by more exacting conditions in industry, but it should make its most effective appeal to the hearts of the people who are striving to do the most good to the largest number.

Some Underlying Principles

At the risk of making this chapter very dull, and I am told that this is a fault which inexperienced authors should avoid at all hazards, I may perhaps be pardoned if I set down here some of the fundamental principles which have been at the bottom of all my own plans. I have undertaken no work of any importance for many years which, in a general way, has not followed out these broad lines, and I believe no really constructive effort can be made in philanthropic work without such a well-defined and consecutive purpose.

My own conversion to the feeling that an organized plan was an absolute necessity came about in this way.

About the year 1890, I was still following the haphazard fashion of giving here and there as appeals presented themselves. I investigated as I could, and worked myself almost to a nervous break-down in groping my way, without sufficient guide or chart, through this ever-widening field of philanthropic endeavor. There was then forced upon me the necessity to organize and plan this department of our daily tasks on as distinct lines of progress as we did our business affairs; and I will try to describe the underlying principles we arrived at, and have since followed out, and hope still greatly to extend.

It may be beyond the pale of good taste to speak at all of such a personal subject—I am not unmindful of this—but I can make these observations with at least a little better grace because so much of the hard work and hard thinking are done by my family and associates, who devote their lives to it.

Every right-minded man has a philosophy of life, whether he knows it or not. Hidden away in his mind are certain governing principles, whether he formulates them in words or not, which govern his life. Surely his ideal ought to be to contribute all that he can, however little it may be, whether of money or service, to human progress.

Certainly one's ideal should be to use one's means, both in one's investments and in benefactions, for the advancement of civilization. But the question as to what civilization is and what are the great laws which govern its advance have been seriously studied. Our investments not less than gifts have been directed to such ends as we have thought would tend to produce these results. If you were to go into our office, and ask our committee on benevolence or our committee on investment in what they consider civilization to consist, they would say that they have found in their study that the most convenient analysis of the elements which go to make up civilization runs about as follows:

1st.   Progress in the means of subsistence, that is to say, progress in abundance and variety of food-supply, clothing, shelter, sanitation, public health, commerce, manufacture, the growth of the public wealth, etc.

2nd.   Progress in government and law, that is to say, in the enactment of laws securing justice and equity to every man, consistent with the largest individual liberty, and the due and orderly enforcement of the same upon all.

3rd.   Progress in literature and language.

4th.   Progress in science and philosophy.

5th.   Progress in art and refinement.

6th.   Progress in morality and religion.

If you were to ask them, as indeed they are very often asked, which of these they regard as fundamental, they would reply that they would not attempt to answer, that the question is purely an academic one, that all these go hand in hand, but that historically the first of them—namely, progress in means of subsistence—had generally preceded progress in government, in literature, in knowledge, in refinement, and in religion. Though not itself of the highest importance, it is the foundation upon which the whole superstructure of civilization is built, and without which it could not exist.

Accordingly, we have sought, so far as we could, to make investments in such a way as will tend to multiply, to cheapen, and to diffuse as universally as possible the comforts of life. We claim no credit for preferring these lines of investment. We make no sacrifices. These are the lines of largest and surest return. In this particular, namely, in cheapness, ease of acquirement, and universality of means of subsistence, our country easily surpasses that of any other in the world, though we are behind other countries, perhaps, in most of the others.

It may be asked: How is it consistent with the universal diffusion of these blessings that vast sums of money should be in single hands? The reply is, as I see it, that, while men of wealth control great sums of money, they do not and cannot use them for themselves. They have, indeed, the legal title to large properties, and they do control the investment of them, but that is as far as their own relation to them extends. The money is universally diffused, in the sense that it is kept invested and it passes into the pay-envelope week by week.

Up to the present time no scheme has yet presented itself which seems to afford a better method of handling capital than that of individual ownership. We might put our money into the Treasury of the Nation and of the various states, but we do not find any promise in the National or state legislatures, viewed from the experiences of the past, that the funds would be expended for the general weal more effectively than under the present methods, nor do we find in any of the schemes of socialism a promise that wealth would be more wisely administered for the general good. It is the duty of men of means to maintain the title to their property and to administer their funds until some man, or body of men, shall rise up capable of administering for the general good the capital of the country better than they can.

The next four elements of progress mentioned in the enumeration above, namely, progress in government and law, in language and literature, in science and philosophy, in art and refinement, we for ourselves have thought to be best promoted by means of the higher education, and accordingly we have had the great satisfaction of putting such sums as we could into various forms of education in our own and in foreign lands—and education not merely along the lines of disseminating more generally the known, but quite as much, and perhaps even more, in promoting original investigation. An individual institution of learning can have only a narrow sphere. It can reach only a limited number of people. But every new fact discovered, every widening of the boundaries of human knowledge by research becomes universally known to all institutions of learning, and becomes a benefaction at once to the whole race.

Quite as interesting as any phase of the work have been the new lines entered upon by our committee. We have not been satisfied with giving to causes which have appealed to us. We have felt that the mere fact that this or the other cause makes its appeal is no reason why we should give to it any more than to a thousand other causes, perhaps more worthy, which do not happen to have come under our eye. The mere fact of a personal appeal creates no claim which did not exist before, and no preference over other causes more worthy which may not have made their appeal. So this little committee of ours has not been content to let the benevolences drift into the channels of mere convenience—to give to the institutions which have sought aid and to neglect others. This department has studied the field of human progress, and sought to contribute to each of those elements which we believe tend most to promote it. Where it has not found organizations ready to its hand for such purpose, the members of the committee have sought to create them. We are still working on new, and, I hope, expanding lines, which make large demands on one's intelligence and study.

18

Principles of Public Giving

JULIUS ROSENWALD

JULIUS ROSENWALD WAS THE FOUNDER OF SEARS, ROEBUCK, AND
CO. AND A MAJOR CONTRIBUTOR TO Y.M.C.A. AND Y.W.C.A. AS
WELL AS MANY OTHER CHARITABLE ORGANIZATIONS.

When this piece was first published in The Atlantic
Monthly *in May, 1929, it drew considerable response with
particular emphasis on Rosenwald's opposition "to gifts in
perpetuity for any purpose." Numerous replies and articles
relating to Rosenwald's stance appeared in subsequent
issues of the magazine as well as in other publications.
Among the later writings on this thesis is a piece by Daniel
J. Boorstin which is reprinted in the following chapter.
Rosenwald also responded with a second article, "The
Trend Away from Perpetuities," which was published in the
December, 1930, issue of* The Atlantic Monthly.

There are few colleges in the land today which are not striving for 'adequate
endowment.' Museums, orchestras, operas, homes for the aged, hospitals, orphanages, and countless other charitable and remedial organizations, are aiming at the same goal. It was recently estimated that more than two and a half
billion dollars were given to various endowments in this country in the last
fifteen years. The sum is vast, equal to the total national wealth a hundred years
ago, but institutions continue to solicit more and greater endowments, and men
of wealth are encouraging them with ever-increasing gifts.

All of this giving and receiving is proceeding without much, if any, attention
to the underlying question whether perpetual endowments are desirable. Perhaps the time has come to examine, or rather reexamine, this question, for it is
not a new one in the long history of philanthropy.

Reprinted from *The Atlantic Monthly* (Boston, MA: The Atlantic Monthly Company, May 1929) by
permission of the publisher.

I approach this discussion neither as an economist nor as a sociologist, but simply as an American citizen whose experience as a contributor to charitable causes and as a trustee of endowed institutions has given him some insight into the practical side of the problem. My only purpose is to raise the question of how best we may aid in the advancement of public welfare.

We can learn more from British experience, which has been more varied as well as longer than our own. Monasteries, in the earlier centuries, received such enormous grants that Edward I and his successors undertook to limit their possessions. Despite these efforts, it is estimated that shortly before Henry VIII secularized the monasteries, between one-third and one-half of the public wealth of England was held for philanthropic use. This first great struggle between the living State and the dead hand indicated, as Sir Arthur Hobhouse has pointed out, that the 'nation cannot endure for long the spectacle of large masses of property settled to unalterable uses.'

This experience was reflected in laws intended to restrict charitable bequests in perpetuity, but the endowment of charities of all kinds continued until there was hardly a community in all England without its local fund. So obvious had abuses become that a Parliamentary Commission was created to inquire into the situation. Its preliminary report, published in 1837, filled thirty-eight folio volumes and listed nearly thirty thousand endowments with a combined annual income of more than £1,200,000.

Those who view endowments uncritically might think the condition of English charities fifty years ago happy in the extreme, for less than 5 percent of the population lived in parishes without endowed charities, all sorts of human needs had been provided for by generous donors, and funds were increasing rapidly. But Mr. Gladstone, who certainly was a humanitarian, rose in the House of Commons to say that the three commissions which had investigated the endowed charities 'all condemned them, and spoke of them as doing a greater amount of evil than of good in the forms in which they have been established and now exist.'

The history of charities abounds in illustrations of the paradoxical axiom that, while charity tends to do good, perpetual charities tend to do evil. James C. Young, in a recent article, 'The Dead Hand in Philanthropy,' reports that some twenty thousand English foundations have ceased to operate because changing conditions have nullified the good intentions of the donors; and a large number of American funds, many of them of comparatively recent origin, have likewise become useless.

When I was a boy in Springfield, Illinois, the covered wagons, westward bound, rolled past our door. The road ahead was long and full of hardships for the pioneers. They were hardy and self-reliant men and women, but many of them were so inadequately equipped that if misfortune overtook them, as it frequently did, they were almost certainly doomed to suffering, and perhaps death.

The worst hardships and dangers of the Western trail had passed in my boyhood, but there was still use, then, for the Bryan Mullanphy fund, established in 1851 for 'worthy and distressed travelers and emigrants passing through St. Louis to settle for a home in the West.' A few years later the trustees could with difficulty find anyone to whom the proceeds of the fund might be given. Some years ago, for lack of beneficiaries, the income had piled up until the fund totaled a million dollars. I have not followed its later fortunes, but, unless the courts have authorized a change in the will, that money is still accumulating, and will accumulate indefinitely. The Mullanphy gift was a godsend in its brief day. The man who gave it found one of the most urgent needs of his time and filled that need precisely. He made only one mistake: he focused his gift too sharply. He forgot that time passes and nothing—not even the crying needs of an era—endures. He deserves to be remembered as a generous-hearted man who realized, perhaps better than anyone else in his generation, that a wealth of pioneer blood and energy was being dissipated in the creation of our American empire. If he is remembered at all, it is more likely as the creator of a perpetuity which lost its usefulness almost as soon as it was established.

Mullanphy's mistake has been made not once but countless scores of times. It has been made by some of the wisest of men. Benjamin Franklin in drawing his will assumed that there would always be apprentices and that they would always have difficulty when starting in business for themselves in borrowing money at a rate as low as 5 percent. In addition, he assumed that a loan of three hundred dollars was enough to enable a young mechanic to establish himself independently. With these assumptions in mind, Franklin set up two loan funds of a thousand pounds each. One was for the benefit of 'young married artificers not over the age of twenty-five' who had served their apprenticeships in Boston, and the other for young men of similar situation in Philadelphia. The accumulated interest as well as the principal was to be lent out for a hundred years. By that time, Franklin's calculations showed, each thousand pounds would have amounted to £135,000. One hundred thousand pounds of each fund was then to be spent. The Boston fund was to be used in constructing 'fortifications, bridges, aqueducts, public buildings, baths, pavements or whatever may make living in the town more convenient for its people and render it more agreeable to strangers.' In Philadelphia, he foresaw that the wells which in his day supplied the city with water would become polluted; accordingly, he proposed that Philadelphia's fund should be used for piping the waters of Wissihicken Creek into the city. Fortunately, Boston provided herself with pavements, and Philadelphia herself with a water supply, without waiting for Franklin's money. Great as his intellectual powers were, he had miscalculated at every point. The class he proposed to benefit gradually became nonexistent; therefore the funds failed to accumulate as rapidly as he had anticipated. At the end of a hundred years, instead of the $675,000 he had expected in each fund, there were only $391,000 in Boston and $90,000 in Philadelphia, and meanwhile the good works which he had chosen as the grand climax of a career devoted to good works had long been provided.

Benjamin Franklin was a wise man, and so was Alexander Hamilton; yet it was Hamilton who drafted the will of Robert Richard Randall, who in the first years of the last century left a farm to be used as a haven for superannuated sailors. A good many years ago the courts were called upon to construe the word 'sailor' to include men employed on steamships. Even so, the fund for Snug Harbor, I am assured, vastly exceeds any reasonable requirement for the care of retired seafarers. The farm happened to be situated on Fifth Avenue, New York. Today it is valued at thirty or forty million dollars.

I have heard of a fund which provides a baked potato at each meal for each young woman at Bryn Mawr, and of another, dating from one of the great famines, which pays for a half a loaf of bread deposited each day at the door of each student in one of the colleges at Oxford. Gifts to educational institutions often contain provisions which are made absurd by the advance of learning. An American university has an endowed lectureship on coal gas as the cause of malarial fever. In 1727, Dr. Woodward, in endowing a chair at Cambridge, England, directed that the incumbent should lecture for all time on his *Natural History of the Earth* and his defense of it against Dr. Camerarius. It did not occur to the good doctor that his scientific theories might eventually become obsolete; yet, with the passing of years and the progress of scientific knowledge, the holder of the chair had to admit his inability to comply with the founder's instructions and at the same time execute Dr. Woodward's plain intent— namely, to teach science. The list of these precisely focused gifts which have lost their usefulness could be extended into volumes, but I am willing to rest the case on Franklin and Hamilton. With all their sagacity, they could not foresee what the future would bring. The world does not stand still. Anyone old enough to vote has seen revolutionary changes in the mechanics of living, and these changes have been accompanied and abetted by changing points of view toward the needs and desires of our fellow men.

I do not know how many millions of dollars have been given in perpetuity for the support of orphan asylums. The Hershey endowment alone is said to total $40,000,000 and more. Orphan asylums began to disappear about the time the old-fashioned wall telephone went out. We know now that it is far better for penniless orphans, as for other children, to be brought up under home influence. The cost of home care for orphans is no greater than the cost of maintaining them in an orphanage. But the question is not one of cost, but of the better interest of the children. Institutional life exposes them needlessly to contagion, and is likely to breed a sense of inferiority that twists the mind. The money which the dead hand holds out to orphan asylums cannot be used for any other purpose than maintaining orphan asylums; it therefore serves to perpetuate a type of institution that most men of good will and good sense no longer approve.

To protest twenty-five years ago that orphans were not best cared for in asylums would have been considered visionary; fifty years ago it would have been considered crack-brained. There is no endowed institution today which is more firmly approved by public opinion than orphanages were within the lifetime of any man of middle age. Let that fact serve as a symbol and a warning to those who are tempted to pile up endowments in perpetuity.

There is another and to my mind no less grievous error into which many givers still are likely to fall. They conceive that money given for philanthropic purposes must be given, if not for a limited object, then at least in perpetuity: the principal must remain intact and only the income may be spent. The result has been, as many a trustee knows, that institutions have become 'endowment poor.' Though they have many millions of dollars in their treasuries, the trustees can touch only the 4 or 5 percent a year that the money earns. There is no means of meeting an extraordinary demand upon the institution, an extraordinary opportunity for increasing its usefulness. Research suffers; museums are unable to purchase objects that never again will be available; experiments of all sorts are frowned upon, not because they do not promise well, but because money to undertake anything out of the ordinary cannot be found, while huge sums are regularly budgeted to carry on traditional and routine activities. And nothing serves more successfully to discourage additional gifts than the knowledge that an institution already possesses great endowments.

As a trustee of the University of Chicago, I know how difficult the problem is. Opportunities for purchasing libraries or for extending the work of some department into new fields are continually coming before us, and though we have endowments of $43,000,000 we have frequently been unable to authorize the use of even a few thousands for some object which would add much to the University's resources and usefulness, to say nothing of its prestige. We may not even convert the principal of our endowments into books or men, which are the real endowment of any university.

A number of years ago the University started collecting more endowment. I did not contribute to the fund, but instead turned over a sum of which the principal may be exhausted. That fund, I am assured, has been of considerable service. It has been used for such diverse purposes as the purchase of the library of a Cambridge professor; for paying part of the cost of Professor Michelson's ether drift experiments; for reconstructing the twelve-inch telescope at Yerkes Observatory; for a continuation of research in glacial erosion in the state of Washington, and for research in phonetics. If the fund had been given as permanent endowment, it is obvious that some of the objects could not have been achieved. The men who desired to undertake experiments and research might have been forced to postpone their investigations; the books purchased might have been scattered among a dozen libraries, never to be reassembled. It is true that money disbursed now will not yield income to the University fifty years hence, but it is also true that fifty years hence other contributors can be found to supply the current needs of that generation.

I am convinced that the timidity of trustees themselves is often responsible for their inability to spend principal. Donors would in many cases be willing to give greater discretion to trustees in such matters if they were asked to do so. A notable example in point is the consent by Mr. Carnegie, more than ten years ago, to the current use of funds which he had given originally for endowment to Tuskegee Institute. At a time when this school was in desperate need of money, I proposed at a meeting of the board of which Honorable Seth Low was chairman and Theodore Roosevelt was a member that we request Mr. Carnegie to permit us to spend not only the interest but also a small portion of the principal of his gift. My suggestion was at first frowned upon. Finally the board agreed, and a letter, dated January 24, 1916, was sent to Mr. Carnegie by Mr. Low which read in part as follows:

> I am writing to submit to you a suggestion which has been made to me by one or two of my fellow trustees of the board of Tuskegee Institute. Mr. Rosenwald, in particular, who is a generous supporter of the Institute, feels very strongly that a permanent endowment fund is less useful than a fund the principal of which can be used up in fifty years, his idea being that every institution like a school ought to commend itself so strongly to the living as to command their interest and support....In accordance with this suggestion, I am writing to ask whether you would be willing to permit the trustees to use, each year, at their discretion, not more than 2 percent of the principal of the fund which you so generously gave some years ago toward the endowment of the Institute. It is always possible that within the lifetime of the next generation industrial training for the negro race will be assumed by the state or national government. Should any such change or any unforeseen change in conditions take place, a fund so firmly tied up in perpetuity that the principal cannot be touched, except possibly through an act of the legislature, might be a disadvantage rather than an advantage.

To this Mr. Carnegie's secretary, Mr. John A. Poynton, replied on February 23, 1916, giving Mr. Carnegie's approval to the suggestion in the following terms:

> Mr. Carnegie has given careful thought to the proposal that your trustees be permitted to use each year a portion of the principal of the fund which he contributed toward endowment. In establishing his foundation Mr. Carnegie has favored the plan of giving the trustees and their successors the right to change the policy governing the disposition of the principal as well as interest when to them it might seem expedient, believing it impossible for those now living to anticipate the needs of future generations. Mr. Carnegie would be happy to have the trustees of Tuskegee assume a similar responsibility in connection with the fund which he contributed toward the endowment of that institute, and asks me to say that he is willing to have a small percentage of the principal used annually for current expenses if three fourths of the members of your board should decide in favor of such a plan.

Here is evidence that Mr. Carnegie might have relaxed the terms of his other gifts had he been asked to do so. It was not the donor but the trustees who were timid. (I have seen trustees act in much the same way in matters of financial administration. Men accustomed to investing a large part of their private fortunes in sound common stocks have felt that as trustees they must invest only in first mortgages or bonds. Of late a good many boards of trustees have enjoyed a change of heart, to the vast benefit of the institutions they serve. But that is a digression.) In some of the institutions with which I am best acquainted, funds given with no strings attached have been added to the perpetual endowment as a matter of course. It is a noteworthy fact, though not as widely known as it should be, that the Rockefeller foundations are not perpetuities. If any of them today are wealthier than at their establishment, it is not because the trustees are not free to spend principal when the occasion rises. As a matter of fact, I am told these boards have expended about seventy-five million dollars of their capital or special funds, and it is probable that at least two of them will disburse all of their principal funds within another decade or two.

I am opposed to gifts in perpetuity for any purpose. I do not advocate profligate spending of principal. That is not the true alternative to perpetuities. I advocate the gift which provides that the trustees *may* spend a small portion of the capital—say, not to exceed 5 to 10 percent—in any one year in addition to the income if in their judgment there is good use at hand for the additional sums. Men who argue that permission to spend principal will lead to profligate spending do not know the temper of trustees and the sense of responsibility they feel toward funds entrusted to them; nor do they appreciate the real difficulties which face donors and trustees of foundations in finding objects worthy of support. I am prepared to say that some of the keenest minds in this country are employed by foundations and universities in seeking such objects; yet, when a real need is discovered, it often cannot be met adequately, simply because of restrictions placed on funds in hand.

The point has been raised that great institutions must have perpetual endowments to tide them through hard times when new money may not be forthcoming. Those are precisely the times when it is most important to have unrestricted funds which will permit our institutions to continue their work until conditions improve, as they always do. A great institution like Harvard ought not to have to restrict its activities merely because its income for one reason or another has been temporarily curtailed. The spending of a million or two of principal at such a time is not imprudent. Sound business sense, indeed, would commend it.

I am thinking not only of university endowments, but also of the great foundations established to increase the sum of knowledge and happiness among men. Too many of these are in perpetuity. It is an astonishing fact that the men who gave them— for the most part, hard-headed business men who abhorred bureaucracy—have not guarded, in their giving, against this blight. I think it is almost inevitable that as trustees and officers of perpetuities grow old they become more concerned to conserve the funds in their care than to wring from those funds the greatest possible usefulness. That tendency is evident already in some of the foundations, and as time goes on it will not lessen but increase. The cure for this disease is a radical operation. If the funds must exhaust themselves within a generation, no bureaucracy is likely to develop around them.

What would happen, it might be asked, if the billions tied up in perpetuities in this country should be released over a period of fifty or one hundred years? What would become of education and of scientific research? How could society care for the sick, the helpless, and the impoverished? The answer is that all these needs would be as well provided for as the demands of the day justified. Wisdom, kindness of heart, and good will are not going to die with this generation.

Instead of welcoming perpetuities, trustees, it seems to me, would be justified in resenting them. Perpetuities are, in a measure at least, an avowal of lack of confidence in the trustees by the donor. And it is a strange avowal. The trustees are told that they are wise enough and honest enough to invest the money and spend the income amounting to 4 to 5 percent each year; but they are told in the same breath that they are not capable of spending 6 to 10 or 15 percent wisely.

If trustees are not resentful, it is because they know that donors of perpetuities are not thinking in those terms. Sometimes perpetuities are created only because lawyers who draft deeds of gifts and wills have not learned that money can be given in any other way. More often, probably, perpetuities are set up because of the donor's altogether human desire to establish an enduring memorial on earth—an end which becomes increasingly attractive to many men with advancing years.

I am certain that those who seek by perpetuities to create for themselves a kind of immortality on earth will fail, if only because no institution and no foundation can live forever. If some men are remembered years and centuries after the death of the last of their contemporaries, it is not because of endowments they created. The names of Harvard, Yale, Bodley, and Smithson, to be sure, are still on men's lips, but the names are now not those of men but of institutions. If any of these men strove for everlasting rememberance, they must feel kinship with Nesselrode, who lived a diplomat, but is immortal as a pudding.

There has been evolution in the art of giving, as in other activities. The gift intended to meet a particular need or support a particular institution in perpetuity was generally approved, but is now outmoded. There are evidences that all perpetuities are becoming less popular, and I look forward with confidence to the day when they will become a rarity. They have not stood the test of time.

To prove that I practice what I preach, it may not be out of place to say that every donation that I have made may be expended at the discretion of the directors of the institution to which it is given. The charter of the foundation which I created some years ago provides that principal as well as income may be spent as the trustees think best. This year, as the management of this fund was being reorganized, I was anxious to make sure that the trustees and officers would meet present needs instead of hoarding the funds for possible future uses. I have stipulated, therefore, that not only the income but also all of the principal of this fund *must* be expended within twenty-five years of my death. This I did in the following letter to the board of trustees, approved and accepted by the board at its meeting in Chicago on April 29, 1928:

> I am happy to present herewith to the Trustees of the Julius Rosenwald Fund certificate for twenty thousand shares of the stock of Sears, Roebuck and Company.
>
> When the Julius Rosenwald Fund was created and sums of money turned over, it was provided that the principal should be spent within a reasonable period of time. My experience is that trustees controlling large funds are not only desirous of conserving principal, but often favor adding to it from surplus income.

I am not in sympathy with this policy of perpetuating endowment, and believe that more good can be accomplished by expending funds as trustees find opportunities for constructive work than by storing up large sums of money for long periods of time. By adopting a policy of using the fund within this generation we may avoid those tendencies toward bureaucracy and a formal or perfunctory attitude toward the work which almost inevitably develop in organizations which prolong their existence indefinitely. Coming generations can be relied upon to provide for their own needs as they arise.

In accepting the shares of stock now offered, I ask that the Trustees do so with the understanding that the entire fund in the hands of the Board, both income and principal, be expended within twenty-five years of the time of my death.

I submitted this letter, in advance, to a wide circle of men and women experienced in philanthropy and education, anticipating a good deal of dissent. There was almost none. Twenty years ago when I, among others, spoke in this vein, our ideas were considered visionary; today they are receiving an ever wider approval.

I believe that large gifts should not be restricted to narrowly specified objects, and that under no circumstances should funds be held in perpetuity. I am not opposed to endowments for colleges or other institutions which require some continuity of support, provided permission is given to use part of the principal from time to time as needs arise. This does not mean profligate spending. It is simply placing confidence in living trustees; it prevents control by the dead hand; it discourages the building up of bureaucratic groups of men, who tend to become overconservative and timid in investment and disbursement of trust funds. I have confidence in future generations and in their ability to meet their own needs wisely and generously.

19

From Charity to Philanthropy

DANIEL J. BOORSTIN

DANIEL J. BOORSTIN IS LIBRARIAN OF CONGRESS, A NOTED
EDUCATOR AND HISTORIAN, A LAWYER, AND A PROLIFIC AUTHOR.
HE RECEIVED THE PULITZER PRIZE IN 1974 FOR HIS BOOK THE
AMERICANS: THE DEMOCRATIC EXPERIENCE. MR. BOORSTIN
PRESENTED THE LECTURE FROM WHICH THIS CHAPTER IS
EXCERPTED AT THE UNIVERSITY OF CHICAGO ON OCTOBER 15,
1962, AS PART OF A CELEBRATION OF THE 100TH ANNIVERSARY OF
THE BIRTH OF JULIUS ROSENWALD.

If you are an American interested in education and public institutions and you travel about France today, you find something strangely missing from the landscape. In Paris, of course, you find a host of sites and buildings serving public purposes—from the Champs Elysees, the Place de la Concorde, the Louvre, the Tuilleries, the Petit Palais, the Grand Palais, and the Invalides, to the College de France, the Academie, and the Sorbonne. All over the country, of course you see mairies and parish churches and cathedrals. Along the Loire, on the Cote d'Azure, or scattered elsewhere, splendid chateaux and country estates are monuments to private grandeur, past and present. You are apt to feel puzzled, a bit lost and disoriented, simply because what you see there, like much else in Europe, is classifiable with an unfamiliar neatness. The sites and buildings are, with few exceptions, either public or private. They are monuments of the wealth and power, *either* of individuals *or* of the state. The University of Paris (and there is only one university of Paris) is an organ of the Ministry of Education; the Louvre and the Bibliotheque Nationale are the responsibility of the minister of culture; the schools are run by the national government. Even the most imposing religious monuments—Notre Dame, Chartres, and Mont-Saint Michel, for example—are essentially public, for they have been supported by taxation. The French church has enjoyed privileges which (despite the freedom of religion) have amounted to making it an organ of the state. If you are not in a private building, you are in an institution created and supported and controlled by the government.

In a great American city, by contrast, many—even most—of the prominent public buildings and institutions are of a quite different character. They do not fall into either of these sharply separated classes. Strictly speaking, they are not private, nor are they run by the government. They are a third species, which in many important respects is peculiarly American. They have many unique characteristics and a spirit all their own. They are monuments to what in the Old World was familiar neither as private charity nor as government munificence. They are monuments to community. They originate in the community, depend on the community, are developed by the community, serve the community, and rise or fall with the community.

They are such familiar features of our American landscape that we can easily forget, if we have ever noticed, that they are in many ways a peculiar American growth—peculiar both in their character and in their luxuriance, in what has made them grow and in what keeps them alive and flourishing. I need hardly remind you of such prominent features of Chicago life as the Art Institute, the Chicago Museum of Natural History (sometimes called the Field Museum), the Shedd Aquarium, the Adler Planetarium, the Museum of Science and Industry (commonly called the Rosenwald Museum), and The University of Chicago (founded by John D. Rockefeller). Each of these—in fact, nearly all the major philanthropic, educational, and public-serving institutions of the city (with some conspicuous exceptions)—was founded and is sustained voluntarily by members of the community. One finds comparable institutions in every other American city. Of course, there are numerous hospitals, universities, and other enterprises supported by our government; but these are far more often the creatures of local or state than of the national government. Scattered examples of community institutions of this type are not unique to the United States. Something like them—some of the Oxford and Cambridge colleges, for example—existed even before the New World was settled by Europeans. In one form or another a few such institutions are found today probably in every country in the world, except in Communist countries, where the autonomous public spirit is prohibited. But in extent, power, influence, and vitality our community institutions are a peculiarly American phenomenon.

Here in the United States, even some of our institutions ostensibly run by one or another of our governments are in fact community institutions in a sense in which they are not elsewhere in the world. Take, for example, our "public" schools. In the great nations of western Europe, the schools which are supported by the general citizenry and which anyone can attend free of charge are run not by separate communities through school boards but from the center by the national government headquartered, say, in Paris or in Rome. It was once a familiar boast of the French minister of education that he could look at his watch at any moment during the day and tell you exactly what was being taught in every classroom in the country. Nothing is more astonishing to a European than to be told that in the United States we have no corresponding official and that, except for a few constitutional safeguards (for example, of freedom of religion, or of free entry to public facilities, regardless of race), the conduct of our public instruction is decentralized. It is in local community hands.

Origins of an American Idea of Community: An Old Antithesis Dissolved

This notion of community is one the most characteristic, one of the most important, yet one of the least noticed American contributions to modern life.

In Origin, American Communities Were Voluntary: Communities Arose Before Governments

In western Europe, with insignificant exceptions, men found themselves wherever they were in the nineteenth century because they were born there. The act of choice, of consciously choosing their particular community, had been made, if ever, only by remote ancestors—the contemporaries of Beowulf, William the Conqueror, Siegfried, or Aeneas. On the other hand, because we were an immigrant nation, everybody here, except the Indians and the Negroes and those others who had been forcibly transported, was here because he or a recent ancestor (a father, grandfather, or great-grandfather) had chosen this place. The sense of community was inevitably more vivid and more personal because, for so many in the community, living here had been an act of choice.

In crowded, preempted Europe, with its no-trespassing signs all over the place, the control of governments, by the nineteenth century or even before, covered the map. The decisive contrasting fact, not sufficiently noticed, is that in America, even in modern times, *communities* existed before governments were here to care for public needs. There were many groups of people with a common sense of purpose and a feeling of duty to one another before there were political institutions forcing them to perform their duties. A classic example is the Pilgrims, who landed at Plymouth in November, 1620. Of course, they were held together by a strong sense of common purpose. But since they were landing in an unexpected place—they had intended to land in Virginia and not in New England— they were a community without government. While still on board the *Mayflower,* they were frightened by the boast of their few unruly members who threatened to take advantage of this fact as soon as they touched land. So by the Mayflower Compact they set up a new government. The Pilgrim community thus had preceded the government of Plymouth.

This order of events was repeated again and again in American history. Groups moving westward from New England and other parts of the Atlantic seaboard organized themselves into communities in order to conquer the great distances, to help one another drag their wagons uphill, to protect one another from Indians, and for a hundred other cooperative purposes. They knew they were moving into open spaces where jurisdiction was uncertain or nonexistent. Or take the remote mining towns, founded here and there in what is now Colorado, California, Montana, or Nevada—places where men knew that their silver or golden objects could not be secured unless they managed to stay alive and preserve their property. In all these places men who were already a community formed do-it-yourself governments. Communities preceded governments.

Not least important was this phenomenon in the new western cities. Chicago was to be the greatest, but there were others, like Cincinnati, Kansas City, Omaha, and Denver, which had become flourishing communities before they had well-established, elaborate governments.

This simple American order of experience was to have deep and widespread effects on American thinking about society, government, and the responsibilities of the individual. While Europe was everywhere cluttered with obsolete political machinery, in America *purposes* usually preceded machinery. In Europe it was more usual for the voluntary activities of groups to grow up in the interstices of ancient government agencies. In America more often the voluntary collaborative activities of members of community were there first, and it was government that came into the interstices. Thus, while Americans acquired a wholesome respect for the force of the community organized into governments, they tended to feel toward it neither awe, nor reverence, nor terror. The scrupulous faithfulness with which most Americans pay most of their taxes (even their income taxes!) continually astonished continental Europeans. This is only another vivid reminder that Americans tend to think of Government as their servant and not their master. While we have less faith in government and expect less of it, we also have less suspicion of it.

The Quick-Grown, Fluid Community:
The Booster Spirit

In nineteenth century England a number of cities like London, Birmingham, and Manchester grew with unprecedented rapidity. But this speed was slow compared to the contemporary growth of many American cities, which became metropolises almost before geographers had located them on their maps. The population of Illinois, for example, more than quadrupled between 1810 and 1820, more than trebled between 1820 and 1830, and again between 1830 and 1840. The city of Chicago (then Fort Dearborn), which around 1830 counted a hundred people, by 1890 had passed the million mark. Though it had taken a million years for mankind to produce its first city of a million inhabitants, Americans—or perhaps we should say Chicagoans—accomplished this gargantuan feat within a single lifetime. Similar phenomena occurred not only in Chicago but in dozens of other places—in Omaha, Cincinnati, Denver, Kansas City, St. Louis, and Dallas, to mention only a few.

Such fantastic growth itself fostered a naive pride in community, for men literally grew up with their towns. From this simple fact came a much maligned but peculiarly American product: the Booster Spirit. The spirit which had grown in the nineteenth century was pretty conscious of itself by about 1900 when the word "booster" was invented. In cities of explosive growth, group needs were urgent and rapidly changing. Sewage disposal, water supply, sidewalks, parks, harbor facilities, and a thousand other common needs at first depended on the desires, the willingness, and the good will of individuals. Could people who had very little governmental machinery do these things for themselves and their neighbors? Could they rapidly change the scale and the ends of their thinking about their town? Were they willing? By saying "Yes," they proved that they were a community.

Hardly less remarkable than this sudden intensity of community feeling in upstart cities was the fluidity of the population and the readiness with which people came and went. During a single day in the summer of 1857, thirty-four hundred immigrants arrived in Chicago on the Michigan Central Railroad alone. People came not only from the eastern and southern United States but from Ireland, Germany, and Scandinavia, and, very soon, too, from Poland, Italy, China, and other remote places. People who came so readily sometimes also left soon and in large numbers. Such cities flourished partly because they were distribution points—spigots from which people poured into the sponge-like hinterland.

Thus was nourished the Booster Spirit, distinctively American not only in intensity and volubleness but in the readiness with which it could be detached from one community and attached to another. Booster loyalties grew rapidly; yet while they lasted, they seemed to have an oaklike solidity. Here today and there tomorrow. Chicago today; tomorrow Omaha, Denver, or Tulsa. "But while

I'm here, I'm with you 150 percent." "We'll outgrow and outshine all the rest!" Never was a loyalty more fervent, more enthusiastic, more noisy—or more transferable. This was the voluntary, competitive spirit.

The keynote of all this was *community*. American history had helped empty the word of its connotations of selflessness. Notice how irrelevant were the antitheses of "Individualism" versus "Socialism," "The Man" versus "The State." Governments here were not the transformed instruments of hereditary power. American businessmen were eager and ingenious at finding ways for federal, state, or local government to serve their enterprises—whether they were New England shippers, western lumbermen, transcontinental railroad builders, manufacturers, or simple farmers or merchants. Of course, this was not because they were socialists but rather because, starting from the fact of community, they could not help seeing all agencies of government as additional forms through which specific community purposes could be served.

From Conscience to Community

There are few better illustrations of this central concept—perhaps it might better be called a sentiment—in American life than the history of American philanthropy. And there has been no more effective exponent of the community spirit in philanthropy than Julius Rosenwald, the centennial of whose birth was celebrated on October 15, 1962. I will not try to tell the story of Rosenwald's philanthropies. I will, rather, describe some of the distinctiveness of certain American developments and show how Julius Rosenwald participated in them.

Philanthropy or charity throughout much of European history has been a predominantly private virtue. In most of western Europe the national states and their organs were elaborated before the needs of modern industrial society came into being. The state and its organs had therefore preempted most of the areas of public benevolence, improvement, education, and progress even before the appearance of the great fortunes which modern industry made possible. The creators of the modern state—for example, Queen Elizabeth I in England, Napoleon in France, and Bismarck in Germany—developed arms of the state to do more and more jobs of public service, public enrichment, public enlightenment, and cultural and scientific progress. The charitable spirit was a kind of residuum; it inevitably tended to become the spirit of almsgiving. Of course, everybody was required to contribute by taxes or gifts to state or church institutions. But because the state—and its ancient partner, the church—had taken over the business of wholesale philanthropy, the independent charities of wealthy men were generally left to alleviating the distress of the particular individuals whom they noticed.

By the nineteenth century in France or Italy—even in England—it was by no means easy, though one had the means and the desire, to found a new university (the legislature might not charter it; it might confuse or compete against the state-organized system; it might become a center of "revolutionary" or of "reactionary" ideology; etc.), a new museum, or a new research institute. The right to establish new institutions, like the right to bear arms, was jealously guarded by the sovereign, which, of course, usually meant the single national government at the center.

Meanwhile Christian teachings had long exalted the spirit of charity and the practice of almsgiving. "If thou wilt be perfect, go and sell that thou hast, and give to the poor, and thou shalt have treasure in heaven: and come and follow me...Verily I say unto you, that a rich man shall hardly enter into the kingdom of heaven" (Matt. 19:21-23); "Knowledge puffeth up, but charity edifieth" (I Cor. 8:1); "And now abideth faith, hope, charity, these three; but the greatest of these is charity" (I Cor. 13:13). Charity ennobled the giver; it was more blessed to give than to receive.

The first characteristic of the traditional charitable spirit, then, was that it was private and personal. This fact has made difficulties for scholars trying to chronicle philanthropy, especially outside the United States. Donors have often been reluctant to make known the size (whether because of the smallness or the largeness) of their donations. They have sometimes feared that signs of their wealth might bring down on them a host of the poor, confiscatory demands from the tax farmer, or jealously from the sovereign. For more reasons than one, therefore, charity, which was a salve for the conscience, became an innermost corner of consciousness, a sanctum of privacy. A man's charities were a matter between him and his God. Church and conscience might be intermediaries, but the community did not belong in the picture.

Second, the traditional charitable spirit was perpetual, unchanging, and even in a certain sense, rigid. "The poor," said Jesus, "ye always have with you" (John 12:8). The almsgiver was less likely to be trying to solve a problem of this world than to be earning his right to enter into the next. There hardly seemed to be any problem of means or of purpose. Since it was always a greater virtue to give than to receive, the goodness of charity came more from the motive of the giver than from the effect of the gift. Only a hypocrite, a proud man, or one impure of heart would hesitate while he chose among the objects of the gift.

The philanthropic spirit as it has developed, changed, flourished, and become peculiarly institutionalized in America, has been very different. In some respects it has even been opposed to these two characteristics of the time-honored virtue. Here, again, the dominant note, the pervading spirit, the

peculiar characteristic, has been a preoccupation with community. This transformation of the charitable spirit has been expressed in at least three peculiarly
American emphases.

Community Enrichment:
The Purposes of Philanthropy

The focus of American philanthropy has shifted from the giver to the receiver,
from the salving of souls to the solving of problems, from conscience to community. No one better expressed this spirit than Julius Rosenwald, when he
said:

> "In the first place 'philanthropy' is a sickening word. It is generally looked
> upon as helping a man who hasn't a cent in the world. That sort of thing
> hardly interests me. I do not like the 'sob stuff' philanthropy. What I want to
> do is to try to cure the things that seem to be wrong. I do not underestimate
> the value of helping the underdog. That, however, is not my chief concern
> but rather the operation of cause and effect. I try to do the thing that will aid
> groups and masses rather than individuals."

This view, which we should probably call (in William James's phrase) "tough
minded" rather than hardhearted, has long dominated what has been the peculiarly American charitable spirit.

The patron saint of American philanthropy is not Dorothea Dix or any other
saintly person but rather Benjamin Franklin, the man with a business sense and
an eye on his community. For Franklin, doing good was not a private act
between bountiful giver and grateful receiver; it was a prudent social act. A wise
act of philanthropy would sooner or later benefit the giver along with all other
members of the community. While living in Philadelphia, Franklin developed
philanthropic enterprises which included projects for establishing a city police,
for the paving and the better cleaning and lighting of city streets, for a circulat-
ing library, for the American Philosophical Society for Useful Knowledge, for an
Academy for the Education of Youth (origin of the University of Pennsylvania),
for a debating society, and for a volunteer fire department.

Like Julius Rosenwald, Franklin did not go in for "sob-stuff" philanthropy.
Few, if any, of his enterprises were primarily for the immediate relief of distress
or misfortune. Notice, also, that in Franklin's mind and in his activities the line
between public and private hardly existed. If an activity was required and was
not yet performed by a government—by city, state, or nation—he thought it
perfectly reasonable that individuals club together to do the job, not only to fill

the gap, but also to prod or shame governments into doing their part. A large number, but by no means all, of his activities have been taken over by the municipality of Philadelphia, the state of Pennsylvania, or the federal government. From this point of view the important thing was not whether the job was done by government or by individuals: both governments and individuals were agencies of community. The community was the thing. Notice also that Franklin's opportunity to step into the breach with community enterprises arose in large part because the community was relatively new, because state activities were still sparse—in a word, because the community existed before the government.

Community Participation:
The Means of Philanthropy

While, as we have just observed, the focus of American philanthropy has shifted from giver to receiver, there has occurred another equally important shift in point of view. The clear lines between the roles of the giver and the receiver, which in the traditional European situation were so distinct, in America became blurred. In an American equalitarian, enterprising, fluid society the ancient contrasts between the bountiful rich and the grateful poor, the benefactor and the beneficiary, on which the almsgiving situation had depended, became obsolete. In America a community—the ultimate beneficiary—was increasingly expected to be its own benefactor. The recipient here (who became more difficult to identify as a member of a fixed social class) was now viewed less as a target of individual generosity than as an integral part of the social capital, an item of community investment.

It is not surprising, then, that the time-honored notion that it is more blessed to give than to receive, like some other ancient fixed axioms of charity, began to be dissolved. When you no longer believe the ancient axiom that the "poor are always with you," a recipient is no longer a member of a permanent social class. So far did we move from the old notion; now the ideal recipient of philanthropy was himself viewed as a potential donor. Just as the value of a charitable gift tended to be judged less by the motive of the giver than by the social effect of the gift, so the suitability of a recipient was judged less by his emotional response—his gratitude or his personal loyalty to a benefactor—than by his own potential contribution to the community. A free citizen who receives assistance is no mere receptacle of benevolence; he prepares himself to become a fountain of benevolence.

By a twist of New World circumstances, by the transformation of the charitable spirit, in the United States it often happened that those who received most from an act of philanthropy were also those who gave most. Julius Rosenwald, and some other characteristically American philanthropists, have viewed this as the ideal philanthropic situation. Take, for example, a scene in Boligee, Alabama, in the winter of 1916-17. This was one of the so-called arousement meetings to raise money from the local Negro community to meet Julius Rosenwald's offer of a matching sum to build a simple schoolhouse. We are fortunate to have an eyewitness account:

> "We gathered together in a little old rickety building, without any heat, only from an old rusty stove with the stove pipe protruding out of the window where a pane had been removed for the flue… The Farmers had been hard hit that year as the boll weevil had figured very conspicuously in that community, and most of the people were tenants on large plantations. When we reached the scene where the rally was to be staged, the teacher with thirty-five or forty little children had prepared a program which consisted of plantation melodies… They sang with such fervor and devotion, until one could hardly restrain from crying… The patrons and friends were all rural people, and crudely dressed. The women had on home spun dresses and aprons, while the men in the main were dressed in blue overalls. Their boots and shoes were very muddy, as they had to trudge through the mud from three to four miles… When the speaking was over we arranged for the silver offering, and to tell the truth I thought we would do well to collect ten dollars from the audience; but when the Master of Ceremonies, Rev. M.D. Wallace, who had ridden a small mule over the county through the cold and through the rain, organizing the people, began to call the collection the people began to respond. You would have been over-awed with emotion if you could have seen those poor people walking up to the table, emptying their pockets for a school… One old man, who had seen slavery days, with all of his life's earnings in an old greasy sack, slowly drew it from his pocket, and emptied it on the table. I have never seen such a pile of nickels, pennies, dimes, and dollars, etc., in my life. He put thirty-eight dollars on the table, which was his entire savings."

These were the people who would benefit most from the Rosenwald gift, yet they were the people who in proportion to their means were giving most.

Someone with less faith in his fellow men might simply have given the sums outright without asking any matching funds, for the Negroes of Alabama were surely depressed and underprivileged. In a recent previous year, when the state of Alabama had appropriated $2,865,254 for public education, only $357,585, or less than 15 percent, went to Negro schools—this despite the fact that Negroes made up about half the population of the state. Rosenwald had faith in the Negroes of Alabama—not only in their potentiality but, still more important, in their present determination and their ability to help themselves.

By the time of his death, Rosenwald had contributed to the construction of 5,357 public schools, shops, and teachers' homes in 883 counties of fifteen southern states at a total cost of $28,408,520. Julius Rosenwald's personal contribution was monumental: $4,366,519. But a fact of which he would have been still prouder was that his contribution had induced others to contribute still more.

Adaptation to Community:
The Flexibility of Philanthropy

Faith, hope, and charity were as changeless as God or human nature, but philanthropy must change with its community. American philanthropists were citizens of fast-growing cities with shifting populations, novel enterprises, and as speedy an obsolescence of social problems as of everything else. To do their job, they had to keep their eyes open and their feet on the ground. They had to be alert to new needs which required new investments by everybody in a progressive community.

Julius Rosenwald, who had grown up with the West and with Chicago, was well aware of all this. He warned vain men against seeking immortality by attaching their names to institutions; he reminded them of Nesselrode, "who lived a diplomat, but is immortal as a pudding."

Rosenwald never tired of pointing to the dangers of rigid philanthropy, of gifts in perpetuity for unchanging purposes, which might become a burden rather than a blessing.

Since Julius Rosenwald's day, two new kinds of problems in the application of the American community ideal to philanthropic institutions have become acute. The first has arisen from the vast foundations which appeared in the first decades or our century.

While in many respects these foundations were squarely in the American tradition which I have described, they faced new problems and themselves created some. Many of these are not unrelated to the dangers against which Julius Rosenwald warned, although they arise from some opposite causes. The perpetuities, the rigidities, and the bureaucracies against which Rosenwald inveighed were in charities whose purposes were too specific and hence likely to become obsolete. But the foundations which dominate the scene nowadays are extremely general in their purpose. The public dangers which arise from them come precisely from the fact that there is no prospect that they will ever become obsolete. The Ford Foundation's purpose is to serve the public welfare.

Spontaneity, drift, fluidity, and competition among American institutions have given our future much of its vitality. Some of the dangers which come from the new large foundations spring from the very vagueness and generality of their purposes as well as from their sheer size. They have already become powerful, independent, self-perpetuating institutions. They are in the wholesale—some might say the "mail-order"—philanthropy business. Instead of encouraging latent energies in the community, they are naturally tempted to initiate projects; and the more spectacular and more novel are often most attractive from a public relations point of view. They show few signs of that self-liquidating tendency that Rosenwald rightly insisted to be a feature of a healthy foundation.

The entry into our language of certain phrases is a clue to the changing spirit of our large-scale philanthropy and to the new dangers. We all have heard of the "foundation executive"—a person who makes his living from administering philanthropy, from inventing, developing, and publicizing worthy projects. He is often a refugee from academic life; he is seldom underpaid (at least by academic standards); ideally, he is a person of driving energy, of aggressive organizing power, and of all the affable virtues. He is a new breed of the American college president, another expert on things in general, who has the new advantage of being able to exert his affability on the disbursement rather than on the collection of funds. But some might ask whether one such breed is not enough and perhaps all that our culture can stand. Amusement is sometimes expressed by professors when they find themselves solemnly presenting their appeals for support of their research to foundation officials who left university life precisely because they were unable to produce research which satisfied these very same professors.

Another telltale phrase which has entered our vocabulary is the so-called "foundation project." Generally speaking, a foundation project must be collaborative; it must have defined and predictable results; it must be noncontroversial; and yet it must have some popular interest. The fact that we in academic life know what kind of project will appeal or will not appeal to the foundations is one of the worst things that can be said about them. Generally speaking, instead of being an incentive to the initiative of individuals or communities, our largest foundations have tended to foster (as, indeed, they created) the vogue for concocted projects cast in the foundation mold. Thus foundations become freezing agents in the world of scholarship and of community projects. Their proper role is as catalyst.

An even larger new problem has arisen in the mid-twentieth century from our efforts to apply our philanthropic spirit abroad. At least since the Marshall Plan (or European Recovery Plan, which between 1948 and 1951 helped western European countries bolster their economies by gifts and loans to the amount of 12.5 billion dollars), and the "Point Four" program, outlined by President Truman in his Inaugural Address of January 20, 1949, followed by large programs under the succeeding presidents of both parties, the role of philanthropist-to-the-world (or to the free, or potentially free, world) has been irrevocably assumed by the United States.

Two dangers lie in our new role, seen in the perspective of our peculiar national history. The first is that—in our enthusiasm to do good, in our optimism, our desire to encompass the world in our community, and to put the best light on everything we do—we may confuse ourselves into assuming that charity and self-interest are always necessarily consistent. In this confusion we not only fail to see the clear dictates of our national self-interest but becloud our purer acts of charity with suspicions of Machiavellism.

The second danger here arises from the peculiar character of American life, in which, as I have said, the idea of community has been central. In the United States our distinctive philanthropic institutions have been neither wholly public nor wholly private; they have been acts of community, depending for their success and their meaning on the triple ideas of community enrichment, community participation, and adaptation to community. If philanthropy has arisen in America out of our poignant and pressing sense of community, does it follow that elsewhere in the world the sense of community itself can arise merely or even mainly from outside acts of philanthropy?

Our phenomenal success and our phenomenal energies in developing philanthropic institutions for our own community may mislead us into overlooking how much that success has depended on the preexistence here of a sense of community. From being a single aspect of American domestic institutions, philanthropy—the charitable spirit—in its transformed American shapes has become the leading feature of our relation to the world. Not merely the prosperity but the very survival of the United States may now depend on our ability to see where charity ends and where national self-interest begins—on our ability, in Julius Rosenwald's words, not to be overwhelmed by "the 'sob-stuff' philanthropy," but to look hard at "the operation of cause and effect" and to "try to cure the things that seem to be wrong." This will depend not only on whether we can train a few thousand Peace Corpsmen or a few tens of thousands of administrators of foreign aid but on whether we can look unashamedly (as Rosenwald did) at the limits of our capacity to help others and on whether we can—even at some risk to ourselves—share Rosenwald's faith in the ability of other peoples and future generations to solve their own problems.

20

Stories of Notable Givers

ARNAUD C. MARTS

ARNAUD C. MARTS SERVED AS PRESIDENT OF THE FUNDRAISING COUNSELING FIRM OF MARTS AND LUNDY, INC. AND OF BUCKNELL UNIVERSITY.

"This thing of giving," said George F. Burba, "I do not understand, any more than you do, but there is something about it that blesses us.... Those who give most, have most left.... I believe that everyone who dries a tear will be spared the shedding of a thousand tears.... I believe that every sacrifice we make will so enrich us in the future that our regret will be that we did not sacrifice the more....

"Give—and somewhere, from out of the clouds, or from the sacred depths of human hearts, a melody divine will reach your ears, and gladden all your days upon the earth."

One day I sat in the parlor of an eighty-year-old friend who had just made a gift of $100,000 to a college, and who was experiencing the usual exhilaration of such an act. Suddenly he pointed to a man of his own age who was walking by. "See that old coot?" he said. "He has the same amount of money I have, but I feel sorry for him, poor chap."

"Why?" I asked.

"Because he has never learned how to buy any happiness with his money. All his life he has played one game. It has been his lifetime game to be worth more on December 31st of each year than he was on January 1st. So far as I know, he has won that little game every year. Now he's eighty—and he's miserable. Think what fun he could have if he'd only given away a little of his money now and then to help his fellow men. Too bad! Poor old man! Too bad!"

What, indeed, is it that inspires a man to take a substantial sum from his private capital and freely give it into the treasury of a philanthropic institution for the service of others?

Reprinted from *Philanthropy's Role in Civilization: Its Contribution to Human Freedom*, Chapter 2, by Arnaud C. Marts (New York: Harper and Brothers, 1953). Copyright ©1953 by Harper & Row, Publishers, Inc. Reprinted by permission of the publisher.

Some men give again and again. Others seem incapable of doing so, though their possessions may have become a source of responsibility and anxiety. Some know how to give both liberally and wisely, and derive deep satisfaction from the results. Others form the habit of keeping all they possess, and appear pleased at having been able to resist the temptation to give. They often manage to persuade themselves either that the cause is foolish, or none of their concern. Cynicism supports such an attitude.

But what are the motives that lead to giving?

Raymond Moley says something in his book, *How to Keep Our Liberty*, that applies in this connection, although he is speaking of political action by citizens in support of "nonmaterial" American ideals:

> "People are moved by many impulses other than those with roots in stomachs and pocketbooks. Human beings are endowed with the sentiments of idealism, loyalty and pride associated with the home, the family, the local community, friends, ancestry, tradition, religion and patriotism."

Evidently they must be rooted deep in human nature.

If we recount the stories of a few notable gifts that have become a part of the fiber of our nation, it may shed light on the motive power behind benevolent giving.

A Boy from Maine

Gardner Colby was a boy whose seagoing father had died leaving his widow—scarcely twenty-five years of age—with a family of four and no means for their support. The ten-year-old Gardner was earning a few pennies by working in a potash plant in Waterville, Maine.

Also in Waterville was a new-born college, chartered as the Maine Literary and Theological Institution, whose first president, the Reverend Dr. Chaplin, was a kindly man who befriended and aided the little Colby family. In 1820, when the institution celebrated the erection of its first building, the whole village joined in the jubilation. A lighted candle was placed in each of the many windows in the front of the building and the villagers looked on the spectacle with awe. It was a sight to thrill a youth befriended by the president of this wonderful institution.

The little family moved away to struggle and advance elsewhere. Gardner prospered—first as a small merchant, then as a wholesale merchant, an importer, a manufacturer, a railroad president, and a capitalist.

One Sabbath morning as he sat in his church pew in Massachusetts, a chance word from the preacher strangely moved him. To illustrate a point, the minister recalled an episode from his early life—the picture of Dr. Chaplin coming bowed and dejected from the home of a wealthy man in Portland, repeating over and over, "God save Waterville College! Waterville College must not perish!" Before his death Dr. Chaplin's efforts had indeed saved the college for the time being, but by 1864 the ravages of the Civil War had so reduced its resources that it seemed as if nothing short of Providence could prevent its closing.

At the next commencement season Gardner Colby came to Waterville with a message. He offered the college $50,000 for endowment on condition that $100,000 be obtained from other friends. In two years' time the gift was claimed. Some years later Waterville College became known as Colby College.

What led this New Englander to give so generously while all about him others were easily evading the same appeals? Was the motive power compounded of childhood memories of a valiant mother, or of gratitude, or of an inner desire to give evidence to the people of Waterville that the poor young widow and her family had in them the stuff that wins? Above and through it all, was there not a deep-rooted love of God and mankind?

In the South

General Samuel C. Armstrong had a firm philosophy: it was "Subtract hard work from life and in a few months it will all have gone to pieces. Labor—next to the grace of God in the heart—is the greatest promoter of morality, the greatest power for civilization." It was his philosophy and his vision that gave new direction to Negro education in the South with the establishment, in 1868, of Hampton Institute in Virginia—an institution destined to prove of incalculable consequence to the Negro race and to the total pattern of American social life.

General Armstrong was the son of a Congregational missionary to Hawaii who had learned, from his observation of educational work there, practical methods which might be applied to the training of a race totally unfamiliar with the academic educational process. With the financial aid of the American Missionary Society, Hampton Institute offered Negro youths instruction of an intensely practical sort. It comprised training in the most common and useful forms of labor—helping the Negro to fit himself for life in spheres where he was most likely to live it.

In 1881, Booker T. Washington, a graduate of Hampton Institute, founded Tuskegee Institute in Alabama, fashioning his school after Hampton. Before long fifteen smaller institutions sprang up as offshoots of Tuskegee. Thus, the new lead which philanthropy at Hampton had given furnished the direction and drive for the main educational efforts in behalf of the Negro race for the next half century.

In the same year that General Armstrong established Hampton another man took a great step in aiding education in the South. Imagine the moral influence of George Peabody's act, in 1867, in establishing the Peabody Education Fund with an initial gift of $3,000,000—and much more added later—with his statement that the purpose was to reestablish an educational system in the South for both white and black.

The announcement of this gift had a profound influence in assuaging public passions. To make the announcement, Mr. Peabody wisely called together at Washington a group of the most distinguished men of both North and South. In the Brady photograph of the conference we see General Grant standing side by side with Governor Aiken of South Carolina, and Winthrop of the Federal Congress and Rives of the Confederate Congress sitting side by side.

Here is a contemporary account of the meeting:

> After reading his deed of gift to them for the children of the South, there is a solemn hush, and then it is proposed that the blessings of Almighty God be called upon this solemn act. They kneel there in a circle of prayer—the Puritan of New England, the pioneer of the West, the financier of the metropolis, and the defeated veterans of the Confederacy. With bended knee and touching elbow, they dedicate this great gift. They consecrate themselves to the task of its wise expenditure. In that act and in that moment, not quite two years after Appomattox, is the first guaranty of a reunited country.

Others took up the cause of Negro education. John F. Slater of Connecticut made a gift of a million dollars in 1882; Daniel Hand, also of Connecticut, gave a like amount in 1888. Starting in 1902, the Rockefeller family began a system of giving to Negro education that has approximated a hundred million dollars. There were also large gifts from Andrew Carnegie and his foundation. In 1917, Julius Rosenwald of Chicago contributed more than fifteen million dollars; and during the 1920 decade there were gifts and bequests of millions of dollars from George Eastman of Rochester and scores of other philanthropists. Rarely has there been a nobler outpouring of devoted gifts for a single cause, continuing to this very day.

A Michigan Pioneer

Here is a story worth notice—not because it is extraordinary, but because it is so natural, so typical, so indigenous to America.

Edward K. Warren was born in 1847 in a village parsonage in Vermont. While still a lad, the family moved to Michigan—recently admitted to statehood and very much a pioneer region. The vigorous father presided over "home missionary" churches. The equally vigorous son was raised on the three R's, a fourth R—religion—and lots of hard work.

While running a country store, where he learned that whalebone was getting scarce, and that bone in women's corsets had an uncomfortable habit of breaking, he invented an inexpensive and flexible substitute made out of the springy quills of turkey feathers. He named it "featherbone." He got a mechanic to help design machinery, and in 1883 set up a little factory in his home town of Three Oaks.

For a while it was tough sledding. One day when things looked dark he promised the Lord that if He would see him through this financial crisis, he would "tithe" for the rest of his life. Young Warren came through, and set to work tithing and working with the Lord in any way he could. He seems to have taken as an everyday motto, "Let us do with our might what our hands find to do."

The business prospered, and the profits began to bear fruit in many directions. Mr. Warren helped to rebuild the local Congregational Church and remained its lifelong pillar. Tremendously interested in Sunday Schools, he boosted the work of the International Sunday School Association, became its president, and organized the international convention in Jerusalem in 1904.

Loving his village, his region, and his state, he steadily expanded his interests and activities. The factory was the chief source of his fellow townsmen's livelihood. His bank and his store and his farm rendered useful service. He acquired large holdings of native woods and dunes shoreland along Lake Michigan, setting up a Warren Foundation to look after their use. Before his death he had the satisfaction of giving an assembly site and buildings to the Congregational Church for summer conventions. Warren's Woods—a tract of primeval forest—was later deeded to the State of Michigan as a laboratory for the botany department of the University of Michigan and for the general use of all students and the public. There has also been set up in perpetuity a Dune State Park for the enjoyment and education of the people of Michigan, also by deed to the state.

Finally, Mr. Warren conceived the idea of gathering together in a folksy sort of museum, located in Three Oaks, every possible relic and reminder of the local pioneer civilization that he and his father had seen develop. He visited other museums like that of the University of Wisconsin, got expert help, and realized his dream. Now, some years after his death, this unique collection is being moved to Lansing—given to Michigan State College.

If these acts are called philanthropic, to him they were as natural as raising and caring for his family. Many such men and women—never celebrated in national news columns—have similar fruitful lives, passing on the by-products to their fellow citizens.

North Carolina Farm Boy

In the year 1856 there was born on a farm in North Carolina a boy who was to give $80,000,000 to philanthropy, and to find in his giving the supreme happiness of a life of many triumphs.

Let us go back to "Buck" Duke's parents and to the father whose homely maxims James B. Duke quoted all through his life. The father, Washington Duke, started as a hard-working farmer near Durham, North Carolina. Only six months of his life had been spent in school. A man of the utmost integrity and good native intelligence, he was deeply loyal to the Methodist Church and its ministry. Religion was a vital part of his life. James Duke said in later years: "My old Daddy always said that if he amounted to anything in life, it was due to the Methodist circuit riders who so often visited his home, and whose preaching and counsel brought out the best that was in him. If I amount to anything in this world I will owe it to my Daddy and to the Methodist Church."

When the Civil War was ended, Washington Duke returned to his family to find he had lost everything and that his Confederate money was worthless. All he had left were two blind army mules which had been given him, fifty cents, and a small shanty for shelter. His daughter Mary was housed with the neighbors, and Washington and his two sons, Buck and Ben, slept in the shed. There they discovered that the soldiers had overlooked something—a quantity of good leaf tobacco. And in an old log barn the Dukes started their first factory, pulverizing the tobacco with flails and proudly labeling bags of prepared tobacco *Pro Bono Publico*.

Loading the *Pro Bono* onto a covered wagon drawn by the two blind mules, the father and his two sons began an itinerant life of bartering at the crossroads. When Buck was eight years old another of his duties was to load a bag of grain on a mule's back and carry it to the mill to be ground into flour. The water slipping through the millrace entranced him, and he lay in the grass by the hour watching the water pour over the big wheel. He longed to own a water mill.

Soon the tobacco business was a great success and the three children were sent away to college—Buck going to Eastman Business College in Poughkeepsie, New York, where he worked day and night with boundless enthusiasm. At fourteen, he was made the manager of his father's factory; at eighteen, he was admitted to partnership; and by the age of thirty he was in New York, opening up a vast new market.

And now he had time for that boyhood dream—water power. His experiments in harnessing the swift waters of his native state resulted in vast power developments and ever-greater revenue for the Duke fortune.

The father's interests were turning to a small Methodist institution in Randolph, North Carolina—Trinity College. In 1890, Washington Duke offered $85,000 for a set of new buildings, if the little college would move to Durham. The move was made and Mr. Duke gave hundreds of thousands of dollars to Trinity before his death in 1905.

His son Buck continued to give lavish sums to Trinity, realizing, as he did so, a lifelong desire to serve God and humanity. Prompted by intense love for his father, deep loyalty to the Church, and patriotic attachment to his state, he set up the great Duke Endowment of approximately $40,000,000 for the betterment of the institutions and the people of the Carolinas. In particular, he provided vast sums for a university to be named after his father, Washington Duke. Trinity College was expanded into Duke University to meet the conditions of the gift.

Thus, the swiftly moving waters of his native state turn the wheels of productive industry and earn, year after year, the funds which bring education and well-being to the people of his own beloved section of America. They build homes for orphans, they help build and maintain rural Methodist churches, they provide pensions for aged Methodist circuit riders, and thus establish a living monument of eternal service to Washington Duke.

Scientific Genius from Ohio

Charles M. Hall, son of a Congregational minister, was born in 1864 and spent his youth in the little college town of Oberlin, Ohio. He was a studious, earnest boy, deeply interested in chemistry and inventions. As a lad, he fell into the habit of seeking out the college's professor of chemistry, F.F. Jewett. He would come to buy a few cents' worth of tubing or test tubes or other experimental material, and then disappear to carry on his private experiments at home.

When later he entered the college as a student, Professor Jewett quickly recognized the unusual quality of his work, and soon they were working side by side, exploring the mysteries of chemistry.

One day Professor Jewett said to his students, "If anyone should invent a process by which aluminum could be made on a commercial scale, not only would he be a benefactor to the world, but he would also be able to lay up for himself a great fortune."

Young Hall was thrilled by the challenge. Patiently he worked at the problem throughout college. With the help and encouragement of Professor Jewett, he rigged up one electric battery after another and tried every variation of method, until one morning after graduation—in the woodshed laboratory he had fitted out at home—he discovered the secret of producing aluminum on a commercial scale. Upon this epoch-making invention was built a vast, essential industry and, inevitably, a sizable fortune.

Charles Hall early began to turn the overflow of his energy and means to the service of his Alma Mater, serving on its board of trustees and making numerous and continued gifts toward its expanding program. His interests outside business covered a wide cultural range—religion, education, music, and the fine arts. He turned over his personal art collection to Oberlin.

He died young and unmarried—just under fifty—and left his great estate in three parts: one to Oberlin; one to Berea College in Kentucky; and one to education and missions in the Orient, a work dear to the hearts of his parents.

Oberlin's share set the college on the road to a position of substantial endowment and expanded influence. Thus, the lad who found his inspiration and his help in the modest little brick laboratory blessed his Alma Mater with a matchless gift out of the abundance which his genius and her influence had created.

The Secret Partner

Another notable story appeared, with the above title, in *Time* magazine of August 4, 1952, under the section devoted to philanthropy. The story was also featured, with pictures, in *Life*.

According to the account in *Time*, Claud H. Foster of Cleveland, a retired inventor-manufacturer who recently gave away $4,000,000, lays his business successes to the fact that if you are "in tune with the secret partner, He'll do something for you." The secret partner, of course, is God. Foster expressed himself as feeling strongly that "something was done for him" quite beyond his own efforts.

The account mentioned three instances. At fourteen, he had phenomenal success with four acres of early potatoes, which providentially were spared any frost, brought $1,800, and enabled him to pay off a debt that had haunted his father for years.

At nineteen—strangely combining his skills as a machinist and a self-taught trombone player—he invented an auto horn that worked off the exhaust and gave out several musical notes. This "Gabriel Horn" made him $150,000.

Then he hit upon the big thing—a shock absorber for autos. Here, again, the idea seemed to come to him out of the blue, as he watched a boat approaching a dock. As he now recalls it, his attention was directed by his secret partner "to a workman who was wrapping a rope around a pile, snubbing the boat." It gave him the idea for the first successful auto shock absorber—the Gabriel Snubber. The company expanded and netted him a million dollars a year, and brought an offer of ten million dollars which he turned down, saying the company was not worth that much. He later sold out for $4,000,000 and retired to spend much of his time in a $3,500 house he built on the shore of Lake Erie.

Here is the last of the story as told by *Time*:

> *"The Big Surprise*. Since Foster felt he had only been the instrument of his partner in making his fortune, he gave much of it away. But he still thought he had too much, since 'my needs are small.' Last week Foster invited many of his old friends—along with representatives of educational and charitable institutions— to a party in Cleveland's Hotel Statler. He promised them the 'surprise of your life.'

> After they had all dined well on filet mignon, Foster arose. One by one the representatives of fifteen Jewish, Catholic and Protestant charitable institutions and Western Reserve University were asked to step to the head table, where Foster sat with a happy smile on his face. At the table each one was handed a big check or a batch of securities. When the give-away party was all over, Foster had handed out $4,000,000.

> "Said he: 'Too many institutions get their money from dead men. I wanted to see them get it. I have no more use for the money. You can take it all, but leave me my friends.'"

In the State of Pennsylvania

Why do men give? For many reasons. We find some of the answers in these notable cases of generosity. And here I want to add one more story—that of a man who said to the author, "You give *your time*, and I'll give *my money*."

In 1935, when the trustees of Bucknell University persuaded me to become part-time president after I had declined election as president, I agreed to spend Thursday and Friday of each week at the college in Lewisburg, Pennsylvania, while continuing my duties as president of the firm of Marts and Lundy, Inc., in New York City.

Like many other colleges in the 1930s, Bucknell was suffering acutely from lack of funds, and I early asked the members of the board of trustees to help me find new supporters for the college. A trustee, Senator Andrew J. Sordoni of Wilkes-Barre, immediately thought of a neighbor: seventy-five-year-old Daniel C. Roberts, retired official of the Woolworth Company. Mr. Roberts, as a boy in Watertown, New York, had been a clerk in the same general store where Frank and Charles Woolworth, Fred Kirby, Frederick Weckesser, Seymour Knox, and other creators of the modern mass-merchandising chain store were clerks, and together they had built the great Woolworth chain. Mr. Roberts and I were introduced.

A friendship sprang up, and with it new plans for the development and strengthening of Bucknell. The main college building had burned down in 1932 and still lay in ashes, a capital debt of $700,000 hung over us, and the institution was operating at a sizable deficit. Mr. Roberts soon came to understand and appreciate the president's efforts to bring new life and resources to the college while at the same time carrying his own business responsibilities in New York City. One day he invited me to lunch. And, as luncheons go, this proved to be no ordinary date.

When it was over, Mr. Roberts asked me to go down to the bank with him. There he handed over to me Woolworth stock worth $100,000. He had committed an act of faith. With this help, we were able to raise the other $300,000 needed to rebuild Old Main.

Not long afterward I was invited to lunch with him again, and again was given securities worth $100,000—with which to hack away at the mountain of debt, which was completely paid off a few years later. Mr. Roberts next gave $150,000 toward a gymnasium. Then a new engineering building had to be built in order to gain accreditation for Bucknell's engineering departments, and Mr. Roberts responded with $250,000, again in stocks, toward that objective.

About that time the pressure of double duties upon me was becoming heavy. I was expecting to relinquish the Bucknell duties, when without warning at a college chapel service, a petition was presented to me—signed by each of Bucknell's 1,200 students—urging me to continue as president. The next day Mr. Roberts repeated this urging and said, "Let's you and me help those Bucknell boys and girls—you give your time, and I'll give my money."

During the next two years before his death, he gave another $250,000, which helped to build the Ellen Clark Bertrand Library dedicated in 1951, and several thousands more for the Bucknell Junior College (now Wilkes College) at Wilkes-Barre. In five short years he had become the largest single benefactor of this century-old Pennsylvania college.

Before he died in 1940 he said to me, "You helped me invest my money in young people while I was still alive and could see it at work. You have brought me some of the greatest happiness of my whole life."

When I retired from the presidency of Bucknell in 1945, and the trustees expressed appreciation for the progress made, I stated that most of this would have been quite impossible except for Daniel C. Roberts. It was an honor to be able to say: "To the modest, generous gentleman, Daniel C. Roberts, who backed me with his gifts and who thus encouraged many other friends to make generous gifts also, and who would not even permit me to reveal his name until it became absolutely necessary to do so, Bucknell owes an incalculable debt of gratitude."

Today, on the Bucknell campus, the central building of Old Main is named the Daniel C. Roberts Hall—a name which will remain on the lips of thousands of young Americans for generations to come as they walk in and out of this beautiful building in their quest for growth of mind and spirit.

21

The Unique Contribution of the Volunteer

RUTH DODD

RUTH DODD, PROMINENT VOLUNTEER FOR MANY CAUSES, IS
PARTICULARLY NOTED FOR HER SERVICE AND ADVOCACY EFFORTS
ON BEHALF OF CHILDREN AND FAMILIES.

Young as social work is, it has a glorious heritage, and unless the lives of professional and volunteer workers are enriched by the consciousness and knowledge of it, the future will suffer an impoverishment in its ideals.

To read the life of St. Francis, *The Little Flowers* and *The Mirror of Perfection,* is to get a glimpse of life lived joyously as an adventure of the soul; to see Poverty as his glorious bride is to think of it not as a thing that cramps us but as something that frees us from the material bonds for the wider life of the spirit. No sensitive soul can apprehend even a little of the Franciscan spirit without a deep stirring within. He is a saint of the Catholic Church, the glory of Italy, but he is also the possession of all of us who in this latter day are working in a spirit of love for our fellow men. He is the first great volunteer, one who chose or willed to leave a life of ease, pleasure, and earthly success for one of service, toil, and self-abasement.

Follow Vincent de Paul through the long, patient years of almost unbelievable toil in the dark places of a Paris preparing for the Revolution. Here is a place where the volunteer should pause and study Mr. Vincent's experiments with his Ladies of Charity and his Sisters of Charity. He must have gone through most of the motions in regard to volunteers that are familiar to us: the high hopes, the discouragement when the eagerness of those who are attracted by the novelty of a new experience disappears in the face of hard work. We are

Reprinted from *Volunteer Values,* Chapter I, by Ruth Dodd (New York: Family Welfare Association of America, 1934) by permission of the publisher.

glad that he had the comfort of watching the increasing bands of Sisters of Charity—those simple souls from the country who, under his inspiration and guidance endured every discipline and hardship and sight of suffering to nurse the sick and relieve the poor.

It was a different Paris two centuries later, after the Revolution, when Frederick Ozanam gathered his group of young Catholics about him to oppose the rising tide of irreligion and atheism. His answer to the taunt of "Show us your works" was the formation of the St. Vincent de Paul Society. Very like our own friendly visitors his young followers were; their conferences have a familiar sound, and the "Alms of Advice" is still a good watchword.

But, Anglo-Saxons that we are, it is to the English group that we turn as to our own people. The first of them, that sturdy old Scotchman, Thomas Chalmers, sowed the seeds that later bore fruit in the charity organization movement. His district plan of a manageable area where his deacons (strange name for volunteers!) could know the people as neighbors know one another, is one of the basic ideas of modern social work.

Lord Shaftesbury's fight for the children in the mines and factories and Florence Nightingale's fight for better care of the sick should give fresh courage to those working against odds for social reform through legislation.

Those young men who, fresh from the influence of Jowett and Balliol College, brought the best of Oxford to the East End of London—Arnold Toynbee and Edward Denison—are the connecting link between Shaftesbury and the group that formed the Charity Organisation Society of London in the '60s.

Octavia Hill was the pattern of all volunteers: her loving spirit knew no barriers between people, her neighborliness was the simple, inevitable way, and her gifts were the bestowal of the things of the spirit—beauty, friendship, opportunity. The high ideals with which the Charity Organisation Society began were due to her and Denison and others of that remarkable group who founded one more society because there were already too many.

The young barrister, Charles Loch, was the first full-time worker, the prototype of the later professional social worker. Up to this time, all effort and experiment had been of volunteer origin; there was no sense of social work as a new profession to be classed with law or medicine. But when we see Charles Loch, at the age of twenty-six, relinquishing his chosen career of law in order to give all his time to the development of the Charity Organisation Society, we know that a definite step forward has been taken. Almost at once he began to train workers to take the positions that were demanding them and a new profession was born.

So, it all began with a volunteer; and it was the intelligent volunteer looking about at the chaos of social life in big cities that called into being the trained worker. To the vision of these pioneers we owe the beginnings of the present scientific attitude of social work—the realization that in such a complicated world it was necessary to throw overboard the previous kind-hearted individual helping of the neighbor, and substitute for it a more highly organized science of helping, which would be congenial to the highly organized type of civilization we were entering.

Still more to their credit is the fact that, after several decades of operating the newly formed agencies of various sorts themselves, these pioneer volunteers of the last century realized that they did not have the time to study the many implications of their service sufficiently, and hence gave the impetus to the founding of some of the first schools of social work.

The World War indicated how much even an untrained person with intelligence and a desire to help might be able to do. In the reports of the National Conference of Social Work from the beginning of this century until 1917 there were only scattered mentions of the volunteer; often several years of the Proceedings indicated no recognition of his services. In 1917 the Conference convened the day after the initial military registration: in eight different addresses there was some discussion of the volunteer in social work and in one there was the suggestion of a training camp for compulsory social service.

In 1926, Miss Mary Goodwillie told a group of volunteers: "The future of volunteer work seems to be threatened and weakened by certain new conditions: First, by the growth of community funds where the burden of the work is shared by so many that it is felt by few; second, by the professional excellence of the trained worker which makes the admiring volunteer ask, 'Where do I come in?' and the efficient professional worker ask, 'Why do I need to be bothered?'; third, by the distractions of modern life in cities which leave so little time for any one thing; and last, by the increase in comforts and luxuries which is slowly making us soft and unwilling to do the hard thing."

Volunteering is no longer a polite gesture made at the cost of a few odd hours. It is a responsibility requiring a substantial block of time and the exercise of intelligence and energy. Working with volunteers is no longer an endurance test for the professional. It is a challenge to her skill in interpreting social work as a living, breathing art, rich in human values and in adjusting personalities to its practice.

The volunteer can make three contributions to her organization that the professional cannot make. First of all she brings to the staff a renewed sense of the worth-whileness of the task. At best there are many days when the hard-driven professional wonders if the game is worth the candle, if we are making any real headway commensurate with our expenditure of physical and spiritual energy. But if these earnest volunteers believe it worthwhile and cheerfully sacrifice their leisure to help the work along, then surely we can keep our end up.

The second unique contribution of the trained volunteer is her influence on the standards of social work in the community. One such volunteer almost single-handedly won over a whole board to keeping a trained staff to head up the emergency work instead of throwing all its resources pell-mell into a breadline and soup-kitchen. That volunteer will be a board member some day, with her training and intelligence influencing policies which may affect the welfare of her whole community.

This leads right into the third unique contribution of the volunteer—her capacity as an interpreter of social work. Of course the paid worker is armored with loyalty and faith in her profession and its work, but the fact that she is supported by that profession sometimes weakens her as its protagonist. When charges of red tape, overhead, and all the rest are tossed about, it is your volunteer who can best say, "But don't you see that red tape is just a way of not jumping at conclusions, a way of getting at basic facts in the interest of justice?"

The volunteer comes into social work anxious to learn, eager for training. As she advances in training and responsibility she creates by reason of her contacts a new current of lay interest and understanding. By her championship of standards she molds citizen attitudes. By her spirit of humility, her willingness to start at the bottom of the ladder, she generates a similar spirit in others to seek, not a post of authority, but a niche of usefulness in social work. How far the ripples of her influence spread depends on the quality of training the professional social worker gives her, the degree of understanding and skill we add to her enthusiasm and good will. If we make her a true partner, sharing in the responsibilities and obligations which after all are not the exclusive concern of the paid workers, we shall swell those ripples of influence into lasting currents.

Volunteers have learned to know what the work is. They grasp its possibilities and realize the handicaps to which the professional workers are subjected because of the limitation of resources. They, with a fresh vision, see the aims of the agency. They may be used as modern interpreters of its method and ideals. One contribution for which volunteers have always been conspicuous will be increasingly needed: that is, their quality of pioneering—a sort of adventurous leadership that rushes in where angels fear to tread. What better antidote for stagnation could be found than this confident idealism of the volunteer?

Will volunteers retard and impede our attainment by giving an amateurish "charity" tinge to social work? To answer this, glance at the other professions: law, engineering, and architecture—all dealing with comparatively inanimate matter— do not use volunteers. But medicine, education, and the church—the three great professions dealing with the body, mind, and soul of human beings—frankly depend upon volunteers for many features of their work. Is it then logical to expect that social work, dealing with all three—mind, body, and soul of human beings—should dispense with volunteers? More than any of the other three human professions, social work will continue to need them for interpreters if for nothing else.

It should be an accepted policy of the family society to plan deliberately to recruit, train, and use on a volunteer basis young men and women. Professional schools of social work should include in their training of students a conscious treatment of the value, use, and training of volunteers, making it clear to the students that volunteers are an integral part of their organization and should be considered as of equal importance with their professional staff workers.

Where social work is financed largely by public funds and is rather directly under the control of publicly elected officials, the continuance of the program depends greatly upon the feeling of organized support for the work from the general public. Volunteers may serve a public agency in at least five capacities:

1. To interpret the community to the workers, that the standard of case work may be adjusted to the understanding and characteristics of the people.

2. To interpret the work to the community.

3. To help local people acquire an objective attitude toward their unadjusted members.

4. To broaden the field of service, where the volume of work is greater than one person can handle, by sharing the responsibility.

5. To develop a type of organization necessary for the permanent stability and progress of the work.[1]

Miss Richmond, in her chapter on friendly visiting in *The Long View*,[2] says that the charitable impulse is a fine thing, perhaps the very best thing we have in the world, only it must have organization and direction. To give organization and direction to this impulse is the challenge which, when met, will bring to us and the volunteer untold gains in enlarged sympathies, keener understanding, and readier response.

Professionals and volunteers have a common goal—to serve those needing our help. To achieve this, we must more closely cement our partnership and develop our sense of team-play, for both the professional and the volunteer are in the field to stay, and their highest potentialities should be developed in a spirit of mutual helpfulness.

Notes

1. For additional material on the volunteer in a public agency, see Dr. Hertha Kraus: "Lay Participation in Social Work from the Point of View of Public Agencies," *Proceedings*, National Conference of Social Work, Kansas City, 1934 (reprints available from the Family Welfare Association of America); Linton B. Swift: *New Alignments between Public and Private Agencies*, Family Welfare Association of America, 1934, p. 47.

2. Russell Sage Foundation, 1930.

22

American Philanthropy and the National Character

MERLE CURTI

MERLE CURTI IS A NOTED HISTORIAN, EDUCATOR, AND WRITER.
HE RECEIVED THE PULITZER PRIZE IN 1944 FOR HIS WORK,
GROWTH OF AMERICAN THOUGHT.

In 1875 Thomas Wentworth Higginson, better known for his championship of the slave and of women's rights than for linguistic scholarship, reported that the term philanthropy had appeared for the first time as an English word in *The Guide to Tongues*, published in 1628. The word was simply "Philanthropie; Humanitie; a loving of man." Dryden, in apologizing for his use of the word philanthropy, declared that it had been introduced into English because there was no indigenous word to connote precisely the meaning of the Greek original. Colonial scholars who read in the original such writers as Isocrates, Xenophon, Epictetus, Plutarch and Polybius, knew the word in its Greek form, but the word philanthropy was not generally in English until the time of Addison.[1]

The term found some favor among disciples of the Enlightenment, but it came into common use only in the middle decades of the nineteenth century. It meant the love of man, charity, benevolence, humanitarianism, social reform. To cite an example from the hundreds at hand, Theodore Parker spoke of John Augustus as a philanthropist. This illegitimate, eccentric Lexington shoemaker had, Parker declared, earned the title by giving help to the helpless and love to the unlovely; more concretely, by bailing thousands out of jail, keeping hundreds from crime and redeeming countless fallen women.[2] In the minds of some of Theodore Parker's contemporaries the term suggested a meddling, hypocriti-

Reprinted from *American Quarterly* 10 (Winter, 1958), pp. 420-437, by permission of the author and publisher. Copyright ©1958 by the Trustees of the University of Pennsylvania.

cal do-gooder. It was no doubt this image that old Count Gorowski had in mind when he cautioned a young lady against mixing with anyone of that class. "Marry thief!" he said, "marry murderer! But never marry philanthropist!"[3] But the more usual meaning was that given in a pamphlet written by Linus Pierpont Brockett in 1864 bearing the title "The Philanthropic Results of the War in America." The author identified the term with charity, benevolence, the love of one's needy fellow men without thought of personal advantage.[4]

After the Civil War certain leaders in the American Social Science Association agreed that philanthropy implies the impulse to relieve a situation, in contrast with social science, which presumably endeavors to present poverty and other social problems by probing behind effect to cause.[5] But this use of the term did not entirely catch on. When, early in our own century, the New York Charity Organization Society established a professional training program for social workers, the new institution was called "The School of Philanthropy."[6]

Yet even at this time the word philanthropy had come to mean, to many Americans, large-scale giving by such men of great wealth as Peabody, Carnegie and Rockefeller. This of course is the sense in which the word is most commonly used today, despite the distaste both Carnegie and Rockefeller had for being called philanthropists. It might be argued that the change in the meaning of the term from benevolence and humanitarianism to large-scale giving reflects a shift in our society to a greater emphasis on the role of wealth.

What indeed has been the relation of philanthropy to the national character? Many social scientists of course reject the validity and usefulness of the concept of national character. Yet the belief that there is a cluster of more or less distinguishing American traits and values has persisted through our history, varying in expression from time to time, from place to place, from subculture to subculture. In general, however, there has been agreement that the American national character has emphasized practicality and efficiency; and that it has equated successful achievement with individual freedom, individual effort, individual responsibility and a wide variety of choices. At the same time voluntary association with others in common causes has been thought to be strikingly characteristic of American life.

Other generalizations about "the American character" have been almost as commonly accepted. Americans have commonly identified public and private interest and needs—an identification made the easier by the national plenty and by social mobility. The national character has included an emphasis on equality both as a right and a fact. It has attached importance to the status and role of women. It has assumed the possibility and desirability of progress toward general well-being through the effort and cooperation of individuals, with the aid of education. It has, despite secular interests, found in religion and morality a rationale and a motivating power. Finally, American values have set much store on process, rather than on the finished product: the assumption has been that America is creative, not merely traditional and imitative.

Not all students of our national character have included philanthropy as a component. If mentioned, benevolence or philanthropy is passed over lightly in the studies of Constance Rourke, David Riesman and Max Lerner. But these writers and also the Kluckhohns and others do give a place in the American value system to benevolence or closely related traits.

Among historians, Turner was appreciatively aware of the role of philanthropy although he did not dwell on it. The Beards, in *The American Spirit*, devoted some thoughtfully discriminating pages to the theme. One is somewhat surprised to find that David Potter, in the stimulating study of the national character in which he makes plenty the key, stopped short of linking this with philanthropy. On the other hand, Arthur M. Schlesinger, Sr., writing in 1953, declared that "unlike Europe, the United States has fathered few misers...The successful...have shared their money with others almost as freely as they made it, returning at least part of their substance to channels of social usefulness through munificent gifts and bequests." This philanthropic streak in the national character, an index of the pervasive spirit of neighborliness, appeared early and has in our own day reached fabulous dimensions. "It is," continued Professor Schlesinger, "another of the distinguishing marks of the American way."[7]

Support for the thesis that American philanthropy reflects the national character also comes from our more thoughtful foreign visitors. Tocqueville was not the first of these to comment on the spirit of mutual helpfulness in America, but no one before him had stated it so cogently. The French social philosopher did not believe that there was less selfishness among Americans than among Europeans. He did hold that in America selfishness was more enlightened; when an American asked for the help or cooperation of his fellow citizens, it was seldom refused. It was apt to be given generously and with great goodwill. Whereas in most civilized nations a poor wretch might be as friendless in the midst of a crowd as the savage in the wilds, in America, in case of accident or calamity, "the purse of a thousand strangers" poured in to relieve the distress of the sufferers. "Equality of condition," Tocqueville said, "while it makes men feel their independence, shows them their own weakness; they are free, but exposed to a thousand accidents; and experience soon teaches them that although they do not habitually require the assistance of others, a time almost always comes when they cannot do without it."[8]

American generosity and mutual helpfulness, traits conceded by many of our most severe critics, were the subject of a striking comment on the part of a later distinguished visitor. "In works of active beneficence, no country has surpassed, perhaps none has equalled the United States," wrote James Bryce in 1888. "Not only are the sums collected for all sorts of philanthropic purposes larger relatively to the wealth of America than in any European country," Bryce went on, "but the amount of personal interest and effort devoted to them seems to a European visitor to excel what he knows at home." This informed admirer thought religious impulses in American life largely explained this trait.[9]

Sixty years later Harold Laski, whose critical analysis of our institutions reflected a socialist bias, conceded the striking generosity of well-to-do Americans in endowing education, research and the arts. In speaking of American giving to Europe and Asia in hundreds of thousands of donations, great and small, Laski insisted that no one was "entitled to speak of the material-mindedness of Americans unless he can produce an instance of comparable and continuous generosity from European experience."[10]

As yet no careful historical and statistical study has been made to test this assumption which has from time to time been challenged by Americans themselves. No one can now say what proportion of men of wealth at given periods saw fit either during their lifetime or in making their last wills to give generously to philanthropic causes. The evidence at hand does show that many people of wealth gave little to philanthropy.[11] It also seems clear that in the nineteenth century a reputation for philanthropy sometimes rested on giving less than two percent of an estate. We know that Americans have reacted various ways to reports of failure to help the less fortunate. Some merely shrugged their shoulders with indifference. Others offered rather limp apologies. Some were openly disapproving. Such, for example, was the phrenological-minded sculptor who was finishing a head of A.T. Stewart, the fabulously rich New York merchant, when he discovered how very little his subject left to charity. He lost no time in remolding the cranium, leveling off the bumps of benevolence and idealism and building up those indicative of acquisitiveness and all the selfish and animal propensities![12]

Until fuller and more precise knowledge is available about the kind and extent of American philanthropy as compared with that in other countries one must indeed be cautious in discussing philanthropy and the national character. Yet a tentative thesis may be suggested at this time, mainly that while American patterns of giving for religion, welfare, education, health, science and the arts owe much to British and continental example, they have, apart from the question of magnitude, relfected a distinctively American character. They have also helped shape that character. In other words, philanthropy has been both index and agent.

To make such a claim is not to deny that the Old World heritage is basic in American philanthropy. The very word, one recalls, and the idea for which it stands, came from the Greeks. American philanthropy owes much to the ancient Jewish doctrine which taught rules about the duty of giving and the right of those in need to receive. It is hardly too much to say that Jewish, Catholic and Protestant doctrines and practices have been central in the development of philanthropy in America. From the time of the Puritans and Quakers in early seventeenth-century America to our own day it would be hard to overstate the influence of the religious emphasis on the value of individual life, regardless of status, of the injunction to feed the hungry and clothe the naked, of the teaching that man is his brother's keeper. The Pauline doctrine that one is only a steward for the wealth God has given him has profoundly influenced American giving. Habits of giving among those who had relatively little to give have owed a great deal to the missionary movement. Even today somewhat over half of all individual giving finds its way into the church envelope, collection plate or treasury of church-related institutions.

American philanthropy has also operated within a frame of English common and statutory law.[13] The colonists brought with them the Elizabethan poor laws; and the Victorian modifications of these laws influenced our charitable practices. English law guided us in our use of the will, the bequest, the perpetuity and the foundation. The English philosophy that he who gives should control, crystallized by Locke, exerted far-reaching influence in America.

Americans have a notable record in giving for disaster relief at home and abroad; but we did not invent this practice. In 1676, for example, the good ship *Catharine* left Dublin laden with meal, wheat, malt, butter and cheese, to be distributed to all in the three New England colonies who stood in need by reason of the disasters accompanying King Philip's War.[14]

Colonial support for schools, colleges and hospitals followed in good part the British pattern of voluntary private support.[15] A Britisher named Wilson preceded Franklin in establishing loan funds for worthy mechanics. In founding parochial and general libraries, charity schools, and in promoting religious and moral instruction among Indians and Negroes, the British-supported Society for the Propagation of the Gospel in Foreign Parts adapted British giving to special needs and conditions in the colonies and in so doing established a pattern later followed by the Americans themselves.

Nor did British influence on American philanthropy end here. It provided an example of a new approach to the relief of poverty and distress. Isabella Marshall Graham, coming to New York from Scotland in 1796, proceeded to found the Society for the Relief of Poor Widows and Small Children, an agency similar to one that Bernard and Wilberforce had just established in London for the relief of the poor. Mrs. Graham likewise established and devoted her entire time to the Orphan Asylum Society and the Magdalen Society, the first organization of that sort in the young Republic.[16] Much later the influence of the

Manchester *laissez faire* school in general and of Dr. Thomas Chalmers of Glasgow in particular were important in the development in the 1830s and 1840s of American voluntary associations for the urban poor.[17] All these activities were associated with the idea that public charity pauperizes and demoralizes the recipient. Nor should one forget the wealthy and childless English scientist, James Smithson, who set an example to well-to-do Americans to give generously for the advancement and diffusion of knowledge.

Yet such British activities and influences should not obscure the fact that for a few decades before the Civil War Americans won an international reputation for leadership in benevolent enterprises. European leaders came here to study prison reform, institutions for the handicapped and agencies for the diffusion of knowledge. In the Old World itself, the writings and achievements of our Franklins, Livingstons, Quincys, Rantouls, Manns, Grays and Sumners found admirers and imitators.

In 1867, however, *The Nation*, in reviewing the recent international congresses on charity and philanthropy, sadly admitted that Americans in this field were no longer read and quoted in Europe as they once had been. The wind blew in the other direction. The growing emphasis in Britain on organization, cooperation, nonduplication of effort, districting, friendly visiting, in short, on scientific method in charity, was reflected in the post-Civil War decades in America in the Charity Organization Movement. The movement in England for model tenements was felt on our side of the Atlantic and the influence of Toynbee Hall on the American social settlement movement is of course well known.[18]

If the idea of national character is valid, one would expect that the philanthropic ingredients transferred to our shores from the Old World would be interrelated in a distinctive pattern. We would also expect to find the key to this in unique or characteristically American experiences.

Our federal system has surely given American philanthropy some of its hallmarks. The legislatures and courts of the several states have emphasized the need of a flexibility which they did not see in British precedents. New York's repudiation of certain aspects of the English law of bequests and Samuel J. Tilden's full failure to appreciate this in bequeathing a large part of his fortune to a trust for a public library, resulted in lengthy litigation and the defeat of Tilden's full purpose.[19] One finds different laws from state to state on the incorporation and degree of public control of charitable institutions and foundations and on bequests and exemptions from taxation for giving. Unlike Britain, then, the United States long had no unified legal code affecting charitable giving in every part of the country. The federal internal revenue legislation, to be sure, has in its provisions for tax-deductible gifts come in many respects to serve as such a code.[20] If on the one hand the diversity of state legislation and court decisions on bequests and gifts has made for uncertainty and confusion, it has also made possible some flexibility and experimentation.

In opening the door to state rights and functions, the federal system has until yesterday minimized the role of the central government in assuming any great responsibility for welfare, education, research and the arts.[21] Since the states themselves have, until our century, supported only a few hospitals, welfare agencies and colleges and even fewer art galleries and museums, private citizens have shouldered the costs for such local institutions—in the Old World all these have long enjoyed the support of the national government.

Separation of church and state as well as the federal system has shaped American philanthropy. In the Reformation the new state churches or governments in continental Protestant Europe took over the role of the medieval church in supporting hospitals, schools and universities. The Anglican Church was something of an exception in not taking on such far-reaching functions. In America separation of church and state meant that, in the absence of any one state church, the large number of voluntarily supported churches have maintained colleges, orphanages, hospitals and similar agencies. Although America has followed England in the last decades in moving toward the continental pattern of state support of welfare agencies, our long experience with voluntary maintenance of charitable and educational institutions has encouraged Americans to feel that there are unique values in such nongovernment operations. These include the control by laymen rather than by experts of privately supported hospitals, art galleries, colleges and welfare institutions. Still another by-product has been the encouragement of competition between rival institutions for gifts and, more recently, of cooperative and highly organized fund-raising.

American philanthropy in greater degree than that of Europe has emphasized the idea of self-help, whether in giving on condition of the matching of gifts or in loans to students to be paid back. This is related to our creed of individual responsibility and achievement, supplemented by mutual aid. It is to be further explained by the concept of plenty. Americans rejected the Old World notion that the poor must always be with us and taken care of by charity. This stress on self-help in philanthropy was functional to the social fluidity that has characterized the industrial growth of our cities and also the frontier process.

American cities, like those of Europe, bred conditions that inspired relief and philanthropic endeavor. But in America the concept of self-help and mutual aid was strengthened by the existence of immigrant groups and by the limited role of local government through long stretches of our municipal history. Thus immigrants, uprooted and often in need until adjustments were made, organized mutual self-help societies, one of the earliest being the Scots Charitable Society in Boston (1657). National and racial pride, related to our cultural pluralism, also help explain why other groups that formed sub-cultures took care of their own: the Jewish groups, the Chinese, the Mormons to cite only the more striking examples. All this gave a special tone to American charities.[22]

The frontier and the related concept of plenty have also given an American accent to the philanthropic heritage from the Old World. One of the first major philanthropic efforts in the East was inspired by a fear on the part of the established order of "western irreligion" and political deviancy, together with a Puritan sense of obligation to do something about it. But the influence of the frontier on philanthropy was not merely in giving an incentive to the organization of the so-called "benevolent empire" of home missionaries and college founders in the West.[23]

The problems involved in settling new areas did, as Tocqueville noted, not merely favor neighborly cooperation in time of need and trouble—they made it necessary. An example from the frontier history of Trempealeau County, Wisconsin, will illustrate the point. When young William Lincoln became ill and died during the winter of 1853, the neighbors provided what medical and religious services the boy received. Neighbors dug a grave. One, Stuart Butman, laid out the body. In the absence of a minister, two neighbor girls sang a hymn. No money was needed to pay for these services. In reenforcing over and again this tendency to help others and in making ever evident the horizons of plenty, the frontier must have encouraged generosity.

Moreover, the social mobility which the frontier fostered, along with our industrial development, made it hard for rising men and their wives to be sure of their social status. This uncertainty encouraged some to take part in charitable and philanthropic activities to win social recognition. Biographies of philanthropists suggest that in some cases giving was motivated by status considerations. In a fluid society like ours, one not only had to make his place but to keep it by further achievement, such as putting success to socially approved uses. If some men of wealth gave quietly, even anonymously, others enjoyed having their gifts publicized and basked in the limelight of community approval.

The American emphasis on individual achievement and on sustained activity to that end has also given a distinct stamp to large-scale giving. Having spent untold effort in getting rich, having tasted the sweets and boredom of extravagant spending, some, driven by a never-ceasing lust to achieve, turned to philanthropy. Carnegie and Rockefeller, each relatively frugal in what he spent on himself, set their hearts on giving with the imagination, organization and efficiency that had marked their activities in steel and oil.

This desire to realize the efficiency which is allegedly so American explained in part the rise of professional middlemen in the philanthropic process. The prototype was the lean and tireless agent that the nineteenth-century college hired for a pittance to travel over the land begging for contributions to keep the wolf from the classroom door. In due course professional administrators of welfare agencies and fundraisers appeared. So did the foundation official and the chronic solicitor of funds from the foundation. Frederick Keppel, an early head of the Carnegie Corporation, loved to tell of the college president who on one occasion announced that he had not come to ask for anything that day. "How much is it," asked Mr. Keppel, "that you don't want to ask for?"

Less familiar among the middlemen of philanthropy who seem to be in the American character have been the counselors to the rich in the matter of giving. One thinks of such preachers as the Reverend William Willcox who guided the Boston merchant Daniel Stone and his wife in giving a two-million-dollar fortune to church-related colleges scattered over the land. One recalls the Reverend Charles Force Deems and the Reverend Frederick T. Gates, whose role in Vanderbilt and Rockefeller giving was crucial. The list of lawyers and bankers who counseled on matters of giving is likewise a long one.

One pioneer figure, neither a preacher, banker nor lawyer, devoted his later years to publicizing unwise or misguided giving and to counseling, without charge, potential donors. Alvin M. West, who made a fortune in California, was shocked on learning that state laws prevented Los Angeles from accepting Colonel Griffith G. Griffith's donation of land for a public park valued at a million dollars. West's search for frustrated donors and unwise giving continued through the first three decades of our century. His list came to include the Sailor's Snug Harbor, whose trustees were unable to spend the income of an early nineteenth-century bequest for a home for seafaring men. West publicized the whittling away of a great part of a St. Louis fortune left for the relief of travelers headed westward in prairie schooners. The courts finally decided, under the *cy pres* doctrine, that the residue might be used to support the Travellers Aid Bureau in railway stations. Then there was the attorney general of Massachusetts who left money to Harvard, Yale and Columbia for the development of "sound public opinion against the tendency to take woman out of the home and to put her into politics"—each institution turned down the gift! Again, the Christian Science Church in Portland refused a gift to establish the White Shield Home for Wayward Girls because the donor had not appreciated the import of an Oregon law requiring the inmates of all homes to be medically examined. By the mid-1920s West estimated that of the approximate $500,000,000 annually given for philanthropic purposes a good proportion was either wasted in duplicating adequate facilities, in inviting disgruntled kinfolk to challenge wills in court with ensuing costly litigation or in passing by truly useful causes.[24]

The effort to bring philanthropy into tune with the national penchant for efficiency has resulted in its rapport with big business. Partly for reasons of tax consideration, partly to enlist public favor and partly to prove the continuing creativity of American business, great firms have increased corporate giving until it has now become a highly specialized function with its own counselors and techniques.[25]

The effort to make philanthropy efficient and socially useful does not exhaust the ways in which American traits, values and actualities have influenced patterns of giving. It has been assumed that American women have played a more telling role in decision-making, in civic enterprises and in spending, than those of most other countries. Certainly this has been true in the American Red Cross. In charity and welfare, women's influence has incontestably been notable. In counseling husbands and sons on giving, and in themselves dispensing their inherited wealth, American women have been active agents in philanthropy. Out of hundreds of names, those of Sophia Smith, Phoebe Hearst, Valeria Stone, Nettie Fowler McCormick, Ellen Scripps, the Phelps-Stokes sisters, Mrs. Stephen Harkness and Elizabeth Milbank Anderson are representative.

One cannot draw a sharp line between American philanthropy as an index of the national character and as an agent of it. But let us examine the claim that in extending the idea that America stands for the creative process, philanthropy has given content and reality to the national character. The argument is that philanthropy, in shifting from the lady bountiful type of amelioration to pioneering in education, research, welfare and social policy at home and abroad, has helped realize national values.

This contention has met with sharp criticism. One criticism has linked a good deal of philanthropy with inefficient and unwise giving, with the dead hand. In addition, muckrakers, progressives and socialists contended that large-scale giving placed far too much power over public policy in the hands of a few men whose fortunes after all had been created only because of prevailing social and economic conditions. It was argued that philanthropy was intended to patch up the shortcomings in the existing order and thus to preserve a status quo that did not deserve preservation.[26] Verbal evidence issuing from donors and particularly from middlemen solicitors gives some support to this statement.[27] It is also true that only a very small proportion of total giving challenged the status quo. The few sizable gifts to the abolition, women's rights and temperance crusades were overshadowed by small rank and file contributions. This was also true of the peace movement until the twentieth-century munificence of Ginn, Bok, Ford and Carnegie. In finding angels such as Tom Johnson and Joseph Fels, Henry George's crusade was more fortunate than most reform causes: its shadow was to be prolonged by the Robert Schalkenbach Foundation. The socialist crusade found some support from such well-to-do benefactors as Gaylord Wilshire and J.G. Phelps Stokes. Both socialists and communists received donations from the American Fund for Public Service, established in the early 1920s when Charles Garland refused on conscientious grounds to keep a million-dollar fortune he inherited. But this was certainly an exceptional foundation.[28]

Many critics felt that philanthropic support of Negro education put a premium on vocational training and retarded the development of liberal and professional education. Nor was the *New Republic* without cause when, in commenting on the Eastman and Duke benefactions, it asked why large gifts to higher education mainly concentrated on institutions of no particular reputation for pioneering. Among the ranks of philanthropists themselves Richard T. Crane criticized giving to higher education and to the mere beautifying of parts of cities while the disadvantaged poor struggled against great odds in grim slums.[29] Certainly much philanthropy was not aimed at remedying basic factors in poverty.

But there was another side of the coin. Emphasis on voluntary initiative in spotting social evils and taking the first steps to remedy them has helped give America her national character. It was private initiative and support that pioneered in constructive efforts to meet the problem of juvenile delinquency, to establish public parks and recreational centers, to build model tenements as pilot examples and to launch many other civic improvements. The roster of pioneers, both donors and those who gave themselves, is a very long one.[30]

When a group of progressive-minded merchants made possible the introduction of scientific study in our colleges in the mid-nineteenth century, a new era in our educational history was under way. The names of Lawrence, Sheffield, the younger Agassiz, Bussey, Peabody, Lick, Ryerson, Scripps and countless others made possible some of the most notable scientific work in our universities. Private initiative also got under way much needed vocational training, as the names of Rensselaer, Cooper, Pratt, Drexel and Carnegie, to name only a few, suggest. And philanthropists also made possible the establishment of the first professional schools of mines, business and journalism. All these philanthropic initiatives give support to the thesis that philanthropy has helped shape national character in creatively meeting new problems, in implementing the idea that America is process rather than finished product.

Without belittling the part of the state universities in opening the door of higher education to women, this innovation owes a great deal to such philanthropists as Cornell, Durant, Vassar, Goucher and Sophia Smith. In the making of an American university tradition, Cornell, Hopkins, Clark, Rockefeller and the educational leaders associated with them played a leading part. So did the generous donors who made possible the transformation of Harvard, Columbia, Princeton and Yale. The Stanfords, the Vanderbilts, the Candlers and the Dukes helped build a university tradition on the West Coast and in the South. The thesis that philanthropy responded to and helped develop the creative impulse in the national character found further support in the introduction of art and music in American higher education. The Carnegie Foundation pioneered in establishing professors' pensions. [31] The Carnegie Foundation and the Rockefeller foundations revolutionized medical education and research.[32] More recently, the innovating process found further expression in the support of various foundations for the area programs, including American studies. Imaginative too was the backing given by a New Jersey merchant and his sister to the establishment at Princeton of the Institute for Advanced Studies.[33] Finally, no one will doubt that American scholarship would be much the poorer were it not for the libraries associated with the names of generous givers at Harvard, Yale, Columbia and Princeton, and for such great collections as the Newberry, the Crerar, the Morgan, the Huntington and the Folger.

Our public schools have been a truly popular achievement. Yet much that is now taken for granted in our educational programs owes a major debt to philanthropy in implementing the national idea of equality of opportunity. Antislavery men and women dug deep into their purses to finance the first southern schools for Negroes during and after the Civil War. A Connecticut industrialist, John Slater, following in the footsteps of George Peabody, established a fund which did much for Negro education in the South. Daniel Hand, George Foster Peabody, the General Education Board, the Jeanes Fund and the Rosenwald Fund prepared Southern opinion for a more adequate public support for Negro schools and piloted many telling improvements in the meantime.[34]

But the stimulus given to building educational opportunities for Negroes was by no means the only constructive contribution by which philanthropy helped realize the onward and upward theme in our national character through our public schools. A Massachusetts industrialist established the first teacher training institute through an initial gift conditional on state support.[35] The education of the blind, the crippled and the deaf was incorporated into public education only after private philanthropy pointed the way. This was also true of manual training and of school health programs.[36]

In adult education, too, private philanthropy laid the groundwork in helping people who wanted to know. In providing for the institute in Boston bearing his name, John Lowell was a creative giver. Dozens of self-made men, poignantly regretting their own deficiencies in early education, founded public libraries in their home towns long before Carnegie entered the stage. Yet the 2,811 Carnegie libraries, given on condition of community maintenance, marked a new era in the world of reading. The contributions of the Carnegie Corporation and of other foundations to adult education have both stimulated public action, improved the quality of that which existed and added new dimensions to the movement.

Except during the New Deal, government has played a negligible part in opening the world of art and music to adult Americans. The example of William Corcoran in providing a building for his art collection and in making it available to the public has been followed by far too many to catalogue their names and evaluate their collections. But it may be appropriate to mention Phillips, Freer and Mellon at the nation's capital, the Fricks, Whitneys and others in New York, and the Tafts, Holdens, Walkers, Nelsons and Johnsons in the several cities which now support or contribute to the support of the notable collections these men and women assembled. So, too, our botanic gardens and museums of natural history sprang in most cases from philanthropic gifts. Finally, the great development of musical taste and talent in America cannot be separated from the pioneer support given to the Boston Symphony by Henry Lee Higginson and the generous gifts of well-to-do men and women in New York, Philadelphia, Baltimore, Chicago, Rochester, Cincinnati and Los Angeles. What Otto Kahn and others did for opera, what Elizabeth Sprague Coolidge did for chamber music, and what Eastman, Curtis, Juilliard, Presser and others did for musical training, has been both pioneering in character and significant in effect.

Philanthropy has also forwarded several values in the American creed by broadening the base of contributions to social welfare, to medicine, to health and, of course, to religious life. The democratizing of giving not only reflects, but has added substance and method to democratic faith and practice. Here the roots are deep for at the time of the great fire in Boston in 1760, many people both in the surrounding towns and in neighboring colonies contributed to the relief of sufferers.[37] In later disasters, whether fires, droughts, floods, pestilences, cyclones or earthquakes, the participation in giving tended to become broader and broader. In part this mass giving owed much to the zeal of the churches in promoting both home and foreign missions—enterprises that required sustained general support from the faithful. In part it was related to the prevalence of plenty and to the relatively high standard of living.

The democratization of giving has not, however, been a merely automatic process. The zest for organization and for "drives" has become increasingly characteristic of American behavior. Parenthetically, this zest owes much to such newspapers as the New York *Herald* and the New York *Tribune*, and to such religious organs as De Witt Talmage's *Christian Herald*, as anyone who reads the sensational appeals for sending street urchins to fresh air camps and the even more sensational appeals for disaster relief, can appreciate. In our own century the Red Cross and the proliferating number of organizations designed to stem mortality in tuberculosis, infantile paralysis, cancer and heart ailments have also designed unique campaigns for fundraising.[38] The experience of John Price Jones in mobilizing opinion in World War I for putting across the liberty loan drives was transferred to a professional fundraising organization which in the 1920s conducted successfully one campaign after another for universities and colleges in the interest of faculty pay, scholarships, plant and endowment.[39] The Community Chest and United Givers are still more recent examples of both high-pressure salesmanship and of wide participation in giving more or less voluntarily.

One of the byproducts of the newer techniques of fundraising has been misrepresentation. Worse, racketeering cloaked as philanthropy exploited millions of givers. This dishonest exploitation for profits of American generosity has no doubt reflected one aspect of American character; but the effort to curb it no less reflects that ambivalent phenomenon.[40]

Both in terms of objects of giving and the wide-scale participation, the evidence at hand suggests as tenable the hypothesis that philanthropy has both reflected and helped create an American middle way between a type of capitalism characteristic of the Old World, in which owners surrender little of what they have unless forced to do so, on the one hand, and socialism on the other. With due respect for minority opinion in each situation, it is interesting to note that the first Congressional investigation of foundations on the eve of the First World War criticized them for alleged effects in consolidating an existing status quo; and that the Reece committee in McCarthy's time damned them for the support they had presumably given to an un-American collectivism.[41] In relieving class and group tensions and in facilitating the growth of social well-being, philanthropy has in a sense been the American equivalent for socialism.

We are today deeply concerned with the American reputation abroad and with the best ways and means by which America can contribute to strengthening the western heritage of freedom. A close study of the history of our past experience in voluntary giving to relieve suffering from famines in Ireland, Russia, China and India, earthquakes in Sicily, and malaria and other plagues in many places, as well as study of projects to initiate and strengthen educational enterprises and to rehabilitate depressed areas, reveals much of importance in our effort to realize the American mission in the large world. The story is one of failure, partial failure, partial success and amazing success. It is a story of what missionaries, foundations, private donors, the American Friends Service Committee, CARE and dozens of other agencies have undertaken and carried through—more or less. The story both reflects a significant facet in the American character and provides testimony to the degree of creativity and effectiveness our philanthropy has enjoyed when it has traveled abroad.

Perhaps in the magnitude of giving, and certainly in the patterns of philanthropy that have found expression here, American experience in philanthropy has both expressed American character and at the same time has helped to shape it. It will be worth watching the future to see how a plant so rooted grows.

Notes

1. Thomas Wentworth Higginson, "The Word Philanthropy," *Freedom and Fellowship in Religion* (Boston: Roberts Brothers, 1875), pp. 323-37. The Abbe de St. Pierre, writing in 1725, used the word *bienfaisance* as the equivalent for the Greek "philanthropy," *The Nation*, IV (April 18, 1867), p. 309.

2. John Weiss, *Life and Correspondence of Theodore Parker* (2 vols.; New York: 1864), II, 329-30.

3. Higginson, *Freedom and Fellowship in Religion*, p. 336.

4. *The Philanthropic Results of the War in America. By an American Citizen* (Linus Pierpont Brockett), (New York: Press of Wynkoop, Hallenbeck, and Thomas, 1863), pp. 3 ff.

5. Henry Villard, "Historical Sketch of Social Science," *Journal of Social Science*, I (1869), 5.

6. Daniel Coit Gilman, "Special Training for Philanthropic Work" (Address at the Annual Meeting of the Charity Organization Society of New York, January 27, 1905), in *The Launching of a University* (New York: Dodd, Mead & Co., 1906), p. 365.

7. Arthur M. Schlesinger, "The True American Way of Life," *Saint Louis Post-Dispatch*, Part Two (December 13, 1953), 3.

8. Alexis de Tocqueville, *Democracy in America* (The Henry Reeve Text...now further corrected and edited...by Phillips Bradley [2 vol.; New York: Alfred A. Knopf, 1945]), II, 175.

9. James Bryce, *The American Commonwealth* (3rd ed.; 2 vols.; New York: The Macmillan Co., 1909), II, 723.

10. Harold J. Laski, *The American Democracy. A Commentary and an Interpretation* (New York: The Viking Press, 1948), p. 725.

11. In an article entitled, "American Millionaires and Their Gifts" a writer, presumably the editor of *The Review of Reviews: an International Magazine* (VII, February 1893, 48-60), reported the results of his request to correspondents in various cities to rate those of the 4,047 millionaires living in their city—the basis of the inquiry being the list of millionaires in a special supplement of the *New York Tribune Monthly*, IV (June 1892). For the text and illuminating interpretations see Sidney Ratner (ed.), *New Light on the History of Great American Fortunes* (New York: Augustus M. Kelley, Inc., 1953).

12. Henry Clews, *Fifty Years in Wall Street* (New York: Irving Publishing Co., 1908), pp. 533-34.

13. B. Kirman Gray, *A History of English Philanthropy* (London: P.S. King and Son, 1905); Amos G. Warner, *American Charities* (New York: Thomas Y. Crowell & Co., 1908), pp. 389-98.

14. Charles Deane, "The Irish Donation in 1676," *The New England Historical and Geneological Register*, II (1848), 245-50.

15. Beverly McAnear, "The Raising of Funds by Colonial Colleges," *Mississippi Valley Historical Review*, XXXVIII (March 1952), 591-612.

16. Mrs. Joanna Bethune, *The Life of Mrs. Isabella Graham* (New York: J.S. Taylor, 1838); *The Power of Faith; Exemplified in the Life and Writings of the Late Mrs. Isabella Graham of New York* (New York: Kirk and Mercien, 1817).

17. *Chalmers on Charity. A Selection of Passages and Scenes to Illustrate the Teaching and Practical Work of Thomas Chalmers, D.D.*, Arranged and edited by N. Masterman, M.A. (Westminster: Archibald Constable & Co., 1900); *The Christian and Civic Economy of Large Towns*, Abridged and with an introduction by Charles R. Henderson (New York: Charles Scribner's Sons, 1900).

18. "Philanthropy in America and Europe," *The Nation* IV (April 18, 1867), 309. See also Robert Bremner, *From the Depths. The Discovery of Poverty in the United States* (New York: New York University Press, 1956), pp. 207-8.

19. Alexander C. Flick, *Samuel J. Tilden* (New York: Dodd, Mead & Co., 1939), pp. 513 ff.

20. Daniel S. Remsen, *Postmortem Use of Wealth* (New York: G.P. Putnam's Sons, 1911); Harvey W. Peck, *Taxation and Welfare* (New York: The Macmillan Co., 1925); Carl Zollman, *American Law of Charities* (Milwaukee: Bruce Publishing Co., 1924); and F. Emerson Andrews, *Corporation Giving* (New York: Russell Sage Foundation, 1952).

21. For the story of federal support of scientific research see A. Hunter Dupree, *Science in the Federal Government. A History of Policies and Activities to 1940* (Cambridge: The Belknap Press, 1957).

22. Edwin Wolf and Maxwell Whitman, *The History of the Jews of Philadelphia from Colonial Times to the Age of Jackson* (Philadelphia: The Jewish Publication Society of America, 1957).

23. Merle Curti, *The Social Ideas of American Educators* (New York: Charles Scribner's Sons, 1935), pp. 688-70; Clifford S. Griffin, "Religious Benevolence as Social Control, 1815-1860," *Mississippi Valley Historical Review*, XLIV (December, 1957), 423-44.

24. Alvin West, "Biographical Clippings," Hanover Bank and Trust Company, New York City.

25. F. Emerson Andrews, *Corporate Giving* (New York: Russell Sage Foundation, 1952); Berrien C. Eaton, Jr., "Charitable Foundations, Tax Avoidance and Business Expediency," *Virginia Law Review*, L (November, 1949), 809-61 and (December, 1949), 987-1051.

26. Morrison I. Swift, *Vicarious Philanthropy* (No place, ca. 1904), pp. 23-24; *The Nation*, IX (November 11, 1869), 406-7; Robert J. Ingersoll, "The Three Philanthropists," *North American Review*, CLIII (December, 1891), 661-71; Hubert Howe Bancroft, *Retrospection: Political and Personal* (New York: The Bancroft Co., 1912), pp. 452-53; United States Congress, Senate, *Industrial Relations:* Final Report and Testimony submitted to Congress by the Commission on Industrial Relations created by the Act of August 23, 1912. 64th Congress, 1st Session, Senate Document, No. 415 (11 vols.; Washington: Government Printing Office, 1916).

27. Samuel Gompers, "Shall Education be Rockefellerized?" *American Federationist*, XXIV (March, 1917), 206-8; Wayne Andrews, *Battle for Chicago* (New York: Harcourt, Brace & Co., 1946), pp. 162-63; Ferdinand Lundberg, *America's Sixty Families* (New York: The Citadel Press, 1946), pp. 320-73.

28. New York *Times*, January 14, 1924, March 16, 1925, March 8, 1926, March 25, 1929.

29. Andrews, *Battle for Chicago*; "Goose Step and the Golden Eggs," *New Republic* (December 24, 1924), pp. 106-8.

30. See, again, Bremner, *From the Depths, passim*. See also Daniel C. Gilman (ed.), *The Organization of Charities, being a Report of the Sixth Section of the International Congress of Charities, Corrections, and Philanthropy, Chicago, June 1893* (Baltimore: The Johns Hopkins Press, 1894); George S. Hale, "The Charities of Boston," Justin Winsor (ed.), *Memorial History of Boston* (4 vols.; Boston: James R. Osgood & Co., 1881), IV, 641-74; Frances A. Goodale (ed.), *The Literature of Philanthropy* (New York: Harper & Bros., 1893); Alexander Johnson, *Adventures in*

Social Welfare being Reminiscences of Things, Thoughts and Folks during Forty Years of Social Work (Fort Wayne, Ind.: Fort Wayne Printing Press, 1923); and William H. Matthews, *Adventures in Giving* (New York: Dodd, Mead & Co., 1939).

31. Robert M. Lester, *Forty Years of Carnegie Giving* (New York: Charles Scribner's Sons, 1941), pp. 45, 82; Howard J. Savage, *Fruit of an Impulse: Forty-five years of the Carnegie Foundation, 1905-1950* (New York: Harcourt, Brace & Co., 1953).

32. Raymond B. Fosdick, *The Story of the Rockefeller Foundation* (New York: Harper & Bros., 1952), pp. 81 ff, 93 ff; The Rockefeller Foundation, Annual Reports, 1913; Carnegie Corporation of New York, *Reports of the President and Treasurer, 1922.*

33. Abraham Flexner, *I Remember, An Autobiography* (New York: Simon & Schuster, 1940), pp. 356 ff.

34. George R. Bentley, *A History of the Freedmen's Bureau* (Philadelphia: University of Pennsylvania Press, 1955), pp. 34, 31 ff, 63 ff; Jessie Pearl Rice, *J.L.M. Curry. Southerner, Statesman, and Educator* (New York: King's Crown Press, 1949); Horace Mann Bond, *The Education of the Negro in the American Social Order* (New York: Prentice-Hall Inc., 1934), p. 133; Ullin W. Leavell, *Philanthropy in Negro Education* (Nashville, Tenn.: George Peabody College for Teachers, Contributions to Education, No. 100, 1930); *Charleston News and Courier,* October 7, 1880 (on Daniel Hand); Benjamin Brawley, *Doctor Dillard and the Jeanes Fund* (Chicago: Fleming H. Revell Co., 1930); George Foster Peabody Papers, Library of Congress; Phelps-Stokes Fund, *Negro Status and Race Relations 1911-1946: The Thirty-Five Year Report of the Phelps-Stokes Fund* (New York: Phelps-Stokes Fund, 1948); Edwin R. Embree, *Investment in People: The Story of the Julius Rosenwald Fund* (New York: Harper & Bros., 1949).

35. Curti, *Social Ideas of American Education,* p. 113.

36. Ashton R. Willard, "The Rindge Gifts to Cambridge," *New England Magazine,* n.s. III (February 1891), 733 ff; W.R. Odell, *Gifts to the Public Schools* (New York: William R. Odell, Publisher, 1932); Allie Boyd, *Philanthropy in the Form of Gifts and Endowments for Elementary and Secondary Education* (Master's thesis, University of Chicago, 1928); "The Des Moines House of Dreams," *School Executives Magazine,* LI (January 1932), 207-25; Milbank Memorial Fund *Quarterly,* (1940); *Annual Reports of the Milbank Memorial Fund, 1922-1925,* especially Report for 1922, pp. 65-69.

37. Extract from Green and Russell's *Boston Post Boy and Advertiser,* No. 136, March 24, 1760, in *New England Historical and Geneological Register,* XXXIV (July 1880), 288-293; *Boston Gazette and County Journal,* March 24, 1760; Documents and correspondence relating to the Great Boston Fire, Manuscript Division, Boston Public Library, MS. 806.

38. Foster Rhea Dulles, *American Red Cross. A History* (New York: Harper & Bros., 1950); Richard Harrison Shryock has set a standard for such studies in his *National Tuberculosis Association, 1904-1954* (New York: National Tuberculosis Association, 1957).

39. John Price Jones Manuscript Collection, Baker Library, Harvard University. See also John Price Jones, *The American Giver* (New York: Inter-River Press, 1954).

40. "Charitable Rackets," *Social Service Review*, XXVIII (March, 1954), 87-88; Jerome Ellison, "Who Gets Your Charity Dollars?", *Saturday Evening Post*, CCXXVI (June 26, 1954), 27 ff; Bernard Thompkins, "When You Give—Are You Being Taken?" *Colliers*, CXXXIII (June 25, 1954), 90-93.

41. United States Congress, Senate, *Industrial Relations*. Final Report and Testimony submitted to Congress by the Commission on Industrial Relations created by the Act of August 23, 1912, 64th Congress, 1st Session. Senate Document No. 415 (11 vols.; Washington: Government Printing Office, 1916); John E. Lankford, *Congressional Investigations of the Philanthropic Foundations, 1902-54* (Master's thesis, University of Wisconsin, 1957).

23

Liberation and Stalemate

DAVID RIESMAN

DAVID RIESMAN, AUTHOR, LAWYER, SOCIOLOGIST, AND TEACHER,
ALSO WROTE THE LONELY CROWD: A STUDY OF THE CHANGING
AMERICAN CHARACTER (1950). HE IS CURRENTLY A PROFESSOR IN
THE DEPARTMENT OF SOCIOLOGY AT HARVARD UNIVERSITY.

The United States has never been as homogeneous as those who talk about a "mainstream" of White Anglo-Saxon culture like to believe, for even within these once-dominant groups there were marked differences among, for example, Congregationalists, Presbyterians, and various branches of Methodism; Quakers, Dutch Reformed, Scotch-Irish Protestants, Huguenot French, and many German Lutherans have been lumped by history in with the so-called "mainstream." What is also left out is the minority tradition of fatalism both among some New England writers and intellectuals and among white Southerners, as well as among evangelical sects which did not share the general belief in the identity of doing well and doing good.

But on the whole, among what might be called the club of the white males, there was more liberty and more equality in the sense of lesser deference, than there had been in Europe, and there was hope that progress would bring both more liberty and more equality. But as immigration increased (especially of those from non-Protestant cultural traditions, including many who distrusted the legitimacy of the governments of their nation-states, or, as in the case of Southern Italians, hardly knew they had a nation-state), differences of customs and beliefs led to the symbolic crusades Joseph Gusfield describes concerning what it means to be an American, who is entitled to offer the preferred definition, and hence who is to have more liberty and equality and who is to have less.

Excerpted by Professor Riesman from his article in *The Uses of Controversy in Sociology*, edited by Lewis A. Coser and Otto Larsen (New York: The Free Press, 1976), pp. 20-25. Reprinted by permission of the author and publisher.

In the affluent decades from 1948 through the 1960's, there was a series of symbolic crusades as well as pragmatic movements by previously excluded groups demanding their share of education, medical, occupational, and other resources. While in the American past, as S.M. Lipset contends, the seesaw between the demand for more liberty and the demand for more equality has been a persistent continuity, the glamorous invitation offered by affluence made it seem possible to achieve simultaneously more liberty, more equality, and more democracy. A series of previously unmobilized groups entered the political arena, sometimes making use of civil and occasionally uncivil disobedience: first white Southerners objecting to desegregation; then previously unorganized blacks, followed by other minorities of color and then by white ethnic groups; elite and then less elite college students; and currently, activist, liberationist women.

In my (all too often fallible) judgment, the women's liberation movements are not a passing fad among highly educated white upper-middle-class women and some of their male contemporaries. Bachofen, Engels, and Veblen argued in the last century that matriarchy was an even older system of authority than patriarchy. However, while attacks on patriarchy have a long intellectual history, and feminist movements among bluestocking pioneers a long social and political history, I would contend that the present situation is neither recapitulation nor simple progression, but represents strong elements of discontinuity. The discontinuity reflects the momentum and scope of the women's movements and their impact on both sexes and many aspects of social, institutional, and personal life.

For generations there have been isolated women, protected by high status, who could defy the conventions of their sex because of the eccentricities allowed their social class. Even in an older America there have been such women: sometimes high-status Bohemians like Amy Lowell or brave reformers such as the Grimke sisters or, in other ways, Jane Addams; and of course in the fight for suffrage women resorted to civil disobedience and other tactics then considered shocking. The social hierarchy helped give scope to Eleanor Roosevelt, Frances Perkins, and other less well-known women as recently as the 1930s. But the New Deal, followed by the Second World War, helped undo the residual social hierarchies, and the baby boom, after the war, along with the affluence that made it possible, enhanced by the suburban spread which had begun much earlier, and egalitarianism, subjected women to same-sex inhibitions even if they were college graduates, and as well educated as their menfolk, or better. They could have *jobs* before the first child came and after the last had grown and flown, but were discouraged by both sexes from entering traditionally male *careers*. As recently as 1963, when Alice Rossi proposed a more equitable division of gender roles in work and in family life, at a conference sponsored by the American Academy of Arts and Sciences, a number of liberal male and female participants regarded her propositions as outre.[1]

The more radical wings of the women's movements shock many today. They are often seen by the general population as an aspect of other crusades by affluent and provocative young people, as in the earlier drug cults, in the antiwar movement, or in countercultural activities generally. But in fact, these radical wings are in part a reaction *against* these other movements of protest: a number of college-educated women discovered that, in the civil rights and New Left crusades, they were being led and often exploited by domineering men under the guise of liberation and emancipation. Women also adapted a tactic, namely the consciousness-raising group, which mixed the age-grades, and helped, or perhaps occasionally overpersuaded, women to reinterpret their situation as one of deprivation and subordination to male chauvinism.[2] Indeed, lacking any obvious territoriality such as some nationalist blacks, Spanish-speaking groups, and American Indians possess, these women found that they had forcibly to separate themselves from a network of relations to men as fathers, brothers, sons, lovers, and to create a metaphorical territoriality. The result has been to inaugurate profoundly unsettling changes in attitudes toward the family and the role of the sexes on a far larger scale than could be accomplished or often even imagined by the earlier isolated pioneers.

There are participants and observers who believe not only that marriage as an institution is endangered, but that it should be. My own surmise is that marriage in some form is likely to survive in America, but it would seem unlikely that gender roles will lapse back into former taken-for-granted patterns. There is already a minority of husbands taking major responsibility for running households while their wives are the major breadwinners—an occasional pattern founded not on ideology but necessity at the economic bottom of society. Among the educated, the hope is widespread that men and women can choose their roles, and that women's liberation movements are leading to men's liberation from competitiveness, from the tyranny of the clock, from Max Weber's "iron cage," and other constraints. But I am inclined to think that the iron cage is worldwide (and that we are more likely to run out of iron than of cages); the vision I once held that a general relaxation of habits of work was possible for Americans may in the short term be quite unrealistic. It would increase the politically explosive effects of inflation to the extent that this is brought about by lowered productivity. I believe that in the years of scarcity ahead, we shall need more than ever to exert ourselves to produce, and may not be able to afford the slackening of the work ethic, and of the need for achievement which must be distinguished from competitiveness and the need to dominate and surpass others. Many women who would consider themselves in the forefront of the women's movements would agree with this, maintaining that women have historically been producers, while men, as Veblen contended, have been sportsmen and gamesmen, more concerned with display than with craftsmanship. But the more countercultural implications of other wings of the women's movements which would reorganize work and family in a more relaxed way, could in the world economy prove too costly.[3]

As more women attend college, and as more children of both sexes are raised in college-educated families, and as more working mothers adapt their views of what is proper to their actual behavior, the circles widen in which some aspects of liberationist ideology are accepted. Daniel Yankelovich's 1974 study comparing college and noncollege youth asserts that there is a "sharp cleavage in views and values now separating college and noncollege women," but his data indicate the degree to which noncollege women accept some tenets which in an earlier day would have been considered heretical; for example, only half of the noncollege women regard having children as an important personal value (nearly a third of college women do), and 38 percent of noncollege women do not regard having children outside of formal marriage as morally wrong.[4]

In a way, what is surprising is that in the symbolic clashes and crusades among cultural classes, so much of Middle America has responded to provocation, not by active violence, but by a slowly growing tolerance coupled with irritated bewilderment. In race relations, for example, except where urban villagers object to forced integration and busing, and also (like other city dwellers) to crime, poll data I have seen (as in the work of Andrew Greeley) show rising racial tolerance, notably so among Catholics. There is also a rise in acceptance of new styles of dress and behavior, including sexual freedom and communal modes of life. The Yankelovich survey reported that, except for the cleavage over women's liberation, many values of the counterculture of 1969 have now reached noncollege youth. Undoubtedly, as with other publicized movements of participatory protest, the women's movements have been deeply offensive to many rural and working-class as well as some middle-class Americans. For these movements appear to delegitimate the role of housewife or part-time or periodic job-holder in comparison with women who pursue careers. Volunteer activity is denigrated, sometimes because capable women were given subordinate positions in organizations led by men, but also in groups such as the League of Women Voters and PTA which have served as social cement not only for participants but for the entire society. Similarly, to the extent that housework is volunteer labor, "unliberated" breadwinner males are told that they are exploiting the unpaid labor of their wives.

Because the women's movements do not stand in isolation from other protest movements, the possibility of continuing class cleavage (despite the emphasis on sisterhood) and backlash exists; but one could argue that the women's movements are currently losing their revolutionary significance and becoming in some measure accepted in all cultural classes. The devotees of Herbert Marcuse would call this repressive tolerance or co-optation, whereas I would regard it as mutual infiltration among groups only partially insulated from each other.

There are pockets of insulation nonetheless, illustrated by the sometimes violent boycott of "modernist" textbooks in Kanawha County, West Virginia, and in the prosperous condition of some of the colleges controlled by evangelical Protestant sects which emphasize Biblical literalism, though at times with little training in theological fundamentals. The fundamentalist churches flourish, while liberal Protestant and Catholic leaders come under attack for preaching up-to-date versions of the Social Gospel. It would be as unwise to take the post-Viet Nam and post-Watergate victory of liberal Democrats in the 1974 Congressional elections as representing a new liberal consensus in the United States as it was earlier to overestimate, as I did, the appeal of right-wing symbolic crusades to working-class voters whose current concerns are more with inflation and the sagging economy than with assaults on their traditional familistic values by the women's movements and other causes advanced by educated minorities. Although the several states of the federal system have lost much of their bulkhead or insular quality that so attracted Justice Louis D. Brandeis, the political apathy of large numbers of potential voters currently offers a certain buffer against the coalescence of the pockets of right-wing extremism whose inhabitants Governor Wallace and former Governor Reagan are trying to mobilize on a national basis.

II

In the judgment of people from more hierarchical societies, Americans have appeared as they did to Tocqueville, less deferential—although he thought America in principle governable thanks to freedom of association, talent in forming voluntary associations via the free press, the social cement provided by religion, and the restraint of the semiaristocracy of the legal profession. (He also presciently feared a possible oligarchy of manufacturers, although the America he visited was still largely preindustrial, and he recognized that the evil of slavery might shatter the nation.) Moreover, the fact that young Americans often had more education than their parents (or were more "American" if the latter were immigrants) and the invitations offered by the frontier and the West and in the cities early gave rise to attitudes hostile to authority as well as to authoritarianism. However, one example may illustrate the discontinuity involved in the increasing loss of credibility by authorities drawing their legitimacy from the society rather than from personal charisma or glamor.

The Civilian Conservation Corps was created under the New Deal to put unemployed youth to work building firebreaks and trails under the discipline of noncoms often drawn from the military services. The CCC were willing to obey the noncom types who supervised them; whereas Peace Corps Volunteers, mostly but not entirely college-educated, disparage those involved in their training and their deployment overseas—the noncoms of this small agency for volunteers. I have also pondered the CCC in connection with proposals, most recently put by the Panel on Youth headed by James Coleman, that young people be put to work in constructive volunteer employment rather than stored in schools or left to roam on the streets.[5] In small enclaves, there have been groups of young people who cleaned up a neighborhood, or Sierra Club members who helped work to clear firebreaks in the forests. In the 1930s young men obeyed the authority of noncom types even if they disliked the work and hated the boss. Of course, not all of them obeyed; there were always Huckleberry Finns.

The affluence of recent decades, however, made Americans of all ages able to say openly what children like to say to adults: "You're not the boss of me!" But neither are they bosses of themselves in terms of self-restraint. And as more and more people have sought their shares in America, their ability to cancel each other out both in symbolic terms and often in pragmatic results—that is, their inability to arrive at trade-offs regarded as for the time being equitable—has led people to feel less potent or efficacious, and hence to blame authority for such evident stalemates as the inability of all industrial, democratic societies to control simultaneously inflation and unemployment (though in terms of unemployment, America's record is among the worst). The anti-Viet Nam war elites were successful in destroying the authority of the "best and the brightest"— now a term of sarcasm—who helped invent, support, and justify the war. (It is now becoming part of accepted history whereas it is in fact mythology, that only the "best and brightest" got us into Viet Nam, forgetting the role of Cardinal Spellman and a number of other people in the China lobby and many in the Democratic Party, ordinary political leaders—and not all M.I.T. or Harvard-trained intellectuals—who were afraid of the Democratic Party's being accused of "losing Southeast Asia," not to speak of the Strategic Air Command and other military services wanting a piece of the action. It is a kind of Northeastern Quadrant vanity to overemphasize the local "best and brightest." But the anti-war elites are themselves fragmented, and indeed often opposed to elitism as such, and almost certainly unable to replace the authorities, many of them still in positions of responsibility, whose legitimacy has been undermined.) Yet this fragmentation of power seems to me most dangerous in controlling the atom, only slightly less dangerous in controlling responses to a lower standard of living. Believing as I do in surprises and discontinuities, I think it conceivable that the mood of the country can change—but it may not change in time for us to find acceptable ways of managing a country of over 200 million energetic people pursuing both private and group destinies of material ambition as well as evangelical mandates.

In view of the perilous situation we have reached, we need not only intelligent and responsive local and national leadership but the willingness to follow it. Governors and mayors who have raised taxes to meet essential services have almost invariably been voted out of office, while those who have borrowed money to pay off voters (mostly middle- and working-class, organized in unions and pressure groups, rather than poor) have survived politically, like those Americans who so amazed Tocqueville by going through bankruptcy and emerging with reputations unscathed. Another long-run legacy is the endemic cynicism concerning the promises of politicians, which in turn leads to gullibility vis-a-vis those politicians who pretend to be against politics, against government itself.

However, thoughtful policy-makers who are not exploiters of voters' resentments, fears, and paranoias are, along with many of the rest of us, puzzled as to what would be politically feasible courses of action that could set limits on the spiraling struggle of contending blocs to keep up with or outrun inflation by shifting its terrible penalties to others. After the euphoria which gripped many in the late 1960s, we are in a period when there are few imaginative human prospects, including visions of alternative societies which are realistic in the sense that they might be achieved, given who we are and what we have made of ourselves in the world. We can learn of course from the experience of other nations and we should, but I do not see models for us, or indeed for the planet, which are particularly helpful for the American case. The visions of the New Left, whether these looked outward to other countries or inward to native American radicalism, failed in this respect by oversimplification and then, feeling more powerless than was often in fact justified, resorting in a few instances to terror. But we also need at the same time something very different, namely, not visions, but faith in the ongoing human enterprise including a restored belief in the virtue of "thinking small," taking some difficult incremental steps along but a single dimension. The counterculture has sometimes done this in providing examples of life of greater simplicity and concern for the environment, even though it has often surrounded such practical steps with rather vague and perhaps endearing visions of a communal society which might fit a country the size of Denmark.

But of course to "think small" is not enough. America has always been in danger of reaching to limits of the antagonistic cooperation of its competing and coexisting parishes of interest and passion. It has astonished me that the Civil War, though seared and enshrined in the memory of Southerners, has made such a small impression on most of the country concerning the capacities for civil strife of a massive sort, and the companion danger of seeking to cope with internal fragmentation by a new surge of American nationalism. Nationalism, with its ethnic variants, remains perhaps the strongest ideological power in the world, although nation-states seem to be losing their monopoly of violence to guerrillas willing to die for their cause—who may themselves some day acquire nuclear as well as conventionally horrifying weapons. At the same time, the history of the human race exhibits extraordinary resiliency and adaptability. Human beings became settled agriculturalists (and thus capable, as Lewis Mumford reminds us, of organizing megamachines to build such monumental things as the pyramids) only a few thousand years ago. Agriculture and civilization did not disappear, even though particular lands, tribal groups, and cities were destroyed through the centuries by waves of "barbarians" and nomads. If we do not destroy the carrying capacity of the planet in a nuclear catastrophe or some biological equivalent, one can be encouraged by the resiliency human beings have shown in developing high cultures, even as old empires have fallen.

Yet we must also prepare ourselves for the possibility that we will not have organized enough technological substitutes for current fossil fuels and other shrinking resources, and hence to find ways of maintaining our civilization on a different level of consumership, without destroying the creativity of entrepreneurs while evoking the resourcefulness and if need be the stoicism manifested in wartime and in many families during the Great Depression of the 1930s.

I am thinking now in terms of decades, for I can conceive of another spurt of economic growth in the United States although not of one which will end inflation and even more rapid depletion of resources than our husbandry and ingenuity can replace. Robert Bellah sees hope, not so much in the civil religion of a largely Protestant and ancestral America, but in what he terms the new religious consciousness (sometimes oriented toward harmony with nature) emerging especially among young people shopping for sects he and others have studied in the Bay Area.[6] But I doubt if necessity is an adequate mother for religious invention. And even such morally compelling leaders as the slain martyrs, Robert F. Kennedy and Martin Luther King, Jr., did not command the full assent of, I would suppose, more than a bare majority of Americans. Indeed, if a charismatic leader came along to respond to our hungers and dilemmas, we would probably fear him or her, especially when what our present situation calls for are "complexifiers" and not the "terrible simplifiers."

When I reflect on history, I cannot be sanguine about the future of any particular nation-state, legatee of crumbling empires—certainly not about the United States. But I also gain from history, as already suggested, a kind of religious faith in the human enterprise as a whole: its tenacity and powers of recovery—including recovery of past wisdoms and great works of art and science, and of the potential in men and women to stretch themselves to the limit of their abilities at once in moral and intellectual terms. These abilities are more than enough to cope with the current human prospect, created as it has been by the ingenuity as well as the greed of our contemporaries and of earlier generations. Mind is not at the end of its tether.[7]

Notes

1. Alice Rossi, "A Modest Proposal," in Robert J. Lifton, ed., *Woman in America* (Boston: Beacon Press, 1964).

2. Jo Freeman, *The Politics of Women's Liberation: A Case Study of an Emerging Social Movement and Its Relation to the Policy Process* (New York: David McKay, 1975).

3. Arlie Hochschild provides a persuasively argued alternative view. Arlie Hochschild, "Inside the Clockwork of Male Careers," in Florence Howe, ed., *Women and the Power to Change* (New York: McGraw-Hill, 1975), pp. 47-80.

4. Daniel Yankelovich, *Changing Youth Values in the Seventies: A Study of American Youth—Summary Report* (Mimeo, 1974).

5. Panel on Youth, *Youth: Transition to Adulthood*, Report of the Panel on Youth of the President's Science Advisory Committee (Chicago: University of Chicago Press, 1974).

6. Robert N. Bellah, "A New Religious Consciousness," in Glock and Bellah, eds., *The New Consciousness* (Berkeley: University of California Press, forthcoming).

7. Lionel Trilling, *Mind in the Modern World* (New York: Viking Press, 1973).

24

The American As Reformer

ARTHUR M. SCHLESINGER, SR.

ARTHUR M. SCHLESINGER, SR., NOTED HISTORIAN, EDUCATOR,
AND AUTHOR, CO-EDITED WITH DIXON RYAN FOX THE 13-VOLUME
HISTORY OF AMERICAN LIFE SERIES (MACMILLAN, 1927-1950).

The Historical Climate of Reform

"I wish to offer to your consideration some thoughts on the particular and general relations of man as a reformer." Ralph Waldo Emerson thus opened a famous address in 1841 on the first great upsurge of social reform in United States history. At the time American society along the seaboard was two centuries old. The people had subdued the savages, reshaped their physical environment, won political independence, established representative institutions, founded towns and cities, developed agriculture and trade, entered upon manufacturing. The country had attained a provisional maturity, and despite the more primitive conditions on the western frontier, thinking men were taking stock of the achievements and conducting what the speaker called a "general inquisition into abuses." And so, as Emerson went on to say, "In the history of the world the doctrine of Reform had never such scope as at the present hour." It seemed to him that every human institution was being questioned— "Christianity, the laws, commerce, schools, the farm, the laboratory"— and that not a "town, statute, rite, calling, man, or woman, but is threatened by the new spirit."[1]

A hundred years afterward, Emerson's words sound as if they had been uttered of our own age, though whether the spirit of reform be deemed a threat or promise is a matter of personal opinion, and Emerson's other remarks attest that he himself regarded it as vital to social health. Between his time and ours, of course, much has happened. Cycles of reform and repose have come and gone until by a giant turn of the wheel the American people again find themselves in a period when in the history of the world the doctrine of reform had never such scope as at the present hour. In venturing to treat Emerson's theme a century later I need hardly say that I do so without Emerson's intuitive wisdom and philosophic acumen. Instead, I bring to it the poorer gifts of the historical scholar, those of the foot soldier rather than of the air pilot. I can only hope that the longer span of national experience since his day, plus the historian's special approach, will add something, however slight, to an understanding of the conditions and nature of the reform impulse in the United States.

The reform urge has obviously not been an American monopoly, nor has the nation ever been immune to struggles for human betterment elsewhere. In particular there has been a like-mindedness with England. The colonists were deeply indebted to the mother country for their notions of individual liberty and free institutions, as well as for that "salutary neglect"—Burke's phrase—which enabled them to develop these conceptions yet farther. Even after Independence this kinship continued, as it has to the present time. Ideologically America has never been isolated from Europe nor Europe from America, and the cross-fertilization of ideals and practices has yielded mutual benefit.[2]

The United States, however, until very recent times has nearly always set the pace for the Old World in reform zeal. The outstanding exception has been in solutions for the social maladjustments arising from industrialization, where Britain as the older country faced these problems in acute form before America was hardly aware of them. The English, for example, led in factory legislation, the mitigation of child labor and the legalizing of trade-unions. Another but less conclusive instance in a different field was England's earlier abolition of Negro servitude. The two governments, obeying a common impulse, acted simultaneously in 1807 to outlaw the African slave trade; then Britain ended human bondage throughout the Empire in 1833, whereas the United States waited until 1865. This delay was not due to any lack of will on the part of American humanitarians, however, but to the fact that the circumstances in the two lands were so very different. In England's case the institution existed some thousands of miles away. Moreover, Parliament had full power to deal with it, and the colonies affected were in a static or decaying economic condition. In America, on the other hand, slavery not only existed at home, but it was anchored in state and local law and was recognized by the federal Constitution. It was also bound up, directly or indirectly, with the material welfare of a large part of the nation. Nonetheless Britain's action inspired the immediate formation of the American Anti-Slavery Society and so threw the American movement into higher gear.

In the case of most other social innovations, however, America has stood at the forefront. Thus (white) manhood suffrage was attained in the United States by the middle of the nineteenth century but not in England until the early twentieth. In like manner America outstripped the older country in regard to liberty of the press, the separation of church and state, the abolition of barbarous punishments, restraints on the liquor traffic, public education and prison reform, not to mention other achievements.

The basic reason for the generally faster pace of reform may be found in two conditions. In the first place, men were not burdened to the same extent by the weight of tradition. Less energy had to be used in tearing down the old and revered, more was left for building anew, and the large measure of self-government enjoyed even by the colonists simplified the process. As Emerson put it on one occasion,

> America was opened after the feudal mischief was spent, and so the people made a good start...No inquisition here, no kings, no nobles, no dominant church...We began with freedom, and are defended from shocks now for a century by the facility with which through popular assemblies every necessary measure of reform can instantly be carried.[3]

The second factor was the kind of people who emigrated to America, not only the original settlers but also their successors, the far greater number of immigrants. Early or late, these transplanted Europeans were men who rebelled against conditions as they found them in their homelands—against a class society, against religious, political and economic oppression—and, unlike their more docile neighbors, they carried their rebellion to the point of going to a distant continent where life was strange, dangers abounded and new careers must be sought. The departure of such folk slowed down the impetus to change at home, just as it tended to quicken it in the adopted country.

Given these two circumstances, the surprising thing is that the tempo of reform in America was not far more precipitate. As Anthony Trollope observed with particular reference to the Revolutionary era, "This new people, when they had it in their power to change all their laws, to throw themselves upon any Utopian theory that the folly of a wild philanthropy could devise...did not do so."[4] He attributed this caution to their inherited English practicality, but there was more to it than that. By starting life in a new state they acquired a new state of mind. Those who had fled from religious bigotry could now worship as they wished, those who had suffered political discrimination were generally free to vote and run for office, while all could make an easier living and attain a greater human dignity. To revise an old proverb, nothing sobers like success. The owner of property, however eager to improve society, has a personal investment in orderly change, and under conditions of self-government a legislative body is, as Emerson remarked in the essay just quoted, "a standing insurrection, and escapes the violence of accumulated grievance."[5]

In other words, virtually every newcomer to America underwent a sea change. No matter how desperate his lot had been in Europe, he quickly displayed what impatient extremists despise as a middle-class attitude toward reform. Being even surer of the future than of the present, he could not love innovation for its own sake, or be willing to risk all existing good in a general overturn. Hence he threw his weight on the side of piecemeal progress.

The national preference for evolution over revolution, whether the revolution be peaceable or violent, has given the United States midway in the twentieth century the reputation abroad of being the last bulwark of conservatism. The kaleidoscopic disruptions of the two world wars have driven Europe to extreme measures of recovery and social reconstruction. By communists the American method of progress is contemptuously dubbed 'bourgeois liberalism,' while even the democratic Socialists of Western Europe find little good in our way of making haste slowly.[6] Yet the mass of Americans remains unconvinced. In their own lifetime they have witnessed a Square Deal followed by a New Freedom followed by a New Deal and then a Fair Deal, each yielding social gains, and they know that the flame of reform burns as fiercely as ever and is as menacing to special privilege. Until events demonstrate the failure of this pragmatic approach, they may be counted upon not to try any different method.

Another historical factor working against headlong change has been freedom of speech and print. Practiced even in colonial times, it was enshrined in the basic law of the states and nation after the Revolution. Liberty of expression may not at first seem a moderating influence, since it is an open invitation to all malcontents to agitate their grievances. But that is just the point. For orderly progress it is better that crackpots rant in public than plot in private, and the very act, moreover, subjects their beliefs to comparison with the more constructive ideas of others. Only in this way can the critics be criticized, their proposals cut down to size, and an appropriate course be arrived at democratically.

Infringements on freedom of utterance almost invariably defeat their purpose either by attracting attention to the cause involved or by creating indignation over the denial of constitutional rights. For example, the murder of the abolitionist editor Elijah Lovejoy and the 'gag resolution' of the House of Representatives against antislavery petitions brought to the antislavery standard countless persons who had been unmoved by the woes of the Negro.[7] Our wisest conservatives have always understood this function of free speech. Alexander Hamilton, Daniel Webster, Charles E. Hughes and Wendell Wilkie, to name no others, championed the liberty to express views which they themselves hated. Through this process of keeping the windows of discussion open, many a plausible reform has died of exposure, while others, more responsibly conceived, have won their way to public acceptance.

In the remainder of this excellent review, Schlesinger examines "whence has American reform derived its abiding vitality?" He indicates that "many rivulets have contributed to the stream, some with constant flow and others intermittently."

Schlesinger identifies religion as by far the most potent source. Other factors are:

- **Europe's Age of Enlightenment.** *Schlesinger adds,* "These eighteenth-century avowals of human excellence and man's boundless capacity for progress found instant and permanent lodgement in America, where they confirmed common observations as well as the more enlightened religious teachings."

- **The Declaration of Independence.** *Quoting Mary Antin, Schlesinger explains,* "What the Mosaic Law is to the Jews, the Declaration is to the American people. It affords us a starting-point in history and defines our mission among nations....Up to the moment of our declaration of independence, our struggle with our English rulers did not differ from other popular struggles against despotic governments. Again and again we respectfully petitioned for redress of specific grievances, as the governed, from time immemorial, have petitioned their governors. But one day we abandoned our suit for petty damages, and instituted a suit for the recovery of our entire human heritage of freedom; and by basing our claim on the fundamental principles of the brotherhood of man and the sovereignty of the masses, we assumed championship of the oppressed against their oppressors, wherever found....The American confession of faith, therefore, is a recital of the doctrines of liberty and equality."[8]

- **Great National Crises.** "In periods of general social dislocation, injustice long endured becomes intolerable, and men in their despair may even seek a passport to Utopia."

- **Innovation Encouraged by Regionalism.**

- **The Authority of the Constitution** by which the Federal Government has been able to Achieve Reform.

The Reform Impulse in Action

Schlesinger begins this important chapter with the preamble: "The history of reform," observes Emerson, "is always identical, it is the comparison of the idea with the fact." And that idea, as he says elsewhere, "is the conviction that there is an infinite worthiness in man, which will appear at the call of worth, and that all particular reforms are the removing of some impediment."[9] This faith in mere humanity derived its spiritual strength, as we have seen, from what forward-looking men regarded as both divine and natural law. But how was the idea to be put into effect, the impediment removed? At this point the friends of reform have usually divided. All might agree on the need of a social change and yet differ bitterly, even irreconcilably, over how to accomplish it. It should not be surprising that isms breed schisms considering the type of rebellious mentality upon which such movements draw.

Much of the chapter then traces the various approaches to abolition—"The conflicting attitudes of men seeking with equal earnestness the same good"— ranging from the passive resistance of Thoreau to "apostles of excitement and vehemence such as William Lloyd Garrison and ultimately to the insurrectionist John Brown."

Schlesinger summarizes: Men took their stand, as they always do, for a complex of reasons—logical, psychological and traditional—some of which they understood and some they did not; they were prisoners of their time and place. As Henry Ward Beecher remarked, Garrison "did not create the anti-slavery spirit of the North: he was simply the offspring of it."[10] That spirit reflected the convictions of a people who, with no economic stake of their own in slavery, fortified their social outlook from the New Testament, the Preamble of the Declaration of Independence and their daily practice of human equality.

The final parts of the chapter deal with the role of political parties as agents of voluntary effort, too often a neglected topic in discussion of the independent sector.

With rare exceptions the purpose of reformers is to induce favorable action by some governmental authority: the legislature in the case of a state, Congress in the case of the nation. In order to kindle the necessary outside support the humanitarians in the first half of the nineteenth century set the example of creating a host of nation-wide voluntary bodies, each with its special palliative or panacea. As described by a contemporary, the first step was to choose an "imposing" designation for the organization; the second, to obtain "a list of respectable names" as "members and patrons"; the next, to hire "a secretary and an adequate corps of assistants"; then "a band of popular lecturers must be commissioned, and sent forth as agents on the wide public" and the press be "put in operation"; finally, "subsidiary societies" must be "multiplied over the length and breadth of the land."[11] So thoroughly did these crusaders work out the pattern of reform organization and propaganda a hundred years ago that later generations have found little to add beyond taking advantage of new communication devices such as the movies and the radio.

The American two-party system, however, has posed constant difficulties for reformers. The reasons for this twofold political alignment need not be considered here, though it is worth noting that it is historically a characteristic of English speaking peoples as contrasted with other nations. The point is that this duality seldom engenders the polarization of convictions which might theoretically be expected: 'me-tooism' is no mere modern phenomenon. The established parties wish to stay established, and to do so they are forced to seek a formula which will bring the many different regions and interests together in an acceptable progam, as well as to unite the liberals and conservatives within their own ranks. They strive for the common denominator, to please as many as possible and offend as few as possible, with the result that compromise and evasion become the rule. As an old-line politician is quoted as saying, "Let me make the deals and I care not who makes the ideals."

Whatever objections may exist to this practice, the major parties have, with the tragic exception of 1860, always succeeded in inducing the public too accept the outcome of elections, and even in that lone instance they had staved off the sectional crisis for forty years. Walter Lippmann, indeed, has extolled this habit of opportunism as the "noblest achievement of democracy," for it means that "the solidarity of the people in a free society is stronger than their division into parties" and "that their capacity to find common ground is stronger than all the

many interests that divide them." He holds that "a nation, divided irreconcilably on 'principle,' each party believing it is pure white and the other pitch
black, cannot govern itself."[12]

This may be conceded as true in an absolute but not in a relative sense. A
more venturesome attitude by the two parties toward pathbreaking social and
economic ideas in line with the American reform tradition would clearly not
endanger democracy. On the contrary, it would buttress it by giving the voters a
clearer alternative at the polls, by enhancing party responsibility and by tend-
ing to keep the government more nearly abreast new needs. Reformers have
always rejoiced when a Jackson or Wilson or Roosevelt defied political
orthodoxy, but such occasions have been few, occurring only when abuses had
accumulated to a point where they could no longer be ignored.

To counter the customary practice of the old parties, reform groups have
from time to time launched their own parties. The earliest of these date from
before the Civil War, but their real flowering came later. The 1872 election was
the first with as many as three minor parties; the 1900 campaign had nine; and
1948 saw seven.

Broadly speaking, these organizations have been of four types. One series
comprised what may be called single-track parties, of which the Prohibition
party, founded in 1869, alone still survives. Other specimens in the later nineteenth century were the Greenback party (1876-1884); the Anti-Monopoly party
(1884); the Equal Rights party (1884-1888), which ran a woman for President to
dramatize the fact that women could not vote; and the United Christian party
(1900), which aspired to put the name of Christ in the United States Constitution. With the exception of the Prohibitionists none of this breed outlasted more
than a few elections, and no new ones of note have arisen in the twentieth
century.

The second sort consisted of parties urging the demands of occupational
interests, notably the farmers and the wage earners, the two great groups
disadvantaged by the rise of Big Business. Working within the reform tradition,
they sought governmental intervention to assure them some of the personal
dignity and economic independence which their forebears had enjoyed. The
agrarian parties—the Populists in 1892 are the best example—proposed such
steps as free silver, the government ownership of railroads and the popular
election of senators. The Labor Reform party (1872) and the Union labor party
(1888), for their part, asked for measures like shorter hours, factory legislation
and currency reform.

Such efforts, however, collided on the one hand with the western farmers'
sentimental attachment to the Republican party and on the other with the
hostility of key labor leaders to hazardous political adventures. Moreover, the

best hope for success lay in uniting the two occupational interests, but attempts to do so never got far. The farmers, rooted in the soil, distrusted the landless wage earner, and being obliged by the nature of their task to toil when necessary from dawn to dusk, they could no more sympathize with the desire of urban workers for shorter hours than the latter could with the farmers' desire for higher crop prices. The Farmer-Labor party of 1920 and La Follette's Progressive party in 1924 tried to bridge the gap, but neither outlived the single election.[13]

The third variety of these movements aimed at displacing the capitalist system. The first Marxist party appeared in the campaign of 1892, and by 1900 there were two in the field. Unlike the other instances, the socialist doctrine was imported from Europe and appealed largely to naturalized citizens still thinking in European terms. At its peak, in 1920, the Socialist party, the stronger of the two, mustered 920,000 votes, most of them undoubtedly of a protest rather than an ideological character; and both groups have continued to function to the present time.[14] Meanwhile, under the spell of the Bolshevik revolution in Russia, a leftist offshoot in 1919 formed the American Communist (originally the Workers) party, whose leaders have come into repeated conflict with the courts on charges of conspiratorial methods, allegiance to a foreign power and an intent to overturn the government by force. The Communist vote, however, has never exceeded 103,000 (in the Depression election of 1932), and in the last two campaigns—1944 and 1948—the party has not even ventured to run presidential candidates under its own label.[15]

The final kind of minor party is represented by temporary splits from one or the other of the established groups. Since the Civil War this has happened about every twenty years, the outstanding cases being the Liberal Republican party of 1872 (which joined with the Democrats in that election); the Gold Democrats and Silver Republicans in the 1896 contest; Theodore Roosevelt's Progressive party in 1912; and the Dixiecrats in 1948.[16] The cause in each instance was a clash of principles or personalities or both. It should be noted, however, that the splinter party is not necessarily animated by reform ideals, as witness the Dixiecrats who left the Democratic fold over the question of Negro rights.

As for the three other types of parties, their idealism cannot in most cases be questioned, but their reform effectiveness can. Historians have stressed the utility of these movements in ventilating unpopular issues and in arousing sufficient voter support to cause the old parties to espouse the proposals. Though the educational function undoubtedly exists, it seems small as compared with the widespread and unflagging efforts of private nonpolitical bodies to promote the same objects. Thus, though minor parties have agitated such causes as woman suffrage, farm relief and factory legislation, the real work of mobilizing opinion has fallen to powerful nonpartisan groups whose spiritual lineage goes back to antislavery times.

Nor is it clear that these parties have done much to impose reform views on the regular parties. Only twice in modern times have they marshalled sufficient strength to break into the electoral college. True, on the first occasion, in 1892, the Populist victories frightened the Democrats into adopting a free-silver plank in the 1896 campaign; but the disastrous outcome of this action, besides failing to accomplish the supposed reform, steeled old-line politicians against similar third-party threats in later years. On the second occasion, in 1924, when La Follette polled some electoral votes (and 16.5 percent of the popular ballots), the effect on the older organizations was negligible.[17] The real aim of minor parties, of course, is to become major parties, but this has never happened since the Republicans, starting in 1854 as a third party, became in their first presidential election the second party. One wonders if the marvel can ever be repeated in view of the difficulties of tradition, organization, finance and legal impediments, all of which are infinitely greater than they were a century ago.

To some extent, moreover, minor parties have done positive harm to reform. By their very nature they tend to drain strength from the more progressive of the old parties, since they recruit voters who, come hell or high water, want the whole loaf instead of only part. In a close race they may even defeat the more liberal party and thereby bring on worse evils. A notable instance—to go back to antislavery days—is the election of 1844 when the Liberty party won enough votes in New York State to assure James K. Polk a plurality over Henry Clay and thus give the presidency to one more hated foe, who in due course instigated the Mexican War and added more potential slave territory to the Union. In the 1948 contest the Wallace Progressives could only have hoped to undercut the Democrats and so bring into power the more conservative of the major parties. And according to the ordinary operation of American politics they should have succeeded; but in this miracle election the Democratic nominee triumphed without the support of either New York, where the Wallace vote threw the state to Dewey, or of the Solid South.[18]

Because of the shortcomings of the third-party method, reformers in recent years have turned increasingly to the pressure-group device. This was a technique borrowed from the enemy, for Big Business had long demonstrated its efficacy in obtaining tariff legislation and other special favors. It involves systematic lobbying, high-powered propaganda to convert the public, campaigns to get out the vote and contributions to the war chests of existing parties. Though reform organizations may be hampered by smaller funds, they possess equal zeal, and the method enables them to take their demands direct to legislative bodies and administrative officers, to bore from within the major parties, and while assisting friends, to threaten enemies with political extinction. Besides, whenever a need is felt with sufficient intensity, an organization can be created and set functioning in a matter of days or weeks. In the national scene the current activity of organized labor in regard to the Taft-Hartley Law illustrates the pressure-group tactic.

Today the number of these groups for all purposes in Washington has come to compose a veritable third house of Congress. In 1942 a total of 628 maintained offices there, a majority of them for what their sponsors regarded as reform objects. Four years later Congress took official cognizance of the situation by requiring the agents to register, with a statement of their purposes, source of income and expenditures.[19] By 1948 more than 1100 were listed, outnumbering the elected members of Congress almost three to one. In this manner the reform spirit has developed a concentrated energy and effectiveness undreamed of by Garrison and Phillips in the more primitive days of the Republic.

Though the 1946 law has deprived the system of its more obvious abuses, the thoughtful may still wonder whether it conduces to the greatest good of the greatest number. There is not the direct responsibility to the voters as in the case of political parties, and, moreover, some causes succeed better than others merely because of stronger financial backing. These are weighty objections, yet it should be remembered that the reform movement, even in its simpler stages, displayed similar features. The principal difference today is that, in a country highly organized in every other field, reform itself has had to take on a highly organized character. In the battle of the giants, with all points of view represented, including the opposition to reform, we citizens of a free society may expect truth and enlightenment to continue to emerge and the nation be correspondingly the gainer.

Notes

1. "Man the Reformer," *Works* (Boston, 1883-1887), I, 217, 218, 220.

2. See A.M. Schlesinger, *Paths to the Present* (New York, 1949), pp. 147-177, 181-183.

3. "The Fortune of the Republic" (1878), *Works*, XI, 410-411. For a similar analysis, see George Gibbs, *Memoirs of the Administration of Washington and John Adams* (New York, 1846), I, 1.

4. *North America* (New York, 1862), 218. J.T. Adams amplifies this point in *The Epic of America* (Boston, 1931), pp. 99-100.

5. "The Fortune of the Republic," *Works*, XI, 411.

6. For an example of the latter attitude, see H.J. Laski, *The American Democracy* (New York, 1948), and for an American expression of a similar point of view, John Chamberlain, *Farewell to Reform* (New York, 1932).

7. As R.B. Nye says in *Fettered Freedom: Civil Liberties and the Slavery Controversy* (East Lansing, 1949), p. 251, the net effect of these and other infringements "was to gain for abolition a body of supporters who thought less of the wrongs of the slave than of the rights of the white man....The antislavery movement flourished under persecution."

8. "They Who Knock At Our Gates" (Boston, 1914), pp. 3-7.

9. *Works* (Boston, 1883-1887), I, 237 ("Man the Reformer"), 258 ("Lecture on the Times").

10. Garrisons, *Garrison*, III, 364.

11. *Protestant Jesuitism* (New York, 1836), pp. 53-54, written anonymously by Calvin Colton, who regarded such bodies disapprovingly.

12. "Mr. Churchill and Me-Tooism," *Boston Globe*, January 26, 1950. Herbert Agar presents the same thesis in *The Price of Union* (Boston, 1950).

13. K.C. MacKay, *The Progressive Movement of 1924* (New York, 1947), estimates that La Follette polled somewhat more than half his strength from the farmers.

14. The older and weaker party was the Socialist Labor Party. Until the ultimate goal is reached, the Socialist party has always urged a long list of timely reforms—such as woman suffrage, a graduated income tax and social security—which have attracted bourgeois liberals. For example, compare the dues-paying membership of 108,000 in 1919 with the vote polled by the Socialist ticket in the next year's election. H.W. Laidler, *Social-Economic Movements* (New York, 1944), p. 591.

15. The Communist ticket in 1940 polled 49,000 votes. The party membership in 1950 was 55,000, according to J. Edgar Hoover, director of the FBI. *New York Times*, May 3, 1950.

16. To some extent La Follette's Progressives in 1924 and Wallace's Progressives in 1948 were also chips respectively off the Republican and Democratic parties.

17. In addition, three splinter parties have captured electoral votes: the Liberal Republicans in 1872, in combination with the Democrats; the Progressives in 1912; and the Dixiecrats (the States' Rights party) in 1948. Theodore Roosevelt would not run a second time on the Progressive ticket because he said the voters were naturally Republicans or Democrats. *Works* (New York, 1923-1926), XXIV, 416.

18. J.D. Hicks believes that "in possibly half a dozen instances the third party vote has snatched victory from one major party ticket to give it to the other." "The Third Party Tradition in American Politics," *Mississippi Valley Historical Review*, XX (1933-1934), 26. It is only fair to note that the Prohibition vote in 1884 is often

credited in this manner with defeating Blaine in New York and thus bringing into the White House Grover Cleveland, the champion of clean government, a low tariff and civil-service reform; but the Mugwump revolt of independent Republicans was probably the more decisive factor. See A.M. Schlesinger, *The Rise of the City* (New York, 1933), pp. 400-401.

19. Most of the states had taken similar action earlier, the Massachusetts statute dating from 1890 and Wisconsin's from 1899.

25

The Negro in Retrospect and Prospect

MARY MCLEOD BETHUNE

MARY MCLEOD BETHUNE WAS A NOTED EDUCATOR AND CIVIL
RIGHTS REFORMER. SHE SERVED AS A SPECIAL ADVISOR ON
MINORITY AFFAIRS TO PRESIDENT FRANKLIN D. ROOSEVELT AND
AS PRESIDENT OF THE NATIONAL ASSOCIATION OF COLORED
WOMEN. SHE RECEIVED THE THOMAS JEFFERSON AWARD IN 1943.
THIS ADDRESS WAS ORIGINALLY DELIVERED BY MS. BEHUNE AT
THE ANNUAL MEETING OF THE ASSOCIATION FOR THE STUDY OF
NEGRO LIFE AND HISTORY IN NEW YORK CITY IN OCTOBER, 1949.

A decade ago, or even five years ago, few would have predicted that the position of the Negro in world affairs would have attained its present significance. The world has been moving rapidly. Well might we pause, then, today to view the Negro in retrospect and prospect.

My splendid audience, here, will join with me in paying tribute to the builders of earlier days, who laid the foundation for today's advance. But we shall not stop over-long to praise our warriors, Louverture and Peter Salem; our churchmen, Allen, Bryan and Garnett; our statesmen, Frederick Douglass and Grimke; or our educators, Booker T. Washington and Lucy Laney, for their greatest tribute, their greatest monument—the greatest monument to all our black heroes since the Negro first set foot in the New World—is the influence which you and I, my friends, are wielding in the world today.

Those of us who are a little older will recall that as we arrived at maturity and took our places as participants in the immediate world about us we quickly learned that we were regarded as a "problem." We spent our early years as adults with the term "Negro problem" dragging at our feet—slowing our steps.

Reprinted from the *Journal of Negro History* 35 (January, 1950) by permission of The Association for the Study of Afro-American Life and History, Inc. (ASALH).

Always we heard discussed the question of what the world's *controlling minority must do about us*. Always—in religion, in education, in employment, there it was—what must be done with the "Negro element?" The pattern of our education, for better or for worse, was worked out *for* us. Someone else decided what we should study, and, outside of the Negro denominations, where we should pray.

We oldsters must take off our hats to ourselves, that through those trying years we did not lose sight of our objectives under the tremendous pressures exerted to induce us to accommodate ourselves to the acceptance of what was clearly illogical and untenable in human relations.

Out of the many fine developments of that period, that one fact stands out sharply —it was a period of pulling ourselves together; of girding our minds and our spirits for an aggressive struggle against the forces of reaction—of timorous people afraid of their future; afraid of their own form of government; afraid of their fellowmen!

We recently went through a revival of the colonization projects and of panicky back-to-Africa proposals, with the Marcus Garvey movement gathering considerable strength among the frustrated of darker hue before it finally collapsed. We had already gone through the separate-as-the-fingers period in which paradoxically the growth of a great educational philosophy paralleled in its initiation and development that of a less-far-sighted social philosophy of appeasement to separatists.

All this represented the thinking of those not yet grown up to the implications of a practicing democracy—to the implications of spiritual and social progress at a time when our country was assuming its place as a world power— was fast moving into position as *the greatest* of world powers!

This represented the days when we were outgrowing our twenties and thirties and forties—and some of us our fifties—when we began in larger numbers to pull to pieces this "Negro problem," this "color problem," to analyze its parts, to determine what manner of phenomenon was dogging our footsteps. We were determined to find out how much of this "problem," if any, was basic difference, and how much of it was suppression and inhibition and fear—and WHOSE!

These were the days when Negro leadership concluded at long last that what the Negro had to deal with, first and foremost, was not so much his own thinking as the stereotyped, nervous thinking of the world's non-colored minority! And with that conclusion the so-called "Negro problem" ceased to drag at our feet.

We took the pieces of that "problem" and spread them out on the conference table of the world. We looked at them dispassionately and objectively and said to the world:

"See here! Here is the difficulty! The difficulty is the hard, democratic way of life that you are unwilling to face; the way of life that is not for the self-satisfied or the indolent, or for the smug, or for the fearful who have faith only in themselves—but the only way that leads to peace among neighbors or among nations."

And there came a period of transition in the world's thinking. The world began to worry about us—about what we "wanted"—which was a sign of progress. And we began to know more surely just what we wanted. It has been only five years since fourteen of us produced, on request, a volume of essays called *What The Negro Wants*, edited by our friend, Rayford W. Logan, and published by the University of North Carolina Press. In 344 pages of comment and analysis, eleven of which were mine, we succeeded in saying that we want precisely what everybody else wants, and find no good reason for being apologetic about it.

We were supposed to represent all shades of thought. What shade I was supposed to represent I do not know. But when we were all through itemizing our "wants" and laid them on the table, the only person remotely apologizing for that list was the publisher, and I doubt if his dissent convinced even himself of the value of further hedging!

How has "the Negro," as the term is used, arrived this close to unity? The answer might well be summarized in the reply of a leader who has retained his poise and objectivity, when asked for his opinion of a fellow-Negro who had thrown his controls to the wind. It was simply a difference of reactions, he replied. We all want the same things. We all intend to get them. We've all been hurt, and the hurt affects us in different ways. That was a sensible, factual answer—a statement to which all citizens of the world must sooner or later face up. It reflects a healthy trend away from denunciation of those who have difficulty in functioning in the midst of racial pressures, and a growing will and desire to find a common denominator on which to base constructive, concerted action.

These hurts are sometimes very useful, and serve us better than we sometimes realize. They have drawn us together. They have drawn friends to us. They have made us organization-minded. They have solidified us and our organizations with the organizations of others, on an intelligently aggressive front.

The movement of the Negro worker from the farms of the South to industry, especially Northern industry, has increased his consciousness of the power of organization. He has been forced to observe the operations of unions—those which have excluded him as well as those which have welcomed him. He has watched his fellow-worker bargaining for himself—on all fronts. He has learned that he, too, has resources of value. He has learned that when he offers his wares as an individual, he is a *peddler*. When he offers them as an organization, he is a *power*.

So, as the eyes of the Negro have opened to his own significance as a power, and the burden of his morale-destroying label as a "problem" has begun to fall away from him, his fellow-Americans, his fellow-citizens of the world, have begun to see the futility of attempting to keep him forever in bondage, in any kind of bondage, however polite the name by which it may be called—parallel culture, separate but equal, or racial integrity. And of the last mentioned it might be said that it is a theory practiced least by those who proclaim it most, with results in hybrid population which preclude argument!

We know that the franchise has not been extended solely from altruistic motives. But in an era of government by pressures, we have constantly improved our techniques in the application of pressures, and so have pushed back, steadily, the areas of unrepresentative government.

We may agree or disagree with any given cause or opinion, but the fact of growing unity of effort remains. Conscientious objectors picket the French Embassy to protest the imprisonment, in France, of another conscientious objector. There is a Negro among them. The steel workers bargain for increased benefits. There are many Negroes among them. The president of a great steel company comes out and talks with these workers, to get their views at first hand. Veterans, teachers, domestic workers, farm workers, university women, men and women of many interests, are united for service to humanity on many fronts. Negroes are a part of organizations representing all of these without racial distinction. And while there will be need for special effort by and with Negroes, to enable them to move fully and freely in the normal life of this country, which is *their* country, so long as any obstructions remain—the concept is rapidly gaining ground that their needs as first-class citizens are indistinguishable from the needs of any other first class citizens, and that the objectives of all are identical.

All racial barriers, as such, may not fall, today or tomorow, but they will not be able to stand long, before the determined advance of citizens of all races, shedding their cumbersome, outgrown racial complexes, in their march toward democratic living.

There have been some very interesting developments in this stretching-out process. One of the most interesting has been the gradual disappearance of the one-spokesman concept. Negroes now listen with great respect, not to just one or two people who can "speak for" them, but to many people who speak with authority, not from pinnacles, but from vantage points gained by mingling, observing and working with the masses.

Consequently, their fellow-citizens who are public servants, from the highest post in the land to the most obscure, also listen with respect, to a growing body of Negro leadership which does not necessarily "think alike," on ways and means, but which holds with remarkable consistency to a common objective.

Trends in world affairs have broadened our vision of the world, and the world's vision of us, and have forced a larger measure of thinking upon the masses.

The terrible lessons of world conflict have educated all of us. The youth from our firesides, for whom we have worked and prayed and sacrificed, have gone to the end of the earth to battle with other youth. *Where* did they go? For what *reason* did they go? Will they have to go again? What influences are abroad in the world that keep the peoples of the world at one another's throats— that have made compulsory military service a normal expectancy for the youth of this generation? What can we do about these influences? What controls can we use?

And then the boys who lived to return to us—what were their observations and reactions to other parts of the world—to other peoples, some of whom we called "friends," some of whom we called "allies," some of whom we called "neutrals," and some of whom we called "enemies"—but all human beings, like ourselves, with special problems, about which, heretofore, we had not known too much, nor had been too much concerned?

It did something to us! It took us out of ourselves! We saw something bigger than we had before envisioned. Our thinking expanded and became less subjective. Our sphere of action broadened. We did not forget that we were Negroes but the fact became less important, to us and to others.

The advent of the Atomic Age flattened out a great deal of race consciousness among all peoples. It eliminated at one sweep, the zones of "safe living"—the places where it was possible for one part of the world placidly to ignore any other part. Ideologies became more important than race. Mankind began regrouping itself around ideologies rather than around color. The mass of Negroes found in the democratic ideal, freedom to work out progress in an imperfect world.

The Negro press immediately recognized the scope of this enlarged interest, and met it by sending sage and seasoned writers to every corner of the globe to report their findings on social, economic and political functioning, in other world areas with heavily mixed populations.

Acceptance of our more cosmopolitan interests and growing economic strength is reflected in the advertising seen in publications slanted to Negro readers, and not infrequently in national publications slanted to all of Main Street. Negro mothers, Negro babies, Negro scientists, Negro skilled workers,

Negro glamour girls, Negro athletes and entertainers greet one from advertisements promoting everything from baby food to automobiles—bidding for the dollars earned and spent by the darker brother.

This concession to our buying power did not just *happen*. It is the result of the skillful, persistent assembling and presentation of authentic data on the Negro by Negro advertising folk, to whom we may well take off our hats.

The concession to Negro buying power has been followed, and we say this advisedly, by concession to Negro thinking, power and influence through organizations in which Negroes have interest. In the academic world, administrators, teachers and taught have found that intellect, like disease, knows no barriers of race. Either it is there or it is not. If it is there, it should be available to all. To make it available to all, educational institutions in increasing numbers are seeking the best brains available in sciences, in the humanities, in the arts, to impart knowledge to those who seek it, regardless of the race of the scholar who possesses it.

In the academic world, the student, young or old—the serious seeker of truth and wisdom with which to live more adequately—is determinedly pushing aside the specious arguments of separation. He is saying that if he is to live successfully in a world of people whose origins are as varied as their complexions, he must know these people. In order to know them, he is seeking them out—seeking to enter schools known as "Negro schools." As many of us know, this is true in very many places even in the Deep South; and, contrary to superficial opinion, those who are applying are not "transplanted Yankees." For the most part they are sons and daughters of the South, girding themselves, understandingly for life in a changing world. At Howard University, in Washington, white students have registered this year from as far south as Houston, Texas, and as far north as Massachusetts—to learn and to learn to live.

Hardly any cause of consequence essays to go before the public, these days, without recognition of the influence of the Negro minority by acquisition of one or more Negro members on its staff to serve as liaison officers in contacts with special organizations.

A professional organization which has pointedly avoided Negroes in its membership, in spite of noteworthy achievements of Negroes in its field, suddenly becomes "Negro conscious" in the midst of a fight on social legislation of which it disapproves and hastily appoints a Negro to its directing body. It was an attempt to replace like color with like interests. And while the action will probably change few minds, its implications are food for thought—we are no longer PEDDLERS!

In the fight for civil rights led by the President of the United States, government has bowed to the inevitable. In some areas, it has bowed graciously; in other areas, grudgingly. But the few outposts that have undertaken to ignore or evade official directives are clinging to another lost cause. "The Army," to quote one leading daily publication, "will continue to manufacture a Negro problem for itself, so long as it employs criteria of race rather than ability, anywhere along the line." And the same holds true for every branch of government and every phase of civilian life.

Without indulging in self-applause, we can very well turn for a brief moment at this point in our march forward and view, with a feeling of so-far-so-good, the gains we have made and held. As mature people we shall waste no time in over-admiration. Long stretches of the road to the full life we shall achieve still lie ahead. But we are traveling with our eyes open and our wits about us, and in traversing the unseen stretches ahead we shall have the benefit of techniques developed and proved in conquering the rough terrain behind.

As the Negro moves out in his newly recognized capacity as a power to be reckoned with, it will be well to remember that not only courage but caution has a place in progress. The caution of which I speak does not mean fearfulness of new ideas, or of putting them into action. It means avoidance of the not-too-good American tendency of those too impatient, too emotion-swayed, or just too lazy-minded to weigh men and measures objectively, to brand, denounce and attack. We shall live more harmoniously if we learn to do without the cliches and shibboleths and catch words which clutter and confuse our thinking.

I would caution that when the opportunity to advance a step presents itself, we should take that step and thank God for it, whether we consider the motive behind it to be dictated by love, by justice, or by expediency, provided only *that there is no booby-trap behind it.*

The caution of which I speak would call for a more general facing of facts calmly and courageously. This great organization with which we are meeting, today, has pioneered, under the leadership of Carter Godwin Woodson, in providing us with many of the facts necessary to progress. My kind of caution would call for acceptance of the responsibility of being informed; for strengthening of moral character; for an increase in formal and informal education at the expense of personal sacrifice, as G. I. benefits wane. It would call for an increase in religion, not to "drown our sorrows," but to inspire our souls; not as an "opiate," but as a balance-wheel—as a recognition that mankind does not know all and will never know all, and does have and can rely upon a spiritual objective.

I firmly believe that the world is on its way toward greater unity, that this country is on its way to a fuller realization of democracy, and that the part of the Negro in both movements is one of increased strength and significance.

The one world toward which we are rapidly moving will not, I think, be a world of one race, or a world of one thought, but a world of mutual understanding, respect and tolerance, based on knowledge of ourselves and knowledge of our neighbors. In such a world as this we are entering, not race, but racial barriers will disappear, because in spite of D.A.R.'s, Gray Ladies, and other groups who avoid their fellowmen, there will be too much work in the world to do for any group to waste time in building futile fences around the fears of economic or intellectual competition, or challenge to their self-assumed controls, which lead to their rigidity and keep them perpetually out of step with progress.

The progress of the world will call for the best that all of us have to give. And in giving it we shall continue to move on in the directions indicated by individual aptitudes and abilities, knowing that the world is gradually recovering from the long sickness of mind—the unbalance—which has heretofore kept its peoples living in little camps of isolation, intolerance and suspicion.

Whether or not possession of the atom bomb by this country or many countries will mean the end of civilization, only God knows. But I feel that we should daily rejoice in the certainty that it has caused many people to regard their neighbors — across the street and across the world—with a more friendly eye, and has marvelously stimulated fresh interest in the application of the Golden Rule.

I see no cause for discouragement, in viewing the years ahead. Democracy in this country is neither dead nor dying. As every mother knows, the pangs of childbirth are keenest just before the child is born. If our hurts are great, now; if our country is torn with controversy over the expansion of social responsibility, over the acceptance of civil rights, it is because a new and more powerful democracy is being born, to serve more greatly the people of all races, of this country, and of the world.

26

Achieving Civil Rights

JOHN HOPE FRANKLIN

JOHN HOPE FRANKLIN HAS WRITTEN AND LECTURED
EXTENSIVELY ON BLACK HISTORY AND RACIAL EQUALITY IN
AMERICA. DR. FRANKLIN HAS BEEN RECOGNIZED AS ONE OF THE
NATION'S LEADING HISTORIANS. HE COFOUNDED THE BLACK
ACADEMY OF ARTS AND SCIENCES.

*In this final section of Franklin's "A Brief History," the
author outlines the development of the civil rights
movement through the 1960s and early 1970s.*

One of the most significant chapters in the recent history of Negro Americans
has been the development of new techniques to achieve old goals. In the 1960s
many people—white and Negro—began to consider the possibility of taking
matters into their own hands by direct action. They had seen violent direct
action at work in the emergence of the white citizens' councils and the revival of
the Ku Klux Klan to fight, with every means at their disposal, the enforcement
of desegregation decisions. It now occurred to some Negroes that they might
accelerate the enjoyment of their rights through nonviolent direct action. In
1956, a year before the passage of the Civil Rights Act, the Negroes of
Montgomery, Alabama, began to boycott the bus lines of the city to protest the
abuse of Negro passengers by white drivers, including Mrs. Rosa Parks, who
had refused to move to the back of the bus. They called for a more satisfactory
seating practice on the buses and the employment of Negro drivers on buses
serving predominantly Negro sections of the city.

As the boycott continued, the white community became outraged. Some
ninety Negroes were indicted under a 1921 anti-union law forbidding conspiracy
to obstruct the operation of a business. Their leader, the Reverend Dr. Martin
Luther King, Jr., was the first to be tried. He was found guilty. Immediately he

Excerpted from Dr. Franklin's chapter, "A Brief History," in *The Black American Reference Book*,
edited by Mabel M. Smythe (Englewood Cliffs, NJ: Prentice-Hall, Inc., 1976) by permission of the
publisher. Copyright ©1976, Prentice-Hall, Inc.

served notice of appeal, while the bus company sought to settle the problem before it became bankrupt. The Montgomery Negroes finally won their battle; and the effective weapon of boycott gained popularity as Negroes of Tallahassee, Atlanta, and Nashville successfully put it to the test.

Soon other organizations were committing themselves to direct, nonviolent action. Within the next few years numerous groups, most of them interracial, became active. Among them were the Congress of Racial Equality (CORE), the Southern Christian Leadership Conference, and the Student Nonviolent Coordinating Committee (SNCC). These were backed up by other groups who gave aid and comfort to those involved in direct action. Among them were the NAACP, the National Urban League, the Southern Regional Council, numerous religious groups, and labor and civic organizations.

On February 1, 1960, four students from the Negro Agricultural and Technical College of Greensboro, North Carolina, entered a variety store, made several purchases, and sat down at the lunch counter and ordered coffee. When they were refused service because they were black, they remained in their seats until the store closed. This was the beginning of the sit-in movement, which spread rapidly through the South and to some places in the North. In the spring and summer of 1960 thousands of young people, white and black, participated in similar peaceful forms of protest against segregation and discrimination. They sat in white libraries, waded into white beaches, and slept in the lobbies of white hotels. Many of them were arrested for trespassing, disorderly conduct, and disobeying officers who ordered them off the premises. A southern journalist labeled the sit-ins "the South's new time bomb," and observed that young Negroes were infused with a new determination to risk violence to acquire some of the rights they believed were due them. When Negro students were criticized for their actions, they placed a full-page advertisement in the white *Atlanta Constitution*, in which they said, "We do not intend to wait placidly for those rights, which are already legally and morally ours, to be meted out to us one at a time." Black students and their white colleagues were on the march to secure their rights. As a result, literally hundreds of lunch counters across the South began to serve Negroes; and other facilities began to open up. Whenever their efforts were not successful, they boycotted white businesses or engaged in "selective purchasing," thus bringing to bear another effective weapon to secure their rights.

In May, 1961, an even more dramatic attack on segregation and discrimination was undertaken by CORE. It sent Freedom Riders through the South to test segregation laws and practices in interstate transportation. In Alabama an interracial team was attacked at Anniston and Birmingham. Although Attorney General Robert Kennedy was obviously somewhat annoyed by the aggressiveness of these unorthodox fighters for civil rights, he ordered the Federal Bureau of Investigation to look into the matter and made it clear that the Freedom Riders would be protected. In the summer of 1961 the jails of Jackson, Mississippi, and other southern communities were virtually filled with Freedom Riders who had been arrested for alleged violation of the law. The federal government kept a sharp eye on these proceedings, sending some 400 United States marshals to Alabama to restore order, and securing an injunction to prohibit any attempt to stop, by force, the Freedom Riders from continuing their test of bus segregation.

At about the same time the Negroes of Albany, Georgia, began to protest their plight by marching through the streets and holding large mass meetings. Hundreds were arrested, and the white officials of the city were adamant in their refusal to discuss the situation with black leaders. In the two years that followed, marching, picketing, and public demonstrations were taken up by Negroes in Atlanta; Danville, Virginia; Cambridge, Maryland; and many other communities. In March, 1963, for example, the Negroes of Leflore County, Mississippi, began to march in order to dramatize a voter registration drive sponsored by the SNCC. In April, 1963, Dr. King inaugurated forty days of marching in Birmingham, Alabama, during which more than 2,500 Negroes were arrested. The Birmingham marches inspired scores of others in the North and South, some of which were attended by violence and rioting. These demonstrations also served the purpose of focusing attention on the Nation of Islam (Black Muslims), who used the marches as a means to point out one of the basic tenets of their position: that the United States would never grant equality to Negroes. Negroes, therefore, should reject any semblance of cooperation with whites and turn their attention to the development of their own culture as well as their own political and economic institutions. While the Nation of Islam was not large in numbers, it gained both popularity and respect, even among many who rejected its program.

In the year of the centennial of the Emancipation Proclamation the first stage of the civil rights revolution reached its peak. The numerous successful demonstrations and marches suggested to the leadership that one massive march on Washington might dramatize to the nation and to the world the importance of solving the problem of the status of the Negro in the United States once and for all. Preparations were made to carry out the march on August 28, 1963. All of the major Negro organizations joined in formulating the plans, and they were joined by scores of other organizations, white and black. A wide-eyed world watched as a quarter of a million blacks and whites converged on Washington from all over the United States, by every conceivable mode of transportation and under every conceivable auspice.

Washington had never seen such a day as this. The businesses in the down-town area closed, not out of respect to the marchers but because of the fear of rioting and looting. Most of the federal employees took the day off, some to participate in the march, others to get as far from the center of things as possible. Before the impressive memorial to Abraham Lincoln the civil rights leaders spoke: Whitney Young, Roy Wilkins, Martin Luther King. From his jail cell in Louisiana, James Farmer, Director of the Congress of Racial Equality, sent a message. Mahalia Jackson sang. Ministers, movie stars, radio commenta-tors, college students, thousands of organizations, and ordinary citizens partici-pated. The President of the United States cordially received the leaders, while other marchers called on their representatives and senators. The nation looked on via television, and the entire world would later see in the newspapers and on the newsreels the most remarkable testimony in behalf of the equality of man-kind ever made in this or any other country. One important figure was absent. Fifty-odd years earlier he had assumed the leadership in the fight for equality. On the eve of the march, W.E.B. DuBois, now a citizen of Ghana, had passed away in Accra.

Two months before the march, President Kennedy had asked Congress to enact laws that would provide a legal guarantee to all citizens of equal access to the services and facilities of hotels, restaurants, places of amusement, and other establishments engaged in interstate commerce; empower the attorney general to start school segregation suits when requested by someone unable to do so; authorize broad federal action to stop discrimination in federal jobs and ac-tivities financed wholly or in part with federal funds; create a Community Relations Service to act as a mediation agency in communities with racial tension; and make it clear "that the Federal Government is not required to furnish any kind of financial assistance to any program or activity in which racial discrimination occurs."

The President's message of June 19, 1963, is not only an historic document, a veritable landmark in the history of the drive for equality. It is also the best available summary of the unfinished business of democracy in 1963. In it, President Kennedy deplored the fact that Negroes did not have equal access to public accommodations and facilities. "No one has been barred on account of his race from fighting or dying for America—there are no 'white' and 'colored' signs on the foxholes and graveyards of battle. Surely, in 1963, one hundred years after emancipation, it should not be necessary for any American citizen to demonstrate in the streets for the opportunity to stop at a hotel, or to eat at a lunch counter in the very department store in which he is shopping, or to enter a motion picture house, on the same terms as any other customer." With regard to segregated schools, he said, "Many Negro children entering segregated grade schools at the time of the Supreme Court decision in 1954 will enter segregated high schools this year, having suffered a loss which can never be regained. Indeed, discrimination in education is one basic cause of the other inequities and hardships inflicted upon our Negro citizens."

Those who marched on Washington in August, 1963, were doing what they could to emphasize the importance of enacting the legislation the president called for. More than that, they were expressing their continuing faith in the efficiency of democratic institutions in righting the wrongs of centuries as well as giving themselves a new lease on life through a process of self-purification. But those who marched were under no illusions and were not blindly optimistic. As soon as they returned to their respective homes, they continued their fight. In New York and Chicago they urged an end to *de facto* segregation in the schools. In Birmingham they called for some tangible indication of good faith on the part of the city administration. In Placquemine Parish, Louisiana, they called for obedience of the law regarding the rights of citizens to register and vote.

When President Kennedy was assassinated on November 22, 1963, many civil rights leaders as well as ordinary citizens thought that the cause of civil rights had suffered a permanent setback; and many were disconsolate. The manner, however, in which the new president, Lyndon B. Johnson, counseled with Negro leaders, the numerous instances during his early days in office in which he pledged himself to fight for equality, and his unequivocal stand in favor of a strong civil rights bill without crippling amendments was a source of considerable optimism. With the Senate majority whip, Hubert H. Humphrey, in charge of the bill and with strong bipartisan support, Congress preceded to enact the strongest civil rights bill that had ever been passed. The very process of enactment was historic, in that a majority of the members of both parties supported the bill, thereby making it possible for the Senate to invoke closure and cut off the bitter-end marathon filibuster conducted by a bloc of southern senators.

It was a great day of rejoicing, therefore, when President Johnson signed the new civil rights bill on July 2,1964, in the presence of congressional and civil rights leaders. The chances for the enforcement of the bill were substantially increased when several prominent southern senators who had fought its passage called for southerners to obey the new law. The appointment of Leroy Collins, former Governor of Florida, as the first director of the Community Relations Service, was widely hailed as an auspicious beginning in the effort to gain acceptance of the law, despite the fact that one prominent southerner called him a "renegade Confederate." As expected, there was vigorous initial opposition to the bill in some quarters, but the prompt declaration by a federal district court that the bill was constitutional and the refusal of Supreme Court Justice Black to suspend its enforcement contributed to the decrease of such resistance. Consequently, Negroes began to eat in restaurants and register in hotels in many parts of the South where hitherto they had not found it possible to secure service.

Perhaps it was the general improvement of the climate of race relations that brought about desegregation steps in the months following the enactment of the civil rights bill of 1964. The summer had witnessed some ugly manifestations of racial unrest as rioting erupted in New York City, Philadelphia, Chicago, and several New Jersey cities. But civil rights leaders were quick to point out that these were not civil rights riots but the angry outbursts of poverty-stricken, jobless people living under intolerable conditions in the city slums. There had also been numerous incidents of violence in the South—including the mysterious murder of three civil rights workers in Mississippi and the brutal slaying in Georgia of a Negro educator returning from reserve-officer training to his home in Washington. But the process of desegregation continued. Segregated public facilities in many parts of the country bowed to the new law, and the pace of school desegregation began to increase noticeably.

The issue of civil rights became an important matter in the presidential campaign of 1964. While the civil rights bill that year had received generous bipartisan support in Congress, the man who became the Republican nominee for the presidency, Senator Barry Goldwater, had voted against the bill on the ground that he regarded certain parts of it as unconstitutional. This gained him strong support in many parts of the South, but it alienated virtually all Negroes—even those who had been lifelong Republicans—from the Republican nominee. If the votes of the so-called white backlash—those opposed to the Negro's vigorous drive for equality—drifted to the Republican party, there were those that President Johnson and his supporters called the frontlash—supporters of civil rights—who joined the Democratic ranks.

The breaking down of racial barriers in hotels and coffee shops did not bring with it the sense of satisfaction and fulfillment that some had expected. Not even the passage of the Civil Rights Act of 1964 or the Voting Rights Act the following year succeeded in inspiring real hope and optimism among Negro Americans. The places that opened their doors to serve them were inordinately slow in modifying their employment policies to provide jobs above the menial category for blacks. The enforcement machinery of the Department of Justice seemed, at times, helpless in the face of the stern opposition of local whites to any change in voting patterns. Indeed, where Negroes gained the vote and even public office, the acceptance of change on the part of whites was often grudging and without grace. Eight years after the passage of the Civil Rights Act, moreover, there was conclusive evidence of racial discrimination as high up as in some of the federal cabinet offices. Small wonder that many black Americans concluded that there was no serious intention on the part of white Americans to commit themselves or the nation to racial equality.

A major source of dissatisfaction and pessimism was the grinding poverty that most blacks experienced in a land of superabundance. Even as employment opportunities opened for some, the unemployment rate among Negroes was still pitifully high. In 1970 unemployment averaged 7 percent among blacks, versus 3.8 percent among whites. In 1968 the average black high-school graduate earned less than the average white with no high-school training. A black with four years of college had a median annual income of $7,744, compared with $8,154 for the average white who had completed only high school.

Poverty was the lot of millions of black sharecroppers who remained in the rural areas as well as those who came to the city. But urban poverty seemed more painful as well as more visible in the rat-infested, dilapidated slum tenement, the vain search for employment, the delinquency of the young, and the temptation toward crime on the part of the elders. The cost of 13.2 billion dollars for public welfare in 1971 was a dramatic reminder of the persistence of poverty in the United States. While far more whites than blacks were on welfare, most discussions of the problem seemed to make the erroneous assumption that only blacks were involved to any considerable extent.

Many racial confrontations of the early 1960s were surprisingly peaceful, although groups like the White Citizens Councils and the Ku Klux Klan frequently instigated a measure of violence. It was a hit-and-run form of violence marked by snipings that tried the patience of even the more conservative elements of the black communities. Many civil rights workers in the South, black and white, were the victims of snipers' bullets. Scores of Negro churches and other meeting places were bombed, sometimes with loss of life. In the later years of the 1960s the conditions of life in the northern and western ghettos slowly pushed blacks to the breaking point of despair. Rioting, accompanied by looting, burning, and loss of life erupted in many places, notably in Los Angeles and Rochester in the summer of 1965 and in Detroit and Newark two years later.

While the Black Muslims were among the first to state categorically their disillusionment with white America, they were soon joined by others. Young blacks who had worked with CORE and SNCC became convinced of the pervasive nature of American racism and wondered if the door of opportunity had not been permanently closed to them. Soon many of them began to challenge the United States and its institutions. It was this mood that led Stokely Carmichael, Chairman of SNCC, to propound in 1966 the doctrine of Black Power. In its most positive sense, Black Power meant the promotion of black self-determination, self-respect, and full participation in all decisions affecting black people. Carmichael insisted that only the full use of Black Power would force whites to deal with blacks on a basis of equality.

Emotions of despair, frustration, and defiance merged to produce a new, fierce breed of black militants no longer willing to compromise in the fight for freedom and equality. Indeed, many were no longer interested in equality in the white man's world. Directing their attention to the masses of blacks, the militants urged their fellows to reevaluate the theory and practice of American law and convention, since these, they insisted, had worked so poorly for them. Theory and practice were white; values in American society were white; and the goals of American democracy were white. Blacks, they argued, should begin to search for their own identity, not among white groups and institutions, but among darker peoples wherever they could find them.

Some black Americans began to focus more attention on African dress and wore their hair "natural." Some followed the lead of Malcolm X and other Black Muslims and adopted African or Arabic names, or used an X in place of their surname to show that they had broken all connections with white America. Some rejected the term *Negro* arguing that it was a relic of slavery, and expressed a strong preference for *Black* (often capitalized) or *Afro-American*. They began to demand control of the institutions in the black community, including the schools; and in some communities, such as the Ocean Hill-Brownsville section of New York City, moves to seize this control led to conflict among blacks as well as with whites. In 1970 some sixteen million blacks belonged to various Christian denominations, but many of them were moving away from a religion of a white Madonna and a white Christ to one more consonant with their pride in race.

The literary manifestations of the new militant mood were wide-ranging, indeed. In the fifties, such prize-winning writers as novelist Ralph Ellison, poet Gwendolyn Brooks, and essayist and novelist James Baldwin had been concerned with the difficulties that black Americans experienced as they confronted American society in general. But if their analyses suggested an urgency they seldom approached desperation. In the sixties, such writers as Eldridge Cleaver, Don Lee, and LeRoi Jones would be more unsparing in their indictment of American society and more far reaching in their suggestions for solutions. The new mood called for the total control of the black man's destiny by black men and went on to propose the complete remaking of American institutions.

As professional writers concentrated on the problems of Negroes in American society, they joined the swelling ranks of those who were calling greater attention to studies of the black man's past and present. Negroes had been systematically excluded from the study of history, they argued. Thus virtually nothing was known of their past contributions, while conventional approaches had rationalized the exclusion of blacks from the enjoyment of citizenship and full equality. Now, as they demanded equality of opportunity in American life, they demanded that schools and colleges introduce courses in black history, black literature, black sociology, and the like. Soon large numbers of educational institutions at every level were responding to the demands of students, parents, and leaders and were establishing programs of black studies of varying degrees of quality and effectiveness.

As Negro Americans made a strong bid to focus on—even to glorify—the history and traditions of darker peoples, many began to reject American values, institutions, and practices. Some saw in government, the police, and the armed services the symbols of their own oppression. As the United States became more deeply involved in the war in Vietnam, blacks began to denounce the conflict as a war against darker peoples and a diversion of national resources that could better be used to wipe out poverty and racial discrimination. Conflicts between white and black soldiers in Southeast Asia and Europe confirmed their view of the armed services as a racist institution. When Cassius Clay, the heavyweight boxing champion, took the Black Muslim name of Muhammad Ali and refused induction into the armed forces in 1967, he was convicted for refusing the draft and was stripped of his title. This embittered many Negro Americans who viewed it as further evidence of racism. In 1971 the United States Supreme Court reversed the draft conviction; but by that time Muhammed Ali had lost millions of dollars because he was unable to defend his title and had suffered untold humiliation. It was not until October, 1974, that Ali enjoyed some vindication upon regaining his title by knocking out George Foreman in Kinshasa, Zaire.

The assassination of Martin Luther King, Jr., on April 4, 1968, not only shocked and saddened many Americans, but it proved once again to most Negroes that some whites would go to any lengths, including murder, to frustrate legitimate black aspirations. Since 1955 King had been the central figure in the struggle of black Americans for equality and dignity. In 1968 he went to Memphis to assist the sanitation workers of that city in their quest for higher wages and better working conditions. As he stood on the balcony of his motel room he was struck down by a rifle shot. The news of King's death sent young blacks into the streets in more than a hundred cities in what one commentator called "a widespread convulsion of disorder." There were several days of rioting, looting, and burning in Washington, Chicago, Baltimore, Kansas City, and many other places. Before it was over some 55,000 troops had been called out and 46 persons had died.

In March, 1968, a month before King's death, the National Advisory Commission on Civil Disorders had observed that "our nation is moving toward two societies, one black, one white—separate and unequal." King's death and its aftermath seemed to confirm that somber observation. The capture of James Earl Ray, an escaped convict, and his confession that he had murdered Dr. King, perhaps could have eased the tension. But Ray's swift trial and sentencing to life imprisonment, with no attempt to determine whether others were involved, merely contributed to the Negro Americans' lack of confidence in the fair, even-handed administration of justice.

The assassination of presidential candidate Robert F. Kennedy in June, 1968, was another severe blow to black America. Both major parties had appeared to be softening their earlier stands on civil rights, but Kennedy had won enormous support in the black community by his hard-hitting attacks on poverty and racism. When the Democrats nominated Hubert Humphrey as their standard-bearer, most blacks supported him, for they had no enthusiasm for Richard Nixon, the Republican candidate; and they were repelled by the raucous segregationist stand of George Wallace.

Negro Americans were generally disappointed with the new Republican administration. President Nixon's efforts to aid the development of "black capitalism" seemed halfhearted. Blacks criticized his welfare program as inadequate. They were disappointed with many of his appointments and were especially appalled by his nomination of Florida's G. Harold Carswell to the Supreme Court; and they were among those who successfully fought the nomination. They were angered by the Nixon administration's move to repeal important provisions of the Voting Rights Act of 1965 and by the President's opposition to busing children to break down school segregation. When he waited for more than a year to comply with the request of the entire Negro membership of the House of Representatives to meet with him, many blacks regarded it as a studied insult to the whole Negro community.

By this time many Negroes were blaming not merely the president or the federal government for existing conditions, but the entire system. Even when they played by the rules of the political game and won, whites refused to abide by the rules. When Richard Hatcher was elected mayor of Gary, Indiana, some all-white sections investigated the possibility of seceding. When Charles Evers became mayor of Fayette, Mississippi, whites began to leave the town. When the leading challenger in the Los Angeles mayoralty race turned out to be a black city council member with an impeccable record of public service, whites rallied to the support of the white incumbent whom they had bitterly criticized, and returned him to office. The system seemed not to work for blacks as it did for whites.

The bitterest indictment of existing racial practices was made by a new group, the Black Panther party, which had been founded on the West Coast by two young men, Huey P. Newton and Bobby Seale. Newton declared that the only culture worth holding on to "is revolutionary culture." In his best-selling *Soul on Ice*, and other writings, Black Panther leader Eldridge Cleaver denounced American racism and the system that produced it. Panthers urged full employment, decent housing, black control of the black community, black studies in the schools and elsewhere, and an end to every form of repression and brutality. In the ghettos the Panthers established centers to provide food and health services for the poor, including hot breakfasts for school children.

Soon the Black Panthers were involved in numerous encounters with the police. In the public mind their possession of arms and their willingness to countenance violence overshadowed everything else. Several leaders, including Newton and Cleaver, were charged with killing policemen. Newton was sent to prison, but in 1970 the conviction was set aside; and Cleaver left the country while out on bond. Meanwhile, public officials seemed determined to deal more harshly with the group, and the director of the Federal Bureau of Investigation, J. Edgar Hoover, pronounced the Panthers to be dangerous and subversive. There were numerous shoot-outs and other bloody encounters. In 1968 a number of off-duty policemen assaulted several Panther party members who had come to a Brooklyn courthouse to observe a trial involving other members. In December, 1969, two party leaders were killed in Chicago in a predawn raid by police who were looking for arms. When it became known that only one shot came from within, it was clear that the raid was less than a shoot-out, and charges against other Panthers present were dropped.

In many parts of the country it appeared that public officials had overextended their fight against the Panthers; consequently, many charges against the latter did not hold up. In May, 1971, several Panthers in New York were cleared of a bomb plot, while in the following month twelve were cleared of charges of murdering a New York policeman. In New Haven murder charges against Bobby Seale and a local Panther leader were dismissed. In Oakland charges of murder against Huey Newton were dropped after two juries were unable to reach a verdict.

Even if more members of the Black Panther party were winning their freedom in the courts, many blacks remained unconvinced that it was possible to secure justice in or out of the courts. In 1970 Angela Davis, a former teacher at the University of California at Los Angeles and an admitted communist, was charged with implication in a courtroom shoot-out in California. Many blacks insisted that Miss Davis was the victim of harrassment for political views and she became something of a heroine before her trial and acquittal in 1972.

George Jackson, the best known of the trio charged with murdering a guard in Soledad prison, was killed in an alleged attempt to escape prison, but the others were later acquitted. Large-scale violence such as occurred at the Attica prison in New York, where almost forty black inmates were killed in 1971, was an indication to many that racism was as rampant in the administration of prisons as in the administration of justice.

It was the deep feeling of disappointment and frustration in the Negro American's quest for equality that sparked the calling of the National Black Political Convention that met in Gary, Indiana, March 10 to 12, 1972. From every part of the country Negro Americans came to Gary to exchange views on the strategy for improving the condition of their fellows. The meeting had the endorsement of the Black Political Caucus, composed of the Negro members of the House of Representatives, the Southern Christian Leadership Conference, and People United to Save Humanity (PUSH), the Southern Christian Leadership Conference's breakaway group, headed by the Reverend Jesse L. Jackson. With LeRoi Jones and Mayor Richard Hatcher assuming leading roles, the group canvassed virtually every facet of economic, social, and political life in the United States. Even when the group had difficulty in reaching agreement regarding the means by which they could best achieve their goals, they manifested a remarkable unity in the manner in which they condemned "rampant racism" in the United States.

The "Political Coming of Age," as *Ebony* magazine described the posture of Negro Americans in 1972, was seen in the determination of the Black Political Convention to ignore party labels in supporting candidates. It could also be seen in the presence of 209 Negro Americans sitting in 37 state legislatures (by April, 1974, the figures were 236 and 41, respectively) and pressing for the enactment of laws designed to improve the condition of blacks. And it could be seen in the action of Shirley Chisholm, the first Negro woman member of Congress, in seeking the Democratic presidential nomination by competing in several state primaries. Finally, it could be seen in the realization of black political leaders that their role could be decisive in the national election, and in their resolution to use that role as a lever to bring about significant improvement in the status of their people.

After the 1974 elections, black members sat in 45 state legislatures and their number in Congress had risen to sixteen in the House, four of them women; the lone black senator had retained his seat. The national television exposure in 1974 of Representative Barbara Jordan of Texas, John Conyers of Michigan, and Charles Rangel of New York—all Democrats—in the House Judiciary Subcommittee hearings on Watergate confirmed the new image of black political figures as active participants on issues unrelated to race.

In spite of the claims to improvements made since World War II, racial inequities in American life remained persistent and flagrant. The period of affluence, during which minority gains appeared possible without apparent cost to the white community, disappeared into accelerating inflation and a deepening recession in the midseventies; and unemployment, as in earlier periods, was much higher among blacks than among whites; and recent efforts to increase minority employment in industry, on university faculties, and in executive recruitment programs, were increasingly being undone by seniority rules and reduction of force. Antiblack violence seemed not to subside, and antiwhite violence among blacks seemed to be on the increase. For any group at any level to resolve the conflicts that had such a long history and so much tragedy appeared extremely difficult. Relations between the races continued to be the most critical domestic problem of the twentieth century. Black people hoped for a better future, but in view of the disappointments of the past they looked with apprehension toward that future.

27

The Last Days

INEZ HAYNES IRWIN

INEZ HAYNES IRWIN HAS WRITTEN EXTENSIVELY ON ALICE PAUL,
THE FOUNDER OF THE NATIONAL WOMAN'S PARTY, AND ON THE
WOMEN'S MOVEMENT. SHE RECEIVED THE O. HENRY PRIZE IN
1924.

In 1917 occurred the great leap forward in the activity of the Woman's Party; in swift succession came the picketing; the burning of the President's words; the Watchfires of Freedom. And Headquarters from 1917 on—as can be easily imagined—was a feverishly busy place. From the instant the picketing started, it grew electric with action. As for the work involved in making up the constant succession of picket lines —

It was not easy at an instant's notice to find women who had the time to picket. But always there were some women willing to picket *part* of the time and some willing to picket *all* of the time. Mary Gertrude Fendall was in charge of this work. That her office was no sinecure is evident from the fact that on one occasion alone—that memorable demonstration of March 4, 1917—she provided a line of nearly a thousand. Of course, too, as fast as the women went to jail, other women had to be found to fill their places. In those days Miss Fendall lived at the telephone and between telephone calls, she wrote letters which invited sympathizers to come from distant States to join the banner-bearing forces. Those women who could always be depended on for picketing were, in the main, Party sympathizers living in Washington; Party workers permanently established at Headquarters; organizers come back suddenly from their regular work. But volunteers came too —volunteers from the District of Columbia and from all parts of the United States. In the winter, as has been before stated, picketing was a cold business. The women found that they had to wear a surprising amount of clothes—sweaters and coats, great-coats, mufflers, arctics and big woolly gloves. Many of the pickets left these extra things at

Reprinted from *The Story of Alice Paul: And the National Woman's Party*, Chapter XVII, by Inez Haynes Irwin (Fairfax, VA: Denlingers Publishers Ltd., 1964) by permission of the publisher.

Headquarters and the scramble to disengage rights and lefts of the gloves and arctics was one of the amusing details of the operation of the picket line. Banners took up space too; but they added their cheering color to the picture.

When the arrests began, the atmosphere grew more tense and even more busy. But just as—when trouble came—a golden flood poured into the Woman's Party treasury, so volunteer pickets came in a steadily lengthening line. Anne Martin had said to the Judge who sentenced her: "So long as you send women to jail for asking for freedom, just so long will there be women willing to go to jail for such a cause." This proved to be true. Volunteers for this gruelling experience continued to appear from all over the country. Mrs. Grey of Colorado, sending her twenty-two year old daughter, Nathalie, into the battle, said:

> I have no son to fight for democracy abroad, and so I send my daughter to fight for democracy at home.

It interested many of the Woman's Party members to study the first reactions of the police to the strange situation the picketing brought about. Most of the policemen did not enjoy maltreating the girls. Some of them were stupid and a few of them were brutal, but many of them were kind. They always deferred to Lucy Burns with an air of profound respect—Miss Lucy, they called her. But a curious social element entered into the situation. Large numbers of the women were well known Washingtonians. The police were accustomed to seeing them going about the city in the full aura of respected citizenship. It was very difficult often, to know—in arresting them—what social tone to adopt.

Mrs. Gilson Gardner tells an amusing story of her first arrest. In the midst of her picketing, an officer suddenly stepped up to her. He said politely: "It is a very beautiful day." She concurred. They chatted. He was in the meantime looking this way and that up the Avenue. Suddenly, still very politely, he said: "I think the patrol will be along presently." Not until then did it dawn on Mrs. Gardner that she was arrested.

Later, when the Watchfires were going, Mrs. Gardner was again arrested while she was putting wood on the flames. There was a log in her arms: "Just a minute, officer," she said, in her gentle, compelling voice, and the officer actually waited while she crossed the pavement and put the remaining log on the fire. Later, when Mrs. Gardner's name was called in the court, she decided that she preferred to stand, rather than sit in the chair designated for the accused. The policeman started to force her down. Again she said, in the gentle, compelling tone: "Please do not touch me, officer!" and he kept his hands off her from that time forth.

Of course, the unthinking made the usual accusation that these women were doing all this for notoriety. That was a ridiculous statement, whose disproof was easy. The character and quality of the women themselves were its best denial. The women who composed the Woman's Party were of all kinds and descriptions; they emerged from all ranks and classes; they came from all over the United States. The Party did not belong exclusively to women of great wealth and social position, although there were many such in its list of membership; and some of these belonged to families whose fortunes were internationally famous. It did not belong exclusively to working women, although there were thousands of them in its ranks; and these represented almost every wage-earning task at which women toil. It did not belong exclusively to women of the arts or the professions; although scores of women, many nationally famous and some internationally famous, lent their gifts to the furtherance of the work. It did not belong exclusively to the women of the home, although scores of wives left homes, filled with the beauty which many generations of cultivation had accumulated—left these homes and left children; and although equal numbers left homes of a contrasting simplicity and humbleness—left these homes and left children to go to jail in the interests of the movement. It may be said, perhaps, that the rank and file were characterized by an influential solidity, that they were women, universally respected in their communities, necessary to it. It was an all-woman movement. Indeed, often women who on every other possible opinion were as far apart as the two poles, worked together for the furtherance of the Federal Amendment. On one occasion, for instance, on the picket line, two women who could not possibly have found a single intellectual congeniality except the enfranchisement of women stood side by side. One was nationally and internationally famous as a conservative of great fortune. The other was nationally and internationally famous as a radical. In other words, one stood at the extreme right of conservatism and the other at the extreme left of radicalism. It was as though, among an archipelago of differing intellectual interests and social convictions, the party members had found one little island on which they could stand in an absolute unanimity; stand ready to fight—to the death, if it were necessary—for that conviction.

Some of the stories which they tell at Headquarters to illustrate the Pan-woman quality of the Party are touchingly beautiful. There is the case, for instance, of a woman government clerk, self-supporting, a widow, and the mother of a little girl. Every day for weeks, she had passed that line of pickets standing silently at the White House gates. She heard the insults that were tossed to the women. She saw the brutalities which were inflicted on them. She witnessed arrests. Something rose within fluttered...tore at her....One day when Alice Paul was picketing, this young woman, suit-case in hand, appeared before her. She said "I am all ready to picket if you need me. I have made all the necessary arrangements in case I am arrested. Where shall I go to join your forces so that I might picket today?" She was arrested that afternoon and sent to prison.

Two other government clerks, who appeared on the picket line, were arrested and jailed. They appealed to the government authorities for a month's leave of absence on the score of their imprisonment. All these three women, of course, ran the risk of losing their positions. But in their case the instinct to serve their generation was stronger than the instinct to conserve any material safety. It is pleasant to record that they were not compelled to make this sacrifice. Others, however, suffered. A school teacher in the Woman's Party, for instance, lost her position because of her picketing.

If the foregoing is not denial enough of the charge, common when the picketing began, that these women were notoriety-seeking fanatics, perhaps nothing will bring conviction. It scarcely seems however that the most obstinate antagonist of the Woman's Party would like to believe that delicately reared women could enjoy, even for the sake of notoriety—aside from the psychological effect of spiders and cockroaches everywhere, worms in their food, vermin in their beds, rats in their cells—the brutalities to which they were submitted. Yet many women who had endured this once, came back to endure it again and again.

One of the strong points of the Woman's Party was its fairness. In reference to the President, for instance, Maud Younger used to say that the attitude of the Woman's Party to him was like that of a girl who wants a college education. She teases her father for it without cessation, but she goes on loving him just the same. Another strong point of the Woman's Party was its sense of humor on itself. They tell with great delight the amusing events of this period—of the grinning street gamin who stood and read aloud one of the banners, *How long must women wait for liberty?* and then yelled: "T'ree months yous'll be waitin'—in Occoquan."—of a reporter who, coming into Headquarters in search of an interview, found a child sliding down the bannisters. Before he could speak, the child announced in a tone of proud triumph: "My mother's going to prison."

A story they particularly like is of that young couple who, having had no bridal trip at the time of their marriage, came to Washington for a belated honeymoon. They visited Headquarters together. The bride became so interested in the picketing that she went out with one of the picket-lines and was arrested. She spent her belated honeymoon in jail, and the groom spent his belated honeymoon indignantly lobbying the Congressmen of his own district.

Later, when they were lighting the Watchfires of Freedom on the White House pavement, the activity at Headquarters was increased one hundred-fold.

The pickets themselves refer to that period as the most "messey and mussy" in their history. Everything and everybody smelled of kerosene. All the time, there was one room in which logs were kept soaking in the pervasive fluid. When they first started the Watchfires they carried the urn and the oil-soaked logs openly, to the appointed spot on the pavement in front of the White House. Later, when the arrests began and the fires had to be built so swiftly that they had to abandon the urn, they carried these logs under coats or capes. The White House pavement was always littered with charred wood even when the Watchfires were not going. Once the fires were started it was almost impossible to put them out. Kerosene-soaked wood is a very obstinate substance. Water had no effect on it. Chemicals alone extinguished it. Amazed crowds used to stand watching these magic flames. Often when the policemen tried to stamp the fires out, they succeeded only in scattering them.

It was an extraordinary effect, too, when the policemen were busy putting out one fire, to see others start up, in *this* corner of the Park, in *that* corner, in the great bronze urn, near the center.

Building a fire in that bronze urn was as difficult a matter as it seems. A Woman's Party member, balancing out from a stairway window at the top of the house at Headquarters, had noted how boldly the urn stood out from the rest of the Park decoration...

At three o'clock one morning, Julia Emory and Hazel Hunkins, two of the youngest and tiniest pickets, bore over to the Park from Headquarters several baskets of wood which they concealed in the shadows under the trees. The next problem was to get a ladder there without being seen. They accomplished this in some way, dragging it over the ground, slow foot after slow foot, and placed it against the urn. At intervals the policeman on the beat, who was making the entire round—or square—of the Park, passed. While one girl mounted the rudder and filled the urn with oil-soaked paper, oil-soaked wood, and liberal libations of oil, the other remained on guard. When the guard gave the word that the policeman was near, the two girls threw themselves face downward on the frozen grass. It is a very large urn and by this stealthy process it took hours to fill it. It was two days before they started the fire. Anybody might have seen the logs protruding from the top of the urn during those two days, but nobody did.

The day on which the urn projected itself into the history of the Woman's Party, the Watchfires were burning for the first time on the White House pavements. The street and the Park were filled with people. A member of the Woman's Party, passing the urn, furtively threw into it a lighted asbestos coil.

The urn instantly belched flames which threatened to lick the sky. The police arrested every Woman's Party member in sight. All the way down the street as the patrol carried them away, Hazel Hunkins and Julia Emory saw the flames flaring higher and higher.

"How did they do that?" one man was heard to say. "I've been here the whole afternoon and I didn't see them light it."

Twice afterwards fires were started in the urn. For that matter, fires were started there after the police had set a watch on it.

Hazel Hunkins, young, small, slender, took the urn under her special patronage. One of the pictures the Woman's Party likes to draw is the time Hazel was arrested there. She had climbed up onto the pedestal and was throwing logs into the pool of oil when two huge policemen descended upon her. The first seized one foot and the second seized the other; and they both pulled hard. Of course in these circumstances, it was impossible for her to move. But she is an athlete and she clung tight to the urn edge. Still the policemen pulled. Finally she said gently, "If you will let go of my feet, I will come down myself."

Later asbestos coils were introduced into the campaign. This—from the police point of view—was more annoying than the kerosene-soaked logs; for they were compact to carry, easy to handle, difficult to put out, and they lasted a long, long time.

Another picture the Woman's Party likes to draw is of Mildred Morris starting asbestos coils. With her nimbus of flaming hair, Miss Morris seemed a flame herself. She was here, there, everywhere. The police could no more catch up with her than they could with a squirrel. One night, with the assistance of two others, she—unbelievably—fastened some asbestos coils among the White House trees; but to her everlasting regret the guards found them before the illumination could begin.

The stories they tell about arrests at this time are endless. Little Julia Emory, who was arrested thirty-four times, is a repository of lore on this subject.

They were a great trial to the police—the arrests of these later months. While under detention, the pickets used to organize impromptu entertainments. This was during the period, when at their trials, the Suffragists would answer no questions and the court authorities were put to it to establish their identities. They related with great glee how in his efforts to prove Annie Arniel's identity, a policeman described one of their concerts in court.

> And then, your Honor, that one there said, "We'll now have comb solo from a distinguished combist, who has played before all the crowned heads of Europe, Annie Arniel," and then, your Honor, the defendant got up and played a tune on a comb.

When, for instance, Suffragists refused bail, the police did not like to hold them overnight because it was such an expense to the District of Columbia to feed them. Julia Emory describes one evening when a roomful of them, arrested, and having refused to put up bail, were waiting the will of the powers. During this wait, which lasted several hours, they entertained themselves by singing.

Once a policeman came in: "Will you pay your bail if we put it at twenty-five dollars?" "No," answered the pickets promptly. He went out, but later he returned. "Will you pay your bail if we put it at five dollars?" "No." "Then march out."

But those light moments were only foam thrown up from serious and sometimes desperate times. When a crowd of ex-pickets gather together and indulge in reminiscences, extraordinary revelations occur. Looking at their faces and estimating their youth, one wonders at a world which permitted one per cent of these things to happen.

And as for their experience with the mobs...Not the least of the psychological factors in the situation was the slow growth of the crowds; the circle of little boys who gathered about them first, spitting at them, calling them names, making personal comments; then the gathering gangs of young hoodlums who encouraged the boys to further insults; then more and more crowds; more and more insults; the final struggle.

Often of course the pickets stood against the White House fence, an enormous mob packed in front of them, with the knowledge that police protection—according to the orders of the day—might be given them or might not....Sometimes that crowd would edge nearer and nearer until there was but a foot of smothering, terror-fraught space between them and the pickets. Literally those women felt they had their backs to the wall. Occasionally they had to mount the stone coping! Always too they feared that any sudden movement within the packed, slowly approaching hostile crowd might foam into violence. Occasionally, when the police followed orders to protect the pickets, violent things happened to people in the crowd. Catherine Flanagan saw a plain-clothes man hit six sailors over the head in succession with a billy. They went down like nine pins. Yet when after hours of a seemingly impressive waiting the actual struggle came—something—some spiritual courage bigger than themselves— impelled them to hold on to their banner poles to the last gasp. They were big in circumference—those banner poles—but the girls clutched them so tightly that often it took three policemen to wrench them away. Catherine Flanagan had deep gashes on the inside of her palms where her own nails had penetrated her flesh and great wounds on the outside of her hands where the policemen had dug their nails into them. Virginia Arnold's hands and arms were torn as though in a struggle with some wild beast.

Yet, I repeat, Headquarters saw its lighter moments even in those most troubled times. And during those most troubled times, that gay spirit of youth managed to maintain itself. The onlookers marveled at it. But it was only because it was a spiritual quality—youth of the soul, in addition to the youth of the body—that it could endure. During the course of the eight years of its history, the members of the Woman's Party had been subjected to disillusion after disillusion. The older ones among them bore this succession of shocks with that philosophy which a long experience in public affairs engenders. But the younger ones—believing at first, as youth always believes, in the eternal verities, and in their eternal prevalence —witnessed faith-shaking sights and underwent even more faith-shaking experiences.

In their contact with public men, they saw such a man as Borah for instance—perhaps the chief of the Knights of the Double Cross—give the Woman's Party what virtually amounted to his pledged word to support the Amendment and then coolly repudiate it. They saw Moses of New Hampshire play a quibbling trick on them which involved them in weeks of the hardest kind of work, only calmly to ignore his own pledge at the end. They contended with such differing personalities as the cold, cultured mind, immutably set in the conventions of a past generation, of Henry Cabot Lodge; the unfairness, or fatuity, or brutality of such men as Penrose of Pennsylvania, Thomas of Colorado, Wadsworth of New York, Reed of Missouri, Brandegee of Connecticut, Hoke Smith of Georgia.

When the picketing began, they saw outside forces get their Headquarters from them; saw them influence scores of property owners sometimes after an advance rent had been paid, not to let houses to them; saw them try to influence the people who gave money, to withhold such financial support; saw them try to influence the newspapers to be less impartial in their descriptions of Woman's Party activities. As the picketing went on and the burning of the President's words and the Watchfires succeeded it—while they were exercising their inalienable right of peaceful protest — they knew the experience of being harried by mobs at the very door of the President of the United States; harried while the President passed in his carriage through their midst; later to be harried in collaboration by both mobs and police. Under arrest and in prison, they underwent experiences which no one of them would have believed possible of the greatest republic in the world. They were held incommunicado; they could see neither counsel nor Party members. They were submitted to incredible brutalities.

And yet, I have said that spirit of youth prevailed. It prevailed because they were speaking for their generation. They developed a sense of devotion to their ideal of freedom which would have stopped short of no personal sacrifice, not death itself. They developed a sense of comradeship for each other which was half love, half admiration and all reverence. In summing up a fellow worker, they speak first of her "spirit," and her "spirit" is always *beautiful*, or *noble*, or *glorious*, or some such youth-loved word.

Once, when one party of pickets, about to leave Occoquan, was in the dining-room, a fresh group, just sentenced, were brought into luncheon and placed at another table. Conversation was not permitted. Not a word was spoken, but with one accord the released pickets raised their water-glasses high, then lowered them and drank to their comrades.

Yes, that was their strength—spirit of youth. Lavinia Dock said, "The young are at the gates." The young stormed those gates and finally forced them open. They entered. And leaving behind all sinister remembrance of the battle, they turned their faces towards the morning.

28

Mexican-American Organizations

HENRY SANTIESTEVAN

HENRY SANTIESTEVAN, AUTHOR, LECTURER, RESEARCHER, AND
CIVIL RIGHTS ACTIVIST, HEADED THE NATIONAL COUNCIL OF LA
RAZA. HE IS CURRENTLY OWNER AND DIRECTOR OF SANTIESTEVAN
ASSOCIATES.

Organizations are created in order to bring about some form of interaction with their environment, usually with the objective of somehow improving it. Generally, the environments with which Mexican-American, or Chicano, organizations have attempted to interact have been harsh. They have not been conducive to the development and growth of Chicano-organized institutions.

Mexican-American organizations usually have been faced with an "outside" environment of a surrounding, dominant society that was inimical or indifferent to them, and an "inside" environment of a barrio suffering from meager resources and preoccupied with sheer survival.

The repression imposed upon the barrio and its inhabitants by the dominant society for some 125 years has produced internalized pressures and tensions in communities and individuals that have made planned, sustained and coordinated activities, essential to the life and growth of an organization, extremely difficult.

Organized retaliation, ranging from the guerrilla raids of small bands to the military movement of substantial armies, was an early Mexican-American response toward hostile and threatening environments.

Excerpted from Mr. Santiestevan's chapter, "A Perspective on Mexican-American Organizations," in *Mexican Americans Tomorrow*, edited by Gus Tyler (Albuquerque, NM: University of New Mexico Press, 1975) by permission of the publisher.

About the turn of the 20th century, Mexican-Americans, still seeking to find some measure of economic and social release from the harsh pressures of a dominant society, turned to the formation of mutual aid organizations. The Alianza Hispano Americana founded in Arizona in 1894 was an excellent example of a mutualist society. It is still in existence and is one of the oldest. Mutualist societies such as the Alianza attracted members by providing small sickness and death benefits. The mutualist organizations were characteristic of an era of adaptation and accommodation which extended roughly from the early 1900s until about the 1930s. Large numbers of Mexican immigrants coming into the United States in the 1910s and 1920s brought about an increased impetus in the development of societies with mutualistic aims. These groups tended to be oriented toward Mexican consulates and emphasized Mexican culture or nationalism. They served as meeting places where members could get together, share experiences, and help each other cope with the American way of life. Among these groups were La Sociedad Mutualista Mexicana, La Sociedad Ignacio Zaragoza, La Camara de Comercial Mexicana, and La Sociedad Cervantes.

In 1921 one of the most important of these organizations, La Comision Honorifica Mexicana, was founded in Los Angeles by Eduardo Ruiz, the Mexican consul. The original purpose of La Comision was to assist immigrant Mexican nationals until consular aid could be attained. However, it later developed much broader goals and was accepted as a community spokesman, especially in cities and towns with a fairly large and recent middle-class Mexican immigration. Subsequent to the formation of La Comision Honorifica Mexicana in Los Angeles, hundreds of similar chapters were formed throughout the Southwest.

It was no mere coincidence that the mutualist societies began to appear at the same time that a small Mexican-American middle class emerged which was attempting to come to some form of political accommodation with the larger society. These societies did not press for full political participation nor include demands for equality, either between Mexican-Americans themselves, or in terms of the dominant majority.

> Thus, only internal citizens of the United States of Mexican or Spanish extraction, either native or naturalized, were eligible to join. This exclusion by citizenship was meant—and used—as an exclusionary mechanism. The implication was that Mexican-Americans were more trustworthy to Anglos than Mexican nationals and also more deserving of the benefits of American life.[1]

For example, the "exclusion by citizenship" was a policy of the Orden Hijos de America (Order of the Sons of America), founded in San Antonio in 1921. It is interesting to note that the Comision Honorifica Mexicana and the Orden Hijos de America were both formed in 1921 and that the former emphasized its relationship with Mexican culture and nationalism, while the latter placed emphasis on its relationship with America, that is the United States, as evidenced by their names.

The founding members of the Order of the Sons of America came almost entirely from the newly emerging middle class. The social and economic positions of these founding members were precarious, and their policy of adaptation was undoubtedly a reflection of the painful vulnerability of Mexican-Americans during the 1920s. It was a valid decision by the Order of the Sons of America that, in order to survive, it must be as noncontroversial as possible and openly express declarations of loyalty to the United States of America. The policies of accommodation and adaptation were thus in their own way a response to the social and economic pressures of a surrounding and generally repressive society.

A large number of the members were returning veterans who had seen military service during World War I, an experience that had extended their education and experience outside accustomed barrio environments. They returned with strong motivations to educate their fellow Mexican-Americans about their political rights.

> The basic objectives of this organization were to enable Mexican-Americans to achieve acculturation and integration, principally through political action. Ultimately, the Order sought to end prejudice against Mexican-Americans, to achieve equality before the law, to acquire political representation at all levels and to obtain greater educational opportunities, restricting membership to United States citizens of Mexican or Hispanic background. It strongly emphasized that its members learn English and work toward gaining citizenship.[2]

Thus, the Order of the Sons of America and organizations similar to it laid the groundwork for many of the objectives of the Chicano organizations today.

The Order of the Sons of America also was to be a forerunner of one of the most enduring of the Mexican-American organizations—the League of United Latin American Citizens (LULAC)—which still exists today. LULAC was born as a result of an exercise of statesmanlike leadership that brought about the unification of several Mexican-American organizations faced with fragmentation and dissolution.

The Order of the Sons of America had developed internal conflicts which resulted in the San Antonio councils independently reorganizing as the Knights of America. This separation led several Mexican-American leaders, among them Benjamin Garza, a leading figure in the Corpus Christi council of the Order of the Sons of America, to call a meeting. As a result, in August, 1927, a conference was held in Harlingen, Texas, at which time a decision to reorganize was reached. A year and a half later, on February 17, 1929, a unification convention was held in Corpus Christi, Texas, by representatives of the Order of the Sons of America, the League of Latin American Citizens, and the Knights of America. At that convention the League of United Latin American Citizens was born.

Within a few months, LULAC had adopted a constitution stressing the achievement of economic, social, and political rights for all Mexican-Americans as its major goal.

> In its objectives, LULAC sought to end discrimination and mistreatment of Mexican-Americans; to achieve equality in government, law, business and education; to promote education in order to produce more doctors, lawyers, engineers and other professional people of Mexican descent; to develop pride in Mexican ancestry; to promote the learning of English by Mexicans as a means of achieving a greater degree of equality; and to encourage the effective exercise of the United States citizenship by active participation in politics.[3]

The participation in politics as defined by LULAC at that time did not call for an aggressive entry into the political arena, nor for any kind of Mexican-American political participation based on a separate ethnic identity, but emphasized education for "good citizenship."

Adaptation and accommodation was the style in the 1920s and 1930s and LULAC conformed to it in that period. At the time LULAC was organized, a debate was going on in Congress and in the press concerning the "rising tide" of Mexican immigration. In 1929 the Great Depression began and brought the emerging, small Mexican-American middle class to a point of extreme vulnerability.

> Thus, in 1929, to protect themselves from social and economic sanctions, the willingness of Mexican-Americans to assert even minimal political demands was tempered at all times and in all expressions by a desire to reaffirm citizenship and loyalty to the United States. It is not surprising that there was at this time no pressure for Mexican civil rights, particularly if it might have involved any kind of open demonstrations.[4]

Among the expressed aims of LULAC was "to develop within the members of our race the best, purest and most perfect type of a true and loyal citizen of the United States of America." Article I of LULAC's bylaws stated, "we shall oppose any radical and violent demonstration which may tend to create conflicts and disturb the peace and tranquility of our country." Although the development of pride in Mexican ancestry was a primary aim of LULAC and certainly individual members were proud of their ethnic identity, there was no demand upon the dominant society for any form of cultural pluralism.

Such emphasis on conformity to the standards of Anglo society, particularly Texas Anglo society, must be judged in the context of the political milieu of the United States and Texas in the 1920s and 1930s. Both Mexican-Americans and blacks were kept in "their place" by a repressive society with methods that included lynchings. The paternalistic influence of the Anglo *patron* was strong, even carrying with it, at least in the eyes of the patron, the right to dictate to Mexican Americans which organizations they should or should not join. An example is an excerpt from a letter by such an Anglo patron in which he scolded his "Mexican Texas friends" for even forming such a group as LULAC.

> I have been and still consider myself as your Leader or Superior Chief....
> I have always sheltered in my soul the most pure tenderness for the Mexican Texas race and have watched over your interests to the best of my ability and knowledge....Therefore, I disapprove the political activity of groups which have no other object than to organize Mexican Texas voters into political groups for guidance from other leaders.[5]

The "most pure tenderness" of the letter-writing Texas patron was an ironic expression of the most pure hypocrisy. It was written by a member of a dominant establishment that did not hesitate to use any means—from paternalism to force—to maintain the Mexican-American in a position of dependence.

LULAC was to survive—and even gain influence—by following such policies of adaptation and accommodation through the Depression and World War II years.

The years following World War II were to carry LULAC and some new, emerging Mexican-American organizations into increasingly aggressive demands for social and political equality. The development of these organizations in the two decades following World War II occurred in a period of profound social change for the Mexican-American population.

World War II brought hundreds of thousands of young Mexican-American males into the armed services, which took them out of the confining experiences of their home areas, brought them into contact with millions of other young Americans, and carried them literally around the world. Mexican-American young men in the armed services during World War II found themselves in shoulder-to-shoulder contact with millions of other Americans and facing the same dangers, challenges, and demands. They found that not only could they keep up with Americans from all parts of the United States, but could often excel.

The second factor deeply influencing the development of Mexican-American organizations following World War II was the urbanization of the Mexican-American population. The Mexican-American joined in the sweeping historic movement of the American people from the rural areas to the cities, and they joined into it for the same reasons: in search of jobs and economic security. By the end of 1950, some 80 to 85 percent of the Mexican-Americans were living in urban areas.

Still a third factor important in the development of organizations by Mexican Americans following World War II was the fact that many of them were now the third, fourth, and even fifth and sixth generations born in the United States. Mexican-Americans now had some one hundred years of historical experience as an emerging and identifiable minority in the United States.

A fourth factor influencing Mexican-American organizations in the 1940s and 1950s was the extension of the Mexican-American population throughout most of the United States. Migratory labor, railroads, and a search for jobs in the industrial centers of the Midwest, particularly in the steel and auto industries, had carried the Mexican-American far beyond his southwestern home. They had become the second largest minority in the nation.

The stage was set for the emergence of the organizations which would turn the policies of accommodation into programs of action to break through ancient patterns of prejudice and discrimination. The chief method was aggressive and direct participation in political action.

It was in this period that the California-born Community Service Organization (CSO) became an important and meaningful organization. CSO utilized new techniques of larger scale grassroots community organization and put emphasis on appealing to active and increased participation by as many elements of the community as possible. CSO moved to broaden the base of the Mexican-American organization beyond the relatively few and successful middle-class members, as was typical of former organizations. CSO activity recruited blue-collar workers and lower income members, including new arrivals from Mexico. It also admitted some non-Mexican-American members, although these were few.

CSO's intent was to cope with concrete and immediate political, social, and economic problems. An assumption of CSO was that American institutions would be responsive to the needs of the Mexican-American population and changes could be brought about by broad community organization and action. Thus, a prime objective of CSO was to get large numbers of Mexican-Americans to register and vote.

The organization put on large-scale community registration drives, some of which, significantly and probably permanently, increased the number of Mexican-American voters. In Los Angeles, CSO registration attempts in its early organizational phase had the election of a Mexican-American city councilman as its immediate objective. CSO registered some fifteen thousand new Mexican-American voters in the Los Angeles area and its efforts to elect its candidate to the city council were successful. It demonstrated that a Mexican-American organization could successfully organize politically and elect candidates. CSO thus pioneered extensive community and political organization and action in the Mexican-American communities.

Two other political groups founded in the late 1950s developed similar patterns of political action. The Mexican American Political Association (MAPA) founded in California in 1958, and Political Association of Spanish Speaking Organizations (PASSO) organized in Texas, were formed to negotiate with, influence, and/or pressure the political system at the party level. Primary objectives of both MAPA and PASSO were to register Mexican-Americans and get them to vote and to elect candidates to political office.

In the early 1960s, PASSO scored a significant and precedent-shattering victory by electing the mayor and city councilman in Crystal City, Texas, successfully deposing a longstanding Anglo political structure. The Crystal City victory foreshadowed what Mexican-Americans could accomplish politically in communities where they had a substantial population.

Another important Mexican-American organization to emerge after World War II was the American GI Forum. The GI Forum was formed out of protest when a funeral home in Three Rivers, Texas, refused to bury a Mexican-American war veteran in 1948. Formation of the GI Forum was the active response of Mexican-American veterans, notifying the nation which they had served loyally and heroically in World War II that they would not tolerate the indignities of prejudice and discrimination.

The GI Forum quickly began to accent political action and organized intensive "get out the vote" and "pay your poll tax" drives in Texas in the 1950s. Since the repeal of the Texas poll tax, it has continued vigorous voter registration drives and civil rights activities. The GI Forum attempts to be active at various levels of the American political system. Today, it is an important Mexican-American organization with chapters throughout the Southwest and in other parts of the United States.

Thus, the Mexican-American organizations which emerged in the post-World War II period introduced at least three new major factors in their policies and programs:

1. Mass community organization with an across-the-board appeal to all elements of the Mexican-American communities.

2. Direct involvement with the political system.

3. Cooperation with supportive Anglo-American organizations and individuals in the "outside" environment to create supportive alliances for their programs.

The policies of accommodation and adaptation utilized for survival in the midst of a hostile environment by Mexican-American organizations during the 1920s and 30s were dramatically altered by the emerging post-World War II organizations into aggressive demands for civil liberties and political and economic rights.

Instead of accommodating to Anglo-American attitudes and institutions, these post-World War II organizations demanded that those institutions respond to their needs. Mexican-American organizations were thus well on their way to insisting that the American community as a whole accept them and their communities as equals within the American system.

The Chicano Movement: The Second Century Begins

The Chicano movement which erupted in the mid-1960s was a breakthrough of forces that had been building for more than a century. It opened the second century of the Mexican-Americans' persistent, active search for equality and social justice as a major segment of the population of the United States.

It was as if the steady flowing of many streams over long years created a churning river that broke out and over the old banks into new open areas.

The pilgrimage of the farmworkers from Delano to Sacramento in the spring of 1966, which began as a small stream and flowed as a growing river of human concern into the nation's awareness, serves well as the symbol of the beginning of the Chicano movement. The pilgrimage became symbolic of the long and tortured struggle La Raza has had to wage with all its tribulations, tragedies, successes, and failures. The principal participants were Chicano farmworkers. Their bitter struggle to organize and their Huelga became unifying forces for Chicanos from all economic and social levels.

But the farmworkers' pilgrimage to Delano was not the only "beginning" of the Chicano movement.

> The exact beginnings of the movement are obscure. There is some evidence that the Chicano movement grew out of a group of conferences held at Loyola University in Los Angeles in the summer of 1966...The Chicano movement is extremely heterogeneous. Its elements have different aims and purposes...The movement cuts across social class, regional and genera-

tional lines. Its aims range from traditional forms of social protest to increasingly more radical goals that appear as a sign of an emerging nationalism...The dynamic force of the movement is its ideology—Chicanismo—ideology it advanced as a challenge to the dominant Anglo beliefs concerning Mexicans as well as to the beliefs of Mexican-Americans themselves.[6]

Among young adults, the Chicano movement principally has taken the form of new student organizations. Among these groups, which began to appear in 1966 and 1967, are the Mexican American Student Confederation (MASC), Mexican American Student Association (MASA), and the United Mexican American Students (UMAS). Other student groups are the Movimento Estudiantil Chicano de Aztlan (MECHA) and the Mexican American Youth Organization (MAYO), which includes young adults at both the college and high school level and from the communities.

A new sense of the dignity and worth of La Raza inspired by the Chicano movement gave impetus to Chicano youth to demand recognition from educational systems. Some of the young leadership turned to direct action and militant confrontation to achieve their goals. Chicano students staged walkouts in the later 1960s in Texas, Colorado, New Mexico, California, and Arizona. Such student walkouts often became the focal point around which La Raza communities rallied forces and extended their activities. In several areas the student walkouts precipitated reaction from the police. Many student leaders were sent to prison, fined, or placed on probation with the result that some of the student organizations were left without effective leadership and with a demoralized membership. But the student groups reevaluated their structures, planned new tactics and strategies, and continued their attempts to get adequate responses from the educational institutions and to improve their communities' quality of life. Their protests and walkouts undoubtedly had a measure of success in changing educational environments. Today some student groups and young adult leaders have become dynamic and effective forces, not only in the area of education, but also in political activity. Some young adults who were former leaders of student walkouts have moved on to become elected to political office on city councils, boards of supervisors, and boards of education. The leadership of MAYO went directly into political action and organized La Raza Unida as a political party.

Young Chicanos have also been active in developing organizations in addition to campus groups and with other objectives in addition to education. One of these is the Brown Berets, organized in Los Angeles, now active in California and Texas. The Brown Berets believe that by giving the example of a disciplined and committed life based on principles of "carnalismo"—brotherhood—they can unite the community. A similar organization is the Black Berets founded in Mountain View, California, in the late 1960s. Both the Black and Brown Berets in recent years have been involved in action-oriented activities in barrio communities throughout the Southwest.

One of the most active organizations to work with Chicano youth has been the Crusade for Justice, founded in Denver in 1965 by Rudolfo "Corky" Gonzalez. The Crusade for Justice has had considerable influence on Chicano young people through its annual Chicano Youth Liberation Conference, the first of which was held in March, 1969, in Denver.

At the first meeting of the Chicano Youth Liberation Conference, the delegates voted to adopt "El Plan Espiritual de Aztlan," which called for Chicanos to work together to achieve common goals through a revival of the legendary Aztec homeland. Aztlan has become one of the most imaginative and evocative symbols of the Chicano movement. It appeals strongly to Chicanos everywhere and undoubtedly is an expression of the deep psychological need of an alienated and isolated people for a national identity of their own. Mexican-Americans were separated by conquest from one nation, Mexico, and forcibly alienated for more than a century from equal participation and acceptance in another nation, the United States. The Chicanos of today understandably have turned to an image of a "nation" of their own, interpreted through a renaissance of their own historical and cultural heritage.

Thus, the symbol of Aztlan has become the "centerpiece" of Chicano nationalism. Symbols of nationalism of various strengths and types permeate the Chicano movement. The Crusade for Justice and other Chicano organizations make positive use of nationalism to build Chicano identity and pride, and provide an underlying unifying force to organize a wide variety of programs and social services with Chicano perspectives. Among their demands are better housing, relevant education for Chicanos, reformation of the police and courts, greater and more diverse employment and economic opportunities, and land reform.

The issue of land reform thrusts deeply into the history of the Mexican-American. It has been particularly explosive in New Mexico.

In 1963, Reies Lopez Tijerina organized the Alianza Federal de Mercedes (Federal Alliance of Land Grants) in northern New Mexico. By 1964 the Alliance was claiming some six thousand land grant heirs in New Mexico, Colorado, Texas, California, and even Utah, as members. It was expounding a program which emphasized litigation and government action to win the return of land which the Alianza claimed belonged, under old Spanish land grants, to its members or to villages as common land. Most of the problems of Chicanos are derived from the loss of their land to Anglo intruders, the Alianza believes.

By 1966 the Alianza, claiming some twenty thousand members, was laying claim to millions of acres originally owned by Mexican-American village communities. The Alianza proposed to make this land the basis of a secessionist movement through the creation of a Confederation of Free City States. Some of the Alianza members began posting "no trespassing" signs on former land grants. In October of 1966, members of the Alianza attempted to take over part of the Kit Carson National Forest, which they claimed as their own. They proclaimed the Republic of San Joaquin del Rio de Chama. Forest Service rangers ignored their claim for sovereignty, however, and several Alianza members were arrested, including Tijerina. Later, Alianza members raided a courthouse in the small northwestern New Mexican town of Tierra Amarilla. The incident brought the Alianza movement national publicity.

Eventually, however, Tijerina was sent to prison and he lost an appeal to the U.S. Supreme Court. He was released from prison in July, 1971, after serving two years, and parole was granted on the condition that he no longer hold any official position in the Alianza. When his parole was up in 1974, Tijerina had to return to prison, but he received a full pardon in December, 1974. The Alianza continues to press the land issue, demanding that millions of acres claimed as grant land be returned by the federal government. Its activities today are oriented toward filing lawsuits and publishing educational material on the land issue.

During this period of Chicano activism, a group of youthful leaders in Texas who had founded the Mexican American Youth Organization (MAYO) were trying a form of political action that was unique to Mexican-Americans—forming their own political party. Led by Jose Angel Gutierrez—youthful, politically astute founder and former state chairman of MAYO—they established La Raza Unida as a distinct and new political party. La Raza Unida maintains that Chicanos must have their own separate political party in order to achieve self-determination.

> The preamble to La Raza Unida program states the decision of "the people of la raza...to reject the existing political party of our oppressor and take it upon ourselves to form La Raza Unida Party which will serve as a unifying force in our struggle for self determination."[7]

Gutierrez and two other Chicanos ran as candidates of the La Raza Unida Party in the school board elections in Crystal City, Texas, in April, 1970, and won easily. It was the first time the school board had had a Mexican-American majority in this community which was predominantly Mexican-American. Gutierrez was elected president of the board, which immediately established a bilingual education curriculum, started a federal free lunch program, and mandated that discrimination against or neglect of Mexican-American students would not be tolerated. The following spring, La Raza Unida ran two more candidates for the school board and again won, thereby guaranteeing its control of the board for several years to come. Crystal City is the same community where, several years before, concerted political action by Mexican-Americans had gained them control of the mayoralty and the city council, only to lose that control when they were unable to consolidate their political position. The significant victories of La Raza Unida in the board of education elections again made Crystal City a symbol to Chicanos of strength through unified political action.

La Raza Unida went on to win the city council and board of education elections in several other communities and has now established itself on the Texas ballot as a statewide political action party. Following his school board victory in Crystal City, Gutierrez said, "Aztlan has begun in the Southwestern part of Texas." His words underscored the dynamic force of the Chicano nationalism that runs throughout the Chicano movement.

The dynamism of the Chicano movement is also affecting the Mexican-American female—the Chicana.

Chicanas are making increasingly effective efforts to organize and assert their own identity and dignity. Among the many active Chicana organizations are the Comision Femenil Mexicana of Los Angeles; the National Chicana Institute of Tempe, Arizona; the National Chicana Welfare Rights of Los Angeles; the National Institute for Chicana Women of San Antonio, Texas; the National Chicana Businesswomen's Association of Albuquerque, New Mexico; and Barrio Pride, an organization of Chicanas in Phoenix, Arizona, working with subteen and teenage Chicanas.

> Emergence of the Chicana as a strong motivating force within the Spanish speaking community has been in conjunction with that of the Chicano. For this reason her struggle cannot be paralleled with the Anglo woman's fight for rights against the Anglo male. Chicanas have fought side by side with their men in the struggle for equal opportunity in all areas of American life....Women have stepped out of the background into the spotlight as spokesmen of various public meetings. School boards, commissions, city councils, to name a few, have felt the sting of the verbal slaps from irate Mexican American women. Chicanas have shown themselves to be alert, forceful and intelligent and they appear to be a major catalyst in the Chicano community. The aggression on the part of the Chicana toward the Anglo has not been condemned but encouraged by the Mexican American male.[8]

The activist Chicana comes well within the historical tradition of Mexican and Mexican-American women. Their traditional image as always docile and submissive does not coincide with historical accuracy. The Spanish conquistadores tell of meeting women *caciques*—chiefs—leading some of the Indian tribes. The story of "Adelita" as a militant revolutionary is one of the best known and most colorful of the Mexican Revolution. And Mexican-American women have always been formidable figures of strength, leadership, and durability in the long painful trek of their people toward full equality and justice in the United States. It is not surprising, therefore, to find Chicana women of today forming their own organizations, asserting their own independence and identity, and defining their own role in the Chicano movement.

The force of the Chicano movement has also surged through prison walls. Convicts and former convicts (known as "pintos" in barrio language) have formed their own organizations. Two such organizations are Empleo and Pintos, formed in California prisons, dedicated to the rehabilitation of prisoners and to prison reform. The appeal of ethnic pride and identity of Chicanismo has brought a new sense of dignity and worth, and with it new motivations to the unfortunate "pintos" among La Raza.

But nowhere is the Chicano movement penetrating more deeply, influencing organizations and their programs more positively, and bringing about more significant changes than in the barrios. A development of major significance in the Chicano movement is the emergence in the late 1960s and early 1970s of the barrio community organizations.

The barrio and colonia organizations are committed to the improvement of their communities through planned programs in housing, economic development, health services, social services, youth programs, manpower training, and education. These organizations relate directly to problems of the barrios and colonias and involve the community in their organizations and programs. They seek to develop a spectrum of specific programs with identifiable and measurable objectives.

The barrio community organizations are organized as tax-exempt [501(c)(3)] corporations and seek the support of foundations, corporations, churches, federal government, and concerned individuals. They have learned to apply the professional skills and other disciplines necessary to the development of an effective, programmatic organization and at the same time remain relevant and responsive to the needs of the community and its people. They are autonomous organizations formed by and for the people of the community who determine their own agendas.

Notable examples of successful barrio community organizations are the Mexican American Unity Council (MAUC) in San Antonio; the Chicanos Por La Causa (CPLC) in Phoenix, Arizona; the Spanish Speaking Unity Council

(SSUC) in Oakland, California; the Home Education Livelihood Program (HELP) which carries out programs in the rural areas of New Mexico; and The East Los Angeles Community Union (TELACU) and Euclid Foundation in East Los Angeles.

In their short time of existence, these program-oriented community organizations already have scored notable results. Here, briefly, are some of them:

In San Antonio, MAUC, directed by Juan Patlan, recorded a first for local community organizations when it opened a nationally franchised food service drive-in. It has also packaged various other business enterprises, constructed a low-cost housing project, and run a mental health program which achieves unique success in reaching barrio residents.

The SSUC, directed by Arabella Martinez, developed a sixty-one unit low and moderate income townhouse project in Hayward, California, believed to be the first of its type and made possible by a community-based Chicano group in northern California. SSUC also operates successful and efficiently run youth programs, packages business enterprises, and plays an influential role in the general activities of the community.

The CPLC in Phoenix, Arizona, directed by Ronnie Lopez, is an active barrio development organization that has successfully packaged loans for a Mexican-American bakery, developed a restaurant, has completed several homes in its housing program, and is involved in many other projects. CPLC also works closely with the Barrio Youth Project, directed by Sam Ramirez, which conducts a spectrum of training and other programs for young adults, including a printers' training course in their own print shop.

HELP in New Mexico is oriented to rural development, including such projects as self-help housing and a community-based weaving factory which produces colorful ponchos, wall-hangings, and rugs. It is also involved in farmers' cooperative associations, a manufacturing company which produces camper shells for pick-up trucks, and many other business enterprises. The executive director of HELP is Ray Lopez.

In Los Angeles, TELACU and the Euclid Foundation are pursuing similar barrio development programs and have scored notable achievements in housing, packaging of business enterprises, programs for the elderly, and similar activities. Executive directors of TELACU and the Euclid Foundation are Esteban Torres and the Rev. Tony Hernandez, respectively.

Colonias del Valle, directed by Alejandro Moreno, is developing a system to provide water to fifty-two families of a colonia near Donna in Hidalgo County, Texas. Presently, one-eighth of the county's 181,000 residents do not have access to piped water.

In Homestead, Florida, the Organized Migrants in Community Action (OMICA), directed by Rudolfo Juarez, are attempting to provide decent housing for migrant workers. Recently, OMICA's prompt and vigorous action resulted in bringing in medical and other aid for rural families hit by typhoid fever caused by polluted water in the area.

These barrio community organizations and others like them are concentrating on definable, positive programs to achieve concrete results for their communities. Their directors and leadership, as well as their staffs, are generally youthful, have developed excellent professional skills, and are vigorously committed to the permanent improvement of the quality of life in their communities.

Among other organizations are the Mexican American Education Council (MAEC) in Houston, Texas; the Trinity Chicano Coalition in El Paso, Texas; the Guadalupe Organization (GO) in Guadalupe, Arizona; the Corporation Organizada Para Accion Servidora (COPAS) in Santa Fe, New Mexico; OBECA/ Arriba Juntos in San Francisco, California; the Barrio Development, Inc. in Uvalde, Texas; the Arriba Juntos in Corpus Christi, Texas; and the Chicano Federation of San Diego County, Inc., San Diego, California.

These barrio community organizations firmly maintain that they must develop a spectrum of programs so that they will eventually achieve self-sufficiency. They see themselves as developing or facilitating the development of economic bases broad and productive enough so that they eventually will have a major impact on the economy of their communities.

The barrio community organizations, despite the short time they have been in existence, already are having a discernible influence on the direction of an important segment of the Chicano movement. They are developing program-oriented, permanent institutions in the barrios, to serve the needs of the barrios. They are turning around older, outworn policies of accommodating Mexican-American organizations to the attitudes and institutions of the dominant society. They are, instead, developing policies and programs that bring American attitudes and institutions into support of their own agendas.

They are awakening a nation—slowly but steadily—to the creative strengths of a people breaking free from the barriers of prejudice, alienation, and repression forced upon them by a domineering surrounding environment.

As the nation moves into the last quarter of the twentieth century, Mexican Americans are moving into their second century as a major segment of its people. They have stepped boldly onto the national scene. They are demanding to be heard, and they are ready.

Mexican-American organizations are now emerging as national bodies, advocating the interests and expressing the concerns of Chicanos to the nation.

One of the first to appear, the National Council of La Raza (NCLR), was developed in close programmatic relationships with the emerging barrio community organizations. NCLR began in 1968 as the Southwest Council of La Raza, with headquarters in Phoenix, Arizona.

In its first four years of existence, the Southwest Council of La Raza moved to a position of national recognition as an effective new Chicano organization. It assembled training, technical assistance, and funding support for autonomous barrio community organizations, and together with them fashioned a network to channel resources into the barrios.

The field experience of the Southwest Council of La Raza made it clear that Mexican-Americans and the problems they faced were to be found throughout the nation. The Southwest Council of La Raza found it imperative to expand its role to interpret and advocate Chicano interests nationally.

In December, 1972, the Council reorganized as the National Council of La Raza and established its headquarters office in Washington, D.C., and its program operations office in Phoenix, Arizona. NCLR now operates as a national advocacy center for La Raza interests. Its headquarters carries out program liaison services with the federal agencies and provides information, data, and interpretive material on public policies and La Raza activities through *Agenda*, a monthly newsletter and quarterly magazine.

Its program operations in Phoenix include economic development and housing development components. In economic development, the Council has been the major force in the formation of La Raza Investment Corporation (LRIC), a minority enterprise small business investment corporation organized to leverage financial assistance for minority entrepreneurs. In housing, the Council has formed La Raza Housing Development Corporation (LRHDC), which is involved in the training of housing management specialists.

The Council is also preparing to implement a La Raza Educational Development Center (LREDC) to conduct research, develop materials, and provide well-informed advocacy for Chicano educational interests.

The unique combination of a national council working with a network of autonomous, decentralized barrio organizations provides for flexible programmatic approaches on local levels and strong, responsible advocacy of La Raza interests on the national level.

The conditions of alienation and social neglect suffered by the Mexican-American minority in the United States are no longer confined to the border states. They now involve Chicano communities as distant from the United States-Mexico border as Seattle, Chicago, and Detroit.

Over the past fifty years, Mexican-Americans have moved into practically every state of the Union and have formed sizable communities in many of them, particularly in the Midwest. Today, while the bulk of this minority—the nation's second largest—is still anchored in the Southwest, millions of Americans of Mexican descent have spread through the Northwest, Midwest, Northeast, and the South.

Mexican-Americans are now an inextricable part of the total national scene and their organizations are breaking out of traditionally isolated environments to interact with the total national environment.

The Chicano movement's break-out may prove to be its most enduring contribution. National agendas require national organizations. Mexican-American national organizations already are responding.

Mexican-Americans already are opening the next era of their historic struggle for social justice and full equality—the development of national organizations.

Notes

1. Joan W. Moore with Alfredo Cuellar, *Mexican Americans—Ethnic Groups in American Life Series* (Englewood Cliffs, New Jersey: Prentice Hall, Inc., 1970), p. 11.

2. Matt S. Meier and Feliciano Rivera, *The Chicanos: History of Mexican Americans*, p. 143.

3. Ibid., p. 241.

4. Moore and Cuellar, *Mexican Americans*, p. 143.

5. Ibid., p. 144. The letter appeared on March 8, 1929, in the *Hidalgo County Independent*, Edinburgh, Texas.

6. Moore and Cuellar, *Mexican Americans*, p. 149.

7. Meier and Rivera, *The Chicanos*, p. 277.

8. Linda Aquilar, "Unequal Opportunity and the Chicana," *Civil Rights Digest* (Spring 1973): 31.

29

Private Initiative for the Public Good

JOHN W. GARDNER

JOHN W. GARDNER HAS BEEN AN ACTIVE AND DISTINGUISHED
PARTICIPANT IN OUR NATION'S EDUCATIONAL, PHILANTHROPIC,
AND POLITICAL LIFE. HIS NUMEROUS ACTIVITIES INCLUDE
SERVING AS THE PRESIDENT OF THE CARNEGIE FOUNDATION FOR
THE ADVANCEMENT OF TEACHING AND THE CARNEGIE
CORPORATION OF NEW YORK, SECRETARY OF HEW, FOUNDER AND
CHAIRMAN OF COMMON CAUSE, AND A FOUNDER AND CHAIRMAN
OF THE INDEPENDENT SECTOR.

The tax deductibility of gifts to educational, religious, and charitable organizations has a long and honorable history. But recently some critics have questioned the practice, and their arguments have a superficial plausibility. The case is made in roughly the following terms.

Roger D., who is in the 70 percent income tax bracket, makes a gift of $1,000 to Stanford University. If he had not made the gift at all, the government would have taken $700 of the $1,000 in taxes. So in effect only $300 of the gift is out of his own pocket. With respect to the other $700—so the argument goes—he is simply diverting to Stanford money that would otherwise have gone to the United States Treasury. Why, ask the critics, should the government of the United States allow Roger D. to divert to Stanford money that would have come to it?

The purport of the argument is clear: abolish the tax deductibility of such gifts. The critics have not yet advocated that step. They seem bent on whittling away at deductibility rather than abolishing it. But if their arguments are valid, abolition is the logical aim. Then the $700 that would have gone to Stanford will

This essay originally appeared in the 1964 Annual Report of the Carnegie Corporation of New York and is reprinted here by permission of the author.

go to the Treasury and the government can decide what it wants to do with it. The whole procedure has a marvelous surface plausibility. But the consequences would be catastrophic for our private educational, charitable, and religious institutions and would alter profoundly the character of American life.

The first consequence would be that these institutions—universities, hospitals, research laboratories, and the like—which depend on private contributions either would waste away or would become appendages of government. Since many of them are performing essential services for the nation, the latter outcome would no doubt prevail. The vast network of private institutions devoted to education, health, and welfare would then depend wholly on the centralized decisions of the federal government.

For many countries such monolithic central support of all educational, scientific, and charitable activities would be regarded as normal. But for the United States it would mean the end of a great tradition. In the realm of good works this nation boasts a unique blending of private and governmental effort. There is almost no area of educational, scientific, charitable, or religious activity in which we have not built an effective network of private institutions. In all fields (with the exception of religion, of course) governmental and private institutions form a partnership of rare effectiveness in serving the public interest.

The deductibility of philanthropic gifts from taxable income reflects a deeply rooted public policy encouraging private concern for good works. That policy grows out of powerful impulses in the American character and has borne fruit in a way that astounds people of other nations. This year private gifts to educational, religious, and charitable activities will approximate $11 billion. More than 62 million individuals will have contributed to the total.

Back of this is a remarkable attitude on the part of the individual citizen. He is in the habit of accepting some measure of personal responsibility for improving the state of the world. He does not believe that government has the sole responsibility for identifying (or solving) public problems. It has been our public policy to encourage him in that view. Anyone who wants to alleviate the sufferings of his fellow man, dispel the clouds of ignorance, or build a better society is encouraged to try as long as his actions fall within the framework of legally and morally acceptable behavior.

Tax Exemption

Private initiative in good works has been threatened on another front in recent discussions of the tax exemption of philanthropic foundations. Some of the attacks on tax exemption resemble the argument against tax deductibility cited earlier. It is said that the money that is tax exempt would have gone to the

United States Treasury if the exemption had not existed. Therefore, the argument goes, it is public money. And since it is public money it ought to find its way into the federal government's pocketbook, i.e., the Treasury—or at least the spending of it should be subject to government control.

One interesting feature of the argument is that if it should be valid, it would hold equally for all tax-exempt educational, scientific, religious, and charitable organizations. Those who would apply it to foundations today could with entire consistency apply it to universities, hospitals, and churches tomorrow.

Foundations are part of a tradition of philanthropy that is as old as civilization itself. Its beginnings are lost in antiquity. Plato's Academy was an educational foundation. Pliny the Younger endowed a foundation to care for needy children. Special provisions governing property that was dedicated to religious, charitable, or educational uses were commonplace in the ancient world. Our own laws governing philanthropic activities go back to the Statute of Charitable Uses passed during the reign of Elizabeth I. Philanthropic foundations were not uncommon in the American colonies and from the beginning of our national life. Then a little more than fifty years ago the great benefactions of Andrew Carnegie and John D. Rockefeller brought to prominence a new conception of giving. They believed that the foundations should expend their funds in a creative search for new solutions to human problems. They sought not just to cure but to prevent, not just to ease human misery but to get at the causes of that misery. And in doing so, they initiated what many believe to have been the most exciting half century in the long history of philanthropy.

Historically, legally, and philosophically, foundations are part of a larger class of institutions that includes churches, universities, scientific laboratories, hospitals, orphanages, and social welfare organizations. Henry Allen Moe, former president of the Guggenheim Foundation, refers to all members of this class as "foundations." This is not just a matter of arbitrary definition. It is impossible to establish a clear boundary line between what is popularly known as a "foundation" and other varieties of endowed institutions.

All of these varied institutions have traditionally received tax exemption. Since our beginnings as a nation both the federal government and state legislatures have acted to preserve and encourage private initiative in good works. We have always believed that this was worth doing, and tax exemption has been the chief instrument for accomplishing it. Such exemption is not a negative act and certainly not a piece of legislative negligence. It is a positive measure designed to insure that in scientific, educational, religious, and charitable activities there will be multiple sources of initiative and creative diversity. Modern thinking about the value of pluralism in preserving freedom has only served to strengthen our convictions on this point.

It is not necessary to argue, as some have, that nongovernmental institutions can perform certain educational and welfare functions in a manner superior to government. Governmental agencies have done a highly creditable job in many of the areas once covered by private institutions. But most responsible Americans believe that *both* governmental and private roles should be preserved. That is what pluralism implies. If the private institutions are squeezed out, a valuable ingredient in our pluralistic society will be forever lost. That these institutions are not a trivial factor on the national scene is reflected in the fact that in the fiscal year 1963-64, they spent more than $38 billion for health and social welfare programs.

Pluralism also implies that a variety of views will be tolerated, even encouraged. This is worth bearing in mind, because on a number of occasions the tax exemption of foundations has been brought into question when critics differed with the content or conclusions of studies done under foundation grants. In upholding gifts for educational purposes, the courts have not sought to pass on the wisdom of particular educational projects. They have acted on the principle that the advancement and dissemination of knowledge is in itself in the public interest. Thus, a trust to promote a religious doctrine is "charitable" within the meaning of the law of trusts although the doctrine has few adherents. The Catholic Church enjoys tax exemption despite the fact that the majority of Americans are not Catholics. A trust to publish books or give lectures expounding the doctrine of the single tax may be tax exempt, even though the members of the court disagree with the doctrine. An experimental college may enjoy tax exemption even though most higher educational authorities are skeptical about the new methods it is using. One of the advantages of charitable trusts is that they permit the testing of ideas that have not been generally accepted. A university enjoys tax exemption without regard to the popularity of the ideas held by faculty members.

As a matter of fact the very hint that tax exemption should depend on the political popularity of ideas under examination is a fateful step down the totalitarian road. If it were accepted then political forces, operating through the legislature, would have the right to censor every sermon and every college lecture; and that would be the end of freedom of thought in this nation.

Criticism of Foundations

Recent criticism of the foundations, however, has not centered on their substantive activities. It has focused on two questions: 1. Have foundation assets become so large that something must be done to curb further growth? 2. Are the foundations abusing their tax exemption by engaging in improper financial and managerial practices?

The view that foundation assets have grown so vast as to require corrective action is not based on facts. In journalistic accounts of this subject one sees occasional reference to Henry VIII's seizure of monastery lands. That such a comparison could be seriously used is a measure of the confusion that exists. At the time of Henry VIII's action, the total annual revenues of the monasteries was estimated to be somewhat greater, in a normal year, than the total revenues of the Crown. Today the income of foundations is in the neighborhood of *one half of one percent* of federal revenues. Foundations hold between $15 and $17 billion in total assets at market value, a sum which is about three-fourths of one percent of the financial assets of all banks, savings and loan organizations, insurance companies, major corporations, and other wealth holders in this country.

As a matter of fact, foundation grants today account for only about 8 percent of the total annual philanthropic giving from private sources. More than 85 percent of the dollars given annually to philanthropic causes are in the form of individual gifts and bequests.

The growth of foundations is dwarfed by the growth of government expenditures for purposes which were once regarded as philanthropic. In 1913 the federal government spent about $5 million on education, and in that same year Carnegie Corporation spent $5.6 million on various philanthropic projects. In fiscal year 1963-64 the federal government spent about $2 *billion* on education (a 400-fold increase) while Carnegie Corporation spent a little over $12 million. Endowed institutions of all sorts—universities, museums, churches, hospitals, as well as foundations—are losing ground steadily to government-supported institutions.

Accordingly, anyone who worries about balance and pluralism in our society should cease marveling that the Ford Foundation is as big as it is, and take note of how small it is compared to any number of vast governmental enterprises that receive little public criticism. We should be thankful that there are institutions in the private sector that are capable of holding their own as a vital force in our national life. In the same spirit, we should revise our scale of values in thinking of an institution such as Harvard University. The average citizen contemplating the Harvard endowment is awed by the wealth that it represents. But in terms of the tasks to be accomplished today, it is not as rich as it should be. In our populous and complex society there are many tasks that can be done only by institutions with access to large resources.

Closely related to the question of size is the question of whether funds that find their way into tax-exempt foundations are somehow lifted out of the stream of our economy and thereby rendered unproductive. It is an odd accusation. The capital funds of most foundations are invested in a highly conventional way and thereby participate directly in the economy. The bulk of their income goes to educational, scientific, religious, and charitable organizations for current projects of general support, which means that the dollars rest briefly in the hands of the recipients and then are spent—and thereby pumped back into the mainstream of the economy.

The second question is much more serious. Are the foundations abusing their tax exemption by engaging in improper financial and managerial practices? The answer, briefly, is that a few foundations *are* abusing their tax exemption. Most are not.

Rascality is possible in any human enterprise, and philanthropy is no exception. It is clear that some individuals do not hesitate to use foundations as a means of carrying on improper activities (for example, serving the pecuniary interests of themselves or their relatives). Such foundations should be called to account. Congressman Wright Patman has rendered a public service in bringing examples of such impropriety to public attention.

But all foundations should not suffer for the misdeeds of a very few. We all condemn diploma mills, but we do not use their existence as a stick with which to beat our finest universities. We all condemn quack doctors, but we do not use their continued existence as an excuse to harass our leading medical specialists.

Most foundations would wish to impose on themselves a more exacting standard than just to stay technically within the law. They would wish to adhere to the highest standards dictated by ethical considerations and the public interest. But since there is no code of practices for foundations, it is not easy for trustees to know when they are doing the right thing.

What constitutes "good practice"? There are many kinds of foundations, and it is difficult to lay down principles that apply to all. Nevertheless, some things can be said.

First, a foundation should practice full disclosure. The larger it is the more energetically it should disseminate full information on its activities. If it has capital assets of more than $10 million, it should publish a detailed annual report. It should publish the size of its capital fund, its investments, and its income. It should describe each grant, including the purpose of the gift, the amount given, and the identity of the recipient. It should record the names of officers and trustees, and it should give some account of the objectives that guide its operations.

Foundations with assets under $10 million need not be held to such arduous standards. But they should have their books audited annually by a qualified firm of certified public accountants and should furnish the audited figures (including the list of grants) to the Foundation Library Center, a national repository and clearinghouse for information on foundations. And of course they must supply the extensive information required by the Treasury.

The leading foundations have set high standards of public reporting. But some other foundations have *not* been cooperative in providing information to the Internal Revenue Service or to congressional investigators. A number of them are still scandalously negligent with respect to public reporting of their activities. Federal regulations now in force require fairly extensive information from foundations, but the Internal Revenue Service has not always enforced the requirements as vigorously as it might. Effective enforcement of provisions now on the books would do much to establish the principle of full disclosure.

Second, there should be clearly stated rules governing the handling of foundation funds, whether in grant-making or investment. Foundations should not engage in speculation. Foundation trustees and officers should not make either investments or grants that serve their own pecuniary interest or that of relatives or business associates. Such "self-dealing" is intolerable and should be prohibited.

Third, the foundation should produce a reasonable return on its total list of investments. And if it is to enjoy the tax exemption accorded educational, scientific, religious, or charitable activities, it should spend its income to finance such activities. Under normal circumstances, it should be expected to spend all of its income each year.

Finally, it will be necessary to work out with care the relationship between foundations and business firms with which they are related. Some points are clear. A foundation should not own or control a business. If it finds itself— through bequest—owner of a business it should divest itself of control as rapidly as possible.

All of the principles that should govern the relationship between foundations and business firms are not yet crystal clear. Public policy on this matter has not yet been worked out. It is going to require further research and public discussion before we arrive at a sound code of practices for foundations. It is the belief of this writer, for example, that every tax-exempt foundation should have a public board—a board on which a majority of members are distinguished citizens not related to the donor nor associated with him in business. But the consequences of such a requirement should be fully and widely discussed before it is laid down as an unvarying principle of good practice.

The Purpose of Foundations

It is important to be clear—as we have tried to be in the preceding paragraphs— about the things foundations should *not* do. But the great purposes of the foundations are not to be found in such negative considerations. Along with the churches, universities, libraries, and laboratories of the nation, they are committed to aims of central importance to the future of the nation. It is in their capacity to further such aims that they must find their justification. The only respect in which they differ from other tax-exempt institutions is that they lend themselves to a greater flexibility in the channeling of funds for tax-exempt purposes.

All objective accounts of the leading foundations have paid ungrudging tribute to the importance of their contributions. Even their critics freely admit the influence they have wielded—in fact their influence is one of the points in the indictment. Yet if one compares foundation expenditures with the total amount the nation spends on educational, scientific, and cultural activities, one is struck by the very small fraction that their combined spending represents. In 1963 all of the foundations together spent not much more than $800 million; in the same year governmental spending (federal, state, and local) for the same purposes exceeded $70 billion. In other words, foundation spending was a little more than one percent of governmental spending for the same purposes.

How could the foundations, contributing such a modest fraction of the total, have achieved such a reputation for influence and accomplishment? They have been on the whole well staffed, but it is not superiority of staff that accounts for their performance. I believe most serious students of the subject would say that it is due to the effectiveness of the modern foundation as a device for fostering innovation. It is designed to make money go a long way in the service of creativity and constructive change. It is one of the few institutions in our society that can keep itself free to act quickly and flexibly in support of the talented individual or the institution that wishes to undertake an experimental program. Anyone who has had administrative responsibilities knows that one of the great barriers to new developments is that the conventional institution rarely has funds for innovation. Its funds are committed to normal operating expenses. The modern foundation keeps money explicitly for innovation.

The modern foundation is still, as social institutions go, a relatively new invention. Today we must treasure any institutions designed to function flexibly and creatively in a period of rapid change. The foundation is such an institution. It is not only an element in our pluralism; but supporting a wide variety of creative individuals, it contributes to an even greater and more fruitful pluralism. Rather than forcing it to be like other more conventional institutions, let us see what we can make of it.

30

The Nongovernmental Organization at Bay

ALAN PIFER

ALAN PIFER HAS BEEN A LEADER IN THE FIELDS OF NATIONAL
AND INTERNATIONAL EDUCATIONAL POLICY, AS WELL AS
NATIONAL SOCIAL POLICY AND URBAN AFFAIRS. HE WAS A
MEMBER OF THE COMMISSION ON PRIVATE PHILANTHROPY AND
PUBLIC NEEDS AND SERVED AS PRESIDENT OF THE CARNEGIE
CORPORATION OF NEW YORK.

An occupational hazard of philanthropy is repeated exposure to the financial plight of others. While the reaction may at times be a kind of relieved "there but for the grace of God...," more often it is one of deep concern, even anxiety. Why do so many of our private nonprofit organizations seem to have perpetually engrossing financial problems? Why should the men who run them have to spend so much time and effort making the rounds of potential donors, hat in hand, often with disappointing results and always at the expense of their primary administrative and program functions? Has the system for maintaining these organizations become basically unsound?

These are questions that each year become more insistent as the social value of nongovernmental organizations continues to mount in response to the steadily broadening aspirations of our society and to the nation's expanding international commitments. Indeed, the financial uncertainty of these organizations in the face of growing responsibilities and sharply increased costs threatens to limit their future usefulness and undermine the private side of a public-private partnership through which the nation is now accomplishing some of its most important public business.

This essay originally appeared in the 1966 Annual Report of the Carnegie Corporation of New York and is reprinted here by permission of the author.

Definition

The term "nongovernmental organization" is used in several ways and is often ambiguous. As used here, it is arbitrarily limited to those organizations that have a private and nonprofit status but are *not* universities, colleges or schools, hospitals, fully endowed foundations, or religious missions. It includes scholarly, professional, educational, scientific, literary, and cultural associations; health, welfare, and community action agencies; nonuniversity research institutes; agencies providing overseas technical assistance; defense advisory organizations; and agencies that have educational purposes but are not part of the formal educational system. Thus, the term takes in only part of that heterogeneous list of approximately 100,000 organizations that are tax exempt and to which contributions are deductible under federal income tax law.

A few hundred of these organizations have national or international purposes and are individually important to the nation at large. The remaining thousands operate only at the local level but have national significance collectively as a vital part of our system of democratic pluralism. In both groups, but especially in the former, are to be found an ever growing number that derive part of their income, and in certain cases a goodly portion of it, from federal grants and contracts. Some of these organizations have moved into the federal orbit by choice, seeing there new sources of financial support. Others have entered it in response to a call for help from Washington. Still others were created by, or as the result of an initiative from, a federal agency.

The kinds of services offered to government by these private nonprofit organizations are too varied and numerous to catalogue here. Indeed, it is a striking fact that nowhere in the federal government does there exist a central record of these services, the organizations providing them, and the volume of expenditure involved, and even at the department or agency level this information is not readily available. "We just don't look at it that way," is the explanation offered, and so separate statistics are hard to come by.

Nevertheless, the use of nongovernmental organizations to carry out public functions, a rare occurrence before World War II, is now accepted policy in most parts of government. Gone are the days when most people in Washington would agree with the once widely held view that public money should be spent only by public agencies. A more flexible approach to the art of government, which also includes an expanded use of universities and private business firms, is growing steadily.

In the Government's Service

Examples drawn at random from current government operations illustrate the variety and ingenuity to be found in the ways private nonprofit organizations are serving government.

The United States Employment Service of the Department of Labor has recently contracted with the National Travelers Aid Association to provide supportive social services in the relocation of families from areas of labor surplus to areas with a labor shortage. The Office of Regional Economic Development of the Department of Commerce, to assist local industrial growth, purchases research services having to do with new products and new markets from such nonprofit organizations as the Midwest Research Institute, the RAND Corporation, and the New England Economic Research Foundation.

The Bureau of Educational and Cultural Affairs of the Department of State uses the services of the National Social Welfare Assembly for planning and administering travel programs of some foreign visitors to this country. The same bureau has for a number of years relied on the Conference Board of Associated Research Councils and the Institute of International Education to assist in the selection of American scholars and students for research, teaching, and study abroad under the Fulbright Program.

The Agency for International Development employs International Voluntary Services for rural development work in Laos, and the American Institute for Free Labor Development to train labor leaders from Latin America. It contracts with the African-American Institute for a variety of educational services in many parts of Africa, and with the Near East Foundation for agricultural education and extension services in Dahomey. It finances a program under which CARE is assisting Algerian doctors to develop their capability to run an ophthalmological clinic. Peace Corps volunteers are being trained by the Tucson, Arizona, branch of the YMCA for service in Venezuela.

The National Science Foundation under its course content improvement program has given substantial contract support to Educational Services Incorporated for curriculum work in science, mathematics, and social studies. The U.S. Office of Education, under its ERIC (Educational Research Information Center) program, an enterprise that also involves ten universities and two private business concerns, has recently contracted with the Modern Language Association and the Center for Applied Linguistics to set up clearinghouses for information on, respectively, the common and the less taught foreign languages. The Office of Education has also provided contract support to CONPASS, a newly formed consortium of professional associations, including the Association of American Geographers, the American Historical Association, and others, to make possible a continuing appraisal of the $33 million annual National Defense Education Act program of teachers institutes in such fields as foreign languages, geography, English, history, reading, and the arts.

In the poverty field well over half of the 900-odd newly created community action agencies supported by the Office of Economic Opportunity are private nonprofit organizations. The OEO also finances demonstration programs carried out by long established private agencies. An example in the community action area is the Office's support of Project ENABLE, jointly sponsored by the National Urban League, the Family Service Association, and the Child Study Association. A second example is OEO's support of programs of the National Legal Aid and Defender Association. A third is the contract with the YMCA to help meet the costs of a job-training program for young people in the Bedford-Stuyvesant area of New York City. The Department of Labor and Office of Education also contribute to this program.

The Food and Drug Administration has recently engaged the National Academy of Sciences to carry out a reassessment of the efficacy of all new drugs marketed in the years between 1938 and 1962. Previously, at the request of the same federal agency and with funds provided by it, the Public Administration Service, a private organization in Chicago, had made a study of state and local food and drug control procedures to help the federal government determine its area of responsibility.

Government by Contract

These are but a few instances of one aspect of the rapidly growing phenomenon of government by grant and contract. The phenomenon will also certainly continue to grow despite the opposition of some members of Congress, who believe it would be preferable for federal agencies to develop their own internal capacity to take on all the new tasks society is assigning to Washington rather than hire others for this purpose. These critics contend that contracting is no more than a subterfuge by which government gets around its own regulations and salary scales. More importantly, some have real doubts as to how far federal agencies should go in delegating their public responsibilities to private contractors. Can the elected officials of a democratic government, they ask, be held fully accountable to the public for tasks that appointed officials have contracted with others to perform?

This is a fair question. At the same time the greatly increased use of nongovernmental organizations to serve government ends is the product of a powerful and pervasive new force that is not to be denied. This force is the growing complexity of the domestic and international problems with which government must cope — complexity that is rooted in scientific and technological advance, in population growth, in urbanization, in international tensions, and in still other factors. Solution of these complex new problems requires even greater specialization, both of facilities and professional and technical manpower. Government cannot hope to build up and maintain such a capacity within its own bureaucracy. It has no alternative but to buy the specialized help it needs from the universities, from private enterprise, and from the nongovernmental organizations.

Beyond this reason, however, are other sound justifications for the government's use of nongovernmental agencies to carry out the nation's public purposes. These agencies by their very nature should have the kinds of attributes that an alert federal administration needs today, if it is to have an adequate sense of responsibility for the nation's well-being. Not all private organizations have these qualities, but many do. They include the capacity to move swiftly, flexibly, and imaginatively into a new area of critical need; the power to arrive at a disinterested, objective appraisal of a situation free of political influence; the freedom to engage in controversial activities; the ability to experiment in an unfettered manner — and if need be fail; and finally the capacity for sympathetic personal attention to the variety of human problems that beset our increasingly dehumanized world.

A New Partnership

Realizing the need for access to such qualities, Washington officialdom has in recent years authorized an ever greater use of nongovernmental organizations, and Congress has provided the necessary funds to buy their services and support their projects. A partnership has been sealed, as it was between government and universities in scientific research and development. The result is that just as we now have the "federal grant university," so also we have the "federal grant nongovernmental organization." And just as we have learned to worry about the impact on the universities of large-scale, mission-oriented federal support, we must also develop a concern about the impact of this kind of money on the weaker partner in the new alliance between government and the nongovernmental organizations.

At the moment such a concern both within and outside government has not arisen, as it did in regard to the universities. Why? One explanation is simply that the volume of governmental contracting with the private organizations is smaller than it is with the universities. This in turn is explained by the predominant part research and development have played in government's needs for outside assistance and the universities' special — though not exclusive— capability in this area. Federal contract and grant support, much of it for research, now represents a substantial part of the annual income of many of our leading universities. No sensible person in government or the universities can ignore the implications of this development. But among nongovernmental organizations research is a much more limited activity, and no other single area of government dependence on these organizations has yet been great enough to arouse concern.

Nevertheless, important as research and development requirements remain, other types of government needs have been growing rapidly, especially for the kinds of operational and management services that nongovernmental organizations of the types we are considering here may provide more appropriately than universities. As the nation increasingly grapples with its domestic programs of educational expansion, urban blight, poverty, housing, race relations, health, and environmental pollution, as well as with its international responsibilities, the use of the nongovernmental organization must inevitably continue to mount.

Concern developed slowly over the implications of government dependence on the universities for research. Originally federal agencies believed they could simply buy research from the universities as a kind of commodity, much as the army once bought mules. This simple notion was later replaced by a more sophisticated realization that to get the research it needed government would also have to support the research universities wanted to do. There developed, therefore, a dual system of relationships, one based on contracts, the other on grants. Gradually, however, the distinction between the two has faded as the result of changing procedures, until the grant and the contract are now virtually indistinguishable.

More recently the government has recognized that it not only must administer its university research support flexibly but also must help build up the basic long-term strength of the universities. It is doing this through the new institutional grant programs of the National Science Foundation, through general research support and grants for facilities to the medical schools by the National Institutes of Health, through the "sustaining university" grants of the National Aeronautics and Space Administration, and through Office of Education grants to the universities for buildings and equipment.

Finally, in the new international education legislation Congress and the administration are contemplating yet another step. They are now proposing to give general support to universities to enable them to develop the capability with which to provide international technical assistance, not only in research but for training and operational services as well.

Let the Seller Beware

Clearly the university case has been well made. But the same case has never been made for using public money to develop the general capacity of nongovernmental organizations to do their jobs more effectively. The standard government position here is that it is simply buying services as a commodity and has no responsibility for the basic health of the suppliers. Therefore it must not pay for a whit more (and often less) than the tangible products it receives, whether research or services; it must buy at the lowest possible price; and it must limit its support to the program and administrative costs of a carefully defined project with a specified terminal date.

This kind of support is in the long run harmful to the nongovernmental organizations. It tends to produce mushroom growth and to place them in a position where they must continually seek further project support of the same nature to prevent the laying-off of staff and closing-down of programs. Thus, the paths of these organizations become characterized by frequent changes of direction induced by Washington's concerns of the day, rather than deliberate courses set by the organizations' own boards of trustees. This process in turn can diminish the interest of the trustees, and hence their sense of responsibility — which is the very heart of effective voluntary private service in the public interest.

The probability is that project support alone will in time make these organizations little more than appendages of government. What may also develop, since government officials cannot in the very nature of their jobs take consistent reponsibility for the affairs of private organizations, are situations in which responsibility falls somewhere between government and trustees, with no effective check on the activities of staff. The dangers here are obvious.

The management of a nongovernmental organization, guided by its own sense of what is best for the organization, does, of course, have a free choice of whether to accept or reject government contracts. This can be said to be a basic part of management's responsibility. One can say, therefore, that if the organization begins to exhibit hyperthyroid or schizoid tendencies as the result of an overdose of government contracts, it has no one to blame but itself. In practice, however, many organizations have found the rejection of government business extremely difficult because of their unwillingness to appear—and be— unresponsive to the national need. In some instances also it is their own identification of a pressing problem that leads them to take the initiative in seeking government support. Finally, they know that organizations that consistently give a higher priority to their own stability than to venturesome growth run the danger of removing themselves from the battle altogether.

Why have the private nonprofit organizations not come together and made their case to government as the universities did? Perhaps it is merely a matter of not yet having had time. A more likely explanation, however, it that they have no ready means of cooperation, so great is their diversity and so amorphous the field of which they are members. Each of these organizations has a constituency of its own and inhabits a world that rarely intersects or overlaps that of another organization. The men responsible for their affairs often do not even know each other. There has, therefore, never been a concerted initiative for the creation in Washington of a single voice to speak for the interests of the nongovernmental organizations field, a voice such as that provided for higher education by the American Council on Education. Perhaps, given the diversity of the field and its lack of integration, this is the way it has to be, but the result is a babel which amounts to no voice at all.

A New Approach

Were government now to recognize the need for building a long-term service capability in organizations with unique or special talents, it would seem an easy matter for federal agencies to begin to apply to the private agencies on whose services they depend the same principles now applied to the universities. For example, "sustaining grants" to such organizations could provide funds for administrative costs not allocable to contracts. Such grants could also provide "venture capital" for programs which, though not of current interest to the government, would develop the general competence of these organizations, and hence their longer-range usefulness to government.

From government's point of view several problems stand in the way of a new approach of this kind. Many Washington officials and members of Congress who believe in the public-private partnership would still hesitate to see government provide general support to private organizations, because they believe this would turn them into veritable arms of government, thereby destroying the very qualities that make them indispensable. General support, they point out, would oblige government to audit the full accounts and monitor the entire program of an organization being helped, whereas with contract or grant support the auditing and monitoring need apply only to a specific project. Others in Washington disagree with this conclusion, saying that if the will existed, there could be as much latitude in government's approach to the nongovernmental organization as there is in its flexible and generous new attitude toward the universities.

A more serious difficulty from Washington's point of view is that some private organizations seem to be badly run and others are apparently still addressing themselves to yesterday's problems, while still others give the impression of being nothing but lobbying groups promoting the selfish interests of particular professions or occupations. Liberalized financial policies that included such organizations might, it is suggested, simply reward inefficiency, obsolescence, and venality. While the point can be made that government has no business using the services of such organizations anyway, the argument is nonetheless generally persuasive, and it indicates that any change of policy must be applied selectively and with discriminating care.

This argument also points up a fundamental difference between universities and nongovernmental organizations. The very nature of the academic enterprise provides a kind of built-in system of responsibility upon which government can rely. Each scholar is accountable not only to colleagues at his university, including boards of trustees or regents, but also to a wider circle of scholars in his discipline at other universities. And at the institutional level, individual universities are accountable to a national—even international—community. This system of self-audit within the academic enterprise has its moments of failure. But on the whole it is remarkably reliable, and it provides a substantial assurance that the money will not be misspent when government gives public funds to the universities.

Nongovernmental organizations, on the other hand, being more disparate, lacking intercommunication, and possessing no sense of community and tradition do not have such a built-in system of discipline. In their case, responsibility is a more localized matter and lies primarily with their boards of trustees. Government's protection in its grants to these organizations is to make sure that the trustees recognize their responsibility and discharge it. Where the trustees are strong and active, the protection afforded government can, in fact, be even greater than that provided in grants to universities.

Responsibility for Support

Most people in Washington believe responsibility for the basic financial health of nongovernmental organizations lies in the private sector. The rightness of this view cannot be disputed when we think of philanthropy as a broad, undifferentiated activity in which the individual is free to give his dollar, or million dollars, for any purpose he chooses. Along with hospitals and educational institutions, some nongovernmental organizations benefit from this kind of giving. This point of view provides one framework for thinking about these organizations, appropriate for those with purposes that tug at the heart strings—"the sailors, dogs, and children" group, as the British say—but wholly unrealistic in regard to those with less emotional pull.

Another framework is provided by the notion that at least certain nongovernmental organizations are national resources of such importance to the public welfare that their financial health cannot be entrusted to the vagaries of individual philanthropy. Here people in government tend to take the view that financial responsibility lies essentially with the foundations and business, an assumption that neither accepts.

With the exception of a number of quite small, local trusts, most foundations take the position that only in exceptional circumstances is the provision of long-term, general support to an organization justified. They tend to be especially wary if the purpose for which a general support grant is requested is simply to put an organization into a position to accept government project grants or contracts. Indeed, the foundations regard project support as *their* particular province and are not ready to have responsibility for some other role thrust on them. Their funds, they argue, are severely limited in size and must be used for the kinds of experimental purposes for which no other funds are available. While this antipathy to general support may be as disappointing to the nongovernmental organizations as is the restricted policy of government, any other attitude would soon tie up foundations' funds and destroy the flexibility that gives them their unique value.

Within the business community the general rule seems to be that corporate giving, beyond donations to educational institutions, hospitals, and the usual private charities, should be restricted to purposes at least indirectly related to a company's interests. Thus, a firm with markets in Latin America is more likely to support a private organization providing technical assistance there than one with the same purposes in Southeast Asia. Or a company manufacturing agricultural machinery may support an organization concerned with farm life but probably not one involved in, say, the arts. This is understandable. But the net effect is that a number of nongovernmental organizations qualify for little or no support from business at all.

Beyond that is the fact that some companies either cannot or do not choose to give. And for all of them there remains the basic consideration that they are by nature profit-making, not philanthropic, enterprises. So while it may be argued cogently that business firms should support nongovernmental organizations more heavily, there are some good reasons why, for the present anyway, passing the hat among them is a frustrating exercise.

Finally, those in Washington who regard the private sector as having full financial responsibility for the nongovernmental organizations, even organizations essentially serving important public purposes, seem to be less than fully aware of the enormously increased costs today of operating these agencies. Both administrative and program costs have risen drastically, because salaries have had to be raised to meet the competition offered by rising government and academic salaries.

A more fundamental explanation, however, of why the resources of the private sector are no longer adequate lies in the dramatic rise of our national aspirations. Under Great Society legislation we have launched a frontal assault on many of the nation's most grievous social, economic, and environmental problems — in poverty, civil rights, health, education, welfare, urban renewal, and air and water pollution. The nation has taken on enormous new tasks costing hitherto undreamed of sums. The impact on government has been traumatic. And no less forceful has been the impact on private organizations. They, however, lack within the private sector a new source of funds comparable to the new kinds of congressional appropriations available to federal agencies.

While comparisons between nations are always hazardous it would appear that the same type of conscious reexamination of the role of the nongovernmental organization and reassessment of its relationship with government which have taken place in Britain since the appearance there of the Welfare State twenty years ago must now take place in the United States. Influential in the British reexamination have been Lord Beveridge's book *Voluntary Action*, published in 1948, the report of the Nathan Committee in 1952, and the subsequent Charities Act of 1960. From these and other contributions to the debate there have emerged both a reaffirmation of the value of voluntary effort in a democratic society and a new recognition of the interdependence of voluntary and statutory effort in an era of greatly expanded governmental responsibility for social welfare. The reexamination in this country must, however, be extended beyond simply the social welfare field to other areas, such as international education and technical assistance, where nongovernmental organizations are now in partnership with government. Furthermore, the process here will be more complex because, among other reasons, our three-tier system of government provides a greater variety of relationships with the nongovernmental organizations.

The Central Issue

Nonetheless, the real issue is beginning to emerge clearly. Is the nongovernmental organization of the future to be simply an auxiliary to the state, a kind of willing but not very resourceful handmaiden? Or is it to be a strong, independent adjunct that provides government with a type of capability it cannot provide for itself?

If it is to be the latter, and for most Americans the question is one that is likely to admit of no other answer, then we must face up to the difficult problem of how we are to finance these organizations. More can be done on the private side, as private responsibility will — and should — continue. For example, there might perhaps be some advantages to be found in experimenting more widely with the notion of cooperative fundraising which has worked so well for some community chest organizations. But the question must also be raised as to whether responsibility for the general financial health of at least the most important of the nongovernmental organizations should not now be shared by the federal government. Certainly the time has come for a comprehensive and careful study of the problem from both the governmental and nongovernmental sides.

If such a study should confirm the findings suggested by informal evidence and indicate the need for a new approach by government, three problems will then have to be considered: the mechanism for distribution of general support, how such support can be given without comprising the independence of the organizations aided, and how quality can be maintained.

Would a new central mechanism in Washington, created with a broad charter, to act as a sort of analogue to the National Science Foundation, prove feasible as a device for channeling general support grants to the nongovernmental organizations? It would seem so in theory, but there would be many problems that might make the idea unworkable. A more practical approach, but one that also contains potential dangers for the organization seeking funds, would be to have each federal agency decide for itself which organizations it considered essential for its purposes and then determine the amount of general support each should receive. As noted above, such a process would have to be rigorously selective, with a wary eye open for possible incompetents and self-servers. The process would also have to be based on criteria politically defensible to Congress and the public.

Preserving the independence of the organizations aided would not appear to be an insoluble problem, although it may be a more difficult one than guaranteeing the independence of the universities has proven to be. It would require on the part of many people in the administration and in Congress a new attitude of greater trust in the nongovernmental organizations. It would entail new administrative practices, based in some cases on new regulations or even on new legislation but in other cases simply on a more liberal interpretation of existing regulations. Lastly, it would demand of the nongovernmental organizations that they continue to seek a wide diversification in the sources of their income, and linkages to as many constituencies as possible.

Government acceptance of a shared responsibility for the financial health of those nongovernmental organizations on whose services it most depends would not solve the problem of how other organizations, not linked to government, are to be adequately financed in the world of tomorrow. But it would be a specific response to the pressing difficulties of at least some of our most valuable private agencies. If we want to avoid an ever more extensive and powerful federal government, it would seem that we must now, paradoxically, use federal money to ensure that we have a viable alternative — a network of vigorous, well-financed nongovernmental organizations ready to service government but able, in the public interest, to maintain their independence of it. This further financial burden on government may be unpalatable to many. But the logic of it is hard to escape.

31

Reclaiming the American Dream

RICHARD C. CORNUELLE

RICHARD C. CORNUELLE ESTABLISHED THE FOUNDATION FOR
VOLUNTARY WELFARE. HIS WRITINGS ALSO INCLUDE
DEMANAGING AMERICA: THE FINAL REVOLUTION.

*This selection includes excerpts of four chapters from
Cornuelle's* Reclaiming the American Dream. *They are
"The Rediscovery of Independent Action," "The
Independent Sector," "The Failure of the Independent
Sector," and "Big Brotherhood or a Free Society."*

Overwhelmed by the problems of the Depression, we suddenly turned most of
our attention to Washington. In so doing, we unconsciously turned our backs on
the tradition of non-governmental action which had held our dream together for
150 years. We suddenly forgot this tradition, dropped it from our conversation,
almost as if it had never existed.

It quickly became fashionable to speak of American life in terms of only two
"sectors": the *public sector*, which is a prejudicial euphemism for government,
and the *private sector*, which is profit-seeking commerce. We leave out the
third sector in our national life, the one which is neither governmental nor
commercial. We ignore the institutions which once played such a decisive part
in the society's vibrant growth. By assuming a major role in meeting public
needs, thus leaving less to government, this third sector once made it possible
for us to build a humane society and a free society together.

This important third force deserves a name. It is a distinct, identifiable part
of American life, not just a misty area between commerce and government. I
have come to call it *"the independent sector."* After some years of work among
the people and organizations operating in this sector, no other word seems to
express its unique, intrepid character as well as the word "independent."

When I first began to sense the importance of the independent sector, I discovered the best analysis of its function had been written by Alexis de Tocqueville, the young French aristocrat who came to our young nation in the 1830s. His monumental *Democracy in America* provided such prophetic insight into the inner working of this country that generations of scholars have been forced to argue with his conclusions or accept them. They cannot ignore him. Few have improved on his work.

Tocqueville saw the American impulse to act independently on the public business as our most remarkable trait. He marveled not so much at our economic success and our political machinery as at our tendency to handle public business directly and spontaneously. He wrote that our "associations"—his word for independent institutions—were the key to a social system that he deeply admired. He saw the vigor, ingenuity, and enterprise of these associations, and sensed the *boundless* potential of their work.

Yet, as we have seen, the popular writers of our day don't even mention Tocqueville's "associations." People now talk only of the public and the private sectors. The habit is almost as pronounced among conservatives as among liberals, and it seriously limits the vision and action of both. Businessmen speak of America as a free enterprise system, as if this were a total description of our way of life. We do, of course, organize our commercial sector, by and large, on free enterprise principles, but free enterprise isn't an all-purpose social system. To try to make it so is to push it beyond its limits, and thus invite government to do whatever business can't do.

The omission of the independent sector also distorts our discussions of our governmental system. We speak of America as a democracy or a republic. We mean only that the people elect the officials who run the government sector. But political democracy is only a fraction of our heritage. Except where the vote is denied, voting is perhaps one of the least effective acts of the responsible citizen. But to describe America as a democracy implies that voting represents a citizen's total responsibility.

America has been unique, not because we organize our commercial sector on free enterprise lines or because we elect those who control government, although we talk about these things the most. We have been unique because another sector, clearly distinct from the other two, has, in the past, borne a heavy load of public responsibility.

When you push back the curtain that has strangely hidden the independent sector from the public eye, one surprise follows another. You notice dozens of agencies that serve you daily. The sector's dimensions are fantastic, its raw strength awesome.

In a sharpened awareness, people who think government is the only source of welfare suddenly discover new facts. A university faculty member, for instance, will realize that he, along with 180,000 colleagues in 1,300 leading schools, gets his medical insurance and pension rights from Teachers Insurance and Annuity Association, a national independent agency that out-performs state retirement plans. TIAA stands as a visible giant among independent institutions, but many of our independent agencies long ago blended into the social landscape. Under the spotlight, they take on a variety of forms so rich they can be illustrated but never fully described.

Sometimes the independent impulse shows itself in humble, simple ways, as when our new neighbors brought a pot of soup and offered to sit with the baby when we moved into our tract house in San Mateo.

Sometimes it shows itself boldly and professionally, as when the National Foundation for Infantile Paralysis set out to conquer polio with dimes—and did it.

Sometimes the independent sector deals with small pleasures, as when my wife's Garden Guild attends to floral decorations at our church.

But often it deals with grave problems, as when Stanford Research Institute designs weapons systems and strategy on which our defense depends.

Sometimes independent action is impulsive, as when thousands of Americans mailed $600,000 to Dallas Patrolman J.D. Tippit's grief-stricken wife and $78,000 to the assassin's stunned young widow. But often it is highly systematic, as when the Ford Foundation coaches colleges and universities in the complexities of long-range capital planning.

Sometimes the independent sector does menial, dirty work, as when volunteer hospital aides empty the bedpans and bandage the oozing sores of patients in hospitals all across the country. But often it does what is most gracious and aesthetic, as when the Guggenheim family builds a magnificent museum or citizens in Pittsburgh sponsor the display of the work of their local artists in the foyers of business and public places.

Sometimes the independent sector does silly things. The Air Mail from God Mission used to drop Protestant tracts from airplanes on the Catholic villages in rural Mexico. But as often, independent institutions work with great sophistication, as when the Sloan-Kettering Institute develops an effective chemotherapy for some forms of cancer and doggedly continues to search for better ways to fight this killer.

Sometimes independent action shows itself in ugly, perverse ways, as when the Ku Klux Klan organizes a vigilante force to terrorize Negro Americans or the Minutemen drill grimly in their cellars. But more often, it moves with a soul-stirring magnificence, as when Dr. Tom Dooley hurriedly raised money to finish his hospital in the Laotian jungle before cancer drained his life away.

Sometimes independent action is highly individual. Leo Seligman of Memphis, who learned about prison life the hard way in a Nazi concentration camp, has met 786 parolees at prison gates in Tennessee with bus fare, lunch, and a helping hand. But it is often highly organized. The Boy Scouts can tell you to the penny how much it takes to set up a troop.

Independent action is sometimes invisible. Did you know more private than public land is available free for camping? (And California's Redwood Association has launched a program among lumbermen to provide still more public camp sites on private land.) Sometimes the independent sector screams for attention, as when mass media annually harangue us to contribute to United Fund campaigns.

Independent action is sometimes frivolous, as when groups are organized for treks in classic cars or to learn to be amateur clowns. But it is sometimes in deadly earnest, as when the business leaders of Dallas jointly acted to integrate the schools and privately owned public facilities of their city.

Sometimes the independent sector provides our luxuries. Most of our opera houses are independent institutions, and independent symphonies provide cultural leaven in more than twelve hundred American communities. Sometimes it provides desperate necessities, as when Salvation Army centers give a meal and a bed to men who would otherwise sleep hungry in the street.

Sometimes independent action is inane, as when a group sought to make Alcatraz a museum of horrors, its cells permanently occupied by wax replicas of the prison's famous inmates. But sometimes it is forward-looking and ingenious, as when the Upjohn Foundation combined with Systems Development Corporation to work out a national system of finding and communicating job opportunities to the jobless.

The independent sector is a kaleidoscope of human action. It takes a thousand forms and works in a million ways.

The independent sector often puts its resources to work magnificently. It is capable of stunning social accomplishments.

A national private organization, as we have seen, just about wiped out polio.

America's "worst" community, Chicago's back-of-the-yards, the setting for Upton Sinclair's *The Jungle,* long ago took its affairs into its own hands and renewed itself. Saul Alinsky, a leader with a gift for getting results, shaped the harsh drive toward clear goals. The people living back-of-the-yards faced problems that would send most communities screaming to Washington in despair— not enough jobs, slum housing, rats, racketeers, dope, illiteracy. But back-of-the-yards now wins awards because it is so clean and orderly. When a problem comes up, the people solve it. The meat packers who employed many of the people in back-of the-yards are now moving out of Chicago. So the back-of-the-yards Neighborhood Council goes out and recruits new industry. Its main asset? Hard-working people you can count on. The Jungle has become a showcase of independent action. And Alinsky, his methods tested and proved, has turned to organizing the Negro drive to wipe out Chicago's South Side slum.

In Indianapolis, Cleo Blackburn set out to renew a Negro slum. He got the banks to lend money for land and materials. He copied the technical methods of Indiana's prefabricated housing industry—so he could use unskilled labor to build houses. He persuaded a foundation to pay the small cost of a technical center to coach the men on how to work. He organized the slum-dwellers into teams, and together they built their houses. The bank took their work as a down payment—sweat equity, Blackburn calls it. The people have built hundreds of houses this way. They've renewed the face and spirit of their community, which is now driving confidently into a total attack on hard-core unemployment.

On Long Island, an independent organization led by Henry Viscardi, a paraplegic, has helped hundreds of crippled people become completely self-supporting. He restores their spirit and determination, and then, often using specially designed equipment and machinery, offers them solid, soul-satisfying work to do.

The Mormons take care of all the welfare needs of all members, and did so through the Depression.

Alcoholics Anonymous seldom fails to help an alcoholic who actually wants help.

Another independent organization, Recovery, Inc., now helps mental patients rebuild their lives by A.A.'s methods.

Charles Lavin has converted older luxury hotels into apartments and given older people comfortable room and board for as little as $86.50 a month. He made it possible for residents to pay part of this cost by helping with the work.

The independent Sears Foundation puts doctors in rural areas by showing communities exactly how they can attract and hold young doctors.

In 1955, a thirty-seven-year-old Presbyterian minister, Millard Roberts, took charge of Iowa's Parsons College. The college was dead on its feet: it owed creditors $1.2 million; it had only 212 students. Its yearly income was $194,000;

its deficit, $116,000. It valued its plant at $700,000. Faculty salaries averaged $2,800 a year. By 1963, Parsons had paid its long-term debt, its plant was worth $5 million; it had 2,200 students; faculty salaries averaged $13,000; its yearly income was $4,700,000. The percentage of faculty members with doctors degrees had increased from 23 to 80 percent. While other college presidents were standing in line for federal money, Roberts arranged a $4.4 million loan from a bank at going rates to build an even bigger campus.

But the independent sector, in spite of its great strength and sporadically incredible achievements, is rapidly falling behind the burgeoning commercial and government sectors.

What's the trouble? Why is the importance of this vast potential so rapidly declining? Why do we ignore this great and growing strength of the independent sector when we form public policy? Why does a leading economist contend that it is fit only to maintain dog cemeteries and sanctuaries for birds?

The answer is simple. The independent sector is now unreliable. It performs unevenly. Its brilliant achievements stand in contrast to miserable failures, to a stubborn backwardness.

I live in California, but my work often takes me to New York. Every so often, something like this happens: I leave New York at four in the afternoon in a jet that puts me in San Francisco at six-thirty. With luck, I can make a seven o'clock board meeting of the local unit of a private welfare agency with which I've worked for several years. The contrast is incredible. My airline reservation has been handled by a computer; the plane crosses the continent in five hours, safely and comfortably. But at the board meeting I may hear a report on how many lap robes the needlework committee knitted and stitched together the month before. The airline, in the commercial sector, operates in the twentieth century and has made it the jet age. The welfare agency, in the independent sector, still operates in the nineteenth century, and is genially content with rustic methods.

The commercial sector has led the way into radically new technology, new markets, and new forms of organization. The government sector has, by a more recent surge, grown enormously in size and scope. It has even become the largest single customer for computers. But the independent sector did not keep the pace. It stumbled blindly into the twentieth century. It failed to grasp the new demands placed upon it and develop new methods to meet them.

It has become the fashion to wind up books about public policy by talking about the "impact of technology." Like most cliches, this one arises from an inescapable fact. We do live uneasily in what *Fortune* editor Max Ways has termed "The Era of Radical Change," and men's technology powers the change.

It is, of course, tempting to exaggerate the consequences of change. It makes good copy. Writers have made hair-raising predictions about the effects of automation, glibly forecasting that men, displaced by machines, will soon stand idle and obsolete in their own world.

Even more frightening are the predictions that technology will be used to control and homogenize men. Socialist George Orwell's vivid *1984* described a world without freedom, a world in which machines are used as instruments of tyranny to perceive and punish even the most timid expression of individuality. Orwell's book was an honest account of the consequences of the new technology if used by the political system that he described. On the conservative side, Professor Friedrich A. Hayek has pointed out that absolute tyranny has become daily more feasible. Medieval tyrants could exercise sporadic cruelty over their subjects. But sustained, total surveillance by Big Brother, with electronic eyes and brains, has become possible only in recent years. Now it can be done. We will build Aldous Huxley's *Brave New World* if we do not build a free world.

Hayek and Orwell both show us that technology magnifies the threat of tyranny, or, in other words, the coming of a one-sector society. And in the United States, we are almost halfway there. A two-sector society is unstable. Saul Alinsky wanted me to title this book...*3-2-1*, like a countdown. He meant that if a three-sector society becomes a two-sector society, it will then soon become a one-sector society.

We can see the symptoms. We watch liberals and conservatives thrown into acrid but arid conflict. Their valid ambitions clash and destroy each other. Political activity merely strengthens government. Conservatives are doomed to ineffectiveness, liberals driven to expand government or abandon their idealism. And the commercial sector, unprotected, stands naked in a conflict it cannot win.

As the knowledge explosion hastens change, it can only accelerate this grim process. The warfare merely moves to a higher technological level; the Orwellian nightmare becomes a preview of tomorrow.

But the coin has another side. If men carefully and deliberately use new knowledge in the independent sector, they can magnify its effectiveness many times over. The information explosion can be its salvation.

Only our central superstition pushes us in the opposite direction. It is the dogma that only government can make the powerful new technology serve the public. Science will consign us to the Orwellian hell only if government becomes the sole manager of change. Yet the superstition that only government can focus today's technology on social problems has become a mental reflex.

Recently, in the wake of cutbacks in defense contracts for research and development in weapons and the possibility of more cuts to come, there has been speculation about how this excess talent should be put to work. One possibility widely discussed is that this fabulous know-how be applied to public problems— education, mass transportation, air-pollution control, desalting sea water, and reducing urban crime. Arthur Barber, Deputy Assistant Secretary of Defense for arms control, said: "The nation has created in the defense complexes the greatest problem-solving talent of all time. On the other hand, we have enormous problems in many areas of civilian life. It would be tragic not to bring the two together." But who will do it? Many think only government can. The president of one huge weapons corporation says: "Only governments need the large and complex systems we are organized to produce."

If this is true, the conflict which now divides us can only intensify. Liberals, in their eagerness to solve public problems, will insist that government massively apply technology to their solution. Conservatives, seeing in computerized government a multiplied threat to freedom, will intensify their Kamikaze attacks on big government. In such a continuation of the liberal-conservative impasse, men would become the helpless victims of marching robots. Technology would be the means men use to enslave each other, "to fight their way into prison," as English essayist Charles Morgan once put it.

But if, on the other hand, we put our new technology to work in strong drive to rehabilitate the citizen's capacity for public service, the machine will be the emancipator. We can put man's new understanding to work more promptly and effectively than government can. The recent signs of a revitalized capacity for direct action suggests that technological tyranny may not be the wave of the future. Men want to use the machines, rather than be used by them.

The critical question is not, Who can use the technology? but, Who will?

We can build whatever kind of world we want. We can build the good society— prosperous, humane, free—on a scale that defies our present capacity to see the future. Step by step, as the whole society discovers new ways to use its new tools, we can turn them to purposes not yet clear to us. We know that the free economy will provide more and more of whatever people want to buy. We know that we will have more and more free time and more ways to enjoy it. Almost everybody will be able to deepen his life through artistic and creative effort. But the ultimate mark of dignity will be the use of more time, and more resources, on voluntary service. We can, indeed we must, grow as responsible individuals and regain a full sense of human purpose.

The key to these ambitions, I believe, is the independent sector.

Through it, we can restore the supportive circle whereby America originally put its unique emphasis on personal dignity. We can again insure our freedom by limiting the powers of central government. Being free, we can move to ever higher planes of prosperity and ever greater human aspirations. We can, as we learn how, focus our growing prosperity directly and imaginatively on real human needs.

We can reclaim the American dream.

32

The Role of Philanthropy in a Changing Society

COMMISSION ON FOUNDATIONS AND PRIVATE PHILANTHROPY

*The Commission on Foundations and Private Philanthropy
was created in 1968 at the initiation of John D. Rockefeller
3rd. Mr. Rockefeller invited Peter G. Peterson, Chairman
of Bell and Howell, to form a commission of private
citizens which would conduct an objective appraisal of
philanthropic foundations in America and make long-term
policy recommendations. Fifteen distinguished individuals
representing diverse viewpoints were selected and funding
was provided by a variety of nonfoundation sources. The
following selection is the second chapter of the
commission's final report.*

In America these days, nothing stands still in one place for very long. Old systems of thought are unhinged. The legitimacy of most forms of authority is being questioned. People with unredressed grievances and with hopes deferred too long have become impatient with patience. In this strained atmosphere the institutions of philanthropy, like almost all other institutions, face a rising demand that they justify their inner life and their external effects.

The first question asked about them is this: are the dynamics at American philanthropic institutions congruous with America's highest interest? If that first question is ignored, or if it cannot be convincingly answered in the affirmative, then the fate in store for philanthropy could resemble that of the man in the fable who was so abstracted from his own life that he scarcely knew he existed until one fine morning he awoke and found himself dead.

Reprinted from *Foundations, Private Giving, and Public Policy: Report and Recommendations of the Commission on Foundations and Private Philanthropy* (Chicago: University of Chicago Press, 1970) by permission of the publisher. Copyright ©1970 by The University of Chicago.

There are some who may agree "in principle" with the worth of private philanthropy, but, when a crunch is on, they view philanthropy as Lord Melbourne, prime minister of England in the early years of Queen Victoria's reign, viewed religion. "I have," said he, "as much respect for religion as the next person. But things have come to a pretty pass when religion is allowed to interfere with England's interests."

Critics who assert that American philanthropy actually goes against the grain of America's highest interest advance several lines of argument in support of their conclusions.

They say first that philanthropy in America is hardly "pure" in motive, nor is it an evangelical expression of human fraternity. It is tied at the hip bone to tax deductions and, as such, is a self-serving instrument of greater use to the wealthy than to the average taxpayer. Why? Because under existing tax laws, persons in the lower income brackets have little incentive to contribute to charity. But, as a taxpayer with rising income moves into higher tax brackets, the more do deductions for charity increase in importance; the higher his income, the less each dollar he contributes costs him in after-tax income, or, to put it another way, the more these charitable contributions cost the government. Further, only the wealthy, and not people of modest means, are likely to be in a position to gain substantial added tax benefits by giving appreciated property instead of cash to philanthropic institutions. Present tax laws, therefore, foster a concentration of philanthropic giving (especially for nonreligious purposes) in the hands of the rich.

This in turn, so it is argued, means that tax incentives for charitable giving serve the process of "elitism" instead of the cause of "democratic pluralism." It serves that process because wealthy people are free to use billions of dollars to support their eccentricities and hobbies—billions of dollars which would otherwise be absorbed into the pool of government funds for uses approved by a vote of the representatives of the people. No similar freedom or subsidy is available for the less well-to-do. Even when the latter deduct their charitable contributions from taxable income, their margin of freedom is confined to their choice of the organizations which will receive their donations. They will, however, have little say about what is done with the money they contribute. Board members of charitable organizations are more likely to be the larger donors to it.

Second, say the critics, it is wrong to take at face value the claims of philanthropic organizations that, since they are private, they are a more efficient instrument of action than the government, and that there is a commitment behind private dollars which government dollars lack. There may be more important goals and more efficient means to attain them, and in any case there is no guarantee that the private commitment is actually in the public interest.

The freedom of private philanthropic organizations to choose their own goals can lead to redundant or wasteful disbursement, the scattering of seeds that produce only a harvest of dead leaves, and a diversion—into the high costs of public relations and advertising incident to fundraising—of money meant for charitable causes.

The critics then ask a passionate question. When funds are desperately needed to support massive governmental efforts to solve acute social problems, why should tax dollars be lost in the form of charitable deductions for privately selected purposes? After all, the very existence of the tax incentive for philanthropy plainly means that charitable expenditures are not purely private expenditures. They are made partly with dollars which, were it not for charitable deductions allowed by tax laws, would have become public funds to be allocated through the governmental process under the controlling power of the electorate as a whole. Thus, say the critics, in place of a democratic allocation of resources, we have a market place for philanthropy dominated by a plutocracy that can do what it pleases without being called to public account for what it does.

Is there an answer to these lines of argument? The Commission is convinced that there is. At the same time, in formulating its own answering argument, the Commission has taken care to bypass the ambush of three assumptions. It does not assume that private philanthropy is a perfect system that has no need for further, and perhaps substantial, improvement. It does not assume that the system will never have any entries in its record of some follies, excesses, redundancy—and, above all, of some of the failures that are inherent in pioneering, high risk ventures. Least of all does the Commission assume that the system can make a "perfect allocation" of its resources, "accountable in full" to the public—a concept, incidentally, which cannot even be defined precisely, let alone attained.

The heart of the Commission's position, expressed in shorthand form, comes to this. Despite the claims made about how governmental decisions are less "elitist," more "democratic," and "more accountable to the public," the test of practical experience clearly makes a strong *dual* system of private giving *and* government funding a better way to allocate resources for the general welfare than the alternative of relying solely on governmental allocations.

Stated more fully, the Commission's judgment of such a dual system of private giving and public funding rests on the following propositions transposed into the form of beliefs:

1. We believe that the improvement of the material and moral condition of the individual human being is central to our society's outlook.

2.   We believe that just as the health of a muscle depends on its being exercised, the individual braces his freedom and enlarges his perceptions through actions on behalf of others which he initiates voluntarily and for which he is willing to assume personal responsibility.

3.   We believe that a society which encourages a sense among its citizens that they have a reciprocal responsibility for themselves and for others strengthens its own fabric—whereas a society which spurs every man to live in and for himself alone weakens the society by weakening the bonds of fraternity.

4.   We believe that government is destined to play an ever-increasing and indispensable role in areas that have traditionally been served by private philanthropic activity. While a government limited in power to the work of a policeman on the beat was adequate for a society whose frontier ran parallel to the land, it is not adequate for a society whose frontier runs perpendicular to the land in the form of our giant industrial complexes and our great urban areas. Unless the power of government is brought to bear on the salient problems of our highly urbanized and industrialized civilization, the problems will increase, not diminish. It is worth recalling that at the onset of the Great Depression of the 1930s, there were people who felt that the economic collapse would right itself through the curative power of "natural causes" and that private philanthropy in the meantime could take care of people in acute distress. Nothing of the sort was in fact possible, and the reluctance—on doctrinaire grounds—to invoke the power of government in order to revive the economy served only to make the economic distress more acute.

5.   At the same time, we believe that government should not venture to do those things which private citizens and private institutions can do as well or better. Government by its nature must generalize, and it moves toward its decisions slowly. Human life itself, however, is infinitely varied in its nuances, in its perceptions, in the directions in which it moves, and in the pace at which it moves. Our society, therefore, is in obvious need of private philanthropic institutions standing outside the frame of government but in support of the public interest—

just as scouts move in advance of a main body of troops to probe what lies ahead. We need philanthropic institutions which can spot emergent problems, diagnose them, and test alternative ways to deal with them.

This is not to say that private funds should merely provide an increment—even though a relatively small one—to what government is doing. A narrow view of that kind would weaken any justification for the existence of philanthropy as an island of autonomy alongside a system of government funding. It would weaken any justification for the diversion of money that would otherwise become funds in the public treasury. Such diversion—exclusive of the realm of religion, from which the government is constitutionally excluded—is most strongly justified when private philanthropic money is used, not as a substitute for tax dollars, but as a supplement of a special kind that serves the public interest in ways in which the government itself is under various operational constraints.

A major case in point turns on the question of whether social change in our day will be a product of the blind play of accident and force or whether it will result from rational reflection and deliberate choice. If we want it to be a result of rational reflection and deliberate choice, then we need social laboratories where new ideas and social innovation are extremely important—at least as important as technological innovation—and probably even more difficult and less understood. In an era of unprecedented technological innovations, social innovation lags seriously. Yet, there is a suggestive analogy between the way new things are born in the commercial sector and the way the support by private philanthropy for laboratory tests of social innovations can lead to an impressive payoff.

In the commercial sector, success usually starts with a vision, often very personal, of what tomorrow's consumers will want, and whether there are technological possibilities of meeting it. The mere bigness of a large industrial establishment, however, is no guarantee that it will have that kind of vision or will have it exclusively. Large industrial establishments can be the captive of a self-generated consensus which says with great force that a proposed new technology is not workable or that the market does not want it or need it. But this is not always the last word about the matter. An entrepreneur, often small, new, and from an unlikely background, arrives on the commercial scene. He is committed to a vision of how a proposed new technology *is* workable and why consumers of tomorrow will want it and need it. He manages to get access to venture capital—a crucial need. He subjects his judgment to a practical test in the formidable world of real things.

In the social realm as well, the consensus mechanism of the large, established institutions of government are not always the best and are certainly not the only way to innovate measures that lead to orderly social change. In statist societies, governments held in thrall by ideologies and dogmas have irrevocably committed the lives of millions of people to large-scale social experiments— such as farm collectivization—with cruel and costly consequences. Even governments of democratic societies have initiated massive programs on the basis of untested theories. Great expectations were aroused by the claimed benefits of what these programs would lead to. But the expectations eventually collapsed, and the result served only to increase public cynicism about the whole of the political process.

The moral of the story is clear. Just as the technological realm and the commercial realm need the innovative individual and the small firm, so does our social realm need them. It needs the person or the single, small institution to have a new vision of what should and can be done. But who will "sponsor" the necessary experiment with "venture capital"? The innovators must be in a position to choose from among alternative sponsors. If their range of choice is confined only to the sponsorship of the federal government, then the innovative process is bound to suffer a loss of the mobility, diversity, pluralism, and decentralization that are prerequisites of orderly social change. There would be this loss, first, because the inner life of government is strained to the limit in merely trying to find the resources that can meet today's massive and pressing needs. Government is not inclined to focus on the long tomorrow. An administration tends to concentrate its thoughts and efforts to the hard enough task of merely staying afloat in today's storms. It has little reserve strength for any major planning and developmental initiatives bearing on a future in which a new administration will have the responsibilities of power.

It is true that individual states in the American union can be laboratories for social experiments. They are places where "pilot projects" can be put to the test of practice, and successful social inventions can then become, by adoption, the common property of the nation. This, indeed, is a root source of strength for our federal system of government. Yet the problems besetting our society are so many and so complex that we need many different kinds of laboratories where social experiments can be conducted. Private philanthropy can help fill this need.

We have also reached an hour in American history when no institution can cultivate its own garden wall. Walls of privacy have been breached by the daily shocks and eruptions that have swept across American life. The spirit of dissent has spread its contagion across our student population and from there to other sectors of American life. And we deceive ourselves if we think the signs and sounds of distress are limited to an anarchistic handful of young people. If they are not to reach their climax in a war of all against all, we are summoned by this turmoil carefully to consider the ways in which we can convert dissent into a force for constructive action and civil peace.

We must evolve more responsive processes through which our young and disenfranchised can secure a fair piece of the social action, whether or not they can acquire a piece of our affluent *economic* action.

Indeed, perhaps it is fair to say that part of the unrest in our society is due to the paradoxical fact that nothing fails like success—that the more successful we have been in assuring the citizen his physical needs will be met, the more sensitive he becomes to other cravings of his soul and mind, as he yearns to realize his potentialities as a human being. In this yearning, he becomes all the more aware of institutional structures, with their inertia and congealed ideologies. He feels that all these stand between him and his vision of an elevated condition of life.

In this seemingly chaotic and clearly diverse and demanding setting, it is perhaps true that only a pluralistic society can become a responsive one. Philanthropy, we believe, must bring a fresh understanding of what pluralism can mean in American life.

We have said a pluralistic society must be one in which multiple options and multiple initiatives are open to its members. Multiple options more than ever will require a mature understanding of majority and minority approaches, living side by side. Responsive pluralism requires the majority be willing to place itself under a self-denying ordinance *not* to use the weight of its larger numbers to crush the minority's claim for equitable consideration and coexistence. It means conversely that the minority is willing to place itself under a self-denying ordinance not to use for frivolous and vengeful reasons any veto power it has over the desires of the majority.

This delicate balance cannot be legislated. It is a habit of the heart which reminds the citizen that today's majority might well be tomorrow's minority and, of course, that today's minority might well be tomorrow's majority.

Nor is this delicate balance likely to be funded by a majoritarian political process alone. We believe private sector philanthropy must be a major source of support for the multiple options our society offers.

Philanthropy, then, must have sufficient funds, so that it can respond to unmet and still unseen needs of society. Yet, if a Declaration of Independence does not by itself make a people free, neither will more funds by itself ensure philanthropy a defensible and relevant place in American life. To ensure such a place for itself, philanthropy must be independent and must use freedom in responsible and courageous ways. It will ensure nothing if it simply enjoys an easy popularity by applying its weight to the end of having everything stand still.

While we believe that the system of strong dual funding is based on sound theoretical principles, we also believe that it offers pragmatic advantages measurable in dollars and cents. In this connection, two points should be made about the relative "costs" to society of a private charity dollar compared to that of a governmental social dollar. First, the donor contributes part of the gift out of *his own net* worth—even after the tax deduction. Second, any review of cost effectiveness of the private charitable sector must also take into account a factor previously noted—namely, the value of the labor represented by volunteer work on behalf of philanthropies.

In 71 percent of the fifty-odd Chicago charitable organizations we interviewed, the number of volunteer workers exceeded the number of paid employees. If the modest value of three dollars per hour is placed on volunteer labor, then the dollar value of volunteer labor in one out of five Chicago charitable organizations exceeds the total payroll costs. This includes such organizations as the Chicago YMCA, Red Cross, United Cerebral Palsy, and Girl Scouts. A manpower survey recently completed by the Welfare Council of Metropolitan Chicago shows that Chicago agencies received more than a million hours per month of volunteer work for everything from the delivery of services to fundraising. Short of a concrete test, it is hard to say how many of the people involved in the delivery of services would reduce their voluntary work if functions now discharged by private charitable enterprises became a governmental monopoly. It seems fair to guess, however, that there would be a sharp fall–off in the quantity and quality of their efforts.

Values in dollars are not the only means for judging the worth of volunteer work in private philanthropy. Society also gains from the way the individual who voluntarily participates in philanthropic efforts builds up an immunity to a malaise common to our day. It is the malaise of the man who stands frustrated in the face of a thousand things he sees should be done. He wants to help make events become what they ought to be—to repair the broken connections between talk and being heard, between pain experienced and a remedy, between urgent needs and their solution. Yet, in the shadow of a big government he may feel powerless to do any of this by himself. Recoiling, he migrates psychologically out of society. He becomes indifferent alike to any good or evil befalling it and withdraws ever deeper into his private self.

It is otherwise with many individuals who volunteer for the work of private philanthropy. The more they conern themselves with the welfare of other people, the more alive they feel through having absorbed within themselves the throb of the society around them. The individual volunteer cannot do everything he would like to do. Yet when he does with all his might that which lies closest at hand, he is less frustrated because he is rewarded with a sense of his own identity—rewarded because he can see his identity stamped on the face of things he helped turn for the better through his personal efforts. He and society are jointly the gainers, whereas both would be the losers if private philanthropy was foreclosed, and its nondollar values were also wiped out.

The commission, in arriving at its conclusions about the merits of maintaining a dual system of public funding and private support for socially desirable projects, found it instructive to listen closely to a lesson taught by Europe's experiences with philanthropy.

It is enough to say here that, after the secular authorities in European nation-states for various reasons curbed the economic capacity of ecclesiastical organizations to engage in extensive philanthropic activities, the long-range consequences were fourfold. First, the sense of personal responsibility by the individual for the welfare of his neighbor was hobbled. Second, the government staked out a monopoly of decision and initiative in areas which, in American experience, were retained as a preserve for private philanthropic efforts. Third, in contrast to America, where private charitable institutions are often the prime innovators and experimenters in social, scientific, cultural, and educational fields, European society depended for its general welfare almost totally on the decisions of government itself. Fourth, this habit of dependence fostered in Europe the kind of stultifying attitudes and values which, in the archetype case of France, were recently excoriated by no less a person than the premier, Jacques Chaban-Delmas. Said he:

> An octopus, and an inefficient one! That is what—we all know it—the State is becoming, despite the fact that there is a corps of generally efficient, at times outstanding, civil servants. An octopus, I say, for, by indefinitely extending its responsibilities it has gradaully put our entire French society under its paternalism...
>
> The distribution of social subsidies is governed by a narrow legal concept of equality that leads to inequality. On the pretext of not distinguishing between beneficiaries, identically the same assistance is being given to those who have the greatest need of it, those who have only a moderate need of it, and those who have no need of it at all. Result: the initial aims are not achieved.
>
> ...[As] de Tocqueville demonstrated—and this continues to be true—there is a deep-lying connection between the omnipotence of the State and the weakness of community life in our country.

As a result of this situation, each social or occupational group, or rather their representatives, not feeling secure enough to be able to negotiate directly and responsibly with other groups, fall back on the practice of submitting their claims to the State, often complicating their claims with a somewhat veiled rivalry. Thus, all too often a real social dialogue is replaced with an appeal to the State for protection, which only strengthens further the State's control over the life of the people and, at the same time, places an excessively heavy burden on the entire economy.

In addition to what the Commission learned from European experience, sources lying closer to home stressed the worth of maintaining a dual system of public funding and private support for socially desirable projects. The Commission put a specific question to fifty Chicago charitable organizations which have had intimate experience with various kinds of financial support. Would they favor government support for the work done by their own organizations being increased to a point at which there was little or no room for private effort? Almost all replies strongly opposed any such total reliance on public funding to the exclusion of private support. It was observed that, under such an arrangement, social efforts would be affected by every turn in the political winds, by every accident flowing from a change of administration, and by every political scramble for government funds. Further, as the power of day-to-day decisions gravitated to the governmental bureaucracy, an all-too familiar consequence would start to unfold. The realities of local conditions—whether on the side of danger or of opportunity—either would not be seen or might be forced to fit a bureaucratic Procrustean bed.

Autonomous islands of private philanthropy existing side by side with a system for public funding provide indispensable initiatives to change. In the realm of social efforts, such an arrangement corresponds to what we have evolved in the realm of economic efforts—a "mixed economy" arrangement that serves as a model to the world.

THE COMMISSION ON FOUNDATIONS AND
PRIVATE PHILANTHROPY
1968-70

J. Paul Austin
Daniel Bell
Daniel P. Bryant
James Chambers
Sheldon S. Cohen
Thomas B. Curtis
Paul A. Freund
Martin Friedman

Patricia Roberts Harris
A. Leon Higginbotham, Jr.
Lane Kirkland
Philip R. Lee
Edward H. Levi
Franklin A. Long
A.S. Mike Monroney
Peter G. Peterson, Chairman

Staff
Executive Director
Everett L. Hollis

Associate Directors
Fritz Heimann
Walter J. Blum

Assistant Directors
William A. Wineberg
John R. Labovitz

Chairman, Finance Committee
Hermon Dunlap Smith

33

The Third Sector

COMMISSION ON PRIVATE PHILANTHROPY AND PUBLIC NEEDS

*The Commission on Private Philanthropy and Public Needs
was formed in 1973 with the initial impetus again provided
by John D. Rockefeller 3rd who felt that a reliable
empirical data base was needed for the public and the
government to make informed policy decisions. Under the
direction of John H. Filer as Chairman and Leonard L.
Silverstein as Executive Director, the Commission worked
from 1973 to 1975 to gather information, analysis, and
opinions on the function of private philanthropy in our
society and its relationship to government. The
Commission was funded entirely by private sources, but it
maintained a close working relationship with government
agencies at all levels. The following selection is the opening
chapter of the Commission's final report* Giving in
America. *In many ways, the Commission's work
represented a benchmark and therefore, although they
may date the piece slightly, I have not attempted to remove
statistical data describing the sector in 1974.*

On the map of American society, one of the least charted regions is variously
known as the voluntary, the private nonprofit or simply the third sector. Third,
that is, after the often overshadowing worlds of government and business.
While these two other realms have been and continue to be microscopically
examined and analyzed and while their boundaries are for the most part readily

Reprinted from *Giving in America: Toward a Stronger Voluntary Sector* (Washington, DC:
Commission on Private Philanthropy and Public Needs, 1975) by permission of Mr. Leonard L.
Silverstein, Executive Director of the Commission.

identified by experts and laymen alike, the third sector—made up of non-governmental, nonprofit associations and organizations—remains something of a terra incognita, barely explored in terms of its inner dynamics and motivations, and its social, economic and political relations to the rest of the world. As on ancient maps, its boundaries fade off into extensions of the imagination, and a monster or two may lurk in the surrounding seas.

Yet it is within this institutional domain that nearly all philanthropic input—giving and volunteering—is transformed into philanthropic output—goods and services for ultimate beneficiaries. So the Commission has attempted to take the measure of this area, both quantitatively and qualitatively, and has examined the sector's roles and rationales, past, present and future.

The sector as a whole is most broadly defined by what it is not. It is not government — that is, its component organizations do not command the full power and authority of government, although some may exercise powerful influences over their members and some may even perform certain functions of government. Educational accrediting organizations, for instance, exercise aspects of the governmental power of licensing. For that matter, political parties can be considered to be a part of this sector although their relationship to government is pervasive and in many cases—congressional party caucuses, for instance—inextricable.

On the other hand, the third sector is not business. Its organizations do not exist to make profit and those that enjoy tax immunities are specifically prohibited from doing so, although near the boundaries of the sector many groups do serve primarily the economic interests of their members. Chambers of commerce, labor unions, trade associations and the like hardly pretend to be principally altruistic.

The World of Philanthropy

Inside these negative boundaries is a somewhat narrower domain within which the world of philanthropy generally operates, a domain made up of private groups and institutions that are deemed to serve the public interest rather than a primarily self-benefiting one, and it is this narrower area that has been the principal focus of the Commission. This area is legally defined by laws that determine which types of organizations should be immune from income taxes and eligible to receive tax-deductible contributions from individuals and corporations. Under the Internal Revenue Code, twenty categories of organizations are exempt from federal income tax, but most of those that are eligible to receive tax-deductible gifts as well fall in one category of the code, Section 501(c)(3). To qualify for exemption under this section, whose "501(c)(3)" designation has become for the nonprofit world virtually synonymous with tax deductibility, an organization must operate exclusively for one or more of these broad purposes: charitable, religious, scientific, literary, educational. Two narrower aims are specified as well: testing for public safety and prevention of cruelty to children or animals. The code further states that no "substantial" part of such an organization's activities may be devoted to attempting to influence legislation and that the organization may not participate at all in candidates' political campaigns.

But even these boundaries, though narrower than those set by the nongovernment, nonprofit definition, are immensely broad and vague. What is charitable, what educational, what religious? In a time in which new and unconventional religious sects are being born, it seems, almost monthly, which are genuine expressions of the religious impulse that are legitimately protected from both taxes and governmental scrutiny? The Internal Revenue Service, for one, wishes it had an all-purpose definition of religion to work with. When is an activity educational rather than primarily propagandistic (and thus barred from tax-deductible gifts under the current laws)? Considerable litigation and administrative judgment have been devoted to answering such questions. Philosophical as well as legal arguments can be and are raised, moreover, as to whether whole groups of organizations within the tax-exempt categories are truly oriented to the public interest—their justification for tax privilege—or whether they serve primarily to further the interests of a select group.

The Commission has not attempted to establish a definition or principle by which nonprofit, nongovernmental organizations can be judged to be in the public interest and thus a proper concern of and channel for philanthropy. Others have tried to form such a definition, but none has unquestionably succeeded. In any case, a certain flexibility is seen as desirable, both philosophically and legally, in defining the public interest. One of the main virtues of the private nonprofit sector lies in its very testing and extension of any definition of the public interest, so it would be counterproductive to try to establish boundaries in more than a general, expandable sense. Similarly, although this Commission has operated under the rubric of "public needs," no attempt has been made to catalogue, let alone establish any priority scale of, such needs. Like the public interest, the closely related concept of public needs is itself fluid and shifting. A constant and transcendent public need by which the voluntary sector and philanthropy may perhaps be ultimately judged is how effectively they keep abreast of this shifting and how well they are deemed to meet whatever new public needs are perceived.

Likewise, no attempt has been made to attach, and certainly none has succeeded in attaching, a new, better name to the territory under examination, even though none of the existing names is universally admired. Here, and throughout the report, the terms voluntary sector, private nonprofit sector (or simply nonprofit sector for short) or third sector are used interchangeably and in all cases except where otherwise indicated are meant to exclude organizations that primarily serve the interests of their own members.

Dimensions of the Voluntary Sector

What are the dimensions of this sector? To the extent that they have been measured at all, the measurement has usually been only a partial one that looks at the amount of private giving and volunteer activity that goes into nonprofit organizations. Even on this incomplete scale, however, it is clear that the nonprofit sector accounts for a very large amount of time and money. According to estimates based on surveys made for the Commission, at least $25 billion annually is given to various causes and organizations, and an equal amount worth of volunteer work is devoted to philanthropic activity. Yet these figures require some subtraction, and a good deal of addition. For one, a small but significant and growing amount of private giving goes to public institutions, mainly state colleges and universities. On the other hand, a sizable share of the funding of the nonprofit sector comes from the government nowadays, and considerable additional funds come from endowment and other investment income and from operating revenues, including payments to nonprofit organizations by those who use their services—students' tuitions, medical patients' fees and the like. Government funding, endowment income and service charges must be added to the overall ledger of the voluntary sector. When they are, a rough extrapolation from available data indicated the total annual receipts of the private nonprofit sector to be in the range of $80 billion, or half as much as Americans spend on food in a year.

Another measure of the dimensions of the nonprofit sector is the employment it accounts for. Approximately 4.6 million wage and salary workers are estimated to have worked in the nonprofit sector in 1974, or 5.2 percent of the total American workforce for that year. One out of every ten service workers in the United States is employed by a nonprofit organization. The proportion of professional workers is even higher—nearly one out of six.

For a physical count of nonprofit organizations, the Commission has turned to a number of sources. The Internal Revenue Service lists, as of June, 1975, 691,627 exempt organizations, groups that have formally filed for and been accorded exemption from federal income taxes. But that number does not include a great many church organizations which automatically enjoy exemption from federal income taxes without filing, nor does it include numerous small organizations that never feel the need to file for tax exemption. On the other hand, it does include a large number of groups that fall outside the philanthropic part of the nonprofit sector, such as labor unions and fraternal organizations, and it also counts a good many groups that are only active for a short time. One Commission report calculates that a "core group" of traditional philanthropic organizations includes 350,000 religious organizations, 37,000 human service organizations, 6,000 museums, 5,500 private libraries, 4,600 privately sponsored secondary schools, 3,500 private hospitals, 1,514 private institutions of higher education, and 1,100 symphony orchestras. Some other recent calculations: There are 1,000 national professional associations. New York City alone has around 6,000 block associations. And a study of voluntary groups in the town of Arlington, Mass., identified some 350 such groups there, serving a population of around 52,000. This last finding confirms earlier estimates of proportions between community size and the number of voluntary groups, and gives support to the extrapolation that in all, counting local chapters of regional or national groups, there may be as many as six million private voluntary organizations in the United States. A purely intuitive indication that this very large number is feasible can be glimpsed in a minute sample of nonprofit groups. To name a few:

> Bedford-Stuyvesant Restoration Corporation, Phillips Exeter Academy, American Acupuncture and Herbs Research Institute, Senior Citizens Association of Wausau (Wisc.), Talmudic Research Institute, New Alchemy Institute, Aspen Institute for Humanistic Studies, Chapin School Ltd., Citizens Committee on Modernization of Maryland Courts and Justice, Bethlehem (Pa.) Public Library, Visiting Nurse Association of Milwaukee, YMCA Railroad Branch of Toledo, Chinatown (N.Y.) Day Care Center, Zen Center of Los Angeles, Big Brothers of Rapid City, World Affairs Council of Syracuse, N.Y., American Parkinson Disease Association, Bethel Temple of Evansville (Ind.), Metropolitan Opera Company, Fathers Club of Mt. St. Mary's Academy (Watchung, N.J.), Mothers Club of Stanford University, Sons and Daughters of Idaho Pioneers, Family Planning Committee of Greater Fall River (Mass.).

Ultimate Beneficiaries

The arithmetic of the nonprofit sector finds much of its significance in less quantifiable and even less precise dimensions—in the human measurements of who is served, who is affected by nonprofit groups and activities. In some sense, everybody is: the contributions of voluntary organizations to broadscale social and scientific advances have been widely and frequently extolled. Charitable groups were in the forefront of ridding society of child labor, abolitionist groups in tearing down the institution of slavery, civic-minded groups in purging the spoils system from public office. The benefits of nonprofit scientific and technological research include the great reduction of scourges such as tuberculosis and polio, malaria, typhus, influenza, rabies, yaws, bilharziasis, syphilis and amoebic dysentery. These are among the myriad products of the nonprofit sector that have at least indirectly affected all Americans and much of the rest of the world besides.

Perhaps the nonprofit activity that most directly touches the lives of most Americans today is noncommercial "public" television. A bare concept twenty-five years ago, its development was underwritten mainly by foundations. Today it comprises a network of some 240 stations valued at billions of dollars, is increasingly supported by small, "subscriber" contributions and has broadened and enriched a medium that occupies hours of the average American's day.

More particularly benefited by voluntary organizations are the one quarter of all college and university students who attend private institutions of higher education. For hundreds of millions of Americans, private community hospitals, accounting for half of all hospitals in the United States, have been, as one Commission study puts it, "the primary site for handling the most dramatic of human experiences—birth, death, and the alleviation of personal suffering." In this secular age, too, it is worth noting that the largest category in the nonprofit sector is still very large indeed, that nearly two out of three Americans belong to and evidently find comfort and inspiration in the nation's hundreds of thousands of religious organizations. All told, it would be hard to imagine American life without voluntary nonprofit organizations and associations, so entwined are they in the very fabric of our society, from massive national organizations to the local Girl Scouts, the parent-teachers associations or the bottle-recycling group.

Government and Voluntary Association

Ultimately, the nonprofit sector's significance, and any measure of its continuing importance, lies in its broader societal role, as seen in the long history of voluntary association and in what signs can currently be glimpsed of new or continuing directions. To talk of the sector's role in society inevitably means looking at voluntary activity and association alongside of government. Both are expressions of the same disposition of people to join together to achieve a common end, and in much of the United States' experience they have been complementary expressions. But in global terms they often have functioned and do function as mutually competitive forces. No government tolerates all forms of voluntary association; groups that are seen as threatening a country's security or that pursue common criminal purposes are routinely suppressed. The tensions between voluntary association and government run broader and deeper in many parts of the world, however, and have done so through many periods of history.

Sociologist Robert A. Nisbet has written of the "momentous conflicts of jurisdiction between the political state and the social associations lying intermediate to it and the individual." These have been, he writes, "of all the conflicts in history, the most fateful." Such conflicts can be traced at least as far back as democratic Greece and imperial Rome, in both of which societies governments were at times hostile to voluntary association. Imperial Rome, wrote Gibbon, "viewed with the utmost jealousy and distrust any association among its subjects."

The Middle Ages witnessed a flourishing in Europe of more or less autonomous groupings—guilds, churches, fiefdoms—within weak central governments. But modern history can be seen at least in part as being patterned by the return to Greek and Roman affinities for the central, dominant state, with an accompanying discouragement of nongovernmental groups. The foremost philosophers of this monism of the state in modern times were Thomas Hobbes and Jean Jacques Rousseau, and the French Revolution was one of its most exuberant expressions. Charitable, literary, educational and cultural societies were banned in the brittle course of the revolution. "A state that is truly free," declared a legislator of revolutionary France, "ought not to suffer within its bosom any association, not even such as, being dedicated to public improvement, has merited well of the country."

Americans Are Forever Forming Associations

In spite of this inhospitable historical and philosophical setting, "association dedicated to public improvement" found fertile territory in the New World, a land colonized far from the reach of central governments, a vast land that did not lend itself well to strong central government of its own and in frontier areas was slow to adopt even minimal local governments. As historian Daniel Boorstin has observed, America evidenced a profound tendency to rely on voluntary, nongovernmental organizations and associations to pursue community purposes "from the beginning." As this country was settled, he writes "communities existed before governments were there to care for public needs." The result was that "voluntary collaborative activities" were set up first to provide basic social services. Government followed later on.

It is no historical accident that one of the Founding Fathers is nearly as famous for his development of nongovernmental means to public ends as he is for his role in shaping and representing the fledgling republic. Benjamin Franklin's institutions outside of government compose a major portion of the index of the voluntary sector. He was the leading force in founding a library, a volunteer fire department, a hospital, a university and a research institution. An historical survey of philanthropy made for the Commission notes: "Franklin did not invent the principle of improving social conditions through voluntary association, but more than any American before him he showed the availability, usefulness and appropriateness to American conditions."

"The principle of voluntary association accorded so well with American political and economic theories," the survey observes further, "that as early as 1820 the larger cities had an embarrassment of benevolent organizations." Fifteen years later, this propensity to organize became the subject of one of Alexis de Tocqueville's most famous of many famous observations about the new nation:

> "Americans of all ages, all stations in life, and all types of disposition are forever forming associations. There are not only commercial and industrial associations in which all take part, but others of a thousand different types— religious, moral, serious, futile, very general and very limited, immensely large and very minute. Americans combine to give fetes, found seminaries, build churches, distribute books and send missionaries to the antipodes. Hospitals, prisons and schools take shape that way. Finally, if they want to proclaim a truth or propagate some feeling by the encouragement of a great example, they form an association. In every case, at the head of any new undertaking, where in France you would find the government or in England some territorial magnate, in the United States you are sure to find an association."

Evolutions Within the Third Sector

This observation applies to the United States almost as fully 140 years later. Today, in fact, private association appears to be so deeply embedded and to exist on so much broader a scale in the United States than in other parts of the world as to represent one of the principal distinguishing characteristics of American society. Yet the purposes of voluntary organization have hardly remained stationary or of the same relative significance within the voluntary sector over the years.

In a pattern of evolution that has repeated itself in different areas of society, government has taken over many services and functions of the nonprofit sector, and new focuses of nonprofit activity and organization have emerged. Schools, as de Tocqueville observed, were generally founded and run by nongovernmental organizations, often churches, in early America. But soon after de Tocqueville's observations were published in 1835, the public school system began to take hold in the United States, and today only one out of ten primary and secondary school students goes to nonpublic schools. Higher education and aid to the poor correspondingly accounted for more and more nonprofit activity as the nineteenth century progressed. Then, beginning in the late nineteenth century, many of today's giant state universities got their start, and public institutions began to challenge the primacy of private institutions in higher education as well. The private nonprofit sector was the chief dispenser of "charity" well into this century, but in recent decades this function has increasingly been absorbed by government welfare and social insurance programs.

Today we appear to be on the threshold of yet another major expansion by government in an area that until a few years ago was dominated by private nonprofit (and profit) organizations, the health field. A Commission study of philanthropy in this area anticipated that by the mid-1980's more than half of all spending on health in the United States will be accounted for by government programs, with much of the rest flowing through government-regulated private insurance plans.

Underlying Functions of Voluntary Groups

The end purposes of nonprofit activity have changed considerably over the course of American history, therefore, and unquestionably will continue to change. Yet certain basic functions—underlying social roles that have been characteristic of much or all nonprofit activity regardless of the particular service or cause involved—have endured throughout the changes that have taken place. This is not to say, of course, that all nonprofit organizations are performing these functions optimally or even adequately. Indeed, expert research the Commission has received and informal testimony it has listened to suggest that many organizations in the sector fall well short of their capabilities. Yet the same research and testimony is virtually unanimous in finding distinctive functions for the nonprofit sector and in asserting that these functions are today as important as they ever have been to the health and progress of American society, more important in some cases than ever. Among these basic functions are the following:

—*Initiating new ideas and processes.* "...There are critical reasons for maintaining a vital balance of public and private support for human services," asserts a Commission report by Wilbur J. Cohen, former Secretary of Health, Education and Welfare, "not the least of which is the continuing task of innovating in areas where public agencies lack knowledge or are afraid to venture....The private sector is adept at innovation, and at providing the models government needs."

"A new idea stands a better chance of survival in a social system with many kinds of initiative and decision," observes a Commisson study of the health field. Government undoubtedly provides the most fertile arena for certain kinds of initiative and innovation, but certain new ideas, these and other Commission reports indicate, stand a better chance of survival and growth in the nonprofit sector than in the corridors of government.

"The development of the early types of both health maintenance organizations and the physicians' assistance (paramedical aides) programs would never have surfaced if they had required prior public sector consensus and support," says the Commission's health study. Another study—on the role of philanthropy in the environmental field—finds: "The perspective of governmental agencies, even in the research only...agencies..., tends to be limited and dominated by existing and agency views of the problems and alternative strategies for 'solving' the problem....It is difficult to induce...governmental agencies...to undertake new directions for research and analysis." The "pioneering" role of nonprofit organizations has long been recognized. More than half a century ago, Beatrice and Sidney Webb, writing on the "Sphere of Voluntary Agencies," found these agencies capable of "many kinds...of...treatment... the public authorities are not likely themselves to initiate." Nongovernmental organizations, precisely because they are nongovernmental and need not be attuned to a broad and diverse constituency, can take chances, experiment in areas where legislators and government agencies are hesitant to tread.

Once successfully pioneered by nonprofit groups, and having established their legitimacy and worthiness, new ideas and processes can be, and often have been, supported and expanded by government. Birth-control technology, to take a relatively recent example, was pioneered by the nonprofit world in its more controversial beginnings and today is heavily underwritten by many governments throughout the world.

—*Developing public policy.* Standing outside of government, voluntary organizations not only can try out new ideas, initiate services that may be too controversial for government bodies to deal with at early stages, but can exercise a direct influence on shaping and advancing government policy in broad areas in which the government is already involved. Groups specializing in certain policy areas are continually producing research and analysis, information and viewpoints, especially on long-rage policy matters, that may be lacking at times in government circles themselves, preoccupied as they often are with day-to-day operating concerns. A major function of nonprofit groups in public policy development has been to help clarify and define issues for public consideration, both at local and regional levels, as the Regional Plan Association does through its studies and proposals for the New York metropolitan area, or as The Brookings Institution does at the national level. Privately sponsored specal commissions and boards of inquiry have been frequently formed at both levels to focus analysis and attention on issues as diverse as hunger, cable communication and legalized gambling.

—*Supporting minority or local interests*. For many of the same reasons the nonprofit world can experiment with new ideas less cautiously than government, voluntary groups can support causes and interests that may be swept aside by majoritarian priorities or prejudices. The civil rights movement grew out of the initiatives of nonprofit organizations such as the NAACP; the consumer and environmental movements, once the concerns of only a few perceptive or single-minded people, also found their early nourishment in private groups. But the causes need not be—or may not ever come to be regarded as— so large and socially significant. William S. Vickrey, an economist at Columbia University, has written of the "cumbersomeness of public agencies in dealing with relatively small-scale activities," of the impediments facing "high-level decision-making bodies on matters of small magnitude in which they have relatively little basis for judgment." More specialized private agencies may be able to operate efficiently and intelligently within their spheres, may be more sensitive to small-scale problems than government. In the health field, for example, a Commission report notes that nonprofit organizations "can assist in support of health programs for religious and ethnic groups, migratory workers, and racial minority groups which the public sector cannot often address....Private philanthropy will be needed in the future to even out some of the inequities which will invariably occur between different communities, and to respond to the health needs of groups too culturally different to gain adequate public support."

—*Providing services that the government is constitutionally barred from providing*. In the United States, the government is proscribed from entering the broadest area of the nonprofit sector, religion. So there is simply no alternative to the nonprofit sector if religious functions are to be filled at all in this country. Similarly, the Council on Foundations points out in its report to the Commission, the establishment in 1973 of a private nonprofit National News Council to oversee the news media "is an experiment that, if not totally off-limits to the government because of the First Amendment, is clearly not the kind of function that it should or would undertake."

—*Overseeing government*. Alongside government's constitutional inhibitions are its institutional ones. Despite its own internal checks and balances, government can hardly be counted on to keep a disinterested eye on itself. In his historical perspective on philanthropy written for the Commission, historian Robert H. Bremner observes: "A marked tendency of American philanthropy has been to encourage, assist and even goad democratic government—and democratic citizens—toward better performance of civic duties and closer attention to social requirements." The Nathan Committee, which looked at philanthropy in Great Britain a quarter century ago, saw much the same role for voluntary groups. "They are able to stand aside from and criticize state action, or inaction, in the interest of the inarticulate man-in-the-street." As government's role in many areas formerly dominated by nongovernmental groups grows even larger, and the voluntary role grows correspondingly smaller, the monitoring and influencing of government may be emerging as one of the single most important and effective functions of the private nonprofit sector.

—*Overseeing the market place.* While most of the third sector's activity relates more closely to government than to the business sector because of the nonprofit, public-interest common denominator of government and voluntary organizations, the sector does play a role, and perhaps a growing one, in relation to the business world. In some areas, voluntary organizations provide a direct alternative to, and a kind of yardstick for, business organizations. Nonprofit hospitals and research organizations, for instance, operate in competition with close commercial counterparts. A number of nonprofit groups makes it their business to keep a critical gaze on business, including labor union activity, as well. Potentially freer from the influence of powerful economic interests, nonprofit groups can act as detached overseers of the market place in ways that government agencies and legislators are often restrained from doing.

—*Bringing the sectors together.* Nonprofit organizations frequently serve to stimulate and coordinate activities in which government or business or both interact with voluntary groups to pursue public purposes. Organization for community development is one example of this synergistic role. Another is the practice by a group such as The Nature Conservancy of enlisting the help of industry in the form of low-interest loans to buy land for preservation and conservation purposes, land that may eventually be turned over to government ownership. The fact that voluntary organizations have neither commercial interests to pursue nor official status often makes them best suited to act as intermediary or coordinator in activities involving government and business.

—*Giving aid abroad.* In a time of heightened nationalistic sensitivities, especially where official American actions abroad are concerned, nonprofit organizations have been able to offer aid in situations where government help would be politically unacceptable. Workers for the American Friends Service Committee, for instance, were able to remain behind in Da Nang during the North Vietnamese takeover of that city and were able to help war victims there even though the United States government was considered hostile by the city's occupiers. As a Ford Foundation annual report observed a few years ago: "...Our welcome in sensitive areas often derives from the fact that we are not a government."

—*Furthering active citizenship and altruism.* While the previous categories deal mainly with the important roles nonprofit organizations serve for the society as a whole or for certain beneficiary segments of the society, one of the broadest and most important functions voluntary groups perform derives not so much from what they do for beneficiaries as what they do for participants. Voluntary groups serve as ready and accessible outlets for public-spirited initiative and activity—for philanthropy broadly defined. In a complex urbanized and suburbanized society, the individual acting alone can hope to make little impress on community or national problems, is often at a loss to find and help those who need help. Many government agencies have highly structured work arrangements and cannot or do not readily receive the assistance of public-spirited citizens. But those so minded can usually join or can help form a voluntary organization as an effective vehicle for altruistic action, and this possibility itself serves as a constant encouragement to altruism, to an active involvement in public causes, which is of the very essence in a healthy democratic society.

New Frontiers and an Ageless Rationale

These vital roles for voluntary organizations continue to serve and influence areas of society that have traditionally been the concern of the nonprofit sector. In addition, many new or greatly expanded concerns of voluntary activity have emerged in recent years as challenging new frontiers of the sector and of its particular capabilities. "Over the past 20 years," observes Pablo Eisenberg, head of the Center for Community Change, "hundreds if not thousands of new local organizations have been created to deal with issues such as ecology, consumer problems, economic and social self-determination, public-interest law, poverty and neighborhood revitalization...groups with different purposes and structures and, in some cases, constituencies." Indeed, a recent survey indicates that possibly as many as 40,000 environmental organizations alone have sprung up throughout the country, mostly in the last few years. And in a Commission study of philanthropy in five cities, one major conclusion is that "nonprofit, tax-exempt organizations continue to grow in each of the cities studied."

For all the absorptions by government and despite severe financial difficulties of many voluntary organizations, it would appear, in other words, that the impulse to associate is still very strong. Indeed, there are social currents in motion that should be adding fresh impetus and vitality to this ageless expression of man's community with man.

One current is the sense of alienation that modern men and women are widely viewed as experiencing in the face of giant, impersonal institutions or government and business. The generally smaller size and more perceptible humanity of voluntary groups—be they block associations, local chapters of the American Legion or women's rights organizations—would appear to offer at least a partial antidote to any contemporary malaise stemming from feelings of ineffectiveness or unidentity. As Richard W. Lyman, president of Stanford University, wrote recently in an essay entitled "In Defense of the Private Sector," "People everywhere are yearning for the chance to feel significant as individuals. They are yearning for institutions built on a human scale, and responsive to human needs and aspirations. Is this not precisely what we have believed in and worked for, long before it became so popular to do so?"

In addition to responding to an existential yearning, the voluntary sector should appeal more than ever today in terms of its bedrock grounding in the spirit and political philosophy of pluralism—in the idea that society benefits from having many different ways for striving to advance the common weal. The federal government's unavailing efforts to control the economy follow many frustrating social programs of the Great Society and both add to the evidence of our senses that in our increasingly complex society there is no one body, one governing structure, that holds the answers to society's problems, is equipped to find the answers by itself or could put them into effect if it did. In the wake of Watergate, moreover, we are probably less persuaded than ever to stake our destiny totally on the wisdom or beneficence of centralized authority. This sorry and sordid chapter in recent history has dramatically demonstrated the virtues of diffusion of power and decentralization of decision making in public affairs, and it has demonstrated the correlative virtues of a vigorous public-minded and independent sector. The sector ideally should not compete with government so much as complement it and help humanize it, however. Nor because of institutional inertia or self-protectiveness should it or parts of it stand in the way of proper extensions of government into areas where, because of the demands of scale or equity, the private sector simply cannot fill a collective want. The sector should not be at odds with government, in other words, so much as outside of it and in addition to it.

In furtherance of its own role of serving the public interest, government at the same time should actively encourage a large and vigorous voluntary sector that can help carry the burdens of public services. For to operate effectively, and humanely, government must take care not to overload its own mechanisms by attempting to bring every public purpose directly under its direction and control.

The late Walter Lippmann recognized this central importance to government, and to American society at large, of nongovernmental organization. American democracy, he wrote a number of years ago, "has worked, I am convinced, for two reasons. The first is that government in America has not, hitherto, been permitted to attempt to do too many things; its problems have been kept within the capacity of ordinary men. The second...is that outside the government and outside the party system, there have existed independent institutions and independent men..." His observation describes the ultimate rationale for a "third" sector in American society, a rationale that applies as fully for today and tomorrow as it did for yesterday.

COMMISSION ON PRIVATE PHILANTHROPY
AND PUBLIC NEEDS
1973-75

John H. Filer, *Chairman*
Leonard L. Silverstein, *Executive Director*

William H. Bowen
Lester Crown
C. Douglas Dillon
Edwin D. Etherington
Bayard Ewing
Frances Tarlton Farenthold
Max M. Fisher
Raymond J. Gallagher
Earl G. Graves
Paul R. Haas
Walter A. Haas, Jr.
Philip M. Klutznick
Ralph Lazarus

Herbert E. Longenecker
Elizabeth J. McCormack
Walter J. McNerney
William H. Morton
John M. Musser
Jon O. Newman
Graciela Olivarez
Alan Pifer
George Romney
William Matson Roth
Althea T. L. Simmons
Leon H. Sullivan
David B. Truman

Commission Staff
Gabriel G. Rudney, *Director of Research*
Jeanne Moore, *Executive Assistant*
E. B. Knauft, *Assistant to the Chairman*
Judith G. Smith, *Compendium Editor*
Robert E. Falb, *Co-Counsel*
Stuart M. Lewis, *Co-Counsel*
Jerry J. McCoy, *Co-Counsel*

34

The Voluntary Sector: Problems and Challenges

PABLO EISENBERG

PABLO EISENBERG IS PRESIDENT OF THE CENTER FOR
COMMUNITY CHANGE AND CO-CHAIR OF THE NATIONAL
COMMITTEE FOR RESPONSIVE PHILANTHROPY.

*This paper was prepared at the request of the National
Center for Voluntary Action for submission to the
Commission on Private Philanthropy and Public Needs. It
was originally published in the Commission's six-volume set
of research papers.*

There is widespread belief that the voluntary sector is in a state of acute and prolonged crisis. Some attribute this situation to a serious shortage of money and the inability of private groups to finance their growing needs. Others point to the octopodan spread of government, a development that threatens the traditional balance between the public and private sectors. Yet others perceive the voluntary sector as a complex system of organizations often irrelevant to the pressing issues of social and economic survival in the 1970s and 1980s.

An element of insight and truth underlies each of these observations. Each focuses on an important part of the problem and directs our attention to a fundamental dilemma that clouds the future of the voluntary sector. Simply stated, the question is whether the voluntary sector—philanthropy, voluntarism, and private organizations—can meet the changing needs of society with its traditional assumptions, strategies, and operations.

There is a tendency among many observers to cite the proliferation of voluntary organizations, the amount of money spent by private groups, and the vast number of hours contributed by volunteers as tangible evidence that all is well

Reprinted from *Research Papers of the Commission on Private Philanthropy and Public Needs*, Vol. II
(Washington, DC: U.S. Department of the Treasury, 1977) by permission of the author.

with the voluntary sector. There is an Adam Smith quality in this view, reflecting the hope, if not the conviction, that all the parts of the voluntary mechanism are working effectively through a hidden hand on behalf of the public's good.

But statistics are only one indicator of the health of institutions. The quality of performance, the timing and politics of action, the significance of the activity, and the nature of the process are all elements that must be included in any overall judgment of an institution or the private sector in general. These tend to be much more difficult to assess. Little wonder, then, that so little attention has been paid to their evaluation.

The voluntary sector, its goals and functions, can be divided into two major facets. While they overlap, one is essentially private, the other primarily public. The former refers to those not-for-profit activities of individuals and organizations that promote self-betterment, individual professionalism, personal services, and self-fulfillment through participation with others. This side is basically focused on individual wants, needs, and gratifications. The latter, the public side, is chiefly concerned with societal problems and the preservation of our democratic value system, the American ideals of justice, liberty, and opportunity. It is based on a traditional American view of society that has recognized the inherent dangers of big government and assigned to the private sector the responsibility for keeping government open, responsible, and in check.

It is in dealing with its public function that the voluntary sector is particularly derelict in fulfilling its mission and responsibilities.

The past few decades have witnessed revolutionary changes in our institutional arrangements, both domestic and international; in the growth of government and its bureaucracies; in the nation's economic condition, patterns and problems; in the evolution of minority and disadvantaged communities; and in the emergence of unforeseen urban, rural, consumer, and ecological issues.

Not only have vast changes swept the country, but there is ample evidence that our society itself will have to undergo radical surgery if our democratic way of life is to survive. The market mechanism, long the mainstay of economic life, is breaking down and will have to be modified. Poverty has not been eliminated. Social injustice continues. Economic opportunity is undermined by racial discrimination. If the poor aren't getting poorer, they aren't getting much richer. An inequitable tax system perpetuates an inequitable economic social system. Essentially public decisions affecting not only Americans but other countries as well are still being made by private institutions and small groups of individuals. The pressure for distributing power and resources more fairly within our society is building as a result of both internal and external influences.

How to anticipate these changes and where to initiate preventive medicine should and must be the business of the voluntary sector, particularly its innovative components, the foundations and educational institutions. Few philanthropic organizations and private groups, however, appear to have significantly altered their priorities and practices to adjust to recent developments. They remain cautious and conservative, preferring to avoid or ignore these new trends and issues. While the world has moved, they have tended to stand still. Their traditional purpose and current conceptual base have been undermined by the march of events.

The fossilization of traditional practices is everywhere in evidence. Over the past twenty years, hundreds if not thousands of new local organizations have been created to deal with issues such as ecology, consumer problems, economic and social self determination, public interest law, poverty, and neighborhood revitalization; yet philanthropy has made little or no provision for these new vital groups. Many social agencies and volunteer groups continue to serve their clients, old and new, as they have for years, irrespective of changing circumstances and the need for modern strategies and special skills. Nor have philanthropy and many private organizations demonstrated much interest in and concern for the New Federalism with its dangerous implications for responsible democracy at the local level and for the continued vitality of the voluntary sector.

Special attention must be focused, therefore, on the public side of the voluntary sector, on the neglected public social and economic issues which must increasingly become a responsibility of local and national voluntary organizations.

The Expanding World of Private Organizations

During the last two decades the number of private organizations engaged in traditional philanthropy, community service, professional betterment, and social activities has multiplied significantly. Paralleling this growth has been the emergence of a new large group of local and national organizations with different purposes and structures and, in some cases, constituencies. While vocal, active, and productive, these volunteer groups are still struggling to gain acceptability, credibility, and recognition from the voluntary sector in general and the philanthropic organizations in particular.

Although all are concerned with major economic and social problems, they may be divided into two major groups. Many organizations combine the characteristics of both types.

The first is primarily involved in the identification, analysis, and resolution of public issues, local, regional, and national. In contrast to the largely middle-class better government and taxpayer groups of the past, the new groups comprise a wide and growing range of concerns and a rich diversity of class and ethnic backgrounds. Civil rights and antipoverty organizations emerged in the 1950s and 1960s, encouraged by increasing citizen responsiveness to social problems and governmental action. During the past ten years ecology and consumer groups have mushroomed as the threat to our natural resources was perceived and business malpractices became more clearly understood. Major areas of public needs and services have received attention with the creation of special citizen organizations to deal with housing, health, welfare, and community development. Government and budgetary practices are now spurring the creation of new groups interested in municipal performance and program effectiveness. Cutting across these groups and constituencies has been the growth of coalition movements around particular issues appealing to a large and diverse number of organizations.

The second type may be characterized as self-determining organizations that have been created to provide disadvantaged constituencies with those opportunities, services, and influence that have not been available through normal or traditional channels. They may involve a particular neighborhood or section of a city, a special minority community or portion of that community, or persons too poor and disconnected to care adequately for their family needs and rights. Their premise is that neither the public nor private sector will pay sufficient attention to their problems and plight, that they themselves must determine and direct their own development. Economic development corporations reflect this avenue for greater economic opportunities for poor and minority communities. So do many of the cooperatives and cottage industries formed in recent years. Other groups and organizations have turned to social and political strategies for greater power and influence. The traditional social services provided by United Way agencies and government institutions have often neglected disadvantaged communities or delivered services in an ineffectual way. New organizations, more responsive to and directed by these communities themselves, have therefore been created to provide more relevant services to those most in need. Alternative schools, food stamp outreach and sales, community-based health centers, many Headstart programs, and nontraditional manpower programs are examples of this corrective approach to social services.

Without a long tradition of experience and recognition, and premised on the need for and desirability of change, both types of organizations have found the task of supporting themselves extraordinarily difficult. Unlike many other institutions, their financial support has not necessarily been correlated to their performance level. Indeed in some instances high productivity has insured inadequate backing. In a sense, they remain the financial stepchildren of the voluntary sector despite their crucial importance to the nation's economic and social programs.

Nowhere is this more evident than in their relationship with the governmental changes that have been introduced under the rubric of the New Federalism.

The New Federalism and Government Power

The New Federalism, introduced over the past few years, represented a tremendous challenge to institutions concerned with the strength of the voluntary sector. It is altering the relationship between the federal, state, and local governments, as well as the authority and power each exercises. It is redefining the responsibilities of the three levels of government toward the protection of the nation's minority and disadvantaged groups. It has concentrated much greater power in the executive branches of state and local governments without simultaneously strengthening the legislative branches. And it has changed the federal government's attitudes about and policies toward voluntary sector organizations.

The devolution of governmental power and control has been implemented without due regard to the capacity of local governments to exercise these new responsibilities or their willingness to conduct business openly and to be held accountable. Nor have local and state governments been compelled to reform their archaic bureaucratic or procedural practices as a condition of receiving this new public trust. The New Federalism assumes that these governments have the competence to perform adequately or that, if they do not, the exercise of new responsibilities will somehow produce the necessary competence. There is ample evidence that both assumptions are fallacious.

The inroads of the New Federalism have been quiet, subtle, and slow. Much of its foundation has been laid by executive fiat without broad public awareness. Only after two years of operation is general revenue sharing, its most publicized program, beginning to be understood by the general public. The special revenue sharing measures recently introduced are still mysteries to most people. A great deal of what has happened over the past few years has not been the subject of extensive legislative debate or public discussion, even though it will have an enormous impact on community life and priorities everywhere.

The operation of many local governments has traditionally been a relatively closed system. Citizens and community groups have enjoyed little or no opportunity to participate in and influence the priority-setting and decision-making government processes. Local budget procedures are still a mystery to most local organizations and individuals. Public information about city and county activities has been limited and often tightly controlled. A large number of elected and appointed officials have tended to treat the general public more as an obstacle to efficiency than as clients whose interests they are supposed to serve.

Most citizens have never been involved in local government affairs except peripherally at election time. They view their governments largely as remote entities, divorced from their personal lives, secretive in their dealings, and callous to many of their needs.

As long as city and county governments were relatively weak, had to contend with strong independent local authorities and federal programs, and had limited control of much of the money channelled into their jurisdictions, this nondemocratic state of local government affairs was tolerable, if not particularly productive. Citizens, particularly minority constituencies, could look to the federal government and independent institutions and programs for redress and the protection of their rights and interests. Private nonprofit organizations financed directly or indirectly by the federal government and a few foundations could and did provide an outlet for active citizen involvement in local public activities. In short, a balance of power existed which restrained local governments' influence over and control of its citizenry.

The New Federalism has upset this balance of power, tilting it heavily on the side of officialdom and government bureaucracy. Revenue sharing and the concept of Chief Executive Review of proposals, the A-95 system of federal coordination by local public officials, and other shifts have given chief executive officers much greater control over the funds entering their jurisdictions than they have ever enjoyed before.

Even in the areas of program planning and coordination the administration has made it clear that private sector organizations are not to have a role to play. Representation on the A-95 federal review and coordination bodies is limited to governmental representatives; there is no provision for citizen involvement or private sector participation. Citizen involvement has been downgraded in all federal programs. In some it has become merely advisory; in others it has become so permissive a requirement that it is being ignored. The attempt to eliminate OEO and community action as well as the major cuts made in the Model Cities program attest to the difficulties experienced by independent citizen action in recent years in relating to government programming.

Adding momentum to this swing of the power pendulum has been the conscious decision of the administration to end direct federal support and encouragement of private nonprofit groups.

For disadvantaged and minority communities—either ethnic, class, or political—decentralization of government authority and the decategorization of federal grants represents a throwback to the 1940s. They cannot forget that categorical programs and federal strings were introduced precisely because state and local governments could not or would not protect their rights and guarantee them equal economic and social opportunities.

While the local political scene has changed in the past decade or two, it has not changed that much. Elected officials still make decisions based on majority opinion and pressure, and disadvantaged and minority groups know that where they are in the minority their interests and rights are likely to be ignored. The federal responsibility for and guarantees of minority rights and concerns that characterized the 1960s are being attenuated by the New Federalism and its programs. Redress and justice must be sought increasingly at the local level, which is difficult, or through the courts, which takes an inordinate amount of time.

A number of the reforms mandated by the New Federalism were necessary and potentially productive. The categorical grant system was in great need of consolidation and simplification. Local governments, lacking the means with which to be responsive to community needs, required additional resources and authority. Unfortunately, the doctrinaire way in which these reforms and other aspects of the New Federalism has been implemented has not corresponded to the requirements of a responsive government or an interested and active citizenry.

Government has been strengthened at the expense of the voluntary sector, not as a more effective partner to the voluntary sector. Greater power without commensurate capability or public accountability presents a dangerous potential for local corruption and tyranny. The federal government has refused to provide for checks and balances at the local level. Only the voluntary sector can fill this gap.

The Need for Community-Based Organizations

The manner in which general revenue sharing has been allocated and used reflects a number of the problems raised by the simultaneous increase in local government authority and reduction in federal responsibilities and controls.

Although touted as a mechanism for bringing power to the people, general revenue sharing has not perceptibly increased citizen involvement in local budgetary processes or local government matters, except in the relatively few communities that have had access to additional resources, technical assistance, and outside stimuli. Where citizen activity has occurred, it has usually been the result of citizen group initiatives, not those of elected or appointed officials. These officials appear to have little predisposition to open local government processes to greater citizen planning, participation, or evaluation. Despite a few notable exceptions, local officials have tended to neglect the public aspects of their public-service mission.

Nor does it appear that general revenue sharing has channelled a fair share of its funds to the disadvantaged and minority communities. Only 3 percent of the money spent by localities has been channelled into social services for the poor and the aging. Even less has gone into housing, community development, and other programs for the disadvantaged. This is an indicator of the problem that these groups are apt to encounter at the local level in attempting to gain priority attention and service.

Since priorities will be determined increasingly by local officials, mostly through local political processes, those constituencies that exercise the least influence or power will have to organize more effectively to press their case. Where desirable and possible, they will want to join with other similar groups to form more powerful coalitions capable of winning local government attention and programs.

Neighborhood and community groups are therefore assuming new roles: monitoring state and local government programs and performance; assessing community needs as a vehicle for more responsive government action; analyzing and intervening in the local budgetary processes; pressing for governmental reform; and assuming more adequate mechanisms for broad citizen involvement in government affairs. In many cases these additional functions will require capable leadership, specialized skills, and greater resources.

It is ironic that at the very moment when community-based organizations are more needed than ever, they should find themselves more financially strapped. A great number of community groups are dying on the vine. Others have either gone out of existence or are lying dormant, hoping that the trickle of funds can be turned on again. Numerous organizational efforts have died because of a lack of money, while ongoing organizations have had to reduce their program and staff levels and, consequently, their effectiveness.

There are a number of reasons for this state of affairs. The federal government's decision to reduce substantially the direct funding of private nonprofit organizations has taken a heavy toll. The recession has limited the money available through foundations. Churches and unions do not have the funds available for local organizations that they once did. The corporate world, no longer faced by the prospects of rioting and ghetto rhetoric, appears to have retrenched and weakened its commitment to community organizations and change at the local level. And few United Way affiliates have shown much interest in supporting community-based, issue-oriented, and activist organizations or coalitions. Given their broad structure, they are likely to continue the emphasis on traditional social service agencies and the voluntarism of the old school.

The financial prospects for community organizations remain dim. Only the foundations, despite their financial plight, appear to be a promising potential source of money for community groups in the short run. This potential, however, is dependent on the likelihood that the foundations can and will change their priorities.

National Problems and the Need for National Organizations

A vital, effective network of community organizations, ranging from neighborhood groups to local Leagues of Women Voters to antipoverty agencies to better-government groups, will depend not only on adequate resources but on regional and national support systems that can provide a continual flow of information, contracts, and technical assistance. Local organizations, particularly those concerned with public policy issues and intervention, are insulated from what is happening in Washington and from legislative and departmental decisions shaping federal programs. They find it difficult, if not impossible, to keep in touch with community development and model programs in other communities.

The national support and technical assistance organizations, unfortunately, are facing a financial crisis similar to that of their local affiliate groups. Many have had to reduce their budgets drastically. Others that were planning to expand their services to meet new needs have had to curb these plans.

The significance of national organizations is not limited to local groups or local public policies. They have had and will continue to have an important bearing on national policies and the federal government. Just as local governments will require careful watchdogging on the part of community groups, the federal government and its bureaucracies must be held in check by public scrutiny and voluntary organizations.

The record of national organizations active in monitoring the federal government and checking its abuses is already impressive. Civil rights organizations have successfully kept pressure on the government to promote equal opportunity in certain areas and redress discrimination in others. A coalition of private groups succeeded in 1971 in preserving OEO and community action and is once again fighting to maintain an independent federal antipoverty agency. Another coalition, with the help of Congress, forced HEW to modify its restrictive guidelines for social services. And a few national organizations have been successful in bringing the major problems inherent in general revenue sharing to the attention of policy makers and the general public. More, not fewer, national groups must be involved in this continuing effort to keep the federal government open and honest.

In their efforts to influence public policies and satisfy their clients, the national voluntary organizations are constrained by a major deterrent, the provision that 501(c)(3) organizations are prohibited from conducting substantial lobbying. Business, unions, and the federal government itself, however, may lobby without risk to their corporate status. The constituencies represented by nonprofit organizations have equal legitimacy and should be heard by the Congress in its deliberations. Until the Internal Revenue Code is amended to permit voluntary nonprofit organizations to utilize a satisfactory percentage of their resources (15 to 25 percent) for lobbying purposes, these organizations and their constituencies will continue to be discriminated against.

The Foundations and Their Priorities

Although the foundations appear to be the only likely source of immediate financial support for local community organizations and national groups concerned with public policies, their record indicates that they will have to change their priorities drastically to meet this challenge.

Traditionally, the foundations have channelled their funds into established national and local institutions, such as universities, research institutes, cultural and artistic groups, old line agencies, and professional organizations. They have generally avoided grassroots, neighborhood, activist, and social-change-oriented organizations, either low income or middle class. Their stress has been far more on safe, respectable projects than on the cutting edge of public issues and policy. While innovators in research and technology, they have for the most part lagged behind on social and governance problems.

In the 1960s, with the upsurge of community action and the growth of community groups, a relative handful of foundations began to take an interest in community-based organizations and social change. But their numbers never grew appreciably, nor did their priorities rub off on the world of philanthropy. Possibly twenty to thirty foundations, most of them in the East, have borne the burden of supporting community-based organizations. When the amount of money granted by The Ford Foundation is subtracted from the total allocated to these groups and their support organizations, the limited foundation involvement becomes readily apparent.

Two of the most frequently given rationales for not supporting community organizations are the memory of the confrontation strategies of local groups in the 1960s and the constraints imposed by the Tax Reform Act of 1969. The first is based largely on a myth about what actually happened in the 1960s. While a few community organizations did take to the streets to protest social conditions, most of these in an orderly and legal way, the great majority of them went about their neighborhood or community business in a normal manner. It is too easy to characterize the few hell-raising groups as typical of the genre. Moreover, the 1970s bear little resemblance to the 1960s. Community organizations today have different strategies and styles from their earlier counterparts.

The Tax Reform Act, in proscribing political activities by grant recipients, have set some limits on foundation activities. Yet it in no way impedes foundations from giving money to the hundreds of community-based organizations that are not actively engaged in political efforts. Why, then, has it been so difficult for these groups to obtain funds? Why have the League of Women Voters Education Fund and its affiliates been so hard-pressed financially? Why have other middle-class organizations interested in social action and government reform had trouble getting financial support? One reason may well be that many foundations have used the Tax Reform Act to cloak their own priorities and interests. Most were not interested in community organizations, social change, and government affairs before the Act and have not changed their priorities since.

The New Federalism, as has been mentioned, has realigned the relationships and responsibilities between the three tiers of government. Its implementation will affect tax policies, civil rights enforcement, and the services provided for low income and working-class people. It will help determine the direction and nature of development for the next decade. One might reasonably have expected the foundations to take a great interest in this development and to have tested the assumptions behind revenue-sharing programs and the decentralization of government authority. Little such interest has been exhibited. Once again the foundations find themselves in the rearguard rather than the vanguard of the nation's institutional development.

If the family and community foundations have been reluctant to finance projects revolving around public policy and social change, the corporate foundations appear to have established an even more unimpressive record. As the corporations' commitment to urban and community problems wanes, their foundations' policy can be expected to become more, not less, conservative.

The unrepresentative nature of the majority of foundation boards may be one of the major reasons for the foundations' priorities and posture. Heavily weighted toward corporate representatives and family members, foundation boards cannot be expected to reflect either a broad perspective of the country's interests and needs or a progressive view of social and economic change.

The staffs of many foundations also leave something to be desired. Many are selected for those cautious qualities reflected on the boards. Others are appointed because of their corporate or family ties. Few appear to have been activists, community organizers, union officials, or persons with real public policy experience.

If the foundations are to meet the challenge of the 1970s and 1980s, their boards and staffs will have to become more diversified and representative of the society at large. Organizations such as the Council on Foundations will have to accelerate their efforts to educate the foundations about their responsibilities and obligations. Public interest groups and research organizations will need to focus critical attention on the foundations and enter into a dialogue with them.

The Responsibilities of Other Voluntary Organizations

The traditional role of the individual volunteer providing program service time will remain an important social contribution and outlet for personal commitment and energy. That role, however, should be continually subject to analysis and redefinition in order to meet the tests of relevance and high priority. In areas with high concentrations of poor and minorities, the demand for volunteers is likely to be limited to persons with specific skills in business, law, and accounting, or other necessary specialities. In these districts, as well as in urban areas in general, the emphasis may be placed on group action rather than on individual service, on the need to work with and through powerful neighborhood or community organizations that can successfully influence public policies and equalize the distribution of resources. For such organizations, volunteers may prove most useful in soliciting support, both financial and political. More and more volunteers will want to turn from applying band-aids to the symptoms to attempting to change the system itself.

National organizations like the National Center for Voluntary Action and the United Way and community umbrella organizations, such as the local United Ways and Voluntary Action Centers, have a responsibility to help redefine the role of volunteers. They must help channel the energies of millions of Americans to meet changing societal requirements.

All too many local United Ways have not adapted to modern times. The funds they distribute are often not directed at their communities' gravest problems or to the neediest, most meritorious organizations. A large number are still reluctant to take on the most pressing public issues, even though these issues directly affect their client populations. More responsible and aggressive leadership will be required if the United Way organizations are to be a significant local force for progressive change.

The universities and colleges have a dismal record as providers of community resources and services. Endowed with a plentiful supply of trained researchers and student workers, the universities have the skilled manpower voluntary organizations are seeking. Their new rhetoric of community involvement and public service has not been matched by any collective commitment to action from the administration, faculty or, indeed, student level. At the very moment when they are most needed to provide community services, they are either unprepared or unwilling to respond to the challenge.

In general, the great majority of educational institutions have only involved themselves in community-related activities when they were well compensated to do so. The excuse for the "involvement only if paid" approach has been that universities are experiencing budget difficulties and that extra commitments require additional resources. This lame rationale is difficult to accept. Whether professors work with community groups, students become involved in social issues, or administrators encourage public service from the university are not matters of available dollars or additional resources. They depend instead upon educational values, institutional commitment, and quality of leadership. A university or college has the right to decide if a professor's obligation stops with teaching and research or if it goes beyond these tasks to the needs of the community and society in general.

A good number of the problems reflected in the policies and practices of voluntary organizations, whether they are universities, local United Ways, or national organizations, can be traced to their board composition and board involvement. Like foundations, many universities and other institutions have trustees who are unrepresentative of the community at large, representing instead certain established interests. Such representation tends to cultivate caution and conservatism and to limit the fresh air injected into policy deliberations.

Frequently, the board members are trustees in name only. They may be too busy or disinterested, or they may be selected only for their reputation and prestige. Policy making and the affairs of the institution are left entirely in the hands of professional administrators, and the potential for intelligent lay direction and performance evaluation is thereby lost. There is a saying in Washington that the most unaccountable persons in town are the staff directors of the private national organizations. This could just as easily be said of many other administrators in the voluntary sector throughout the country. Until their boards are truly active and functional, these organizations will find it difficult to exercise the influence and produce the results we have come to expect.

Relationship Between the Private and Public Sectors

There has always been an element of tension and uncertainty in the relationship between the voluntary and public sectors. The voluntary sector has acted as a check on governmental excess and corruption while the public sector has regulated the broad framework within which the voluntary sector has operated. This difficult but productive relationship must continue, particularly in view of the dangers inherent in the New Federalism.

There should, however, be a better understanding of what the voluntary sector can and cannot do as well as of the financial problems it can be expected to experience. It is clear, for example, that the economy may prevent philanthropy from raising its expenditure level over the next few years. Foundations, United Ways, and other institutions, therefore, will be forced to choose between maintaining their present priorities or, in order to move in new directions, transferring some of these responsibilities to public bodies.

As a general rule, philanthropic organizations should retain or adopt those programs and issues that cannot or should not be sponsored by governments. The arts and culture, for example, are receiving growing support from federal and state government agencies. Their activities should properly be considered an element of public education to be funded through public funds. There will thus be a decreasing need for foundations to support orchestras, ballets, and cultural institutes, thereby releasing funds for other purposes.

Having divested themselves of these projects, foundations will be in a better position to meet the challenge of supporting public-issues development, community-based organizations and their national support groups, social change experiments, and the monitoring of government performance. For these are responsibilities that governments cannot undertake and with which they should not be entrusted. Science and technology are other activities that could and should receive greater government support and be less dependent on philanthropy, as long as steps are taken to ensure that such basic research will not be subjected to arbitrary political influence.

While citizens and voluntary organizations will have to bear most of the responsibility for holding local government accountable and for the development of public issues, governments should be expected, regardless of their party and philosophy, to put the New Federalism to the test by establishing effective mechanisms for citizen involvement in local planning, program operations, and evaluation.

If this is to be done, the federal government will have to take a strong initiative that it has so far been reluctant to take. Instead of reducing citizen involvement in federal programming, it will have to increase it substantially. If this does not happen, the gap between the voluntary and public sectors will grow, and dissatisfaction and despair with our public institutions will continue to grow dangerously. Guarantees of citizen involvement in government processes will not be sufficient to give many Americans equal opportunities to obtain their piece of the economic and social pie. Community action programs and community economic development corporations (CDCs) have successfully served as institutional vehicles for access to goods, services, leadership training and jobs previously denied to poor, working poor, and minority communities. They must be continued and strengthened, not undermined or eliminated.

Community action agencies and CDCs and related agencies, though funded by the federal government, remain one of the largest voluntary networks in the country. Over 200,000 persons, many of them poor with no previous record of community involvement, are serving on their boards and committees as unpaid volunteers. They deserve support from the voluntary sector. It is ironic that so little support for them has come from two organizations that are in the forefront of the voluntary sector movement, the United Way and National Center for Voluntary Action.

35

The Impact of the Volunteer Sector on Society

DAVID HORTON SMITH

DAVID HORTON SMITH FOUNDED THE ASSOCIATION OF VOLUNTARY
ACTION SCHOLARS AND SERVED AS GENERAL EDITOR AND
RESEARCH DIRECTOR OF THE CENTER FOR A VOLUNTARY SOCIETY,
AN ORGANIZATION WHICH OPERATED IN THE EARLY 1970s UNDER
THE DIRECTION OF JOHN DIXON AND CYNTHIA WEDEL TO
"PROMOTE AND EXPAND THE AWARENESS, UNDERSTANDING, AND
EFFECTIVE UTILIZATION OF VOLUNTEERS AND VOLUNTARY
ASSOCIATIONS IN COPING WITH HUMAN AND SOCIAL PROBLEMS."
DR. SMITH IS CURRENTLY PROFESSOR OF SOCIOLOGY AT
BOSTON UNIVERSITY.

The "voluntary sector" refers to all those persons, groups, roles, organizations, and institutions in society whose goals involve primarily voluntary action. The term "voluntary action" is treated at length in the first volume of this series (*Voluntary Action Research: 1972*), so that we shall not elaborate on its meaning here. Suffice it to say that, roughly speaking, it includes what one is neither made to nor paid to do, but rather what one does out of some kind of expectation of psychic benefits or commitment to some value, ideal, or common interest. The voluntary sector may be roughly delineated in a negative way by contrasting it with the commercial or business sector (sometimes called the "private sector") and with the government or public sector. Another way of describing the voluntary sector is by saying that it is the total persisting social embodiment (in the form of norms, expectations, customs, and ways of behaving) of voluntary action in society.

Our question here is, simply, what impact does the voluntary sector as a whole have on society? There is not sufficient research information to permit one to do an aggregate analysis, building up a picture of the whole by sys-

Reprinted from *Voluntary Action Research: 1973* (Lexington, MA: Lexington Books, D.C. Heath & Co., 1973) by permission of the author. Copyright ©1973 by David Horton Smith.

tematically combining the parts—the kinds of impacts of voluntary action at different system levels we have been examining in part in prior chapters. Instead, we can only do the very sketchiest global analysis, based on a loose inductive logic and general theoretical considerations. In making this very brief and simplistic analysis, we are again more interested in suggesting some lines of possible future research and theory than in being exhaustive or thorough.

Another way of looking at what we are calling the impacts of the voluntary sector is to see the processes behind these impacts and to term them the "functions" or "roles" of the voluntary sector. These processes are not necessary features of the voluntary sector in any given nation, let alone in all nations. But they do represent what the voluntary sector can do and often has done in the past in particular societies at particular times. This is an attempt to help delineate more clearly why there is a voluntary sector in society, much as one might elsewhere discuss the role of government institutions or business or even the family in society. Like all of the latter, of course, the role of the voluntary sector changes over time in a given society and even in human society as a whole. Nevertheless, the impacts of the voluntary sector we discuss briefly below are suggested as very general aspects of the voluntary sector in human society, and hence they are present to at least some degree as long as there is a voluntary sector.

First, one of the most central impacts of the voluntary sector is to provide society with a large variety of partially tested social innovations, from which business, government, and other institutions can select and institutionalize those innovations which seem most promising. The independent voluntary sector is thus the prototyping test bed of many, perhaps most, new social forms and modes of human relations. Where business and government, science and technology are active in the creation and testing of technological innovations, the independent voluntary sector specializes in the practical testing of social ideas. Nearly every function currently performed by governments at various levels was once a new social idea and the experiment of some voluntary group, formal or informal—this is true of education, welfare, care for the aged, building roads, even fighting wars (volunteer citizen militias).

In sum, the voluntary sector has tended to provide the social risk capital of human society. It has been sufficiently free of the kinds of constraints that bind business (the constant need to show a profit) and government (the need to maintain control, and, in societies with effective democracies, the need to act in accord with a broad consensus) so that its component elements (particular voluntary groups or even individuals) can act simply out of commitment to some value or idea, without needing to wait until the payoffs for that kind of activity can be justified in terms appropriate to mobilizing economic or governmental institutions. It is thus the most "error-embracing" and experimental component of society (see Smith with Dixon 1973).

Second, another central impact of the voluntary sector on society has been the provision of countervailing definitions of reality and morality—ideologies, perspectives, and worldviews that frequently challenge the prevailing assumptions about what exists and what is good and what should be done in society. The voluntary sector is that part of society which, collectively, is most likely to say that "the emperor has no clothes." Voluntary groups of various kinds are distinctive among human groups in the extent to which they develop their own ideologies and value systems. If these definitions of reality and morality are sufficiently compelling to people, voluntary groups grow into huge social movements and can change the course of history, both within a given nation (e.g., the abolitionist movement in the early and middle nineteenth century of the United States) and across human society as a whole (e.g., Christianity, Buddhism, democracy, communism).

This kind of impact of the voluntary sector is related to the previous one, but where the former kind of impact emphasized experimentation with social innovation in practice, the present impact emphasizes instead ideological and moral innovation. Where the previous point focused on the social risk capital role of the voluntary sector in society, the present point focuses on the role of the voluntary sector as a gadfly, dreamer, and moral leader in society. Voluntary groups of various kinds are concerned with the generation and allocation of human commitment in the deepest sense. In the process of doing this, the voluntary sector as a whole provides moral and ideological leadership to the majority of human society, and often calls into question the existing legitimacy structures and accepted social definitions of reality of particular societies.

A third major impact of the voluntary sector on society is to provide the play element in society, especially as the search for novelty, beauty, recreation, and fun for their own sake may be collectively organized. Again because the voluntary sector is not constrained generally by such values as profit, control, and broad social consensus, voluntary groups can form in terms of literally thousands of different kinds of common interests. A full array of common interest groups (especially expressive rather than instrumental ones) in an elaborated but still evolving voluntary sector permits (in principle) nearly all individuals to find at least one group that will be satisfying to them. If there is no such group, one or more individuals may form one, if they wish, to reflect their own needs and vision of the play element. Such a group may be formal or informal, large or small, permanent or transient, open or closed, and so forth.

To speak of the play element here is not to speak of something trivial and unimportant. As society becomes increasingly complex and work activity is increasingly structured in terms of large bureaucracies, people's unsatisfied needs for play, novelty, new experience, and all manner of recreation tend to increase. The kind of easy interchange and blending of play and work that could be present in more traditional economies tends to be lost. Under such circumstances, voluntary groups often provide a window of variety and intrinsic satisfaction in an otherwise rather boring or at least psychically fatiguing world of work and responsibility.

Fourth, the voluntary sector also has a major impact on the level of social integration in society. Partly through directly expressive groups, whose aims are explicitly to provide fellowship, sociability and mutual companionship, and partly through the sociability aspects of all other kinds of collective and interpersonal forms of voluntary action, the voluntary sector helps in a very basic way to satisfy some of the human needs for affiliation, approval, and so on. In advanced industrial and urbanized societies, where the family and kinship as well as the local community and neighborhood play a markedly reduced role in providing social integration, affiliations based on common interests can become very important to the individual. Indeed, without the latter kind of voluntary-sector-based common interest affiliations, the resulting rates of individual social isolation in society would lead to even more anomie, alienation, and a variety of attendant social and psychological problems than are now the case. Obviously, the voluntary sector has not been the whole solution to the root problem of social isolation in modern society, yet voluntary groups do play a demonstrable and important part in the solution. And with the feeling of being accepted as a person that the voluntary sector provides (or can provide) to a significant proportion of the population in modern societies goes the correlative provision of positive affect, a major component of human happiness and the quality of human life.

Another aspect of the role of the voluntary sector in providing social integration is the social adjustment "buffering" function that many kinds of voluntary groups provide. When numerous individuals of a certain social and cultural background are for some reason uprooted from their customary societal niches, new voluntary groups frequently emerge to provide these individuals with an insulated or "buffered" special environment for part of their time. Typical examples would be the numerous immigrant associations that sprang up in the United States as a result of successive waves of immigration from various countries (Handlin 1951) or the kinship-oriented associations that emerged to ease the adjustment of rural West Africans to life in large cities (Little 1965).

These kinds of social-adjustment-oriented voluntary groups do not, however, emerge only in the case of physical/geographical changes on a large scale. The voluntary sector also provides a social adjustment "mechanism" to ease the shocks of social dislocations and rapid social changes of all sorts. The voluntary groups involved may cater to a former elite that has been disenfranchised or deprived of its former holdings (e.g., the association of maharajahs of India, which arose to fight for "maharajah's rights" when the Indian Congress stripped them of their traditional privileges and land, substituting a moderate annual stipend). Or the voluntary groups involved may represent a deprived category of persons who are attempting to adjust to changed social conditions that are more conducive to their sharing equitably in the good life as lived in their society (e.g., the early labor unions or black power groups, striving for recognition of their right to exist and to fight for the betterment of the conditions of their constituencies).

On another level, the voluntary sector plays an important integrative role by linking together individuals, groups, institutions and even nations that otherwise would be in greater conflict, or at least competition, with each other. (This and other impacts of voluntary groups are discussed further in Smith, 1966.) At the community level, a variety of voluntary associations will each tend to have as members a set of two or more individuals representing differing and often opposing political, religious, cultural, or social perspectives and backgrounds. The coparticipation of this set of individuals in the same voluntary association can have significant moderating effects on the relationships among these individuals. Similar integrative effects can be found at national levels where several groups from different parts of the country and/or different social and cultural perspectives participate together in a common federation or other national voluntary organization. And at the international level, the joint participation of voluntary groups from otherwise conflicting nations in some transnational federative organization may well have important long-range effects on the relations between the countries involved and on the possibilities of peace in the world.

A fifth kind of general impact of the voluntary sector involves the opposite of the first one, which dealt with the social innovation role of voluntarism. In addition to providing a wide variety of *new* ideas about social behavior, the voluntary sector also is active in preserving numerous *old* ideas. Voluntary action and voluntary organizations have played a major role in history in preserving values, ways of life, ideas, beliefs, artifacts, and other productions of the mind, heart, and hand of man from earlier times so that this great variety of human culture is not lost to future generations. For example, there are in the United States numerous local historical societies that specialize in preserving the history of particular towns and areas. There are nonprofit voluntary organizations that run local museums, libraries, and historical sites. And there are a number of voluntary organizations whose primary function it is to preserve the values of cultures or subcultures that no longer have any substantial power or importance in American society, but that nevertheless represent a way of life of significant numbers of people at some period in history or somewhere around the world (e.g., American Indian groups, in some instances, or immigrant ethnic associations that persist long after the ethnic group involved has been thoroughly assimilated into American culture). The role of municipal, state, and national governments in supporting museums and historical sites grows from the roots of earlier nonprofit, nongovernmental support of such "islands of culture."

Another aspect of the belief/value preservation role of the voluntary sector involves voluntary associations as educational experiences, especially where these associations are attempting to pass on to their members or to the public at large some body of beliefs and values originating in the past. In part this would include many of the activities of most religious sects and denominations, especially insofar as one focuses upon their socialization and indoctrination activities (e.g., catechism classes, "Sunday schools," Hebrew day schools, etc.). In part this function also includes all manner of more strictly educational voluntary organizations, from Plato's Academy (see Peterson and Peterson 1973) to modern Great Books Discussion Groups and so-called "Free Universities."

The various levels of government in the contemporary world have largely taken over the task of education on a broad scale, yet voluntary organizations still are active in supplementing government-run educational systems by filling in the gaps and by prodding these systems to improve or take on responsibility for the preservation of additional knowledge or values. For instance, voluntary civil rights and black liberation organizations have taken the lead in educating both blacks and whites in the United States regarding black history and accomplishments. Gradually, under the pressure of such voluntary associations in the past several years, the public educational system in the United States has been changing to accommodate a more accurate and complete picture of black history, although the process is by no means finished yet. Similar examples could be given with regard to other content areas as well (women's history, American Indian history, etc.).

A sixth major impact of the voluntary sector is its embodiment and representation in society of the sense of mystery, wonder, and the sacred. Neither the business nor government sectors in modern society have much tendency to be concerned with such matters. Many would say that religion today *is* very much a big business; and both business and government support science in a substantial way. Yet precisely in those areas where religion and science almost meet, where the borders of religion are receding under the pressure of an ever-expanding science, the business and government sectors are often *least* involved. Voluntary associations and nonprofit foundations/research organizations are the only groups experimenting seriously with new forms of worship, non-drug-induced "consciousness expansion" and the "religious experience," the occult, investigation of flying saucers, extrasensory perception, etc.

The "heretics" of both science and religion are seldom supported in their work directly and consciously by the business or government sectors. Only through voluntary action and the support of the voluntary sector have the major changes in man's view of the supernatural and its relation to the natural tended to come about in the past. The same has also been true, by and large, for major changes in man's view of himself and of the natural universe in the past. The dominant economic and political (and religious) systems of any given epoch are seldom very receptive to the really new visions of either the natural or supernatural world (e.g., Galileo and Copernicus; Jesus). Voluntary action is thus the principal manner in which a sense of the sacred, the mysterious, and the weird can be preserved and permitted some measure of expression in our otherwise hyper-rational contemporary society.

A seventh impact of the voluntary sector results from its ability to liberate the individual and permit him or her the fullest possible measure of expression of personal capacities and potentialities within an otherwise constraining social environment. All societies have their systems of laws, customs, roles, and organizations that box people in and limit their opportunities for personal expression and personal development. The full extent of societal limitation on people has just begun to be realized in recent decades, spurred in part by the "liberation" movement of women, blacks, the poor, the "Third World" and other disadvantaged or disenfranchised groups. The primary embodiments of the societal barriers and boxes have generally been the economic and governmental systems, although other major institutions of society have played a role as well (e.g., education, the family, religion, etc.).

Voluntary associations and groups, on the other hand, have long been a primary means of at least partially escaping these barriers and boxes. Through participation in voluntary action a wide variety of people have been able to find or to create special social groups that would permit them to grow as individuals. This kind of personal growth has many relevant aspects, but can be summed up generally as "self-actualization," to use a term from Maslow (1954). For some this means intellectual development, the process of becoming increasingly analytical, informed, and self-conscious about the nature of one's life situation and problems. When this occurs for a whole category or group of people, the process is often referred to as "group conscienticization" or "consciousness-raising" (e.g., among blacks, women, the poor). Seldom does such special personal growth occur on a broad scale outside voluntary groups and movements.

For others, self-actualization through voluntary action takes the form of developing otherwise unused capacities, talents, skills or potentials of a more active and practical sort. For many kinds of people, depending on the stage of social, economic, and political development of a society, voluntary associations and voluntary action offer the only feasible opportunity for leadership, for learning to speak in public, for practicing the fine art of management, for exercising analytical judgment, etc. Until very recently in American society, for instance, neither blacks nor women nor the members of certain other disadvantaged groups could hope to develop fully their capacities through the occupational system of the economic or government sectors. Only in voluntary groups of their own making could they seek any kind of fulfillment and self-expression, bound as they were (and in part continue to be) by the prejudices and discrimination of the dominant white, male, Anglo-Saxon Protestants in our society. However this situation is not unique to the United States. There are similar and even different forms of prejudice and discrimination in *all* other societies, varying only in degree and the particular social groups singled out for attention. And in all societies voluntary associations also offer the disadvantaged some chance of enhanced self-development, though these associations must sometimes meet in secret as underground groups if the society in which they are operating is oppressive and does not respect the right of free association.

Voluntary action potentially offers unique opportunities for personal growth and realization of personal potentials not only for those people whom society otherwise deprives, but also for *all* the members of society in certain directions. No matter how free, open, egalitarian, and highly developed the society, there are always limitations of some sort placed on the development of each person by his particular social environment. Any major decision to follow a certain line of personal occupational or educational development, for instance, automatically forecloses a number of other alternatives, or at least makes them highly unlikely. Voluntary associations, however, exist (or can exist) in such profusion and variety that they can provide otherwise missed personal development opportunities to almost any person at almost any stage of life. This is as true for the school teacher who always wanted to learn to fly (and who can join a flying club to do so even at age 60), as it is for the airline pilot who always wanted to write novels (and who can join a writer's club to work toward this end).

Of course, not every person will find the appropriate voluntary association for his or her personal growth needs to be available at the time it is needed. But the voluntary sector as a whole, nevertheless, still serves in some significant degree this general role of providing substantial numbers of individuals in society with otherwise unavailable opportunities for self-actualization and self-fulfillment.

An eighth major impact of the voluntary sector in society is one of overriding importance, relating directly to the first and second impacts discussed above. We are referring to the impact of the voluntary sector as a source of "negative feedback" for society as a whole, especially with regard to the directions taken by the major institutions of society such as government and business. Without "negative feedback," any system is dangerously vulnerable to destroying itself through excesses in one direction or another. Thus, however uncomfortable and irritating they may be at times, voluntary associations and the voluntary sector are absolutely vital to the continuing development of a society.

This systemic corrective role of the voluntary sector is, of course, not carried out by *all* voluntary associations, any more than all voluntary associations are concerned with the play element, value preservation, or the sacred. Yet the small cutting edge of the voluntary sector that does perform the role of social critic is extremely important, usually bearing the responsibility for the continued existence and future growth of the rest of the voluntary sector. In societies where a sufficient number and variety of voluntary groups are *un*able to play effectively their roles as social critics, the dominant governmental and economic institutions may well take over and suppress the entire voluntary sector (e.g., Allen 1965).

In the contemporary United States there are numerous examples of voluntary associations and groups playing this systemic corrective role. All of the cause oriented, advocacy, and issue-oriented groups tend to fall into this category, from the environmental movement to the civil rights movement and women's liberation. The tactics and strategy of such groups cover a broad range from rather traditional lobbying through demonstrations and "be-ins," to direct remedial action such as "ecotage" (sabotage of notable corporate polluters and other "environmental undesirables").

Some of the more imaginative and innovative approaches have been developed in an attempt to modify the business sector, rather than focusing solely on the government sector. For instance, there have been in-depth investigations by Ralph Nader and his associates of particular companies' practices and their relationship to the public interest (e.g., for First National City Bank of New York and for DuPont), counter-management stockholder activity in the public interest (e.g., Project G.M.), dissenting annual reports written to present a full public accounting of a corporation's activities harmful to the general public interest and welfare, class action suits brought by voluntary groups against manufacturers and developers, etc.

When looked at in the particular, such activities (which vary markedly in their success) often seem fruitless and doomed to failure, given the power of the organizations and systems being challenged. Yet when we see these activities of voluntary groups in a larger context, when we sum up these numerous activities attempting to modify and improve the dominant systems and organizations of our society, they take on a very important general meaning. Even if many or most of such system correction attempts by voluntary groups should fail, the continual and expanding pressure being brought to bear by the voluntary sector on the central institutions of society is still likely to have a salutary long-term modifying influence. When the leaders of the business and governmental sectors *know* that "someone is watching," that they will eventually have to account to the public interest for their actions, this awareness encourages greater attention to the public interest rather than merely to narrow, private interests.

When for one reason or another the voluntary sector is not able to operate effectively as a systemic corrective (either because of its own inadequacies or the failure of the leaders of dominant institutions to listen and change accordingly), the usual result in human history has been a broad social revolution (not just a palace revolution or simple coup). When the dominant institutions of any society have ignored for too long or too often the voices of the public interest as expressed by elements of the voluntary sector, revolutionary and usually underground voluntary groups arise and make concrete plans to overthrow the existing system completely. The American, French, Russian, Chinese, Cuban, and other revolutions all attest to this pattern.

Thus, when the voluntary sector cannot make itself heard adequately through the permissible communication and influence channels in a society, certain voluntary groups and movements tend to arise to revamp the whole system, establishing whole new institutional arrangements with their corresponding new channels of influence and communications. Not surprisingly, these new channels generally favor those kinds of persons and groups who were unable to be heard previously (although the kinds of people formerly dominant often end up in as bad a position or worse than that faced by the formerly disadvantaged prior to the revolution). This cycle will tend to repeat itself until a society reaches a point where it is effectively and continuously self-correcting, through the activities of a strong and social-change-oriented voluntary sector, and where its major institutions are basically operating primarily in the public interest of *all* of its citizens (not just its white, male, Anglo-Saxon Protestants, or their equivalents in some societies other than the United States and the British Commonwealth).

The ninth major impact of the voluntary sector worth mentioning here is the support given by the voluntary sector specifically to the economic systems of a society, especially a modern industrial society. Voluntary associations of many kinds provide crucial kinds of social, intellectual, and technical linkages among works in numerous occupations: professional associations increase the effectiveness of most kinds of scientists, engineers, technicians, etc., just as manufacturers' and trade associations support the growth of whole industries. And various kinds of labor unions play their part as well, although many business-men would question the degree to which they "support" the economic system. But labor unions only seem nonsupportive of the economic system when the latter is viewed narrowly from the point of view of an employer interested solely in profit maximization. Labor unions ultimately have to be deeply concerned with the viability of the economic system and productivity of their own mem-bers if they are to survive.

This economic support role of the voluntary sector is usually lost sight of because so many people tend to view all kinds of economic self-interest and occupationally related voluntary associations as integral parts of the business sector. In fact, these kinds of voluntary organizations are quite distinct from the business sector itself, however close their relationship might be to business corporations and occupational activities. The primary purpose of business cor-porations is to make a profit for their owners, whether they are actually involved in running the corporation or not. On the other hand, economic self-interest voluntary associations have as their primary purpose the enhancement of the long-term occupational and economic interests of their member-participants. While corporation employees and professionals are *paid* in salaries, wages or fees for their participation, the members of economic self-interest voluntary associations themselves *pay* for the privilege of belonging to and benefiting from these associations.

The tenth major impact of the voluntary sector we shall note is a rather subtle one: the voluntary sector constitutes an important *latent* resource for all kinds of goal attainment in the interests of the society as a whole. Put another way, the voluntary sector represents a tremendous reservoir of potential energy that can be mobilized under appropriate circumstances for broad societal goals. The role of the voluntary sector in revolutionary situations is but one example of this latent potential. The activity of voluntary association networks in more limited disaster situations is a more common example (Barton 1970). The volun-tary sector and its component associations, groups, and channels of communica-tion and influence make possible the mobilization of large numbers of people on relatively short notice for special purposes (usually in the common interest) without resorting to economic rewards or legal coercion as activating forces. Such a latent potential in the voluntary sector is especially important when neither economic nor political-legal forces can feasibly be brought to bear to resolve some widespread problem situation.

The latent potential of the voluntary sector can be viewed in another way as well. Voluntarism is based on a *charitable grants economy* (donations of time, money, etc.) as contrasted with the coercive grants economy (taxation) on which the government sector operates or the market economy on which the business sector operates. Both of the latter types of economy work well for certain kinds of purposes, but neither works well for the accomplishment of all kinds of purposes in society. In the same way, there are many kinds of purposes and activities (several of which are implicit in the nine major impacts of the voluntary sector reviewed above) for which the charitable grants economy tends to work best.

Now the important latent potential of the voluntary sector is that, under appropriately compelling circumstances (i.e., for the "right" value, goal or ideal), the money, goods, real property, and services mobilized by the voluntary sector through the charitable grants economy can completely overwhelm all considerations of the coercive grants economy and the market economy. For certain goals and ideals, a large majority of society can be induced to "give their all" and to do so gladly, willingly, and voluntarily. This does not occur very often, to be sure, nor does it last very long. But the latent potential is there in any society at any time. With the right spark—usually a charismatic leader with an idea and an ideal—the course of history can be changed in these brief, rare periods of almost total societal mobilization through the leadership of the voluntary sector.

The Negative Side

In describing the foregoing ten types of impact that the voluntary sector tends to have in some degree in any society, we have emphasized the positive contributions that voluntary action makes to society. However, as with any form of human group or activity, voluntary action and the voluntary sector are by no means always positive in their impacts. For every one of the ten types of impact we have noted, there can be negative consequences in certain circumstances and with regard to certain values. Thus, when voluntary associations experiment with new social forms, the failures can often be harmful to specific people and organizations. When alternative definitions of reality and morality are offered, these can be evil as in the case of Nazi Germany and its ideology as generated by the Nazi party, a voluntary association. When voluntary groups focus on the play element, their fun can become mischievous as in the case of a boys' gang that wrecks a school "just for kicks." When social clubs provide a warm and close sense of belonging to their members, they can also create deep dissatisfaction in people who would dearly like to belong but are excluded from a particular club or kind of club.

In the same way, voluntary groups striving to preserve some beliefs or values from the past may be holding on to anachronisms that would be better left to the pages of history books. Clubs whose members chase around seeking flying saucers and little green men from Mars might more profitably spend their time and energy elsewhere with more satisfying results. Organizations that arouse the full potentials of black people—who must then go out into the real world and face a harsh reality of bigotry and discrimination—may or may not be doing them a favor. The kinds of systemic corrections being suggested by cause-oriented and advocacy groups may not be conducive to the greatest good of the greatest number. Economic self-interest voluntary groups often tend to ignore the public interest in favor of an exclusive and selfish private interest. And the latent potentials of the voluntary sector can be mobilized to do evil as well as to do good for one's fellow man.

Conclusion

What then? Our answer is clear: All the more reason to begin a thorough study of the impact of the voluntary sector and voluntary action at all system levels, in all kinds of societies, in terms of all kinds of possible value standards. What we have suggested as major impacts of the voluntary sector only scratch the surface of a very large area for research. We have tried harder to demonstrate what voluntary action *might* do in various areas, rather than what it actually *does* do. We have done more to illustrate the breadth of the present topic than to present a definitive synthesis of the way things are, based upon empirical research. In most areas and for most types of voluntary action we simply do not know what the impacts are because no relevant research exists.

Yet at many levels and in many topical areas the possible impacts are extremely important to human society, past, present and future. Therefore, we would argue that evaluation of the impact and effectiveness/ineffectiveness of all types of voluntary action is one of the highest priority areas for future research on voluntary action. We seem to have much less empirical evidence bearing on such impact questions than we have for almost any other area or subfield of voluntary action research. This situation can be remedied only by a great deal more future commitment to impact/effectiveness research on the part of voluntary action scholars (including the Association of Voluntary Action Scholars itself), voluntary organizations and movements, and funding agencies of all kinds. We sincerely hope this joint commitment will be forthcoming in the next few years.

Notes

1. Allen, William Sheridan. *The Nazi Seizure of Power.* Chicago: Quadrangle Books, 1965.

2. Barton, Allen H. *Communities in Disaster.* Garden City, New York: Anchor Books, Doubleday Company, 1970.

3. Handlin, Oscar. *The Uprooted.* New York: Grosset and Dunlap, 1951.

4. Little, Kenneth. *West African Urbanization: A Study of Voluntary Associations in Social Change.* Cambridge, England: Cambridge University Press, 1965.

5. Maslow, Abraham H. *Motivation and Personality.* New York: Harper and Row, 1954.

6. Peterson, Sophia, and Virgil Peterson. "Voluntary Associations in Ancient Greece." *Journal of Voluntary Action Research* 2, no. 1: 2-16.

7. Smith, David Horton. "The Importance of Formal Voluntary Organizations for Society." *Sociology and Social Research* 50, (1966): 483-92.

8. Smith, David Horton, with John Dixon. "The Voluntary Sector." Chapter 7 in Edward Bursk, ed., *Challenge to Leadership: Managing in a Changing World.* New York: The Free Press, Macmillan and Co., 1973.

9. Smith, David Horton, Richard D. Reddy, and Burt R. Baldwin. "Types of Voluntary Action: A Definitional Essay." Chapter 10 in David Horton Smith et al., eds., *Voluntary Action Research: 1972.* Lexington, Mass.: Lexington Books, D.C. Heath and Co., 1972.

36

The Foundation as an Expression of a Democratic Society

ADAM YARMOLINSKY

ADAM YARMOLINSKY HAS ACHIEVED NATIONAL AND INTERNATIONAL DISTINCTION IN THE FIELDS OF LAW, ECONOMICS, EDUCATION, GOVERNMENT, AND SOCIAL POLICY. HIS NUMEROUS POSITIONS INCLUDED DEPUTY DIRECTOR OF THE PRESIDENT'S ANTIPOVERTY TASK FORCE, PRINCIPAL ADVISOR TO THE COMMISSION ON PRIVATE PHILANTHROPY AND PUBLIC NEEDS, MEMBER OF THE NATIONAL ADVISORY COMMITTEE OF THE INSTITUTE FOR RESEARCH ON POVERTY. HE IS CURRENTLY WITH THE FIRM OF KOMINERS, FORT, SCHLEFER, AND BOYER.

The Foundation in Nondemocratic Societies

I want to begin by discussing the role of the foundation in nondemocratic societies of the past. I think it is plain to all of us that there is no place for the private foundation in a totalitarian society. Where the state is in complete charge of the apparatus of society, competing organizations of any kind are ruled out, and foundations in such form as one finds in dictatorships have little, if any, similarity to the kinds of foundations with which we are familiar and in which we are interested.

The Monasteries

We can, however, learn a bit from the role of the foundations in traditional societies. In the Middle Ages, monasteries served much of the same functions

Reprinted from *N.Y.U. Proceedings of the Fifth Biennial Conference on Charitable Foundations*, edited by Henry Sellin (Albany, NY: Matthew Bender & Co., Inc., 1961) by permission of the author and the publisher. Copyright ©1961, Matthew Bender & Co., Inc.

that foundations serve today; while not totalitarian, they could scarcely be called democratic. But they were preservers and transmitters of culture. They were places of refuge. They were also to a limited extent centers of inquiry.

We cannot talk of free inquiry during that period as during the Renaissance, but certain of the activities that were carried on in the monasteries, even during the darkest of the Dark Ages, were as close as institutions came in that period to the kinds of inquiry which are now encouraged today by foundations, both public and private.

Not only did monasteries perform these functions, but the pattern of their existence was similar to that of foundations today. They existed on sufferance. Yet they continued when other institutions disintegrated. One reason for their survival was their observance of the rule of poverty, a rule that may be honored more in the breach than in the observance by some of our foundations of today.

The Universities

If we move from the medieval monasteries to the early universities during the Middle Ages and Renaissance, we find that their functions in their societies were not dissimilar. In structure and organization, medieval universities were quite unlike public universities in the United States today. They were not created by the state. They were not governed by representatives of society at large. They governed themselves and were self-perpetuating institutions. They were able to survive, again in part because of the unique functions that they performed, and in part because they observed a *de facto* rule of poverty. Moreover, there was an impetus behind them, a force of energy, intellectual energy, if you will, which made itself felt, even in a society which, at the outset of this period, was more anti-intellectual than any modern society.

It is interesting to note, however, that the universities of Europe towards the end of the Renaissance period ceased to be the primary centers of intellectual activity. Thus we find that the early explorers of the natural sciences had to conduct their experiments outside the universities, through the formation of scientific societies, because they could find neither the intellectual support nor the minimal funds that they required from the university corporations. This development may point up the need for foundations to engage in continual self-examination of their aims, purposes and activities today.

The Patron

As a source of support for creative activity, the institutional foundations of the Middle Ages and the Renaissance were supplemented to a great degree, indeed almost replaced, by the activities of individual patrons who operated some of the first fellowship programs. These programs were arbitrary and undisciplined by our standards, but judging by their best products (which seems to me the only way to judge a fellowship program), they were magnificently successful.

If we try to analyze the basis for their success, I think we find it not in their system, because they had none, but in the goals that they pursued. These goals gave first place to individual excellence, without regard to the method by which it was uncovered or rewarded.

Theoretical Basis of the Foundation in a Democratic Society

If we find that foundations during these past periods have been useful in societies which themselves were not committed to the ideals of democracy, on what theory or theories do we tolerate foundations in a democratic society? A private foundation is certainly an undemocratic institution. Despite the pressures of Form 990, it is not answerable directly to the people or their elected representatives. It is not governed by any elected group. Its trustees are normally a self-selected and self-perpetuating body.

I suggest that there are three theories which seem valid for justifying the existence of these nondemocratic institutions in our society.

Faith in the Individual

The first theory goes to the purpose of the foundation and the purpose of the society itself. Both are dedicated to a faith in the basic worth of the individual. This faith is implicit in every activity of a private foundation, just as it is the raison d'etre for every activity of government in a democratic society. It is this community of purpose which provides the essential and primary justification for foundations, without regard for the moment to the form in which they operate.

Pluralism of Decision Making

I do not think, however, that we can put aside the question of form for more than a moment. A democratic society is essentially and necessarily a pluralistic society. Our society is pluralistic even in its form of government. We have not only a geographical pluralism, distinguishing the role of the states and the role of the national government, but also a pluralism in the distribution of power among the three branches of government.

Judicial Analogy

It may be relevant to compare the role of the private foundation with the role of the judicial branch. Here is a branch of the government that has neither the power of the purse nor the power of the sword. Judges in our federal system are not elected. They are appointed for life. Like foundation trustees, whatever their decision, so long as they are on good behavior, they continue in office. They are, in fact, the only federal officials who receive their full salaries after retirement. This provision, which was instituted perhaps to give them a slight nudge towards retirement, may have nothing to do with their independence before leaving the bench, but this independence is unquestioned. The judicial branch is acknowledged as an essential counterbalance in our system. I suggest that in a small way the foundations have a similar role to perform.

Foundations as Expression of Pluralism

Everyone has heard the argument that foundation dollars are taxpayers' dollars. I think this is an argument that clearly defeats itself. There is a deliberate determination here in favor of a kind of pluralism of purpose, since foundation dollars are put outside what might be termed normal democratic processes. These dollars are not subject to the control and disposition of the national government, or of the elected representatives of the people.

Countervailing Powers

There is a third basis on which the existence of foundations, particularly of the larger foundations, is justifiable. Here I refer not to the atomization of power in our society, but to its concentration, in a way that permits one focus of power to be opposed by another focus, which is large enough and strong enough to swing the balance, or, at least, to provide a satisfactory and nearly equal opponent in situations of conflict.

The theory of countervailing power is one that has been developed by J. K. Galbraith in a context of institutional economics. It is a theory, however, that has equal application in the field of political power, and particularly in the field of foundation activity. I suggest that there are three areas in which the countervailing power of foundations, and particularly of larger foundations, is a useful force in our society.

Foundations and Fund-Raisers

The first, and perhaps the most obvious, is the countervailing power of the foundations vis-a-vis the big fund-raisers. When the collector for the latest national drive to eliminate the latest national disease comes around to the door of even the wealthiest individual citizen, there is not a great deal that the potential donor can do about the program that the drive supports. The program has been neatly packaged, and while you can buy a little piece of this or a little piece of that, you cannot, on your own, change the previously planned distribution of funds to be collected among the various elements.

But when even a large fund-raising enterprise approaches a foundation of any size, it is not only possible, it is taken for granted that the fund-raiser will have to discuss his program with the foundation staff. Very likely he will have to make some changes in it, not as a result of compulsion, but simply as a result of the process of exchange of ideas with the foundation people, who are not prepared to buy someone else's idea without being able to contribute a little bit of their own. After all, the justification for the existence of a staff in a foundation implies that not all of the ideas will come from the donee.

Foundations and Universities

There is a similar role that foundations play, vis-a-vis universities. It is one, I think, that foundations themselves are reluctant to acknowledge. The universities, until recently, would have denied it vigorously. But I believe that any interrogation of university presidents and of foundation staffs would reveal that there is a real interplay of ideas, an interplay that depends certainly in part on parity of intellectual strength of the two participants. It depends also on the fact that a foundation, in discussion with a university about a specific program, is able, at the very least, because of its potential contribution, to gain the audience of the people who will be making the decisions.

There is a process of exchange here which enables foundations to bring home to the universities ideas about planning for research projects, curriculum planning, organization of activities—for example between what is done on the home campus and what is done overseas—which have already made real contributions to the planning process, and even to the substantive organization of the university world.

Foundations and Government

Turning to the third contervailing power situation, the opposition between foundations and government, I use this idea of opposition obviously as a constructive notion, not as a negative one. While one might suppose that the government of the United States is so massive an enterprise that not even the foundations can stand up against it, this is not so. Indeed, anyone who has worked on foundation projects with a governmental connection must be well aware that the large foundation is able to demonstrate possibilities to government which may be used by public agencies with great effect.

There is even an example of a very small foundation which was able to undertake a program of internships in public service with the use of quite minimal funds. By conducting the program for a few years, the small foundation demonstrated so successfully to the United States Civil Service Commission the value of the program, that is now being supported by public funds. Thus, here is another area where the countervailing power of the foundation can make a real contribution to a democratic society.

The Activities of the Foundation in a Democratic Society

Since the foundation has a place, or can have a place in a democratic society, let us examine briefly in what general ways the foundations can maximize the values to which a democratic society is dedicated: through programming, through procedures, and through staffing patterns.

Programs

Programs

In the area of programs, it is very important for foundations to be acutely aware of the new directions in which government, particularly, and other segments of our society are moving. As with the foundations that existed in earlier times, it is all too easy to continue to support programs which, while valuable in themselves, are not contributing to the most vital streams of energy and intellectual activity in society today. I refer particularly to three fields here.

Public Affairs

It would be most unfortunate if a division of hard and fast lines was drawn between government activity and foundation activity. The greatest opportunities for foundations are found in a society in which the government is vigorously active and moving ahead. By getting out in front of what government is doing, but close to its interests, foundations can make it possible for government to move into appropriate new fields. There are many new areas where perhaps the time is not quite ripe for a full-fledged government program. An opportunity exists for a proper foundation venture that will point the way for some future government activity.

In these areas it is important not to leave programming to the planners in the agencies in Washington on the theory that they will pick up the responsibility. If the government is not yet doing what it should in a particular field, one of the best ways to encourage public activity is to show the way through private activity.

Communications

What I have in mind here is the whole question of how our society is organized to bring the concerns of those who are guiding events in governmental and quasi-governmental activities to the great mass of the people in general, and to the opinion leaders in the communities throughout the country in particular. It also raises the question of how the reactions and thoughts of our opinion leaders can be communicated up the line to those who are making national and international decisions.

This is an area in which the imagination, the ingenuity and the flexibility of foundations make them particularly able to render a unique contribution, one in which foundations should be one step ahead of government. Such a program requires the foundations to maintain an intimate up-to-date association with governmental and quasi-governmental activities. This association cannot be accomplished if a foundation's programs do not change with changing times. Once achieved, however, such an association is particularly rewarding and important for the foundation as an element in a democratic society.

Civil Rights

This involves not only the problem of race relations, but the rights of every kind of group which is unable to prevail by virtue of numbers. In the protection of minority rights we rely on the guarantees of our Constitution and of our public organization. But there is a role here also for the foundations, as avowed minorities, not as representatives of all the people, to be involved in the problems of all kinds of minorities, and to do so again by the exercise of ingenuity, flexibility and imagination—all qualities that foundations are able to mobilize.

Procedures

Turning from the area of programs to the equally important area of procedures, two aspects of the relationships between foundations and grantees should be discussed.

Grantee Freedom

The first of these is what I call grantee freedom, which all of us are very likely to take for granted. Nevertheless, I think it has to be emphasized and re-emphasized. We do not tell our grantees what to do. We pick people whom we think to be competent to do jobs we think need doing, and then turn them loose to do the job in their own way. I reiterate this because we cannot overemphasize how important it is that we continue to behave in this fashion.

Grantee Responsibility

Together with grantee freedom we have to put a good deal of emphasis on grantee responsibility. One of the reasons why universities have been able to continue in existence through the centuries, despite the radical revolutionary and thoroughly disturbing ideas which are promulgated by their members, is that universities have traditionally maintained that their only function is to provide the forum. The university administration says, in effect, "we just hire the hall."

So long as foundations maintain a similar position, so long as foundations insist that the product of a foundation grant is the product of the grantee and not of the grantor, so long as foundations make it plain that, "we just hire the hall," they will be able to maintain the policy of making grants in controversial areas to permit new ideas to be fathered under their auspices, and to survive even in periods of great hostility to new ideas.

The Individual as Grantee

My emphasis on grantee freedom and grantee responsibility accompanies an emphasis on the value of individual fellowship programs. I mentioned earlier the progenitors of fellowships and the values that we derived and still derive from their efforts. It seems to me that no foundation is too small or too large to undertake the work, worry and nuisance that are involved in making small grants to individuals, whether they are scholars or creative writers, newspapermen or government officials.

These grants are based on faith in the capacity of the individual to make a new and important contribution, even though they are not necessarily part of any overall substantive program. While small in amount, they may require what appears to be an exorbitant percentage in the cost of administration. This kind of activity, however, is at the heart of the faith in the democratic process—faith in the value of the individual to which foundations, particularly in a democratic society, must be committed.

Responsibility in Controversy

The attitudes of foundations in controversial situations should also be discussed in connection with the importance of placing the responsibility for the work of the grantee on the grantee himself. All of this responsibility can never be shifted. Foundations are going to be attacked because a particular grantee has come out with a theory, notion, book, or paper which is displeasing to the powers that be. In a democratic society particularly, foundations have an obligation not to let controversy about the results of their grants deter them from continuing to make grants on their own responsibility.

Staffing

One could speculate whether staffing a foundation in a democratic society is any different from staffing a foundation in an undemocratic society. I suggest, however, that the fundamental dilemma of staffing a foundation, which exists in any situation, is exacerbated in a democratic society because of the objectives to which the foundation and the society are both dedicated. There is a real opposition here, a continuous tension, in choosing people to operate at a staff level between the expert and the generalist, between the originator and the follow-upper.

It is all too easy, in staffing a foundation, to choose the traditional experts, to make them responsible for suggestions or recommendations to the board for a grant-making policy, which at least over a brief span is above criticism because the people who are making the grants are above criticism. On the other hand, it is possible to turn the foundation staff responsibilities over to a group of idea men who are way out in front of everybody, and whose efforts for a while result in a good deal of praise and a little bit of blame, but no permanent residue of achievement.

It seems to me that either alternative is going to get the foundation into trouble, unless it can somehow achieve a balance. This is not a static balance; it is a kind of dynamic balance between traditional expertise and the instinct to turn everything upside down. These two instincts are present to a degree in any society, but they are in a particularly lively state of tension in a democratic society.

They need to be in an equally lively state of tension on the foundation board as on the professional staff.

Conclusion

Not only does a foundation have a useful role in a democratic society. It has, in fact, a series of useful roles. Just as a democratic society brings out the best and the most creative potential in every individual who participates fully in the activities of that society, so also does a democratic society bring out the greatest potential in the private foundation. While it creates challenges and difficulties, as the late, lamented series of congressional hearings demonstrated, a democratic society creates opportunities as well for a genuinely cooperative relationship between the foundations and the other segments of society, which cannot be matched in any other form of social organization.

37

The Third Sector

JOHN D. ROCKEFELLER 3RD

JOHN D. ROCKEFELLER 3RD DEVOTED MOST OF HIS LIFE TO
CHARITABLE AND PHILANTHROPIC ACTIVITIES. IN ADDITION TO
ENDOWING HIS OWN FOUNDATION, THE JDR 3RD FUND, MR.
ROCKEFELLER SERVED AS CHAIRMAN OF THE ROCKEFELLER
FOUNDATION AND THE ROCKEFELLER BROTHERS FUND. HE WAS A
LEADING FORCE IN THE CREATION AND DEVELOPMENT OF THE
LINCOLN CENTER FOR THE PERFORMING ARTS, COLONIAL
WILLIAMSBURG INC., THE ASIA SOCIETY, AND NUMEROUS OTHER
CHARITABLE ORGANIZATIONS.

*This selection was originally published in the March, 1978
issue of* Across the Board *and a condensed version
appeared in the April, 1978 issue of* Reader's Digest.

We Americans have always taken pride in the vitality of our country. Yet, too often we fail to recognize one of the main reasons for that vitality: the fact that we have developed over the two centuries of our existence a remarkable three-sector system.

Two of the sectors are instantly recognizable to everyone—business and government. But the third is so neglected and so little understood that I am tempted to call it "the invisible sector." It is crucial to our way of life. But the fact is that it is eroding before our eyes, and very few people seem to be aware of it.

The third sector is the private nonprofit sector. It has been called by other names, but none is truly adequate and none has caught on. It is for this reason that I refer to it simply as "the third sector."

Certainly it is a paradox that the third sector is omnipresent throughout our society, yet is so taken for granted that it is barely discussed or recognized as an important social force at the national level. Tens of millions of Americans participate every day in third sector activities, by contributing their time or their financial support or both. The sector includes tens of thousands of institutions absolutely indispensable to community life all across the nation—churches, hospitals, museums, libraries, private colleges and universities, theater groups, symphony orchestras, and social service organizations of many kinds. All of these depend for their survival on the voluntary contributions of time and money by individual citizens.

The third sector is also the seedbed for organized efforts to deal with social problems. As the most prominent example, all of the important contemporary "movements" have sprung from it—civil rights, consumerism, women's rights, the environment and many others.

In my own efforts over the years to stress the importance of a healthy third sector, I referred to it as "philanthropy." This was wrong on two counts. First, the semantic problem. Philanthropy is a word that has a certain antiquated air about it, suggesting privilege and coming across as a plaything of the idle rich. A philanthropist is seen as a "do-gooder," at best an anachronism and at worst a luxury rather than a social necessity in these difficult times. Second, the conceptual problem. I have come to realize that philanthropy is actually a misleading term. Philanthropy denotes the act of voluntary giving. It is thus the main support mechanism for the third sector, a means rather than an end. What is really important is the ends that philanthropic giving serves.

Government is supported by taxes, business by its profits. The third sector is supported principally by voluntary contributions. This philanthropic giving totals some $26 billion per year in the United States. Far from being a plaything of the wealthy, more than half of individual giving comes from families with incomes of under $20,000 per year. In addition, a recent study estimates that the equivalent of another $26 billion is contributed annually to society through the voluntary services of literally millions of individuals.

The true value behind such figures can probably best be seen by focusing on a specific example. One way you can do this is to find out the value of volunteer services to a hospital in your community. As a test I asked a secretary in my office to check on the hospital in her community. She came back with an eye-opening report. The Woman's Association of the Morristown Memorial Hospital in New Jersey provides 885 volunteer workers who put in more than 145,000 hours in 1976. These women operate some 45 different services. The revenue-producing services netted more than $1 million over the past five years for the hospital, quite apart from the value of the time of the volunteers and their own financial contributions. In addition, they engage in special fund-raising projects: last year, for example, they organized a "decorator tour" of a nearby mansion in which local merchants and interior decorators contributed their goods and services. The project attracted 500,000 visitors and additional income of $270,000 to the hospital.

The women of Morristown hospital certainly do not think of themselves as participating in the third sector, nor does the person who sends an annual $25 contribution to his or her alma mater. The fact that so much of the third sector is individual, personal and local in nature is one reason why it has not been conceptualized as the important national phenomenon that it is. Another reason is the sheer diversity of it. We tend to think of our own particular interest, whether it be a church or college, or a cause such as women's rights or the environment, rather than seeing what all of these diverse interests have in common.

That common thread is a belief in being of service to one's community and to other people, without relying on government and without any expectation of personal profit. At the heart of the third sector is individual initiative and a sense of caring.

It would miss the point to see the third sector as "holier than thou"—as innately superior to government and business. It is not; it is merely different. The real point is that a healthy democratic society needs all three in an effective and balanced relationship.

But the relationship is out of balance today. We live in an age of big government and big business, while the third sector is gradually eroding. One way to see what would be lost if such a tendency continues is to step back and look at our past, at what the third sector has meant in the development of our country.

One of the most dramatic examples is the abolitionist movement, roughly from 1830 to 1860. Clearly, the ending of slavery was imperative if the United States was to continue and progress as a unified, democratic nation. It was not a movement that could result from the profit motive or from government initiative; it had to spring from the third sector. In terms of sheer courage, the leaders of the abolitionist movement are comparable today perhaps only to the Soviet dissidents for standing on moral principle in the face of overwhelming odds. Some of the names are familiar, such as William Lloyd Garrison and Frederick Douglass. Others are obscure to history—names such as Elijah Lovejoy, killed when a mob sacked and burned the office of his antislavery newspaper in Alton, Illinois, in 1837; or James G. Birney, who was born into a slaveholding family in Kentucky, but decided that slavery was an evil that had to be eliminated. Birney sold his plantations, freed his slaves, and devoted his life to the cause, publishing an antislavery newspaper called *The Philanthropist* in Ohio and running for president on the Liberty Party ticket in 1840.

In the wake of the great success of Alex Haley's book, *Roots*, there may well be many white Americans who would be surprised at the "roots" of their own families in the abolitionist movement. For example, my own maternal grandmother, Laura Spelman, operated a way station on the underground railroad.

The remarkable fact is that throughout most of our history virtually every significant step forward in social progress sprang originally from the third sector. A few examples:

> **Care of the mentally ill:** It was the wisdom and fervor of one woman—Dorothea Dix, in Massachusetts in the 1830s—that led to a national crusade for reform of institutions for the mentally ill and to the gradual assumption by state governments of this responsibility.
>
> **Women's rights:** Elizabeth Cady Stanton, Amelia Bloomer and Lucretia Mott founded the Women's Suffrage Movement in Seneca Falls, New York, in 1848. It is often forgotten that these women sought not only the franchise but also a broadening of economic and other opportunities for women.
>
> **Conservation:** President Theodore Roosevelt was a great political leader in support of conservation, but his cause was aided by many initiatives from the private sector and acts of philanthropy beginning in the last quarter of the 19th century. One result was the creation of the National Park Service in 1916.

One could go on almost indefinitely. I think of the work of Margaret Sanger in founding Planned Parenthood, which is the direct antecedent of worldwide concern and action in respect to the population problem. One of the best examples surely is the founding of Alcoholics Anonymous in 1934 by William Wilson, a Newark salesman. No amount of money could buy the caring relationship of one human being for another that exists within all chapters of AA, nor could any government bureau ever do the job so effectively.

In the early part of this century came the invention of the foundation, which historian Henry Steele Commager has called "an American gift to the world." Foundations are often criticized generally for the errors in judgment of a few of them. But the fact is that there are more than 26,000 foundations in the United States. Their contributions to the well-being of mankind are countless: in education, medical research, agriculture, conservation, population, public television, and virtually every other field of worthwhile human endeavor.

An interesting fact emerges from this brief look at our history. In so many fields of social need, the pioneering work of the third sector has resulted in government's taking over responsibility for extending the services broadly, applying the sanction of law where needed, and assuming the major share of the financial burden. This is right and proper. The third sector, in effect, provides the channel through which American citizens, individually and in groups, can express their values and build a moral consensus for what *should* be sanctioned and broadened by government.

Today the need for that channel is as strong as ever, even in an age of big government, when the annual federal budget alone is rapidly approaching a figure 20 times that of individual voluntary giving. Perhaps the best evidence is the fact that there are major contemporary movements in at least three fields in which the pioneering work was done in the third sector 100 years ago or more— civil rights, the environment and women's rights. There will always be a need for a healthy third sector—to keep government honest, to provide alternative ways to solve problems, to help maintain institutions that should never be taken over by government, to pioneer new needs, and to provide opportunities for the initiative and sense of caring of individual citizens—the indispensable bedrock of a thriving democracy.

There is still plenty of life in the third sector today. To cite just a few examples:

- *The East Kentucky Health Services Center:* Two young Kentuckians had a dream six years ago of finding a way to improve the delivery of health services in the poorest and most rural county of Kentucky. The result today is a modern clinic with a staff of five doctors serving 35,000 patients a year on a budget of $600,000. Not a penny of government money was used.

- *Clarinda—Town of Tomorrow:* This is a goal-setting program operated by citizens in an Iowa town of only 5,000 population to plan and manage the growth of their community.

- *The Gray Panthers:* This national movement based in Philadelphia has 75 local chapters organized to fight discrimination based on age.

- *Southeast Alabama Self Help Association:* This black organization based in Tuskegee has 9,000 members; it has established a credit union and a health center, and is planning housing for members.

- *Urban Home Ownership Corporation:* This nonprofit organization has rehabilitated more than $35 million worth of innercity apartment buildings in New York and is turning ownership over to low-income residents.

There are many instances of corporate support of the third sector. One is the remarkable "Five Per Cent Club" in Minnesota, which was started with the initiative of Kenneth and Bruce Dayton of the Dayton Hudson Corporation in Minneapolis. To be a member, a corporation must make philanthropic contributions each year to the full extent allowed by the tax laws—5 percent of net taxable income. As of 1977, 23 corporations had qualified for membership in the club.

Yet, this must be measured against the fact that a handful of publicly held companies in the entire country contribute 5 percent. The national average hovers around 1 percent. Bruce Dayton recalls how President Lyndon B. Johnson underscored the irony of this when he visited Rochester in 1971: "In spite of the fact that your federal government has seen fit to allow a charitable deduction of 5 percent of your profits," President Johnson said, "the record is quite clear that you business leaders feel that the federal government can spend this money more wisely than you can."

Although examples of individual initiative and participation in the third sector could be cited by the thousands, it still seems that many other Americans have given up. We hear much talk of alienation and withdrawal these days, the feeling that one person's voice or vote or effort does not count, that many of our social problems seem too difficult to solve. If big government can't solve them, the individual citizen might reason, what can I do?

This growing mood is one of the reasons why the third sector is eroding. Another is the shrinking financial base. Earlier, I identified philanthropy as the principal source of financial support for the third sector. But there are two others, and both have inherent limitations—government grants and contracts, and the charging of fees for services. If government support becomes too large a proportion of a nonprofit institution's budget, it will soon lose its independence and become a de facto government institution. And if other third sector organizations, such as colleges, museums, and performing arts companies, keep increasing the price of their services to cover costs, they soon will become indistinguishable from businesses.

This situation means that the oldest form of support, philanthropic giving, is still the most important, for it provides the crucial margin which gives third sector institutions and programs their most precious asset—their independence. Without a vigorous flow of voluntary giving, the third sector would ultimately disappear. It would split into two appendages, one to government and the other to business.

The ominous fact is that the pace of philanthropic giving has steadily lost ground in recent years. While everything else has been going up, individual giving today is running at an annual rate of some $8 billion *less* in real terms than it was in 1960. The result is a growing trend over the past five years of the curtailing of services by churches and private colleges and other institutions, and, in an increasing number of cases, closing their doors altogether. Many of the newer community action programs have perished for lack of funds. Others exist on a starvation budget. The rest have to spend an inordinate amount of time and energy searching for every dollar they can get to continue operations.

Why has voluntary giving failed to keep pace? Certainly the mood of alienation I referred to is a causative factor. But I believe the deeper problem is a failure of leadership in all three sectors. Obviously, many millions of Americans are still involved and do contribute. And many of those who have lost heart could still be reached and challenged if leadership would lead, would understand the need and point the way. But most Americans who make small gifts annually don't realize the cumulative power of their giving, the rich tradition of the third sector in our history and its crucial importance to our way of life. Why should they? No one ever talks about it. We have failed to conceptualize it, to give it any recognizable framework of identity.

Consider, for example, the fact that there are dozens of graduate schools of business and public administration to prepare young people for careers in the two dominant sectors—but not one such school to prepare them for areas in the private nonprofit world.

Leadership in all three sectors is naturally preoccupied with its own responsibilities. Even in the third sector itself, the president of a private college, for example, is concerned about the financial status of his or her own institution and tends not to think in terms of the third sector as a whole. The overriding concern of businessmen is to maintain and improve the profitability of their companies. Government leaders are preoccupied with political decision-making and fire-fighting.

The result is that no one seems to take responsibility for the welfare of the third sector, to appreciate its critical importance to our system and what needs to be done to maintain and strengthen it.

If voluntary giving continues to lag, we will be well on our way toward a two-sector system. When that happens, the trend toward a one-sector system will have begun. Opportunities and incentives for individual initiative will disappear, and the vaunted pluralism of American society will gradually give way to a monolithic system.

Perhaps the saddest feature of all is that our system is changing before our eyes, and our leaders don't seem to recognize how or why. I have an unshakable faith in the ability of the American people to respond, but they must have the understanding, leadership, and policies necessary to generate that response. The only way to change the course we are on will be for leaders in all three sectors to see the problem clearly and to take deliberate steps to restore the vitality and balance of a three-sector system. What must be done is to apply the qualities that exemplify the third sector—the qualities of individual initiative and caring—to the welfare of the third sector itself.

I have increasingly wondered what would happen if our top leadership in Washington fully understood and believed deeply in the importance of the third sector. Instead of taking over more and more third sector functions, either deliberately or by default, the government should play a strong supportive role. This would be manifested not only in specific measures, such as tax policies that would encourage voluntary giving, but also in exercising the myriad ways that all agencies of government could cooperate with and facilitate the involvement of citizens in meeting their own needs and problems.

I have wondered, too, what would happen if business executives, members of corporate boards, and shareholders appreciated more keenly that the welfare of their corporations is inextricably tied up with the welfare of the society as a whole, and that they therefore have a responsibility to understand and support the third sector. The fundamental fact is that the business sector and the third sector are both rooted in the free enterprise system. The best way to preserve that system will be to keep the third sector healthy and strong. Adequate corporate participation would be manifested not only by an increase in contributions, but by a much greater sensitivity to the corporation's role in the community and the impact of its decisions on community life.

If such a change of attitudes were to come about—and I believe it is possible—we would be ready to embark on an American renaissance. We would become a giving society once again, one in which the power of individual initiative is rediscovered and revitalized. We would surprise ourselves and surprise the world, for American democracy, which all too many observers believe is on a downward slide, would come alive with unimagined creativity and energy.

Nothing less than this is at stake.

38

The Third Sector: Keystone of a Caring Society

WALDEMAR A. NIELSEN

WALDEMAR A. NIELSEN HAS HAD A DISTINGUISHED CAREER AS A
SCHOLAR, ECONOMIST, AUTHOR, GOVERNMENT AND FOUNDATION
OFFICIAL, AND STUDENT OF PHILANTHROPY. NIELSEN IS THE
AUTHOR OF THE BIG FOUNDATIONS (1972) AND THE ENDANGERED
SECTOR (1979), AS WELL AS THREE WORKS ON AFRICA.

*The following speech was originally delivered to the 25th
Anniversary Conference of the National Council on
Philanthropy held in Denver in November, 1979, just prior
to the publication of Nielsen's book,* The Endangered
Sector. *It was later reproduced as the first in a series of
occasional papers issued by Independent Sector, the
successor organization to the National Council on
Philanthropy.*

You and I are the bearers and beneficiaries of a very precious—and very peculiar—American tradition.

Its peculiarity lies in the fact that although the institutions that embody it are
all around us and constitute an important part of our lives, we remain largely
unaware of it. The simple statistics about it are not collected; scholars rarely
study it; our teachers don't teach about it. It represents a huge sector of our
American pluralistic system—operating in parallel to the sectors of government
and the business economy—and yet there is not even an accepted name for it.

I shall call it, for want of a better term, the Third Sector. It consists of the vast
array of entities—colleges, churches, voluntary hospitals, philanthropic foundations, symphony societies, scientific research centers and a multitude of others,

---

Reprinted by permission of the author.

both permanent and transitory—whose common characteristics are that they are private, do not operate for profit and are devoted to serving the general welfare, not simply the self-interests of their members or supporters.

To overlook something of the scale of the Third Sector takes some considerable overlooking. For even in quantitative terms it constitutes a considerable part of what James Madison called our "compound Republic." Private nonprofit institutions eligible to receive tax-deductible gifts have annual outlays of more than $80 billion. Some 50 million Americans give to them each year. Some 400,000 of them are registered with and accorded tax privileges by the U.S. Treasury Department. In addition it is estimated that there are some 2 or 3 million functioning private nonprofit groups and associations of a less formal nature. To suggest the degree of precision of our knowledge in this field I should mention that some experts guess the total is not 2 or 3 million but more like 6 or 7 million!

Size however is the least measure of the Third Sector. What it does for the spirit and character of our society and for the freedom and fulfillment of each of us is what matters. Let me count the ways:

First and most obviously the institutions of the Third Sector deliver a range of vital services to very large numbers of Americans of every category:

- Private and parochial schools provide elementary and secondary education to more than 5 million students, rich and poor; white and nonwhite.

- Private colleges and universities, which include some of our finest educational institutions, enroll another 2 million.

- Private centers of scientific research, many of them associated wih private universities, carry on a major part of the search for new knowledge in virtually every field.

- Private cultural institutions—from ballet companies and choral societies to art museums and experimental theatre groups— provide their benefits to a very large and rapidly growing number of Americans.

- Private voluntary hospitals, homes for the aged, and facilities for the handicapped constitute nearly half of the immense national apparatus for health care.

- In the equally large and diverse field of welfare services, private charitable agencies did the pioneering work beginning more than a century ago. Today they remain essential instrumentalities in every community across the continent for the alleviation of human distress. The 37,000 agencies which receive funds from the United Ways of America each year serve an estimated clientele of more than 70 million.

- There are nearly 500,000 local churches and synagogues in this country—from the great cathedrals to humble storefronts. On any given Sunday there are probably more people in churches than the total number of people who attend professional sports events in a whole year.

For a great many of us, many of the most joyous as well as some of the most tearful days of our lives are spent in the institutions of the Third Sector.

The second general function performed by the Third Sector is that it strengthens the other two sectors and makes them work better.

Though we tend sometimes to talk of government, the economy and the Third Sector as separate elements, in reality they are closely interconnected. The economy for example, as Eli Ginzburg and others have pointed out, depends heavily on the other sectors to produce the goods and services demanded by the market. The prosperity of the automobile industry has long depended on an expanding national highway system, which is to say government, and on the training and research activities carried on in the colleges and universities of the nonprofit sector.

In an even more fundamental sense the survival of the American enterprise system may depend upon the corrective and compensatory effects of the Third Sector. Kenneth Boulding has argued that without the benefit of nonprofit activity, the economy would quickly develop "conditions that would be widely regarded as pathological....It might easily produce distributions of income which would be regarded as unacceptable and if carried to extreme might destroy that minimum sense of community and maintenance of order which is necessary to sustain exchange." Arthur Okun has put the matter in even broader terms: "Capitalism and democracy are really a most improbable mixture," he has said. "Maybe that is why they need each other—to put some rationality into equality and some humanity into efficiency."

The institutions of the Third Sector are especially heavily involved with government. In most fields other than religion they operate in parallel with government agencies carrying out similar programs, and very often they are overshadowed by the scale of the government agencies on whose flank they operate. Harvard and Stanford are small institutions compared to the state universities of Michigan, California and New York. They are nonetheless crucially important both because of their own excellence and because they provide a standard of measurement, a stimulus that helps invigorate and improve the complex totality of both public and private higher education. The difference this makes can best be appreciated by those familiar with the centralized, wholly governmental university system of other leading societies including most of the nations of western Europe.

In a number of fields—health care, welfare services and scientific research as well as higher education, government is heavily and increasingly reliant on the utilization of these private service systems—through the mechanisms of grants and contracts—to help carry out legislatively mandated programs. In one sense, therefore, Third Sector agencies are an important instrumentality in the service of government.

But at the same time, private nonprofit institutions—because of their strong constituencies and their tradition of independence—are an important check upon the excesses of government and a corrective to some of its worst deficiencies. In the era of Big Government and at a time when governmental efforts become both more massive in scale and more intrusive in their methods, its collaboration with nonprofit agencies is a means of decentralizaton, of breaking the bureaucracy into smaller units, of testing a variety of approaches and of generating the active participation and involvement of citizens. This can reduce the unresponsiveness of government by repairing broken circuits of communication between it and the citizenry. This in turn can provide an antidote to the sense of powerlessness and alienation felt by considerable numbers of Americans today, particularly the poor, the handicapped and the disadvantaged.

I do not mean to suggest that the benefits of the arrangement all flow in one direction: private nonprofit agencies by their access to government funding and their involvement with official experts are often invigorated and broadened. Neither do I mean to suggest by pointing out the importance of the Third Sector to the better functioning of government and the economy that it is more important than the other major sectors in our pluralistic system. But I do mean to emphasize that in its interaction with them, it adds certain distinctive qualities and characteristics to the mix which check and balance the less fortunate tendencies of the other better recognized and more massive sectors.

A third major function of the Third Sector is that it serves as a humanizing force in every sphere of American society.

One of the main ways by which it does this is by providing outlet for the nearly universal impulse to altruism. The idea of volunteering has acquired in the narcissistic atmosphere of the moment something of an antique ring. Nonetheless it represents a massive living American tradition. Forty to fifty million Americans give their time as volunteers every year. One of the most distinctive and commendable features of our society, voluntarism embodies a profoundly important concept—namely that a good citizen of a decent society has a personal responsibility to serve the needs of others. In that simple age-old proposition lies the essential distinction between a brutalizing society and a caring and responsible one; and the Third Sector is a principal vehicle for carrying the idea into action in the United States.

Another less familiar but equally important means by which it serves to humanize our life is by providing the means of expression for all those spiritual, social and creative needs of individuals that government, the army, the office, the store, the factory and the farm cannot satisfy—that is all the things that do not center on power and authority nor on the production and acquisition of material goods. Private voluntary associations and nonprofit institutions are a wide open super highway along which each of us engage in his or her personal pursuit of happiness.

Consider the infinite and delightful variety of those possibilities:

- If your interest is people, you can help the elderly by contributing to the Grey Panthers; or teenagers through the Jean Teen Scene of Chicago; or young children through your local nursery school; or everyone by giving to the Rock of All Ages in Philadelphia.

- If your interest is animals, there is the ASPCA and Adopt-A-Pet; if fishes, the Isaac Walton League; if birds, the American Homing Pigeon Institute or the Easter Bird Banding Association.

- If you are an old WASP, there is the English Speaking Union and the Mayflower Descendants Association; if you have a still older association with the country, there is the Redcliff Chippewa Fund or the Museum of the American Indian.

- If your vision is local, there is the Cook County Special Bail Project and Clean Up the Ghetto in Philadelphia; if national, there is America the Beautiful; if global, there is the United Nations Association; if celestial, there are the Sidewalk Astronomers of San Francisco.

- If you are interested in tradition and social continuity, there is the Society for the Preservation of Historic Landmarks and the Portland Friends of Cast Iron Architecture; if social change is your passion there is Common Cause; and if that seems too sober for you, there is the Union of Radical Political Economists or perhaps the Theatre for Revolutionary Satire in New York.

- If your pleasure is music, there is a supermarket of choices—from Vocal Jazz to the Philharmonic Society to the American Guild of English Hand Bellringers.

- If you don't know quite what you want, there is Get Your Head Together, Inc. of Glen Ridge, New Jersey. If your interests are contradictory there is the Great Silence Broadcasting Foundation of California. If they are ambiguous there is the Tombstone Health Service of Arizona and the Denver Dumb Friends League.

The landscape of the Third Sector is untidy but wonderfully exuberant. What counts is not the confusion but the profusion. There is literally something in it for everyone.

For some of us, the Third Sector offers instrumentalities for cultural continuity; for others, of cultural change. Nonprofit groups help satisfy the needs of some for individuality and of others for affiliation. For some they are a way of caring for others; for others a way of being cared for. They provide a means by which we amuse ourselves and experience the joy of the arts, and a means for consoling ourselves and healing ourselves. They offer the institutional framework within which we can practice our religious faith. They are the "growing edge" of new social forms and modes of human relations exemplified by the *avant garde* and the counterculture. They offer unobstructed opportunity for each individual to pursue his or her own vision of beauty and truth and they thereby greatly increase the reality of personal freedom.

Fourth and finally, let me turn to another and perhaps the ultimate contribution of the Third Sector to our national life—namely what it does to ensure the continuing responsiveness, creativity and self-renewal of our democratic society.

Some of the institutions of the Third Sector concentrate on the provision of human services, some on the quest for new knowledge, some on the spiritual concerns and self-realization. But another large category operates along the margins of politics. These include grassroots community associations, public interest law firms and reformist groups of every kind.

To some degree these groups represent the organized pestiferousness of the active citizenry on all those issues where the standard organs of representative government including legislatures and political parties do not perform effectively, either because they have become ossified or corrupted. They are stubborn and belligerent protection against nonfeasance and malfeasance by government—what have been called "mediating structures" standing between the citizen and the dangers of bureaucratic and political misconduct.

These multidinous social action movements of the Third Sector are not only bulwarks and defenses, they are also active creative forces for the continuous adaptation of our society to new needs and priorities and for its continuous revitalization. They are the seedbeds from which most important reforms in our country have begun. John Gardner has called them "the first birds off the telephone wire" and he describes the operation in these words: "Very few— almost no—major policy innovations are enacted at the federal level that are not preceded by years of national discussion and debate. The national dialogue is an untidy but impressive process. Ideas that will eventually become the basis for some major innovation in federal policy are first put into circulation by individuals and small groups....The national dialogue that precedes action is primarily a private sector responsibility, particularly in its early stages. The private sector has the pluralism, looseness and free market characteristics necessary to let a hundred ideas bubble up, sift the ones that speak to the condition of the times and let the rest evaporate."

Think for a moment of the great transforming forces for change in our national life over the past 40 years—the civil rights movement, environmentalism, the women's movement, consumerism and the antiwar movement during the Viet Nam period—and ask yourself where they came from. In every instance their origins are to be found not in the technocracy nor the bureaucracy or the political parties but rather in the organized impulse of free groups of ordinary citizens.

Without the opportunity for such manifestations of citizen initiative—outside the usual channels of parties and politics when those become blocked—the American system would progressively lose its resilience and ultimately destroy its own legitimacy. The Third Sector, then, in addition to its other great services to American democracy, is an indispensable, inbuilt adaptive and survival mechanism.

The Third Sector is now in serious difficulty—under simultaneous assault by inflation, government regulation and competition and the negative effects of some misbegotten tax policies. Its own mismanagement of its affairs is another worrisome problem. To preserve its freedom and vitality will require a long, determined and persevering struggle by all of us who are committed to the preservation of a humane, compassionate, and free society in this country. That is eminently worth fighting for.

39

What Kind of Society Shall We Have?

RICHARD W. LYMAN

RICHARD W. LYMAN, A NOTED HISTORIAN AND EDUCATOR,
SERVED FOR MANY YEARS AS PRESIDENT OF STANFORD
UNIVERSITY. HE IS CURRENTLY PRESIDENT OF THE ROCKEFELLER
FOUNDATION.

*The following speech was originally presented at the Fall,
1980, meeting of Independent Sector in Washington, D.C.
It was later published as part of Independent Sector's
Occasional Papers series.*

"What Kind of Society Shall We Have?" might suggest an exhortation to strive for the kind of society we'd like (always assuming that we can agree on that), or an exercise in prophecy: what sort of society does it appear that we're going to get? As writers usually do when confronted with such a situation, I'll do some of each, and maybe my ventures into prophecy will frighten you enough to make you work with renewed vigor in this world in which not only are lots of people not philanthropically inclined, but they don't even think they should be. Indeed, some of them would go still further, and argue for the one proposition that spells death for the independent sector: that government ought to enjoy a monopoly of expenditure for the public good.

Most of what is written on the independent sector stresses an array of its virtues that is by now fairly familiar: its contributions to pluralism and diversity, its tendency to enable individuals to participate in civic life in ways that make sense to them and help to combat that corrosive feeling of powerlessness that is among the dread social diseases of our era, its encouragement of innovation and its capacity to act as a check on the inadequacies of government. These things are important to say, and even to repeat.

Reprinted by permission of the author.

The most sophisticated and effective speeches and writing in support of the independent sector also give some attention to its shortcomings, actual or potential. One thinks of such efforts as John Gardner's widely and justifiably praised talk before the Council on Foundations in May of 1979, entitled "Preserving the Independent Sector," in which he remarked:

> ...it's easy to attribute to the sector a role so romanticized and overblown that it's impossible to live up to. I have read statements on the independent or nonprofit institutions of this country which leave the impression that they are virtually faultless.
>
> We know better. Some nonprofit institutions are far gone in decay. Some are so badly managed as to make a mockery of every good intention they might have had. There is fraud, mediocrity and silliness. In short, the independent sector has no sovereign remedy against human and institutional failure.
>
> Beyond that, it is the essence of pluralism that it produces some things of which you approve and some things of which you disapprove. If you can't find a nonprofit institution that you can honestly disrespect, then something has gone wrong with our pluralism.

Clearly, if we want to strengthen the independent sector and thus preserve it, we must pay attention not only to trumpeting its virtues but to remedying its shortcomings. The organization, Independent Sector, must—and no doubt will— concern itself, in time, with strategies for improving the management of independent sector institutions, and with ways of persuading those who remain unpersuaded that accountability through fee disclosure, the publication of informative and understandable annual reports and so on, is crucial to our survival.

But I do not believe that we can understand the strength of the forces that threaten the survival of the private nonprofit organizations, and of the philanthropy that sustains them, merely by looking at the flaws we can discern in the sector, and moving to remedy them, critically important though that is. I've considered some of the reasons why those forces are as strong as they are. They are not strong because there are a lot of blind or malevolent people out there.

People of good will and movements devoted to human advancement can be part of the problem. For instance, we could go back to the 18th century to some of the ideas of that extraordinarily talented and complicated Irish-born politician and political thinker, Edmund Burke.

Burke has often appeared, in the eyes of liberal opinion, as something of a paradox, or perhaps a simple case of treachery. In the 1760s and '70s, he was an outstanding champion of the North American colonies in their struggle against

King George III (or, as we now see, with the British Parliament of that day). He was also noted for his famous attack upon what he took to be the scandalous misgovernment of India by the British East India Company, another "liberal" cause, whatever historians may now make of the balance of right and wrong in the case.

But when the French Revolution burst out, Edmund Burke quickly became its most articulate, vehement and determined critic, in time abandoning political and personal allegiances of a lifetime to defend what he believed to be fundamental points of principle in opposition to the Jacobin regime across the Channel. His *Reflections on the Revolution in France* was the classic statement of the anti-Jacobin reaction, and was in many ways startlingly prescient, considering that it was published in 1790, long before the excesses of the Terror, the endless procession to the guillotine, or the coming of Napoleon, that quintessential Man on Horseback, to save a society at the cost of severely curtailing its newly won liberties. *The Reflections* were also extreme, at times, and so inclined to minimize the evils of the old regime in France as to lose much of the credibility they might otherwise have had. Burke's lamentations over the fate of Marie Antoinette, for example, led Thomas Paine to utter one of the classic caustic comments of all time: "Burke," Paine said, "pities the plumage but forgets the dying bird."

Yet at the core of Burke's objections and his fears for the future lay a concern that is absolutely central to our purposes, as well as quite consistent with his earlier defense of American liberties. The French Revolution purported to be engaged in sweeping away all of the abuses, irrationalities and inequities of the Old Regime, and putting the citizenry in direct command of the State. To assure the citizen his rights (*she* didn't get *hers*, even from Robespierre, although the Revolution did make a start on the problem), it was necessary to abolish the complex networks of privileges, of semi-private corporate powers, of religious anomolies and feudal survivals that cluttered the ground lying between the individual citizen and the national government. At least so it appeared to the proponents of the Revolution.

But when all of the lesser associations that had bound people together in the complex, multicolored and pluralistic institutional patterns that characterized Medieval and early modern Europe were swept away, so as to abolish privilege and to put the citizen directly in control of the one institution that remained empowered, the national State, would the result in fact be to assure liberty, equality and fraternity? Burke thought not. To him, what he called "the little platoons," the countless other ties between people—religious, civic, cultural, economic, and social—were critically important. If they were abolished or rendered impotent, exposed to the full power of the State through taxation, regulation or confiscation, the individual citizen would find himself ground to bits. His sovereignty would be a hollow shell, a theory not a reality, and his ability to live a life of individuality and meaning would be radically diminished. "With the republic [meaning France] nothing independent can coexist," Burke wrote in the *Second Letter on a Regicide Peace*, published in 1796, the year before his death.

Burke was in this representative of the political thinking that gave us our Constitution, with its separation and attempted balances of powers, rooted in fear and distrust of what people will do when given a clear, direct and unmediated mandate to govern their fellows.

We are all familiar with de Tocqueville's famous exposition on the power of free association in the America of the 1830s. The society which de Tocqueville was so astutely observing was a society built on this foundation. Of course, there were other factors at work besides mistrust of government to cause the power of free association to grow so luxuriantly; the very size and diversity of the young nation were among them. But Burke's attitude, and that of our Founding Fathers, were also crucial.

By the same token, the chief reason why the independent sector is now threatened and its relative power diminished is the long, slow, but seemingly inexorable ᶠ that skeptical attitude toward government.

It may seem stran ᵗ to call the growth of government's role inexorable, in a year when practically everybody seems anxious to curb the powers of government, and it appears that the only way a politician can survive is to denigrate the responsibilities he seeks to have entrusted to him. But if one takes the longer and wider view, it seems clear that popular expectations from government have been growing throughout the world for decades, and show few real signs of diminishing.

As one wry British observer put it, "Americans are asking more and more of a government they trust less and less."

There are various reasons for this. In part, and on the level of theory, it appears that Burke was right. By making the national government more accountable to the people as a whole, the French Revolution created the condition for modern government everywhere to become ever more powerful. The justification for riding roughshod over the interests of particular individuals or groups is ever present: it is the will of the people. No wonder that Burke spent so much time inveighing against casual or superficial or (worst of all) abstract notions of what constitutes a people.

But of course there are other reasons, not so theoretical, difficult indeed to brush aside, for ever-growing dependence on government to make life livable. Vast powers of technology and economics, that no 18th century mind, even the most farsighted, could possibly have anticipated, have grown up, and it is indeed difficult to envisage any agency less powerful and comprehensive than the state able to harness such power and direct it toward the public good. It is significant that so many new governments, new states, have come into existence in the world, and almost without exception have adopted from the outset some form of what might be called state socialism as their structure. As Hans Staub points out in a brilliant article in the summer '80 issue of *Daedalus,* the Journal of the American Academy of Arts and Sciences, even in Switzerland, the "classic standard-bearer" of "total federalism,"

> It is becoming increasingly apparent that the autonomy of the small communities and cantons—in theory the ideal of every freedom-loving person—is breaking down in the face of modern economic realities that call for national or even supra-national regulation.

But we in this country have still managed to preserve, albeit in diminished and new seriously threatened condition, the rich heritage of voluntarism and constructive (as opposed to palliative) philanthropy which this new organization, Independent Sector, exists to promote. What do we need to do to protect and expand on this heritage?

Again, diagnosing its weaknesses and moving vigorously to find remedies for them is an obvious need. So are tireless educational efforts aimed at broadening popular recognition that this heritage exists and is of critical importance. It is amazing, and a cause for some dismay, how many Americans have no awareness of this, and do not know how unusual such a heritage is in the world.

But I would like, at risk of committing a seeming heresy, to suggest one other item for our crowded agenda. John Gardner has noted that a nation having the noble motto, "E pluribus unum," needs to devote a bit more attention to the unum, as against the pluribus. It does seem to me that we are in danger of letting pluralism deteriorate into a self-interested aggregation of groups no longer sufficiently bound together by common values, standards and aspirations to constitute a society. As Robert Wood has remarked, "The atomistic impulse in our political tradition that Louis Hartz identified more than thirty years ago is now incontestably in the ascendancy. The concept of national character—of what it means to be an American —appears to have been effectively shattered by war and political turmoil."

This may be heresy, preached in the very Temple of Pluralism. It may easily be misread as a thinly disguised plea for a return to the melting pot, with all that would connote for minorities only now beginning to achieve their proper place in the sun. It can also be dismissed as what everyone is saying these days. Originality I certainly do not claim for it. But the fact that this *is* the Temple of Pluralism makes this precisely the right place to say it.

The tendency for us all to want desperately some association and some objective to give meaning to our lives and to give us the feeling that we matter and are not helplessly adrift on the stormy seas of 20th century history, with its mass organizations, its dehumanized bureaucracies, and its technology all too often perilously close to being out of control—this is indeed a potent force, and one which gives us the possibility of success in our effort to preserve the networks of institutions that go to make up the independent sector. But networks they must also be, and attention must be paid to the need to search for those elements in our history and our present strengths that bring us together and soften the lines of division amongst us. If all we really mean by "pluralism and diversity" is license to despise one another and to litigate our differences, we shall not prevail, nor will we deserve to.

We've been complaining about excessive government regulation. Such regulation comes about in part because legislators like to legislate and regulators enjoy regulating. But it also comes about because, we, the people, ask for it. Few of us want to be regulated. We are far *less* hesitant about demanding the regulation of others. It's good to remember that, to everyone but ourselves, we are among those "others."

This organization, Independent Sector, is the network of networks. The vision that gave rise to it has emerged only in the nick of time, I believe. It remains fragile. We can't even agree on what attitude to take toward that other independent sector, the for-profit world, also remarkable in its variety and its potential both for good and ill.

But the effort must be made. We must be the very last to hide behind our complexity, or argue that, since the world is incomprehensible, we will concentrate on cultivating our private gardens. We must devote at least some of our time and energy to trying to moderate the divisiveness that has made us the most litigious society in the history of the world, as well as one of the most violent. The promotion of the public good is our justification for being. We must see diversity not as an end in itself, but a powerful means to an end, the strengthening of the total society, and the enhancement of opportunities for all of its members. Whatever the sub-publics to which we own allegiance, let us be quick to recognize the interests of others, and eager to identify the common interest that binds us all.

"What Kind of Society Shall We Have?" No kind worth having if it is not, in some ultimate sense, a single society.

40

Corporate Philanthropy: Historical Background

BARRY D. KARL

BARRY D. KARL IS NORMAN AND EDNA FREEHLING PROFESSOR IN
THE DEPARTMENT OF HISTORY OF THE UNIVERSITY OF CHICAGO.
HE IS CURRENTLY WRITING, WITH STANLEY KATZ, A BASIC HISTORY
OF AMERICAN PHILANTHROPY.

Americans have taxed themselves to provide government services for more than 200 years now—and they began complaining about it as soon as they began doing it. Although the federal government was slow to introduce taxes, state and local governments have a long history of taxation, one that includes heated political debate and periodic taxpayers' rebellions. Citizens who paid taxes felt they could monitor the purchased services, even when they were themselves among the recipients.

The emergence of the modern corporation as a "person" to be taxed raised special problems because the power of corporations to influence public policy was subject to political dispute. Corporations could be taxed in ways analogous to the way in which individuals were taxed; but the corporate power to influence the use of those taxes and the services they bought was suspect. It was more comfortable to assume that the public could control the way corporations influenced public policy, because it was a democratic government that decided how tax money was to be spent.

In a very important sense, corporate giving is based on the idea that corporations should be able to influence public policy directly through the power to decide how their contributions to the public well-being are spent. Disputes

Reprinted from *Corporate Philanthropy: Philosophy, Management, Future and Background* (Washington, DC: Council on Foundations, 1982), pp. 132-135, by permission of the publisher.

over corporate philanthropy rest on different attitudes toward that power, attitudes that range from the belief that business is really responsible only for its profits and its taxes, to the belief that powerful corporations can endanger the public's right to govern. Taxation has served as the uneasy link—never enough to satisfy those who have demanded more from corporations, but more than enough to anger those who have paid them.

The courts tried to resolve the question of corporate philanthropy by permitting gifts to projects that somehow involve that corporation's self-interest. What exactly constituted "direct benefit" became the battleground until relatively recently, when a broad concept replaced a more restrictive version and the stage was set for modern corporate giving programs. Some of the issues raised in the past remain, however, and a closer look at the background may be useful.

The "Direct Benefit" Doctrine

By the end of the 18th century, economists and social theorists began to question the utility of charity as a means of solving the ever-present problem of poverty. Supporting the poor in their poverty only kept them in that condition, it was argued. Although some were beginning to suggest that philanthropy could support efforts to search out the causes of poverty, to end it once and for all, others believed that the use of profits to expand production and provide jobs was the only appropriate way for business to affect social problems. By the end of the 19th century, what historians have called "social Darwinism" combined elements of both beliefs: that only the demonstrably fit deserved to survive, and that some of those who appeared unfit could be improved by science. Contradictory though these ideas may seem, they sustained the growing belief that the role of business in social matters was properly limited to what business did best: producing profits.

At the same time, the growth of the corporation and the diversification of its ownership raised a new range of social and political issues. Fear of the large corporation and political debates over the influence of trusts on national economic policy inclined few to the belief that corporations were instruments for doing good. Even those unwilling to look on corporations as monstrous considered them to be potentially ungovernable and in need of regulatory control. Beneficence was not, after all, thought to be characteristic of captains of industry; no one expected industrial leaders to do anything but lead—sometimes ruthlessly.

In the earlier part of the 19th century the interests of business had been easy to define. Owners of businesses were also members of the communities in which they operated. They expected appeals from organizations run by people like themselves, fellow businessmen and their wives who volunteered their time to help those in need. Unusually cold winters, recurrent epidemics, and hard times served as occasions for reminding the fortunate that their blessings might depend on higher powers. Theories of the stewardship of wealth helped to define the responsibilities of the wealthy: those whom fortune had favored were expected to care for those less lucky.

More concrete considerations also affected the process of giving. A contented labor force and a buying public were essential to the kind of community that business needed, and the poor, the unemployed, the sick, and the uneducated were not equipped to join either one. The existence and the persistence of the unfortunate threatened the stability of the system. At the same time, they represented the failure to achieve the minimum standards of well-being that were promised in political debate. It was thus easy to see a direct relation between the interests of business and the stability of the community, especially in urban areas.

A narrow definition of self-interest contributed to the development of American corporate philanthropy in its early years. For example, railroads were willing to contribute to the building of YMCAs for the workers needed by the rapidly growing railroad system, but more sophisticated conceptions of community planning were viewed with doubt. Only a few railroads attempted to extend their responsibilities from the housing of a workforce to the creation of new communities, although it was understood that these were needed to produce goods and to serve as markets.

Industrial managers who wanted to put company money into workers' benefits were criticized by those who thought such benefits a form of charity that had no place in business. It was not until World War I that changes in the role of labor laid the groundwork for new understanding between industrial managers and workers.

Wartime Philanthropy: The Red Cross Model

The rapidly escalating demands that World War I placed on one of the country's oldest national philanthropies, the Red Cross, raised the issue of "direct benefit." Faced first with the task of aiding the civilian population of war-torn Europe, the Red Cross quickly took over the role of serving the needs of Americans in Europe after the United States declared war in April, 1917. These responsibilities were well beyond the resources of any one organization operating on the prewar charitable scale. Newly formed philanthropic organizations stepped in to help, and the solicitation of contributions from individuals began again with new methods and on a much enlarged scale, but even that was not sufficient. Fund-raisers needed to tap corporate resources, and to tap them fast.

It was clear that this was an exceptional cause, and a shrewd device called "the Red Cross dividend" enabled companies to request authorization from stockholders for a special dividend to be contributed to the Red Cross. In addition, wartime legislation in Texas and New York permitted gifts by corporations, although it was clear that such permission was stimulated by and possibly limited to the war effort. States were thereafter inclined to include such gifts among the powers of corporations; however, although Congress raised the issue in its debates on the Revenue Act of 1919, it explicitly rejected the idea.

Postwar Philanthropy: The Legacy of Reform

By 1920, 30 years' worth of reform legislation had placed increasing responsibility for education, medical care, social welfare, and professional urban management on state and local governments. Such services were a costly strain on the tax bases of many growing metropolitan regions.

By 1921, Internal Revenue Service policy accepted the idea that business donations to charitable, medical, or educational institutions were legitimate if such institutions served the needs of the firm's employees. This change in policy reflected a relaxation, however limited, of the need to prove that such donations were of direct benefit to the company.

During the 1920s, traditional philanthropic organizations joined with the expanding services agencies to form central funding groups and united fund drives. Community Chests and United Way, under various local names, proliferated on a national scale; with wartime Red Cross drives as a model, they sought to adopt in peacetime an effective method of operation learned in the war.

Herbert Hoover was one of the architects of the new method. As Secretary of Commerce, he attempted to persuade industry to fund university research and training. As President he moved quickly, once the Depression had started, to marshal the nation's charitable and philanthropic resources to deal with what he presumed to be a short-term emergency. Despite his efforts, however, the persistence of the Depression rapidly taxed such resources to the breaking point. Unwilling to accept government intervention, Hooever launched a heroic campaign, calling on business leaders and radio and movie stars to help persuade the public to give more to charity.

At this time the legal status of corporate giving was still unclear. Corporate legal advisers were still persuaded that the only safe philanthropy was workers' benefits, and, stretching cautiously, services in the communities in which the workers lived. The principle of "direct benefit" excluded everything else.

In 1934 it was still an open question whether aid to the poor and unemployed qualified as a direct benefit, and the Old Mission Portland Cement Company found itself testing the point in the courts. The company claimed that its contributions to the San Francisco Community Chest were of direct benefit to its business interests because they improved the company's standing among its customers. The Supreme Court, citing what it knew to have been congressional intent in excluding charitable deductions for corporations in 1919, said no.

In response, the Community Chests organized an effective lobbying effort that resulted in amendments to the Internal Revenue Code of 1936, permitting charitable contributions by corporations if they did not exceed "five percentum of the taxpayer's net income as computed without the benefit of this subsection." Thus, Congress effectively created the distinction between a charitable gift and a business deduction, a distinction destined to prove as troublesome as the problem it appeared to resolve. To be sure, companies were prohibited from claiming both charitable and business deductions for the same gift, but making the distinction was not always going to be easy, and corporate lawyers were still inclined to be wary.

Congress may have been more so. The provisions of the 1936 code made it plain that business acting in its own interest, defined as narrowly as possible, was deemed safer than business acting on the basis of some broadly conceived public or charitable interest. The implication was clear. Naked self-interest was acceptable; self-interest concealed under the cloak of charity was a danger.

A New Concept of Self-Interest

Transformations in tax policy during World War II both complicated and extended the view of corporate contributions. The foundation of business donations to war-related charitable activities had been laid in the earlier conflict. Now the excess profits tax, combined with restrictions on consumer goods, led to increased corporate funding of cultural events as a form of institutional advertising. By 1955, the effective ending of the G.I. Bill, which had helped U.S. colleges in the immediate postwar years, raised other questions.

Although it was well-established that corporations could contribute to university research programs that benefited their interests, the role of corporate giving in general budget support and as contributions to capital funding in education remained unanswered. The New Deal change in tax policies remained to be tested by stockholders' suits. When the A. P. Smith Manufacturing Company gave $1,000 to Princeton University, it was sued by a stockholder for damages, and the stage was set for the debate.

In upholding the company's action, the Supreme Court of New Jersey in 1953 not only overturned the "direct benefit" rule, but also the need for enabling legislation. "And since in our view," the Court stated, "the corporate power to make reasonable charitable contributions exists under modern conditions, even apart from express statutory provision, its enactments simply constitute helpful and confirmatory declarations of such power, accompanied by limiting safeguards." The court went on to justify its overturning of "direct benefit" by arguing the social responsibility of corporations as members of larger communities. Philanthropy was not only permissible within the range of corporate enterprise, but quite possibly a condition of public responsibility. The court's appeal to historic change presented the issue clearly:

> When the wealth of the nation was primarily in the hands of individuals, they discharged their responsibilities as citizens by donating freely for charitable purposes. With the transfer of wealth to corporate hands and the imposition of heavy burdens of individual taxation, they have been unable to keep pace with increased philanthropic needs. They have therefore, with justification, turned to corporations to assume the modern obligations of good citizenship in the same manner as humans do.

To argue that *Smith v. Barlow* freed corporate philanthropy from the shackles of "direct benefit" and the threat of stockholder suits is attractive, and to some extent true. However, the Court really translated "direct benefit" into a concept of national interest, for reasons not far removed from the circumstances that justified contributions to the Red Cross in World War I. The Court acknowledged that the nation had then been engaged in a wartime crusade; but in 1953 the United States was "faced with other, though nonetheless vicious threats from abroad which must be withstood without impairing the vigor of our democratic institutions at home." Corporate benefit was to be understood "in terms of the actual survival of the corporation in a free enterprise system." Supporting private institutions of education conformed to the "widespread belief throughout the nation that free and vigorous non-governmental institutions of learning are vital to our democracy and the system of free enterprise."

However, opening new debates on the meaning of "direct benefit" did not resolve the problem of justifying corporate philanthropy or provide corporations with guidelines for giving. Nor, judging by subsequent developments in corporate philanthropy, would it be easy to interpret the changes in methods of corporate giving. An increase in the creation of foundations by corporations suggests a concern with formulating professional methods, but by separating the giving process from direct corporate management. The establishment of the

Exxon Educational Foundation in 1955 is the most dramatic example. But the fact that the 5 percent limit established 20 years earlier did not become anything that could be called a standard for corporate contributions suggests something less than revolutionary in the corporate world's reading of *Smith*.

The history of foundations and their relation to public policy suggests that the problems encountered in raising corporate contributions will be interesting. Foundations have learned that they live in the public eye, despite claims to privacy and of third sector identity, and corporate givers are beginning to learn the same thing. Other lessons can be drawn from the experience of foundations.

First, replacing "direct benefit" with doctrines of public responsibility may not be as easy as it sounds. Foundations' attempts at social and cultural experiments have drawn mixed reviews from experts; and their efforts to bring reform to the United States, let alone the world, have met with sharp attack from those who consider their interests endangered by reform. Direct benefit may seem selfish, but it is safe. It is not going to be any easier for corporations to define what is socially responsible than it is for individuals.

Second, foundations know that their relations with American politics are complex and dangerous. Philanthropic behavior is separated from political action by a very thin line, and philanthropists must be alert to charges that they are using their money to obtain political ends. Congress has persistently tried to forbid foundations to involve themselves in political matters, and foundations have just as persistently argued their right to do good as they see it. It is a hard lesson, but money, even generously and sweetly given, is still power.

Finally, there is a sense in which foundations have always been uncomfortable with such phrases as "general purpose" and "the welfare of mankind." Their search for definition and specificity has taken the form of anxiety about "program," as many put it. Specific programs announced clearly and in good time not only reduce uncertainty among potential recipients but also charges of freewheeling and undue influence among potential critics. There is safety in the narrowing of program, even if it limits the imagination and the spirit of free inquiry. There are safe programs that will not draw hostility from anyone—projects meant to aid sick children, for example—although how much they can enrich understanding of larger intellectual issues may be another matter.

Corporate philanthropists may find themselves facing that problem in reverse. "Self-interest" and "direct benefit" may have been restrictive, but they have served as the touchstones that made justification possible, if not always easy. The power of large corporations has long been one of the bugbears of American politics; but the assumption has been that their power was a power to do harm. What we must now cope with is their power to do good.

41

Corporate Philanthropy— An Integral Part of Corporate Social Responsibility

BUSINESS ROUNDTABLE

The Business Roundtable's "Position On Corporate Philanthropy" was released March 26, 1981, and was subsequently endorsed by the U.S. Chamber of Commerce and the National Association of Manufacturers. This document marked the first time that these major business-oriented organizations so officially and forcefully endorsed the principle that "all business entities should recognize philanthropy both as good business and as an obligation if they are to be considered responsible corporate citizens of the national and local communities in which they operate."

The Business Roundtable believes that corporate philanthropy, primarily through contributions, is an integral part of corporate social responsibility. All business entities should recognize philanthropy both as good business and as an obligation if they are to be considered responsible corporate citizens of the national and local communities in which they operate. In recognition of this position, the Business Roundtable further believes that all businesses should establish appropriate programs to handle philanthropy in a businesslike way.

American philanthropy has traditionally been a pluralistic activity involving private individuals, corporations and foundations. Of these groups, individuals provide almost 90 percent of total contributions, while corporations and founda-

Reprinted from *Business Roundtable* (March 26, 1981) by permission of the publisher.

tions provide the other 10 percent. Corporations, however, are providing an increasingly important share of contributions for educational, health, welfare and cultural activities—a trend which is expected to continue in the future.

Although financial contributions to not-for-profit organizations are an essential element in business philanthropy, participation also encompasses a broader range of activities than has been traditionally accepted or defined by the Internal Revenue Service. For example, corporations frequently assist not-for-profit institutions through loans of employees, donations or loans of equipment and space, volunteer programs, and direct dollar investments in economic redevelopment efforts—all of which may be accounted for as business expenses.

The principal alternative to private philanthropy is government funding, which is considered to be inherently less efficient in the distribution and control of funds for these purposes. The sources of government funds, it must be emphasized, are tax-paying individuals and business enterprise. As businessmen and as individuals it is, therefore, in everyone's self-interest to support society through private social investments rather than through the complex and costly redistribution of tax dollars by government. Accordingly, if the business community is serious in seeking to stem over-dependence on government and still allow the private not-for-profit sector to make the same contribution to society that it has in the past, business must itself increase its level of commitment.

In this regard, it has become increasingly evident that business cannot survive and prosper unless society continues to improve and develop. It should be clear, therefore, that businesses, on behalf of their stockholders, employees, and various other constituencies, have a self-interest in philanthropic activities which serve to strengthen the fabric of society. However, there is evidence that the business community has not fully recognized the value of corporate philanthropy. For instance, the most recent Conference Board estimate is that of the more than two million corporations in the U.S., fewer than 30 percent reported making any charitable contributions.

The Business Roundtable also emphasizes that each firm has the responsibility to manage its philanthropic activities according to the same standards it uses to manage the other parts of its business. These standards apply to not only the quality of the individuals managing this function but also the personal involvement of top corporate officers in the management of these activities.

Further, decisions about the amount and distribution of corporate resources allocated to voluntary organizations and projects must and should be left up to individual companies. Accordingly, the philanthropic programs of businesses will differ depending, for example, on the needs of the communities in which they operate. It is, however, most important that all businesses develop an effective means of assessing these needs and regularly review their corporate giving programs to determine the appropriate level of support for not-for-profit organizations.

The extent of philanthropy by a given business enterprise in a particular year is dependent upon a large number of factors including profitability, investment requirements and capital structure as well as the nature of the business. For this reason, the ability to make contributions is often counter-cyclical to the needs of society and businesses should make an effort to maintain support to their most important philanthropic programs even during economic downturns.

Finally, the Business Roundtable recommends that all companies make public, in a manner they deem appropriate, information on their corporate philanthropic programs. Whatever form is chosen, public dissemination of this information would serve as one means of increasing public awareness of the involvement of business in improving the quality of life.

42

Corporate Social Responsibility— A New Term for an Old Concept with New Significance

WALTER A. HAAS, JR.

WALTER A. HAAS, JR., IS CHAIRMAN OF THE BOARD AND DIRECTOR OF LEVI STRAUSS & CO. AND A LEADER IN PHILANTHROPIC AND VOLUNTARY ACTIVITIES AT THE LOCAL, NATIONAL, AND INTERNATIONAL LEVELS. HE RECEIVED THE JEFFERSON AWARD FOR PUBLIC SERVICE IN 1976.

The new term "corporate social responsibility" refers to a relatively old concept that is being expanded to address an increasing number of societal demands on business. These demands reflect a widely held belief that business lacks a significant concern for how its decisions and operations affect society. The general yet comprehensive nature of the term makes definition difficult. Nevertheless, at Levi Strauss & Co. we believe in the comprehensiveness of the concept, and we wish a concern for society to permeate every level of our company and to become a part of the day-to-day decision-making process.

Leaving aside the definitional problem, most contemporary observers of corporate behavior begin by positing three basic rationales for the acceptance of an expanded role for business in society. These are:

- A moral obligation, usually stated as "the right thing to do"

Excerpted from Mr. Haas' article in *Corporations and Their Critics: Issues and Answers to the Problems of Corporate Social Responsibility*, edited by Thornton Bradshaw and David Vogel (New York: McGraw-Hill, 1982) pp. 133-140, by permission of the publisher. Copyright ©1982 by McGraw-Hill, Inc.

- A self-interest concept, usually stated as "a long-term economic self-interest of a corporation"

- A sociopolitical rationale, usually stated as "a necessity to preserve the private sector"

We believe that all three rationales present compelling arguments for the acceptance of this new role, but for Levi Strauss & Co. our strongest motivation is the moral obligation. Simply stated, we believe that this is the right thing to do. This obligation has been reinforced over the years by a family tradition reaching as far back as Levi Strauss himself. As early as 1850 Strauss established the goals of our company: a quality product, the best possible working conditions for our employees, and community service. Today he would be called socially responsible. Then he was simply called a good man.

Corporate executives develop an idea of what they want their company to be. If this conception remains constant over long periods of time and is institutionalized, it becomes, in effect, a personality characteristic of the corporation. Levi Strauss & Co.'s commitment to a genuine concern for people is a character trait of our corporation which is worthy of being maintained. Our primary concern in this regard is to demonstrate in every aspect of our business and in our dealings with the public that we are a corporation that cares about people. By example and encouragement, our top management has attempted to make the work environment a place where a genuine concern for people could manifest itself. As the leadership of the corporation changes, we've tried to ensure that this concept of what the company should be is maintained.

Part of the challenge revolves around current business operations that give rise to the phenomenon of the "transitory manager." Transitory managers affect the ability to maintain a corporate personality because their present work is not likely to be their lifelong environment. Thus, they lack a vested interest in identifying with or perpetuating a particular corporate trait which they do not believe has broad acceptance or has a significant impact on their careers. Their primary concerns and goals are short-term: daily, weekly, and monthly bottom-line figures. Contemplating sociological and political implications of contemporary social problems and how these will manifest themselves fifteen to twenty years down the road is an alien process for most and is considered irrelevant by some. Encouraging this concern and providing an environment which allows this process to develop is the greatest challenge of top management. At Levi Strauss & Co. we pride ourselves on our ability to attract and retain managers who can grow with our "personality" and our business practices.

Being sensitive to the needs and demands of society and joining in cooperative efforts to help meet those needs is in our long-term economic self-interest. If more companies had anticipated the change in societal values from a desire for greater quantity and diversity of material goods to a concern for the environment and the quality of life, many current environmental regulations might have been avoided. At Levi Strauss & Co., our early commitment to quality produced a consumer loyalty to our product that has certainly been in our long-term economic self-interest.

There are, of course, other reasons why addressing social problems is intimately related to our self-interest. The most important is the improvement in a community's general climate. A community with a wide range of opportunities and services such as good educational, recreational, and cultural activities, a comprehensive health system, social services that care for those in need, and an accessible and fair justice system provides a quality of life we all seek. The cycle is reinforcing: people want to live in a good community and work for a good company, and a company wants to locate in a good community and needs good people.

It is important to remember that the role of business in society has been granted through the consent of the governed. Neither the free enterprise system nor the corporation was legitimized by the Constitution. American political institutions and their response to society's goals will determine the future course of American business. Government regulation of the private sector and curbs on business's independence of action have not occurred in a linear progression upward over the years. Instead, packages of legislation have been passed at periodic intervals and have usually been spurred or accompanied by a general perception, valid or not, of widespread abuses on the part of business. Thus, the degree to which business maintains its present level of independence rests on a willingness to monitor itself and on an ability to discern and react to new societal demands.

When Levi Strauss & Co. started a plant in Vallejo, California, two of the first operators hired were blacks. That meant that new employees coming into the plant saw that that was the way it was. Shortly after that an operator who came from the South complained to me about our policy. I said, "Look, I'm sorry, but that's the way it is. And if you leave, we'll be sorry." She didn't leave.

Then we took a bigger step in the South. Frankly, we didn't have the courage to take it as soon as we had wanted. We just didn't know whether it was right to impose our views. This sounds like medieval times now, but you must put yourself back to that period. We didn't know then whether it was proper to force our views on some of those small Southern towns. But we decided to, and Paul Glasgow, who was then in charge of operations, was quite in tune with this decision.

In Blackstone, Virginia, we weren't attracting enough people to our plant for one reason or another. Paul came to us and said, "I think the time is right to integrate that plant." So we said, "Good. We're with you." He went down and spoke with the powers that be. Blackstone was a small Southern town. He came back and said that they wanted a wall to divide the plant into black and white sections. We said, "No, we're not going to." Then they asked us to paint a dividing line. Again we refused. Then they wanted separate drinking fountains and separate rest rooms. We refused, and they didn't like our refusal. But they swallowed it, and our payroll continued and we expanded.

Of course, when we went into communities in the South, affirmative-action programs were not required by law and weren't even so identified, but we were a relatively important employer in all those communities. These developments go back twenty-five years now. In the end, the economic clout of a potential payroll of several hundred employees overcame any local objections to integration. I think we changed attitudes in many communities.

A lot of my business friends complain that they have trouble with their employees and the unions. Why do we take on this additional burden? "Why bother?" they ask. I guess we do because we believe in it.

We do these things because they seem morally right, and they usually turn out to be good business too. In the Blackstone case we kept a plant going. By having an integrated policy we had a much greater labor pool to draw from, which in a labor intensive industry is important. But our policy didn't start that way. We just had a conviction that integration was right.

One of our first attempts to aid the disadvantaged was a plan to help small retail businesses. We had six small retailers in the general San Francisco Bay area to whom we gave technical assistance. But, you know, it's very difficult for a small business to succeed anywhere today regardless of whether it's minority-owned or not. If small businesses don't have management capability and if they're located in a poor area, they have a hard time getting credit, a hard time getting insurance, and a hard time getting delivery. I'm sorry to say that after several years and a lot of help from others, all six retailers failed.

Next we tried contracting with a manufacturing firm in Oakland named Ghettoes Incorporated. It sounded like an ideal situation: we would provide the technical know-how, and we would buy the firm's products. We loaned it sewing machines and an experienced full-time manager, but that firm eventually failed too.

Then we decided that we'd try giving steady employment to a group of disadvantaged people. We made a study to find an area that had the lowest economic level in the country. I think Greene County, Alabama, came out as the third or fourth poorest county in the United States; it was almost entirely black. We thought by opening a plant there we could provide jobs and improve the whole community by giving people buying power. For a lot of reasons the venture didn't work out as we had hoped. But we felt a responsibility to the people, and thanks to our community affairs department we were able to help organize a group of local black businessmen who took over the operation; so it's still in existence. We found technical assistance for the group and helped it get government contracts. And then we sold it all the equipment in the plant for $100.

I really don't know of any other corporation that would have stayed with this program as we did. I think a lot of people feel as the economist Milton Friedman does: the only responsibility that a corporation has is to make money. I disagree with them completely.

Discussing the limitations of corporate responses to the concept of corporate social responsibility is difficult, if not impossible, in the absence of a consensually accepted definition. If, however, we use "fairness" as a general guideline, we are limited only by prevailing ethical values within the population. Here, too, business can have a leadership role, especially internally, in the type of ethical work environment that it provides for its employees.

In terms of community service, corporations are limited by training, by staff, and by resources. Our most important contribution, requiring the overwhelming majority of our personnel and resources, is the providing of jobs and the production of products. Business executives are not equipped either by education or by background for an easy transition to the service sector. For this reason programs should be developed to help facilitate this area of corporate-public cooperation. As with our primary responsibilities, our new social responsibilities require that a material commitment to professional staff and professional programs be made. In the final analysis, however, the extensiveness of any business's effort must be related to the size and nature of its enterprise.

But to dwell on our limitations is to overlook our potentials. One such potential is to share information more openly with both the public and one's own employees. Levis Strauss & Co. publishes on a regular basis financial information on the Levi Strauss Foundation and on company contributions. We have issued a Worldwide Code of Business Ethics and stressed our commitment to social responsibility in our stock prospectus.

There are numerous other areas, and perhaps the limitations referred to above are only the limits of our imagination. The individual talents subsumed in any given corporation have yet to be tapped. The search for viable ways in which to make those talents accessible to society should and must continue. Government and business must cease being adversaries in the face of social dilemmas and become partners in cooperative solutions. Zealots of philosophical laissez faire economics must become the converts of social realities and social responsibility. If nations, governments, institutions, and individuals are prone to act only in the context of narrowly drawn definitions of self-interest, then the onrushing complexities of global resource scarcity, overpopulation, and environmental degradation will bury the worst and devour the best. Let us hope that the separation and alienation we have known over the last two decades will give rise to a new era when individuals, business, government, and developed and underdeveloped countries will come together to address their need for one another and the common needs of this planet. In this latter regard, we are limited only by our willingness to try, to risk, and to make mistakes.

43

The Social Goals of a Corporation

JOHN H. FILER

JOHN H. FILER, CHAIRMAN OF AETNA LIFE AND CASUALTY,
FORMERLY SERVED AS CHAIRMAN OF THE NATIONAL ALLIANCE OF
BUSINESS AND OF THE COMMISSION ON PRIVATE PHILANTHROPY
AND PUBLIC NEEDS.

I fall a very natural heir to a sincere concern about business's responsiveness to society. Henry Beers, who led Aetna Life & Casualty two decades ago, made one of the earliest statements of the doctrine of corporate social responsibility when he urged business people to give tithes of their time as well as their money for the public good. He was particularly insightful when he suggested that the survival of our economic system may well hinge on the extent to which business practices good citizenship. My immediate predecessor shared this conviction. Surrounded by some of the nation's most serious urban riots in the mid-1960s, Olcott Smith put our company among the leaders in a fight to correct social inequities and to revitalize the spirit and the face of our troubled city of Hartford, Connecticut.

Throughout this period our company and most others viewed social responsibility as an important but separate pursuit, to be taken care of largely by charitable gifts and community programs. Such programs have been valuable and have been welcomed by those who have benefited from them, but business must do far more. I believe that we must bring social responsibility into our day-to-day operations and make it part of business decisions.

Charitable activities, while still vital, are a very small part of what most large corporations can and should be doing as responsible members of our society. The real test of the responsiveness of corporations to society is what they are doing in their basic business to meet the needs of society as well as of their customers.

Excerpted from Mr. Filer's article in *Corporations and Their Critics: Issues and Answers to the Problems of Corporate Responsibility,* edited by Thornton Bradshaw and David Vogel (New York: McGraw-Hill, 1982) pp. 271-276, by permission of the publisher. Copyright ©1982 by McGraw-Hill, Inc.

Trying to bring corporate resources to bear on social issues is a matter of pressing urgency for each of us. We are likely to regret it bitterly in future years if we leave this job to others. As we do affect society, and by that I mean people, in a great variety of ways, we obviously have the power to impact on their lives if we wish to do so. Justice, equality, recognition, freedom, mobility, and self-determination are unevenly distributed in the United States today, and corporate America can either do something about the inequities or be required to do something. We, individually or collectively, cannot solve all these problems, but there are some aspects of most of them we can influence for the better.

I am not suggesting that we focus the total power of the corporate community on curing all our nation's social ills. I suggest, rather, that each corporation give attention to the social consequences of each of its activities and, further, that each corporation examine its own special characteristics, strengths, and particular areas of interest and plan how it may best contribute to the fulfillment of one or more unmet public needs.

I'm not talking about the very big-ticket items, such as environmental protection. These must be handled in large part through the regulatory process as long as ours is a competitive business company. Rather, I'm talking about the myriad of other issues, ranging from the redesign of training programs to the imaginative employment of the corporate contributions budget, to making sure that our customers receive what we promise, and to participating in community development projects.

If we are to do all this successfully, corporations must set social goals just as they set business goals. Setting business goals has never been simple, but setting corporate social goals is far more difficult. With traditional corporate goals, participants have a common understanding of overall objectives. They agree that such things as market share, cash flow, profit growth, quality of product or service, return on invested capital, and the like are legitimate values to seek. The differences of opinion among our managers in these areas are likely to have reasonable boundaries. We are experts dealing with experts, and fortunately the more senior we are, the more expert we are believed to be, so that disagreements get resolved and decisions are reasonably well accepted.

When it comes to social goals, none of us has much qualification or experience. There is no common understanding of what social values corporations should seek. And those set on doing something for the public good seldom have enough conviction that they are right to overrule the objectors, the doubters, and the potential second-guessers, not to mention the vigorous proponents of other corporate goals that seem, on occasion at least, to conflict with social progress.

Because social goal setting is so new, so different at this point, I believe that for now it must be primarily a role of the chief executive. The average manager is conditioned by training and incentive programs to view profit as the solitary goal. Few managers view the pursuit of social goals as necessary to personal success. Therefore, it is up to the chief executive to move the message downward, first through senior management and then into the middle and lower levels of the organization. This must be done as an exercise not of autocracy but of leadership.

Effective social goal setting cannot be mandated in any organization, just as we found that legislating civil rights did not go very far toward changing the attitudes of a vast majority of people. I do not believe that we can tell managers that they must place a set number of social goals in their business plans each year and expect those goals to be pursued. It is more effective, instead, to create a climate in which managers willingly and thoughtfully place such goals in their plans. It has recently been my role to encourage our senior people to see that the social problems they can address creatively through their operations are considered when preparing annual plans and that a like amount of thought be given to addressing people problems as is given to addressing profit problems. Anyone reading our company's annual business goals today would find a sprinkling of social goals mixed in with the traditional profit objectives. We have not, of course, addressed all the social problems that we are able to affect, but we are doing more than we were a few years ago, and we will be doing still more in the years ahead.

To set out and carry out social goals, managers must become educated and sensitized to the needs of the community. In our company we have a formal program which tracks the community and social service activities of our top sixty or so people, those at the vice-presidential level and above. We know who is or has been involved in which activities. If the community needs the particular expertise of one of our executives, we are able to find someone with the necessary knowledge or interest to do the job. In a sense, we act as a broker to get the right people into the type of community service in which they can make the greatest contribution and reap the greatest benefit.

This activity meets community needs, but it helps our organization as well. Very often such assignments are good developmental opportunities for our executives. The executives are prepared for higher-level positions in which they will have increased contact with the public. But more important, these outside assignments sensitize them to the community and its needs. We don't want our senior people sitting in comfortable offices thinking that they know what the public wants from us. We want them out there once in a while, hearing about problems from the people themselves.

I referred earlier to the fact that one reason that social goal setting is so difficult is that few of us have the expertise to determine the direction for appropriate social goals. In an effort to develop this type of expertise within our organization, we have created a staff to analyze public-policies issues. Its assignment is to improve our ability to anticipate emerging issues, to analyze them, and to recommend a response before the initiative is taken from us.

One doesn't have to be a student of our industry to know that the affordability of automobile insurance is a serious social issue. Therefore, the first effort of this staff, undertaken before it was formally constituted, was to examine the affordability problem from an independent perspective that questioned the assumptions of the industry, its critics, and the public. We are now studying the staff report on affordability. It is being discussed and refined, and recommendations in some areas are being implemented. What is most important is that our company now has a clearer understanding of who is hurt most seriously. We know as the result of opinion surveys what the public dislikes about our practices. In short, we have direction. We have a better idea today than we did a year ago as to how we can go about alleviating this problem. If we are to stay in the automobile insurance business as we know it, we will have to do something.

It is important to realize that the setting of social goals is done with mixed motives. Goal setting is not merely a moral or an altruistic pursuit, but it seems to me that it is perfectly legitimate to try to accomplish some worth-while social goal even though at the same time we bring about some favorable influence on our corporation. We must not overlook the fact that our primary function of producing quality goods and services while producing a reasonable profit cannot long be ignored. By the same token, we cannot make this objective our sole purpose and expect to continue earning a reasonable profit.

I've dealt thus far with the voluntary setting of social goals. Sometimes we are not so fortunate as to choose our social goals, usually because we fail to pursue them ourselves. An example is the enactment of civil rights legislation and the ensuing equal-employment-opportunity standards under which we all operate. Equal employment was imposed upon us, but this does not mean that business cannot voluntarily find creative ways to achieve equality as quickly and as genuinely as is possible. I might add that failure to develop and utilize all employees is a waste of a corporation's resources. Such a course satisfies neither morality nor economics.

To assure that our company's affirmative-action objectives are met and, most important, are met willingly, we began in 1974 a series of workshops. The first was a day-long session for managers and supervisors that tried to make them aware of their erroneous assumptions about women and members of minority groups. These workshops tried to deal with the lack of dialogue between managers and their female or minority-group subordinates. They encouraged managers to focus on developing these people in the same way in which they had developed white males in the past.

The following year we introduced a program to complete the dialogue. It consisted of a series of 3-day workshops for women and a similar series for minority employees that were designed to help them evaluate their own attitude toward their careers and set personal and business goals, even if this meant the setting of goals that did not include Aetna Life & Casualty.

These workshops received an overwhelmingly favorable reception from the participants, but progress is perhaps better measured by the fact that almost half of the minority employees and approximately 40 percent of the women who attended have since been promoted. Another interesting statistic is that termination rates are much lower for the 1500 employees who have participated thus far than for those who have not.

While the workshops have been effective, they have also shown us that good intentions are not enough without a working knowledge of equal-employment-opportunity laws throughout the organization. To provide this for our managers, we began in 1979 another series of workshops with emphasis on the law as well as on managerial attitudes. Every manager and supervisor in our company was scheduled to participate in this program.

Corporations have given considerable care to equal employment opportunity largely because government abruptly brought management's attention to the matter. However, we must be equally concerned about all our people. As corporations tend to become more complex and monolithic, it has become easier for individuals to feel powerless in the face of unknown or changeable forces. The individual has primary responsibility for his or her own future, but corporations also have a responsibility to create an environment conducive to career growth, to provide realistic information about opportunities and career paths, and to offer opportunities for training.

Recently we took some steps in this area with a series of career-development workshops for all employees, thus rounding out the program. We have a special session for supervisors to assist them in helping their employees plan rewarding careers. With career planning we hope to give our people an opportunity to take charge of their lives. I believe that this program strengthens them. It also benefits the company because helping people take care of themselves is far less costly and more rewarding than taking care of people throughout their working lives.

In these and other ways our company has strengthened its commitment to making social goals a part of our business practices. We have found it a terribly complex and frustrating task that will not be completed over the short term. However, along with the frustrations there have appeared encouraging signs that may make the going somewhat easier in the future. Among these signs is our company's satisfactory level of earnings, which places us in a very respectable position within our industry. I believe that over the last few years we have proved at least that social and financial goals can be pursued together. While there are those who may disagree, I believe that our company's pursuit of social goals has had a measure of influence on attaining its financial goals as well.

44

We Cannot Live
for Ourselves Alone

VERNON E. JORDAN, JR.

VERNON JORDAN HAS ACHIEVED NATIONAL RECOGNITION AS A
LAWYER, NEWSPAPER COLUMNIST, CIVIL RIGHTS ADVOCATE,
FOUNDATION AND CORPORATE TRUSTEE, AND GOVERNMENT
ADVISOR. HE WAS FORMERLY PRESIDENT OF THE NATIONAL
URBAN LEAGUE AND EXECUTIVE DIRECTOR OF THE UNITED
NEGRO COLLEGE FUND.

*The following selection is drawn from Mr. Jordan's
acceptance speech on receiving United Way of America's
highest honor, the de Tocqueville Award, in April, 1977.*

Few observers have penetrated so deeply into the inner workings of American society than Alexis de Tocqueville. Even today, 146 years after the publication of his "Democracy in America," most of his insights retain a relevance for contemporary society. And among them is this profound comment:

> "Among the laws that rule human societies there is one which seems to be more precise and clear than all others. If men are to remain civilized or to become more so, the art of associating together must grow and improve in the same ratio in which the equality of conditions is increased."

In that brief quote we have the kernel of two themes that permeate de Tocqueville's view of America: the propensity toward voluntary associations to order our lives, and the democratic aspirations for equality. And de Tocqueville wisely links the two; indeed he makes them inseparable. In so doing, he provides us with a framework in which to place our voluntary efforts to improve our communities.

Reprinted by permission of the author. Originally published by United Way of America and subsequently reprinted in *Vital Speeches*, Vol. 44 (June 1, 1977), pp. 493-495.

For just as no man is an island, separate and apart from others, so too, no community can see itself in isolation from other towns and cities, from the nation as a whole, or from countries and peoples far from our borders. In our times especially, we have seen how racial and economic dilemmas penetrate even the most self-contained affluent communities. We have seen the problems of rural poverty and racism become the core problems of our urban crisis, and now we see them becoming an integral part of suburban life as well.

There is no hiding place in the modern world. There can be no isolationism in regard to social problems. If our society is to grow and to prosper, if our civilization is to flourish, then indeed our voluntary agencies must be directed to assuring the equality toward which we have strived.

This is not to de-emphasize the proper role of government. Because government has immense resources, legal powers of persuasion, and is politically accountable, it must hold a central position in marshalling our society's efforts toward political, social and economic equality.

But, as de Tocqueville pointed out, the danger that faces democratic governments is the passivity of the populace: the tendency for individuals to abandon their personal responsibility for social actions. Because the voluntary sector provides the opportunity for personal involvement, it becomes the cement that binds our society together.

Implied in this is the recognition that some sectors have greater needs than others; that our society nurtures and perpetuates pockets of poverty and misery, and that the rational organization of voluntary services should compensate for society's wrongs by concentrating disproportionate resources to sectors where the need is disproportionately large.

Just as our society as a whole lags in its perception of the need to concentrate its resources on the disadvantaged, so too, does the voluntary sector fail to adequately address the greatest needs. American philanthropy in general has not adequately come to grips with its responsibility to engage its energies and its resources in the battle to improve the lives of those most in need of assistance.

Helping those least able to help themselves also illustrates de Tocqueville's observations that self-interest and voluntarism go hand in hand. Americans, he said, "show...how an enlightened regard for themselves constantly prompts them to assist one another and inclines them willingly to sacrifice a portion of their time and property to the welfare of the state."

Enlightened self-interest has to do not only with self-regard, but also with the preservation of society's goals and values, and with the creation of conditions in which all may flourish and share in the responsibilities of citizenship. Neglect of that self-interested effort leads, as we have seen, to racial strife, to abject poverty and the bitterness it fosters, and to the breakdown of rules of conduct and civilized behavior.

What is so often called the urban crisis or the racial crisis is often nothing more than the mass withdrawal from enlightened self-interest to the delusion of selfishness.

It is clear to me that the spirit of enlightened self-interest, and of voluntarism as a means of changing our society, are essential to our nation's future. And linked to this concept of creative voluntarism is the need to encourage voluntary activity among all sectors of the population, and not to restrict participation to those with the time and the resources.

One way to encourage greater participation in voluntarism is to increase the incentives for charitable giving. In its effort to simplify the tax code, the government has inadvertently created disincentives to charitable giving by low and moderate income families. In liberalizing the standard tax deduction, the government has removed the tax savings benefits from seven out of ten taxpayers, overwhelmingly lower income, who do not itemize deductions. In effect, this shifts support for charities to the better-off minority of taxpayers who receive tax rewards for their giving, rewards denied other Americans.

The danger here is twofold—charitable giving may become an elitist function, and many millions of Americans are denied encouragement to participate at the most elementary level of voluntary activity.

To state the problem is to suggest the solution: the tax laws should be modified to provide that those who choose to take the standard deduction should also be allowed to take charitable deductions.

A second means of revitalizing voluntarism is to broaden the perceptions most people hold of voluntary activity to include advocacy.

Voluntarism has been caught in the straitjacket of services. It has become fixated on the concept of service provision to the neglect of advocacy that deals with the root causes that create the demand for those services.

We often consider it the proper role of voluntary activity to provide assistance to those in poor health and in poor living conditions. But the line is drawn at advocating public policy changes in our national health delivery system, or in slum rehabilitation, public housing, and discriminatory housing patterns. And yet without dealing positively with these larger issues, voluntarism forces itself into the position of being a band-aid dispenser for a sick society.

I again refer you to de Tocqueville's linkage of voluntary activity with equality. Separate the two and you separate voluntarism from its essential role in a democratic society.

We cannot forget that when de Tocqueville travelled in America almost a century and a half ago, the nation he celebrated as the most democratic in the world was a slave state, holding black people in bondage. The young Frenchman correctly understood that the contradiction between democratic equality and tyrannical slavery contained within itself the seeds of future explosions. He wrote: "If ever America undergoes great revolutions they will be brought about by the presence of the black race on the soil of the United States; that is to say, they will owe their origin, not to the equality, but the inequality of condition."

Thirty years later this nation was caught in the fires of a civil war, and much of our history since then was shaped by conflict between those who would extend equality to all, and those who would refuse to black people their rightful place as equals in a society of equals. That conflict is still with us. In almost every sphere, black people continue to suffer disadvantage based on race. The laws have changed, customs have changed, attitudes have changed, the racial situation has changed—and improved. But black people are still disproportionately poor, and are still denied adequate housing and equal job opportunities. We are still largely separate and unequal.

This then, is the central problem our society faces. In attempting to deal with the problems of black Americans, we are forced too, to deal with other similarly disadvantaged minorities and with the white poor. For all share the conditions of deprivation in the midst of plenty; all share the need for services and advocacy, and all share the unquenchable thirst for equality.

They cannot be denied. We in the voluntary sector can deny them only at our own peril. We hear from the crevices of our nation's poverty-stricken ghettos, the poignant plea for services and advocacy.

Hear their plea, let your response ring loud and clear.

Respond to that plea for help with commitment and dedication, with a spirit of understanding the proper meaning of enlightened self-interest and the inseparability of services and advocacy on behalf of those in need.

At the core of that positive response must be the understanding that we are all linked together in a complex web of interactions in which our efforts to help others make our own lives more satisfying and more secure. Let us recall the profound words of an American contemporary of de Tocqueville's, Herman Melville, who wrote:

> We cannot live for ourselves alone. Our lives are connected by a thousand invisible threads, and along these sympathetic fibers, our actions run as causes and return to us as results.

It's a long way from the Gate City Nursery and the Butler Street YMCA to the de Tocqueville Award, and it has been a proud and happy journey that was made possible with the help and commitment of others, who not only cared but helped me to care. Therefore I accept the de Tocqueville Award for myself and my United Way agency, but also on behalf of my professional colleagues in the United Way movement who share with me the joy of service. With them, I pledge continued commitment and cooperation with our volunteers

Ours is a joint effort, a cooperative venture. Professionals cannot do without volunteers; volunteers cannot do without professionals, and most importantly, those in need of services and advocacy need us both.

To that end, our duties and responsibilities are clear. We have a charge to keep, a calling to fulfill, a rendezvous with a just and righteous cause.

As we return now to those tasks, may we be steadfast strong and of good cheer. May we neither stumble nor falter, rather let us mount up with wings as eagles, let us run and not be weary, let us walk together children, and not faint.

45

The Meaning of Volunteering

BRIAN O'CONNELL

The People who get involved with public causes open themselves to frustration and disappointment, but—through it all and after it all—those moments of making change happen for the better are among their lasting joys. There's something wonderfully rewarding in being part of an effort that does make a difference. And there's something sparkling about being among other people when they're at their best too.

When any of us take inventory of the meaning of our lives, these special experiences have to be among the high points. Happiness is, in the end, a simple thing. Despite how complicated we try to make it or the entrapments we substitute for it, happiness is really caring and being able to do something about the caring.

In the community sense, *caring* and *service* are giving and volunteering. As far back as the twelfth century, the highest order and benefit of charity was described by Maimonides in the Mishna Torah: "The highest degree; than which there is nothing higher, is to take hold of a Jew who has been crushed and to give him a gift or a loan or to enter into partnership with him or to find work for him, and then to put him on his feet so he will not be dependent on his fellow man."

In a world just thirty years removed from the slaughter of six million Jews, and still rampant with diseases and other indignities of the vilest form and breadth, there is room for concern and caring, charity and volunteering. Indeed, in this still young democracy there is total dependence on citizen determination to preserve the freedoms so recently declared and to extend them to all.

Reprinted from *Effective Leadership in Voluntary Organizations: How to Make the Greatest Use of Citizen Service and Influence,* by Brian O'Connell (New York: Walker and Company, 1980). Copyright ©1976 by Brian O'Connell.

The problems of contemporary society are more complex, the solutions more involved and the satisfactions more obscure, but the basic ingredients are still the caring and the resolve to make things better. From the simplicity of these have come today's exciting efforts on behalf of humanitarian causes ranging from equality to environment and from health to peace.

In the course of these efforts there is at work a silent cycle of cause and effect which I call the "genius of fulfillment," meaning that the harder people work for others and for the fulfillment of important social goals, the more fulfilled they are themselves. Confucius expressed it by saying that "Goodness is God," meaning that the more good we do, the happier we are, and the totality of it all is a supreme *state* of being. Thus, he said, God is not only a Supreme Being *apart* from us, but a supreme state of being *within* us.

Aristotle, too, caught an important part of it when he said, "Happiness is the utilization of one's talents along lines of excellence."

A simpler way of looking at the meaning of service is a quotation from an epitaph:

> *What I spent, is gone*
> *What I kept, is lost*
> *But what I gave to charity*
> *Will be mine forever.*

Whether we want to express the meaning of service in involved ways or prefer simpler forms doesn't really matter. It can be charity or enlightened self-interest or people's humanity to people. These are all ways of describing why we volunteer, why volunteering provides some of our happiest moments, and why the good that we do lives after us.

Bibliography

BRIAN O'CONNELL AND
ANN BROWN O'CONNELL

In pulling together this bibliography, just as with searching for and selecting the chapters for the book itself, I have been keenly aware that in the time available I could not begin to identify all the pieces that deserve to be included. All I can do is provide a listing of many of the pieces I have come across and acknowledge that the result is hardly the definitive compilation.

What I have tried to locate and include, at least in the bibliography, are those good books, chapters, speeches, articles and papers that describe and define this side of American life. This list does not include "how to" books and articles. Though I am encouraged with the growing literature on foundation investments, voluntary agency financial accounting, and the like, such topics do not fit the broader intent of the book and bibliography.

I am prepared that some people will have ready openings to point out gaps and gaffes. For that reason, I considered omitting the list altogether. However, because a large part of my purpose in doing the book was to provide a resource for others who share an interest in the sector and to encourage fuller research, writing, and speaking, it seemed best to leave it in.

In garnering material to consider for the full book and in putting together titles for this list, I drew heavily on the bibliographies and reading lists prepared by Professor John Simon's Program on Non-Profit Organizations at Yale University, Professor Robert Bremner of Ohio State University, The Foundation Center, Professor C. S. Griffin of the University of Kansas, and Professor Merle Curti of the University of Wisconsin. Approximately half of my list represents a winnowing and integration of their contributions. The rest are titles I've come across in bits and pieces, often from the footnotes of the nearly 1,000 pieces I have explored. Almost every good find opened several others, and so it went— and could still go, almost endlessly, making me all the more aware of what I haven't found and what I don't know. I hope the reader will view this list as I do, only a starting point for larger efforts, hopefully soon to come.

1. Abbott, Edith, ed. *Some American Pioneers in Social Welfare: Select Documents with Editorial Notes*. New York: Russell Sage Foundation, 1963.

2. Abernathy, Glenn. *The Right of Assembly and Association*. Columbia: University of South Carolina Press, 1961.

3. Adams, David. "Elite and Lower Volunteers in a Voluntary Association: A Study of an American Red Cross Chapter." *Journal of Voluntary Action Research* 9, no. 1-4 (1980): 95-108.

4. Adams, James Luther. "Civil Disobedience: Its Occasions and Limits." In *Political and Legal Obligation*, Nomos XIL, pp. 293-331, edited by J. Roland Pennock and John W. Chapman. New York: Atherton Press, 1970.

5. Addams, Jane. *Democracy and Social Ethics*. Edited by Anne Firor Scott. 1902. Reprint. Cambridge: Harvard University Press, Belknap Press, 1964.

6. Addams, Jane. "Neighborhood Improvement." *Social Welfare Forum*, 1904, pp. 456-458.

7. Addams, Jane. *Twenty Years at Hull House*. New York: Macmillan Co., 1910.

8. Addams, Jane, et al. *Philanthropy and Social Progress, seven essays delivered before the School of Applied Ethics, Plymouth, Mass., 1892*. 1893. Reprint. Montclair, NJ: Patterson Smith, 1970.

9. Alchian, Armen A., et al. *Economics of Charity*. Institute of Economic Affairs Reading, no. 12. London: Institute of Economic Affairs, 1973.

10. Alderfer, Helen, ed. *A Farthing in Her Hand: Stewardship for Women*. Scottdale, PA: Herald Press, 1964.

11. Allen, Kerry Kenn. "Research on Volunteering and Citizen Involvement: Past Performance and Future Potential." In *Working Papers for Spring Research Forum: Since the Filer Commission*. Washington, DC: Independent Sector, 1983.

12. Allen, Kerry Kenn. "Social Responsibility: The Growing Partnership of Business and Voluntary Organizations." In *Volunteerism in the Eighties*, edited by John D. Harman. pp. 95-110. Washington, DC: University Press of America, 1982.

13. Allen, Kerry Kenn. *The Wichita Experience: Mobilizing Corporate Resources to Meet Community Needs*. Arlington, VA: Volunteer: The National Center for Citizen Involvement, 1978.

14. Allen, Kerry Kenn, ed. *The Shape of Things to Come, 1980-1990: A Report from The National Forum on Volunteerism*. Appleton, WI: Aid Association for Lutherans, 1980. Arlington, VA: Volunteer: The National Center for Citizen Involvement, 1980.

15. Allen, Kerry Kenn; Chapin, Isolde; Keller, Shirley; and Hill, Donna. *Volunteers from the Workplace*. Washington, DC: National Center for Voluntary Action, 1979.

16. Allock, J. B. "Voluntary Associations and the Structure of Power." *The Sociological Review* 16 (March 1968): 59-81.

17. Almand, Gabriel A., and Verba, Sidney. *The Civic Culture*. Princeton: Princeton University Press, 1963.

18. Alperovitz, Gar. "Notes Toward a Pluralist Commonwealth." In *Strategy and Program: Two Essays Toward a New American Socialism,* edited by S. Lynd and G. Alperovitz. pp. 49-109. Boston: Beacon Press, 1973.

19. American Association of Fund Raising Counsel, Inc. *Giving U.S.A.* New York: American Association of Fund Raising Counsel, Inc., 1983.

20. American Council of Voluntary Agencies for Foreign Service, Inc. "The Role of Voluntary Agencies in Technical Assistance." *Technical Assistance Programs,* May, 1953.

21. "American Philanthropy of the Nineteenth Century." *Charities Review* 9 (November 1899): 353.

22. American Red Cross. *I Can*. Washington, DC: American Red Cross, 1981.

23. "Americans Volunteer." Manpower/Automation Research Monograph, no. 10. Washington, DC: U.S. Department of Labor, 1969.

24. Amore, Roy C. *Two Masters, One Message: The Lives and Teachings of Gautama and Jesus*. Nashville: Abingdon, 1978.

25. Anderson, John C., and Moore, Larry F. "The Motivation to Volunteer." *Journal of Voluntary Action Research* 7, no. 3-4 (1978): 120-129.

26. Anderson, Robert T. "Voluntary Associations in History." *American Anthropologist* 73, no. 1 (February 1971): 209-219.

27. Anderson, Robert T., and Anderson, Barbara Gallatin. "Voluntary Associations and Urbanization: A Diachronic Analysis." *American Journal of Sociology* 65 (November 1959): 265-273.

28. Andrews, F. Emerson. *Attitudes Toward Giving*. New York: Russell Sage Foundation, 1953.

29. Andrews, F. Emerson. *Corporation Giving*. New York: Russell Sage Foundation, 1952.

30. Andrews, F. Emerson. *Foundation Watcher*. Lancaster, PA: Franklin and Marshall College, 1973.

31. Andrews, F. Emerson. *Philanthropic Foundations*. New York: Russell Sage Foundation, 1956.

32. Andrews, F. Emerson. *Philanthropic Giving*. New York: Russell Sage Foundation, 1950.

33. Andrews, F. Emerson. *Philanthropy in the United States: History and Structure*. New York: The Foundation Center, 1974.

34. Andrews, F. Emerson, ed. *Foundations: 20 Viewpoints*. New York: Russell Sage Foundation, 1965.

35. Arnove, Robert S., ed. *Philanthropy and Cultural Imperialism: Foundations at Home and Abroad*. Bloomington: Indiana University Press, 1982.

36. Babchuk, Nicholas, and Booth, Alan. "Voluntary Association Membership: A Longitudinal Analysis." *American Sociological Review* 34 (February 1969): 31-45.

37. Babchuk, Nicholas, and Edwards, John N. "Voluntary Associations and the Integration Hypothesis." *Sociological Inquiry* 35 (Spring 1965): 149-162.

38. Babchuk, Nicholas, and Thompson, Ralph V. "The Voluntary Associations of Negroes." *American Sociological Review* 27, no. 5 (October 1962): 647-655.

39. Babchuk, Nicholas, and Warriner, Charles K. Introduction to "Signposts in the Study of Voluntary Groups." *Sociological Inquiry* 35 (Spring 1965): 135-137.

40. Bachrach, Peter. "Interest, Participation and Democratic Theory." In *Participation in Politics*, Nomos XVI, edited by J. Roland Pennock and John W. Chapman. New York: Lieber-Atherton, 1974.

41. Bachrach, Peter. *The Theory of Democratic Elitism: A Critique*. Boston: Little, Brown, 1967.

42. Bakal, Carl. *Charity U.S.A.* New York: Times Books, 1979.

43. Banton, Michael. "Voluntary Associations: Anthropological Aspects." In *International Encyclopedia of the Social Sciences*. Vol. 16, edited by David Sills. pp. 357-362. New York: Macmillan Co. and The Free Press, 1968.

44. Barnes, N. K. "Rethinking Corporate Charity." *Fortune*, October 1974, pp. 168-171.

45. Barzun, Jacques. "The Folklore of Philanthropy." In *The House of Intellect*. New York: Harper & Bros., 1959.

46. Baumol, William J. "Enlightened Self-Interest and Corporate Philanthropy." In *A New Rationale for Corporate Social Policy*, edited by William Baumol, Renis Likert, Henry Wallich, and John McGowan. New York: Committee for Economic Development, 1970.

47. Baumol, William J., and Bowen, William G. *Performing Arts—The Economic Dilemma*. New York: Twentieth Century Fund, 1966.

48. Beard, Charles A., and Beard, Mary R. *The Rise of American Civilization*. Vol. 2. New York: Macmillan Co., 1927.

49. Bennis, Warren G.; Benne, Kenneth D; and Chin, Robert, eds. *The Planning of Change*. New York: Holt, Rinehart & Winston, 1961.

50. Berger, Peter, and Neuhaus, Richard John. *To Empower People: The Role of Mediating Structures in Public Policy*. Washington, DC: American Enterprise Institute for Public Policy Research, 1977.

51. Bethune, Mary McLeod. "The Negro in Retrospect and Prospect." *Journal of Negro History* 35 (January 1950).

52. Biagi, Bob. *Working Together: A Manual to Help Groups Work More Effectively*. Amherst: Citizen Involvement Training Project, 1978.

53. Blaine, Mrs. Emmons. "Can Citizenship Be Fulfilled by Philanthropy?" *The Survey*, July 2, 1910, pp. 542-547. The Charity Organization Society of the City of New York, Publisher.

54. Blake, D. H.; Frederick, W. C.; and Meyers, M. S. *Social Auditing: Evaluating the Impact of Corporate Programs*. New York: Praeger, 1976.

55. Blendon, Robert J. "The Changing Role of Private Philanthropy in Health Affairs." In *Research Papers of the Commission on Private Philanthropy and Public Needs*. Vol. 2. Washington, DC: Department of Treasury, 1977.

56. Blomstom, R. L.; Davis, K.; and Frederick, W. C. *Business and Society: Concepts and Policy Issues*. New York: McGraw-Hill, 1980.

57. Bode, Carl. *The American Lyceum: Town Meeting of the Mind*. New York: Oxford University Press, 1956.

58. Bogen, Boris D. *Jewish Philanthropy: An Expression of Principles and Methods of Jewish Social Service in the United States*. New York: Macmillan Co., 1917.

59. Bolling, Landrum R. *Private Foreign Aid: U.S. Philanthropy for Relief and Development*. Boulder, CO: Westview Press, 1982.

60. Bolling, Landrum R. "Private Philanthropy and International Activities in the Decade After the Filer Report." In *Working Papers for Spring Research Forum: Since the Filer Commission*. Washington, DC: Independent Sector, 1983.

61. Bolling, Landrum R. "Voluntarism and the Public Good." *Saturday Evening Post*, May/June 1979.

62. Bolling, Landrum R. "What Every Trust Officer Should Know About Philanthropy and Foundations." *Trusts and Estates*, December 1978.

63. Bolton, Sarah K. *Famous Givers and Their Gifts*. New York/Boston: T. Y. Crowell & Co., 1896.

64. Bombeck, Erma. "Without Volunteers: A Lost Civilization." From "At Wit's End," Field Newspaper Syndicate, June 24, 1975.

65. Boorstin, Daniel. "The Fertile Verge—Creativity in the United States." Address given at The Carnegie Symposium on Creativity, November 19-20, 1980, Library of Congress, Washington, D.C., 1980.

66. Boorstin, Daniel. "From Charity to Philanthropy." *The Decline of Radicalism*, Chapter 3. New York: Random House, 1963.

67. Boorstin, Daniel. "Missions and Momentum." *The Americans: The Democratic Experience*, Part 10. New York: Random House, 1973.

68. Booth, Alan, and Babchuk, Nicholas. "Personal Influence Networks and Voluntary Association Affiliation." *Sociological Inquiry* 39 (Spring 1969): 179-188.

69. Boris, Elizabeth T. "Research on Philanthropic Foundations." In *Working Papers for Spring Research Forum: Since the Filer Commission*. Washington, DC: Independent Sector, 1983.

70. Bornet, Vaughn Davis. *Welfare in America*. Norman, OK: University of Oklahoma Press, 1960.

71. Boulding, Kenneth E. *The Economy of Love and Fear*. Belmont, CA: Wadsworth, 1973.

72. Boulding, Kenneth E. "Notes on a Theory of Philanthropy." In *Philanthropy and Public Policy*, edited by Frank G. Dickinson. Washington, DC: National Bureau of Economic Research, 1962.

73. Boyd, Floyd, and Vieg, John, eds. *Voluntary Action, Mainstay of a Free Society*. Proceedings of the 1st Conference of the Institute of Public Affairs, Claremont, California, 1949. Claremont: Pomona College, 1950.

74. Boyte, Harry Chatten. *The Backyard Revolution: Understanding the New Citizen Movement*. Philadelphia: Temple University Press, 1980.

75. Bremner, Robert H. *American Philanthropy*. Chicago: University of Chicago Press, 1960.

76. Bremner, Robert H. *From the Depths: The Discovery of Charity in the United States*. New York: New York University Press, 1964.

77. Bremner, Robert H. "Private Philanthropy and Public Needs: Historical Perspective." In *Research Papers of the Commission on Private Philanthropy and Public Needs*. Vol. 1. Washington, DC: Department of Treasury, 1977.

78. Bremner, Robert H. *The Public Good*. New York: Alfred A. Knopf, 1980.

79. Brockett, Linus Pierpont. *The Philanthropic Results of the War in America. By an American Citizen*. New York: Press of Wynkoop, Hallenbeck, and Thomas, 1863.

80. Brost, Diane, and Montana, Patrick J., eds. *Managing Nonprofit Organizations*. New York: AMACOM, 1977.

81. Brown, John Crosby. "Private Giving and Public Spending." *The Atlantic Monthly* 161, no. 6 (June 1938): 813-818.

82. Brown, Richard D. "The Emergence of Voluntary Associations in Massachusetts, 1760-1830." *Journal of Voluntary Action Research* 2 (1973): 64-73.

83. Bryce, James. *The American Commonwealth*. New York: Macmillan Co., 1909.

84. Butcher, Willard C. "Total Corporate Responsibility in the 80's." Remarks delivered at the University of North Carolina, October 16, 1981.

85. Butler, Stuart. "Research into the Impediments to Voluntarism." In *Working Papers for Spring Research Forum: Since the Filer Commission*. Washington, DC: Independent Sector, 1983.

86. Byrne, Frank L. *Prophet of Prohibition: Neal Dow and His Crusade*. Madison: State Historical Society of Wisconsin for the Dept. of History, University of Wisconsin, 1961.

87. Carey, Sarah C. "Philanthropy and the Powerless." In *Research Papers of the Commission on Private Philanthropy and Public Needs*. Vol. 2. Washington, DC: Department of Treasury, 1977.

88. Carnegie, Andrew. *The Gospel of Wealth: And Other Timely Essays*. New York: The Century Co., 1900.

89. Carnegie, Andrew. *Miscellaneous Writings of Andrew Carnegie*. Edited by Burton J. Hendrick. Garden City, NY: Doubleday, Doran & Co., Inc., 1933.

90. Carter, Richard. *The Gentle Legions*. Garden City, NY: Doubleday & Co., Inc., 1961.

91. Cass, Rosemary Higgins, and Manser, Gordon. *Volunteerism at the Crossroads*. New York: Family Service Association of America, 1976.

92. Channing, William Henry. *The Life of William Ellery Channing, D.D.*. Boston: American Unitarian Association, 1880.

93. Chapin, F. Stuart. "Social Institutions and Voluntary Associations." In *Review of Sociology*, edited by Joseph B. Gittler. New York: John Wiley & Sons, 1957.

94. *The Charitable Impulse in 18th Century America: Collected Papers*. New York: Arno Press, 1971.

95. "Charity and Philanthropy." *The Catholic World* 9 (October 1866-March 1867): 434-446.

96. Cheit, Earl F., and Lobman, Theodore E., III. "Private Philanthropy and Higher Education: History, Current Impact, and Public Policy Considerations." In *Research Papers of the Commission on Private Philanthropy and Public Needs*. Vol. 2. Washington, DC: Department of Treasury, 1977.

97. Cicero. *On Moral Obligation (De Officiis)*. Translated by John Higginbotham. London: Faber, 1967.

98. "Citizen Participation in the American Federal System." *Advisory Commission on Intergovernmental Relations*. Washington, DC: U. S. Government Printing Office, 1979.

99. Clark, Merrell M. "In the Image of God." In *Working Papers for Spring Research Forum: Since the Filer Commission*. Washington, DC: Independent Sector, 1983.

100. Clotfelter, Charles T. "Tax Incentives and Charitable Giving." *Journal of Public Economics* 13 (1980): 319-340.

101. Coffman, Harold C. *American Foundations: A Study of Their Role in the Child Welfare Movement*. New York: YMCA Press, 1936.

102. Cohen, Nathan Edward. *Social Work in the American Tradition*. New York: Holt, Rinehart & Winston, 1958.

103. Cohen, Nathan Edward, ed. *The Citizen Volunteer*. New York: Harper & Bros., 1960.

104. Colwell, Mary Anna Culleton. *Philanthropic Foundations and Public Policy: The Political Role of Foundations*. Ph.D. dissertation, University of California at Berkeley, 1981.

105. Commager, Henry Steele. "The American Style of Giving." *Mainliner* 20, no. 12 (December 1976).

106. Commission on Private Philanthropy and Public Needs. *Donee Group Report and Recommendations—Private Philanthropy: Vital and Innovative? or Passive and Irrelevant?* Washington, DC: Department of Treasury, 1977.

107. Commission on Private Philanthropy and Public Needs. *Giving in America: Report of the Commission on Private Philanthropy and Public Needs*. Washington, DC: Department of Treasury, 1975.

108. Connors, Tracy D., ed. *The Nonprofit Organization Handbook*. New York: McGraw-Hill, 1980.

109. Coon, Horace. *Money to Burn*. New York: Longmans, Green & Co., 1938.

110. Cornuelle, Richard C. "A Brief Interpretive History of America's Voluntary Sector." *United Way Annual Report* (1979). Alexandria, VA.

111. Cornuelle, Richard C. *Healing America: What Can Be Done About the Continuing Economic Crisis*. New York: G.P. Putnam's Sons, 1983.

112. Cornuelle, Richard C. *Reclaiming the American Dream*. New York: Random House, 1965.

113. "Corporate Philanthropy—An Integral Part of Corporate Social Responsibility." *Business Roundtable,* March, 1981.

114. Corson, John J., and Hodson, Harry V., eds. *Philanthropy in the 70's: An Anglo-American Discussion.* Washington, DC: Council on Foundations, 1973.

115. Council on Foundations. *Corporate Philanthropy.* Washington, DC: Council on Foundations, 1982.

116. Cousins, Norman. "New Directions for American Foundations." *Saturday Review* 35 (September 13, 1952): 24.

117. Crothers, Rev. Samuel. "The Art of Philanthropy." *Survey,* 1905, pp. 872-873.

118. Cull, John G., and Hardy, Richard E. *Volunteerism: An Emerging Profession.* Springfield, IL: Charles C. Thomas, 1974.

119. Cuninggim, Merrimon. *Private Money and Public Service: The Role of Foundations in American Society.* New York: McGraw-Hill, 1972.

120. Curti, Merle E. *The American Peace Crusade, 1815-1860.* 1929. Reprint. New York: Octagon Books, 1965.

121. Curti, Merle E. *American Philanthropy Abroad: A History.* New Brunswick, NJ: Rutgers University Press, 1963.

122. Curti, Merle E. "American Philanthropy and the National Character." *American Quarterly* 10, no. 4 (Winter 1958): 420-437.

123. Curti, Merle E. "Creative Giving: Slogan or Reality?" *Foundation News* 3, no. 6 (November 1962): 7-10.

124. Curti, Merle E. *The Growth of American Thought.* New York: Harper & Row, 1943.

125. Curti, Merle E. "The History of American Philanthropy as a Field of Research." *American Historical Review* 62 (January 1957): 352-363.

126. Curti, Merle E. "Tradition and Innovation in American Philanthropy." *Proceedings of the American Philosophical Society* 105, no. 2 (April 1961).

127. Curtis, James. "Voluntary Association Joining: A Cross-National Comparative Note." *American Sociological Review* 36 (October 1971): 872-880.

128. Dahl, Robert A. *Pluralist Democracy in the United States.* Chicago: Rand McNally, 1967.

129. Damle, P. R. *Philosophy Today and Other Essays.* Poona, India: Oxford Press, 1965.

130. Davies, John D. *Phrenology, Fad and Science: A 19th Century American Crusade*. New Haven: Yale University Press, 1955. Hamden, CT: Anchor Books, 1971.

131. Davis, Allen F. *Spearheads for Reform: The Social Settlements and the Progressive Movement, 1890-1914*. New York: Oxford University Press, 1967.

132. de Grazia, Alfred, ed. *Foundation for Voluntary Welfare*. Winning essays of the 1956 National Awards Competition of the Foundation for Voluntary Welfare. New York: New York University Press, 1957.

133. de Grazia, Alfred, ed. *Grass Roots Private Welfare*. New York: New York University Press, 1957.

134. de Tocqueville, Alexis. "Of the Use Which the Americans Make of Public Associations in Civil Life." *Democracy in America*, Vol. 2. New York: Alfred A. Knopf, Borzoi Books, 1976.

135. Dick, Jane. *Volunteers and the Making of Presidents*. New York: Dodd, Mead & Co., 1980.

136. Dickinson, Frank G. *The Changing Position of Philanthropy in the American Economy*. Occasional paper, 110. New York: National Bureau of Economic Research, 1970.

137. Dickinson, Frank G., ed. *Philanthropy and Public Policy*. New York: National Bureau of Economic Research, 1962.

138. DiMaggio, Paul. "Cultural Entrepreneurship in Nineteenth-Century Boston: Part 1, The Creation of an Organizational Base for High Culture in America." *Media, Culture and Society* 4 (1982): 33-50.

139. DiMaggio, Paul. "Non-Economic Theories of the Independent Sector." In *Working Papers for Spring Research Forum: Since the Filer Commission*. Washington, DC: Independent Sector, 1983.

140. Dodd, Ruth M. *Volunteer Values*. New York: Family Welfare Association of America, 1934.

141. Dubeck, P. "Membership Experiences and Voluntary Organization Maintenance." Ph.D. dissertation, Northwestern University, 1973.

142. Dulles, Foster Rhea. *American Red Cross: A History*. New York: Harper & Bros., 1950.

143. Dulles, Foster Rhea. *Labor in America: A History*. 2nd ed. New York: T. Y. Crowell & Co., 1960.

144. Dumond, Dwight L. *Anti Slavery: The Crusade for Freedom in America*. Ann Arbor: University of Michigan Press, 1961.

145. Eells, Richard. *Corporation Giving in a Free Society.* New York: Harper & Bros., 1956.

146. Eells, Richard, ed. *International Business Philanthropy.* New York: Macmillan Co., 1979.

147. Eisenberg, Pablo. "Accountability, Accessibility and Equity in Philanthropy: Filling the Research Gap." In *Working Papers for Spring Research Forum: Since the Filer Commission.* Washington, DC: Independent Sector, 1983.

148. Eisenberg, Pablo. "The Voluntary Sector: Problems and Challenges." In *Research Papers of the Commission on Private Philanthropy and Public Needs.* Vol. 2. Washington, DC: Department of the Treasury, 1977.

149. Eisenstadt, S. N. "The Social Conditions of the Development of Voluntary Associations—A Case Study of Israel." *Scripta Hierosolymitana* 3 (1955).

150. Eisenstadt, S. N., ed. *Max Weber on Charisma and Institution Building.* Chicago: University of Chicago Press, 1968.

151. Eitzen, D. Stanley. "A Study of Voluntary Association Membership among Middle-Class Women." *Rural Sociology* 35 (March 1970): 84-91.

152. Elias, Julius. "Relations Between Voluntary Agencies and International Organizations." *Journal of International Affairs* 7 (1953): 30-34.

153. Ellis, Susan J., and Noyes, Katherine H. *By the People: A History of Americans as Volunteers.* Philadelphia: Energize, 1978.

154. Embree, Edwin R. "Timid Billions: Are the Foundations Doing Their Job?" *Harper's Magazine* 198 (March 1949): 28-37.

155. Embree, Edwin R., and Waxman, Julia. *Investment in People: The Story of the Julius Rosenwald Fund.* New York: Harper & Bros., 1949.

156. Emerson, Ralph Waldo. "Man the Reformer." *The Collected Works of Ralph Waldo Emerson,* edited by Robert E. Spiller and Alfred R. Ferguson. Vol. 1. Cambridge: Harvard University Press, Belknap Press, 1971.

157. Epstein, Abraham. "Do the Rich Give to Charity?" *American Mercury* 23 (May 1931): 22-30.

158. "Essays on the Principles of Charitable Institutions." *The Monthly Review* 1, no. 142 (January-April 1837): 574-590.

159. Etzioni, Amitai. *The Active Society.* New York: The Free Press, 1968.

160. Etzioni, Amitai. "New Directions in the Study of Organizations and Society." *Social Research* 27 (Summer 1960): 223-228.

161. Etzioni, Amitai. "The Third Sector and Domestic Missions." In *Emerging Concepts in Management*, 2nd ed., edited by Max S. Wortman, Jr. and Fred Luthans, pp. 401-413. New York: Macmillan Co., 1975.

162. Fallers, L.A., ed. *Immigrants and Associations*. The Hague: Mouton, 1967.

163. Faris, Ellsworth; Laune, Ferris; and Todd, Arthur J., eds. *Intelligent Philanthropy*. Chicago: University of Chicago Press, 1930.

164. Faris, N. A. *The Mysteries of Almsgiving*. Beirut: Kazi Publications, 1966. Lahore: Kazi Publications, 1974.

165. Fellman, David. *The Constitutional Right of Association*. Chicago: University of Chicago Press, 1963.

166. Ferguson, Adam. *An Essay on the History of Civil Society, 1767*. Edinburgh, printed for A. Millar & T. Caddel in The Strand, London, 1767.

167. Filer, John H. "The Role of the Private Sector in Addressing Social Issues." Address given at the annual meeting of the American Council of Life Insurance, November 18, 1980.

168. Filer, John H. "The Social Goals of a Corporation." In *Corporations and Their Critics: Issues and Answers to the Problems of Corporate Responsibility*, edited by Thornton Bradshaw and David Vogel. New York: McGraw-Hill, 1982.

169. Filler, Louis. *The Crusade Against Slavery, 1830-1860*. New York: Harper & Bros., 1960.

170. Finlay, J. R. "Rethinking the Corporate Social Predicament: An Agenda for Mutual Survival." *Business Quarterly*, Summer 1977, pp. 59-69.

171. Flanagan, Joan. *The Successful Volunteer Organization*. Chicago: Contemporary Books, Inc., 1981.

172. Flathman, Richard. "The Rights of Volunteers." In *Volunteerism in the Eighties*, edited by John D. Harman. pp. 55-69. Washington, DC: University Press of America, 1982.

173. Fletcher, C. Scott, ed. *Education for Public Responsibility*. New York: W. W. Norton & Co., Inc., 1961.

174. Flexner, Abraham. *Funds and Foundations: Their Policies Past and Present*. New York: Arno Press, 1976 (©1952).

175. Flexner, Abraham. "Private Fortunes and the Public Future." *The Atlantic Monthly*, no. 156 (August 1935): 215-224.

176. Flora, Peter, and Heidenheimer, Gerold J. *The Development of Welfare States in Europe and America*. New Brunswick, NJ: Transaction Books, 1981.

177. Flynn, John P., and Webb, Gene E. "Women's Incentives for Community Participation in Policy Issues." *Journal of Voluntary Action Research* 4, no. 3-4 (1975): 137-146.

178. Forsythe, David P. *Humanitarian Politics: The International Committee of the Red Cross*. Baltimore: Johns Hopkins University Press, 1977.

179. Fosdick, Raymond B. *Adventure in Giving: The Story of the General Education Board*. New York: Harper & Row, 1962.

180. Fosdick, Raymond B. *The Story of the Rockefeller Foundation*. New York: Harper & Bros., 1952.

181. Foskett, John M. "Social Structure and Social Participation." *American Sociological Review* 20 (August 1955): 431-438.

182. Foster, Charles I. *An Errand of Mercy: The Evangelical United Front, 1790-1837*. Chapel Hill: University of North Carolina Press, 1960.

183. Foster, Stephen. *Their Solitary Way*. New Haven and London: Yale University Press, 1971.

184. *The Foundation Directory*. 8th ed. New York: The Foundation Center, 1981.

185. *Foundations, Private Giving, and Public Policy: Report and Recommendations of the Commission on Foundations and Private Philanthropy*. Chicago: University of Chicago Press, 1970.

186. Fox, Daniel M. *Engines of Culture: Philanthropy and Art Museums*. Madison: State Historical Society of Wisconsin, 1963.

187. Fox, Sherwood Dean. "Voluntary Associations and Social Structure." Ph.D. dissertation, Harvard University, 1952.

188. Frank, L. K. "What Influences People to Join Organizations?" *Adult Leadership* 6 (February 1958): 196.

189. Franklin, Benjamin. "On the Institution in Holland to Prevent Poverty" (1772). In *The Writings of Benjamin Franklin*, edited by Albert Henry Smyth. New York: Haskell House, 1970.

190. Franklin, Benjamin. "On the Laboring Poor" (1768). In *The Writings of Benjamin Franklin*, edited by Albert Henry Smyth. New York: Haskell House, 1970.

191. Franklin, Benjamin. "On the Price of Corn and Management of the Poor" (1766). In *The Writings of Benjamin Franklin*, edited by Albert Henry Smyth. New York: Haskell House, 1970.

192. Franklin, Benjamin. *The Papers of Benjamin Franklin*. Vol. 1, Jan. 6, 1706 through Dec. 31, 1734. Edited by Leonard W. Labaree. pp. 32-36. New Haven: Yale University Press, 1959.

193. Franklin, John Hope. "Achieving Civil Rights." In *The Black American Reference Book,* edited by Mabel M. Smythe. Englewood Cliffs, NJ: Prentice-Hall, 1976.

194. Freeman, Howard E., and Showel, Morris. "Differential Political Influence of Voluntary Associations." *Public Opinion Quarterly* 15 (Winter 1951): 703-714.

195. Freeman, Jo. "The Tyranny of Structurelessness." *Berkeley Journal of Sociology* 17: 151-164.

196. Fremont-Smith, Marion R. *Foundations and Government: State and Federal Law and Supervision.* New York: Russell Sage Foundation, 1965.

197. Fremont-Smith, Marion R. *Philanthropy and the Business Corporation.* New York: Russell Sage Foundation, 1972.

198. Fremont-Smith, Marion R. "Since the Filer Commission: Constitutional and Other Legal Issues." In *Working Papers for Spring Research Forum: Since the Filer Commission.* Washington, DC: Independent Sector, 1983.

199. French, Peter A. "Corporate Moral Agency." In *Ethical Theory and Business,* edited by Tom L. Beauchamp and Norman E. Bowie. Englewood Cliffs, NJ: Prentice-Hall, 1979.

200. Friedman, M. "The Social Responsibility of Business Is To Increase Its Profits." *The New York Times Magazine,* September 1970, pp. 33.

201. Frisch, Ephraim. *An Historical Survey of Jewish Philanthropy: From the Earliest Times to the Nineteenth Century.* New York: Macmillan Co., 1924.

202. Frothingham, Octavius B. *Transcendentalism in New England: A History.* Philadelphia: University of Pennsylvania Press, 1972 (c.1876).

203. Fulmer, Robert M. "Managing Voluntary Associations for the 1980's." *Journal of Voluntary Action Research* 2, no. 4 (1973): 212-215.

204. Galarza, Ernesto; Gallegos, Herman; and Samora, Julian. *Mexican-Americans in the Southwest.* Santa Barbara: McNally & Loftin, 1969.

205. Gallup Organization. *Survey of the Public Recollection of the 1978 Charitable Reduction;* a poll conducted for Independent Sector. Princeton, NJ: The Gallup Organization, 1979.

206. Gardner, John W. "Preserving the Independent Sector." Remarks delivered at the Council on Foundations 30th Annual Conference, May 16, 1979, Seattle, Washington.

207. Gardner, John W. "Private Initiative for the Public Good." *Annual Report of the Carnegie Corporation of New York,* 1964.

208. Gardner, John W. "The Renewal of Societies." Remarks delivered at the International Chamber of Commerce 26th Congress, October 2, 1978, Orlando, Florida.

209. Gardner, John W. "Toward a Pluralistic but Coherent Society." New York: Institute for Humanistic Studies, 1980.

210. Gatewood, Robert, and Lahiff, James. "Differences in Importance of Job Factors Between Managers in Voluntary and Profit Organizations." *Journal of Voluntary Action Research* 6, no. 3-4 (1977): 133-138.

211. Gaylin, Willard; Glasser, Ira; Marcus, Steven; and Rothman, David. *Doing Good: The Limits of Benevolence*. New York: Pantheon Books, 1978.

212. Giamatti, A. B. "Private Sector, Public Control and the Independent University." Baccalaureate address, Yale University, May 24, 1980.

213. Gidron, Benjamin. "Sources of Job Satisfaction Among Service Volunteers." *Journal of Voluntary Action Research* 12, no. 1 (1983).

214. Gidron, Benjamin. "Volunteer Work and Its Rewards." *Volunteer Administration* 11 (1977): 18-32.

215. Gilbo, Patrick F., ed. *The American Red Cross*. New York: Harper & Row, 1981.

216. Gilman, Daniel Colt. "Five Great Gifts." *The Outlook*, August 1907, pp. 648-657.

217. Gilman, Daniel Colt. "Special Training for Philanthropic Work." Address at the annual meeting of the Charity Organization Society of New York, January 27, 1905. In *The Launching of a University*. New York: Dodd, Mead & Co., 1906.

218. Gilman, Daniel Colt, ed. "The Organization of Charities, being a Report of the Sixth Section of the International Congress of Charities, Corrections, and Philanthropy, Chicago, June 1893." Baltimore: The Johns Hopkins Press, 1894.

219. Ginsburg, David; Marks, Lee R.; and Wertheim, Ronald P. "Federal Oversight of Private Philanthropy." In *Research Papers of the Commission on Private Philanthropy and Public Needs*. Vol. 5. Washington, DC: Department of Treasury, 1977.

220. Giovanni Agnelli Foundation. *Guide to European Foundations*. Milano, Italy: Franco Angeli Editore, 1973. Columbia University Press, distributors.

221. Gladden, Washington. "Tainted Money." *Outlook* 52 (1895): 886-87.

222. Glaser, William A., and Sills, David L., eds. *The Government of Associations: Selections from the Behavioral Sciences*. Totawa, NJ: The Bedminster Press, 1966.

223. Glazer, Nathan, and Moynihan, Daniel Patrick. *Beyond the Melting Pot*. Cambridge: The M.I.T. Press and Harvard University Press, 1963.

224. Glenn, John M.; Brandt, Lilian; and Andrews, F. Emerson. *Russell Sage Foundation, 1907-1946*. 2 vols. New York: Russell Sage Foundation, 1947.

225. Goff, Frederick H. *Community Trusts*. Cleveland: The Cleveland Trust Co., 1919.

226. Gold, Doris B. "Women and Voluntarism." In *Woman in Sexist Society,* edited by Vivian Gornick and Barbara K. Moran. New York: Basic Books, 1971.

227. Goldhamer, Herbert. "Voluntary Associations in the United States." In *Reader in Urban Sociology,* edited by Paul K. Hatt and Albert J. Reiss, Jr. Glencoe, IL: The Free Press, 1951.

228. Goodale, Frances A., ed. *The Literature of Philanthropy.* New York: Harper & Bros., 1893.

229. Goodpaster, Kenneth E., and Matthews, John B., Jr. "Can a Corporation Have a Conscience?" *Harvard Business Review,* January-February 1982.

230. Gordon, C. Wayne, and Babchuk, Nicholas. "A Typology of Voluntary Associations." In *The Government of Associations,* edited by William A. Glaser and David L. Sills. Totawa, NJ: The Bedminster Press, 1966.

231. Goulden, Joseph C. *The Money Givers.* New York: Random House, 1971.

232. Gray, B. Kirman. *A History of English Philanthropy.* London: P. S. King & Son, 1905.

233. Greenleaf, William. *From These Beginnings: The Early Philanthropies of Henry and Edsel Ford, 1911-1936.* Detroit: Wayne State University Press, 1964.

234. Greer, Scott. "Individual Participation in Mass Society." In *Approaches to the Study of Politics,* edited by Roland Young. Evanston: Northwestern University Press, 1958.

235. Griffin, C. S. "The Idea of Reform." *The Ferment of Reform, 1830-1860,* Chapter 1. New York: T. Y. Crowell & Co., 1967.

236. Griffin, C. S. *Their Brothers' Keepers: Moral Stewardship in the United States, 1800-1865.* New Brunswick, NJ: Rutgers University Press, 1960.

237. Grubb, Edward. "Philanthropy." In *Encyclopedia of Religion and Ethics,* Vol. 9, pp. 837-840. New York: Charles Scribner's Sons, 1928.

238. Gurin, Maurice G. *What Volunteers Should Know for Successful Fundraising.* Arlington, VA: Volunteer: The National Center for Citizen Involvement, 1981.

239. Haas, Walter A., Jr. "Corporate Social Responsibility—A New Term for an Old Concept with New Significance." In *Corporations and Their Critics: Issues and Answers to the Problems of Corporate Responsibility,* edited by Thornton Bradshaw and David Vogel. New York: McGraw-Hill, 1982.

240. Hale, George S. "The Charities of Boston." In *Memorial History of Boston,* edited by Justin Winsor, Vol. 4, pp. 641-674. Boston: James R. Osgood & Co., 1881.

241. Hall, Peter Dobkin. *The Organization of American Culture, 1700-1900: Private Institutions, Elites, and the Origins of American Nationality.* New York: New York University Press, 1982.

242. Handlin, Oscar, and Handlin, Mary. *The Dimensions of Liberty.* Cambridge: Harvard University Press, Belknap Press, 1961.

243. Hands, A. R. *Charities and Social Aid in Greece and Rome.* Ithaca: Cornell University Press, 1968.

244. Hardy, James M. *Corporate Planning for Nonprofit Organizations.* New York: Association Press, 1972.

245. Harpster, Richard E. *Your Fabulous Volunteers.* Washington, NJ: Washington Emergency Squad, 1980.

246. Harris, James F., and Klepper, Anne. "Corporate Philanthropic Public Services Activities." In *Research Papers of the Commission on Private Philanthropy and Public Needs.* Vol. 3. Washington, DC: Department of Treasury, 1977.

247. Harris, Neil. "The Gilded Age Revisited: Boston and The Museum Movement." *American Quarterly* 14 (Winter 1964).

248. Harrison, Shelby Millard, and Andrews, F. Emerson. *American Foundations for Social Welfare.* New York: Russell Sage Foundation, 1946.

249. Hartogs, Nelly, and Weber, Joseph. *Impact of Government Funding on the Management of Voluntary Agencies.* New York: Greater New York Fund, 1978.

250. Heimann, Fritz, ed. *The Future of Foundations.* (Background papers for the 41st American Assembly, 1972.) Englewood Cliffs, NJ: Prentice Hall, 1973.

251. Held, Virginia. *The Public Interest and Individual Interests.* New York: Basic Books, 1970.

252. Henderson, Charles R. "The Place and Functions of Voluntary Associations." *The American Journal of Sociology* 1, no. 3 (July 1895-May 1896): 327-334.

253. Hesburgh, Rev. Theodore Martin. "Reflections on Voluntarism in America." *Vital Speeches* 46 (June 1, 1980): 484-487.

254. Heusser, D. B. *Helping Church Workers Succeed: The Enlistment and Support of Volunteers.* Valley Forge, PA: Judson Press, 1980.

255. Higginson, Thomas Wentworth. "The Word Philanthropy." In *Freedom and Fellowship in Religion.* pp. 323-327. Boston: Roberts Bros., 1875.

256. Himmelfarb, Gertrude. *On Liberty and Liberalism: The Case of John Stuart Mill.* New York: Alfred A. Knopf, 1974.

257. Hindery, Roderick. *Comparative Ethics in Hindu and Buddhist Traditions.* Delhi, India: Motilal Banarsidass, 1978.

258. Hirschman, Albert O. *The Passions and the Interests*. Princeton, NJ: Princeton University Press, 1977.

259. "The History of American Philanthropy as a Field of Research." *American Historical Review* 62 (January 1957): 352-363.

260. Hogan, Harry J. "Philosophic Issues in Volunteerism." In *Volunteerism in the Eighties*, edited by John D. Harman. pp. 263-278. Washington, DC: University Press of America, 1982.

261. Hollis, Ernest V. "Evolution of the Philanthropic Foundation." *Educational Record* 20 (October 1939): 757.

262. Hollis, Ernest V. *Philanthropic Foundations and Higher Education*. New York: Columbia University Press, 1938.

263. Hopkins, Bruce R. *Charity Under Siege: Government Regulation of Fund Raising*. New York: John Wiley & Sons, Ronald Press, 1980.

264. Horowitz, Helen L. *Culture and the City: Cultural Philanthropy in Chicago from the 1880's to 1917*. Lexington: University of Kentucky Press, 1976.

265. Howard, Nathaniel R. *Trust for All Time*. Cleveland: The Cleveland Foundation, 1963.

266. Hudnut, Robert K. *Sleeping Giant: Arousing Church Power in America*. New York: Harper & Row, 1971.

267. Huggins, Nathan Irvin. *Protestants Against Poverty: Boston's Charities, 1870-1900*. Westport, CT: Greenwood Publishing Co., 1971.

268. Hunter, Floyd. *Community Power Structure*. New York: Anchor Press/Doubleday, 1953.

269. Hyman, Herbert H., and Wright, Charles. "Trends in Voluntary Association Memberships of American Adults: Replication Based on Secondary Analysis of National Sample Surveys." *American Sociological Review* 36 (April 1971): 191-206.

270. Irwin, Inez Haynes. *Story of Alice Paul: And the National Women's Party*. Fairfax, VA: Denlingers Publishers, Ltd., 1964.

271. Jackson, K. O'Brien. "The Role of Voluntary Associations in the Development of the Rural Community." *International Review of Community Development* 21 (December 1969): 199-220.

272. Jacobs, Paul, and Landau, Saul. "The Port Huron Statement." In *The New Radicals: A Report with Documents*. New York: Random House, 1966.

273. James, Estelle. "Comparisons of Nonprofit Sectors Abroad." In *Working Papers for Spring Research Forum: Since the Filer Commission*. Washington, DC: Independent Sector, 1983.

274. James, Estelle. "How Nonprofits Grow: A Model." *Journal of Policy Analysis and Management,* Spring, 1983.

275. James, Estelle. *Outside the State: Voluntary Organizations in Three English Towns.* London: Croom-Helm, 1980.

276. James, Sydney V. *A People Among Other Peoples: Quaker Benevolence in Eighteenth Century America.* Cambridge: Harvard University Press, 1963.

277. Jencks, Christopher, and Riesman, David. "Class Interests and the 'Public-Private' Controversy." In *The Academic Revolution.* Garden City, NY: Doubleday & Co., 1968.

278. Jenkins, Edward C. *Philanthropy in America.* New York: Association Press, 1950.

279. Jenner, Jessica Reynolds. "Participation Leadership and the Role of Volunteerism Among Selected Women Volunteers." *Journal of Voluntary Action Research* 11, no. 4 (1982): 30-31.

280. John Chrysostom, Saint (347-407 A.D.). "Sermon on Alms, Delivered at Antioch." In *Patrologiae Curus Completus.* Series Graeca, vol. 51. Translated from the parallel Greek and Latin texts of the Abbe Migne. New York: New York School of Philanthropy, 1917.

281. Jones, John Price. *The American Giver: A Review of American Generosity.* New York: Inter-River Press, 1954.

282. Jordan, Vernon. "We Cannot Live for Ourselves Alone." *Vital Speeches* 44 (June 1977): 493-495.

283. Jordan, W. K. *The Charities of London, 1480-1660: The Aspirations and the Achievements of the Urban Society.* Hamden, CT: Shoe String Press, Inc., 1974.

284. Jordan, W. K. *Philanthropy in England, 1480-1660.* New York: Russell Sage Foundation, 1959.

285. Kariel, Henry S. *The Decline of American Pluralism.* Stanford, CA: Stanford University Press, 1961.

286. Karl, Barry D. "Corporate Philanthropy: Historical Background." In *Corporate Philanthropy: Philosophy, Management, Trends, Future, and Background.* Washington, DC: Council on Foundations, 1982.

287. Karl, Barry D. "Philanthropy, Policy Planning and the Bureaucratization of the Democratic Ideal." *Daedalus* 105 (Fall 1976).

288. Karl, Barry D. "Research Reports: History and the Future of Philanthropy: Guidelines and Stumbling Blocks." Remarks given at the 1981 Independent Sector National Conference on Philanthropy, Minneapolis.

289. Karl, Barry D., and Katz, Stanley N. "The American Private Philanthropic Foundation and the Public Sphere, 1890-1930." *Minerva* 19 (Summer 1981).

290. Karson, Stanley G. "Social Responsibility of Management." *Nation's Business*, July 1975, pp. 35-37.

291. Katz, Harvey. *Give! Who Gets Your Charity Dollars?* Garden City, NY: Anchor Press/Doubleday, 1974.

292. Katz, Milton. *The Modern Foundation: Its Dual Character, Public and Private*. New York: The Foundation Library Center, 1968.

293. Katz, Stanley. "Research Reports: History and the Future of Philanthropy: Guidelines and Stumbling Blocks." Remarks given at the 1981 Independent Sector National Conference on Philanthropy, Minneapolis.

294. Keniston, Kenneth. *The Young Radicals*. New York: Harcourt, Brace, Jovanovich, 1968.

295. Keppel, Frederick Paul. *The Foundation: Its Place in American Life*. New York: Macmillan Co., 1930.

296. Keppel, Frederick Paul. *Philanthropy and Learning*. New York: Columbia University Press, 1936.

297. Kerr, Baine P. "Remarks on Corporate Philanthropy." Speech presented at the Robert Lee Sutherland Seminar, Austin, Texas, October 4, 1980.

298. Kiger, Joseph. *Operating Principles of the Larger Foundations*. New York: Russell Sage Foundation, 1954.

299. Kimball, Emily Kittle. *How to Get the Most Out of Being a Volunteer: Skills for Leadership*. Phoenix: Jordan Press, 1980.

300. Kirkland, Edward Chase. *Dream and Thought in the Business Community, 1860-1900*. Ithaca: Cornell University Press, 1956.

301. Knauft, E. B. "Functions of the Nonprofit Sector: The Place of the Filer Commission in the Scope and Activities of the Third Sector." In *Working Papers for Spring Research Forum: Since the Filer Commission*. Washington, DC: Independent Sector, 1983.

302. Knowles, Malcolm S. "Motivation in Volunteerism Synopsis of a Theory." *Journal of Voluntary Action Research* 1, no. 2 (1972): 27-29.

303. Koch, Frank. *The New Corporate Philanthropy*. New York: Plenum Press, 1979.

304. Koch, Janet, and Richards, Thomas W. "The Role of Philanthropy in the Environmental Field: Preservation of Natural Lands and Historic Properties." In *Research Papers of the Commission on Private Philanthropy and Public Needs*. Vol. 2. Washington, DC: Department of Treasury, 1977.

305. Kotler, Philip. *Marketing for Nonprofit Organizations*. 2nd ed. Englewood Cliffs, NJ: Prentice-Hall, 1982.

306. Kramer, Ralph M. *Voluntary Agencies in the Welfare State*. Berkeley and Los Angeles: University of California Press, 1981.

307. Krout, John A. *The Origins of Prohibition*. New York: Russell & Russell, 1967 (©1925).

308. Langton, Stuart. "The New Volunteerism." In *Volunteerism in the Eighties*, edited by John D. Harman. pp. 3-21. Washington, DC: University Press of America, 1982.

309. Langton, Stuart, ed. *Citizen Participation in America*. Lexington, MA: D. C. Heath Co., Lexington Books, 1978.

310. Langton, Stuart, ed. *Citizen Participation Perspectives: Proceedings of the National Conference on Citizen Participation, Washington, D.C., Fall 1978*. Medford, MA: Filene School of Citizenship, 1979.

311. Laski, Harold J. *The American Democracy. A Commentary and an Interpretation*. New York: The Viking Press, 1948.

312. Leavell, Ullin Whitney. *Philanthropy in Negro Education*. Westport, CT: Negro Universities Press, 1970.

313. Lerner, Max. *America as a Civilization*. New York: Simon & Schuster, 1957.

314. Lester, Robert M. *Forty Years of Carnegie Giving*. New York: Charles Scribner's Sons, 1941.

315. Levitt, Theodore. *The Third Sector*. New York: AMACOM, 1973.

316. Levy, Reynold, and Nielsen, Waldemar. "An Agenda for the Future." In *Research Papers of the Commission on Private Philanthropy and Public Needs*. Vol. 2. Washington, DC: Department of Treasury, 1977.

317. Lijphart, Arend. *The Politics of Accommodation: Pluralism and Democracy in the Netherlands*. Berkeley: University of California Press, 1968.

318. Lindeman, Edward C. *Wealth and Culture*. New York: Harcourt, Brace & Co., 1936.

319. Linden, Eugene. *The Alms Race: The Impact of American Voluntary Aid Abroad*. New York: Random House, 1976.

320. Lipset, Seymour Martin. *Agrarian Socialism*. Berkeley: University of California Press, 1950.

321. Lissner, Jorgen. *The Politics of Altruism: A Study of the Political Behavior of Voluntary Development Agencies*. Geneva: Lutheran World Federation, 1977.

322. Litwak, Eugene. "Voluntary Associations and Neighborhood Cohesion." *American Sociological Review* 26 (April 1961): 258-271.

323. Loch, Sir Charles S. "Charity and Charities." *Encyclopedia Britannica*. 11th ed. Vol. 5, pp. 860-891. New York: Encyclopedia Britannica, 1910.

324. Loch, Sir Charles S. *Charity and Social Life*. London: Macmillan & Co., 1910.

325. Love, Joseph L. "La Raza: Mexican Americans in Rebellion." *Transaction* 6 (February 1969)): 35-41.

326. Lyman, Richard W. "In Defense of the Private Sector." *Daedalus* 104, No. 1 (Winter 1975): 156-159.

327. Lyman, Richard W. *What Kind of Society Shall We Have?* Occasional Papers Series. Washington, DC: Independent Sector, 1980.

328. Macauley, J., and Berkowitz, L., eds. *Altruism and Helping Behavior*. New York: Academic Press, 1970.

329. McCarthy, Kathleen D. *Noblesse Oblige: Charity and Cultural Philanthropy in Chicago, 1849-1929*. Chicago: University of Chicago Press, 1982.

330. McCarthy, Kathleen D. "Private Philanthropy and Public Needs: The Historical Perspective Since the Filer Commission." In *Working Papers for the Spring Research Forum: Since the Filer Commission*. Washington, DC: Independent Sector, 1983.

331. McCord, David. "Money from Where?" In *In Sight of Sever: Essays from Harvard*. Cambridge: Harvard University Press, 1963. pp. 253-256.

332. MacDonald, Dwight. *The Ford Foundation: The Men and the Millions*. New York: Reynal & Co., 1956.

333. McGill, Michael E., and Wooten, Leland. "Management in the Third Sector." *Public Administration Review* 35 (September/October 1975): 444-455.

334. Macias, Ysidro R. "The Chicano Movement." *Wilson Library Bulletin*, March 1970.

335. McKelvey, Blake. *The Urbanization of America (1860-1915)*. New Brunswick, NJ: Rutgers University Press, 1963.

336. Magat, Richard. *The Ford Foundation at Work*. New York: Plenum Press, 1979.

337. Mansbridge, Jane J. *Beyond Adversary Democracy*. New York: Basic Books, 1980.

338. Manser, Gordon. "Issues and Problems Facing the Voluntary Sector: A Survey of Leadership Opinion." In *Research Papers of the Commission on Private Philanthropy and Public Needs*. Vol. 2. Washington, DC: Department of Treasury, 1977.

339. Manser, Gordon. *The Voluntary Sector in Brief.* New York: Academy for Educational Development, 1979.

340. Maquarrie, John. *Dictionary of Christian Ethics.* Philadelphia: Westminster Press, 1967.

341. Marshall, Helen E. *Dorothea Dix, Forgotten Samaritan.* Chapel Hill: University of North Carolina Press, 1937.

342. Marshall, Maxine. *Volunteers: Hope for the Future.* Nashville: Discipleship Resources, 1980.

343. Marshall, T. H. "Citizenship and Social Class." In *Class, Citizenship and Social Development.* Chicago: University of Chicago Press, 1977.

344. Martin, Samuel A. *Financing Humanistic Service.* Toronto, Canada: McClelland & Stewart Ltd., 1975.

345. Marts, Arnaud C. *The Generosity of Americans.* Englewood Cliffs, NJ: Prentice-Hall, 1966.

346. Marts, Arnaud C. *Man's Concern for His Fellow Man.* Geneva, NY: Marts & Lundy, Inc., 1961.

347. Marts, Arnaud C. *Philanthropy's Role in Civilization: Its Contribution to Human Freedom.* New York: Harper & Bros., 1973.

348. Mason, David E. "The Distinctive Nature of Voluntary Organization Management." *Voluntary Action Leadership* 2 (Spring 1979): 40-42.

349. Mason, Terry. "Symbolic Strategies for Change: A Discussion of the Chicano Women's Movement." In *Twice a Minority,* edited by Margarita B. Melville. St. Louis: C. V. Mosby Co., 1980.

350. Mather, Cotton. "Bonifacius—Essays to Do Good." In *The American Puritans: This World and the Next,* edited by Perry Miller. Garden City, NY: Anchor Books, 1956.

351. Matthews, William H. *Adventures in Giving.* New York: Dodd, Mead & Co., 1939.

352. Maus, Marcel. *The Gift: Forms and Functions of Exchange in Archaic Societies.* New York: W. W. Norton & Co., Inc., 1967.

353. Maves, Paul B. *Older Volunteers in Church and Community.* Valley Forge, PA: Judson Press, 1981.

354. Mavity, Jane H., and Ylvisaker, Paul N. "Private Philanthropy and Public Affairs." In *Research Papers of the Commission on Private Philanthropy and Public Needs.* Vol. 2. Washington, DC: Department of Treasury, 1977.

355. Mayeroff, Milton. *On Caring.* World Perspectives Series, Vol. 43. New York: Harper & Row, 1971.

356. Meek, Peter G. "Self-Regulation in Private Philanthropy." In *Research Papers of the Commission on Private Philanthropy and Public Needs.* Vol. 5. Washington, DC: Department of Treasury, 1977.

357. Melville, Margarita B., ed. *Twice a Minority.* St. Louis: The C. V. Mosby Co., 1980.

358. Meyer, Jack A., ed. *Meeting Human Needs: Toward a New Public Philosophy.* Washington, DC: American Enterprise Institute for Public Policy Research, 1982.

359. Miller, Arthur Selwyn. "The Constitution and the Voluntary Association: Some Notes toward a Theory." In *Voluntary Associations,* edited by J. Roland Pennock and John W. Chapman. New York: Atherton Press, 1969.

360. Miller, Harlan B. "Altruism, Volunteers and Sociology." In *Volunteerism in the Eighties,* edited by John D. Harman. pp. 45-53. Washington, DC: University Press of America, 1982.

361. Miller, Howard S. *The Legal Foundations of American Philanthropy.* Madison: State Historical Society of Wisconsin, 1961.

362. Miller, Lillian B. *Patrons and Patriotism: The Encouragement of the Fine Arts in the United States, 1790-1860.* Chicago: University of Chicago Press, 1966.

363. Miller, Perry. "Do Good." *The New England Mind: From Colony to Province,* Chapter 24. Cambridge: Harvard University Press, 1953.

364. Mills, C. Wright. *The Power Elite.* New York: Oxford University Press, 1959.

365. Millspaugh, Mrs. Charles F. "Women as a Factor in Civic Improvement." *The Chautauquan* 43 (March-August 1906): 312-319.

366. Minkin, Jacob S. *The World of Moses Maimonides.* New York: Thomas Yoseloff Press, 1957.

367. Moe, Henry Allen. "Notes on the Origin of Philanthropy in Christendom." *Proceedings of the American Philosophical Society* 105, no. 2 (April 1961).

368. Montgomery, Dr. Winfield Scott. *Fifty Years of Good Works.* Washington, DC: The National Association for the Relief of Destitute Colored Women and Children, 1914.

369. Moore, Joan W. "Patterns of Women's Participation in Voluntary Associations." *American Journal of Sociology* 66 (May 1961): 592-598.

370. Moquin, Wayne, and Van Doren, Charles, eds. *A Documentary History of the Mexican Americans.* New York: Praeger, 1971.

371. Mount, May Wilkinson. "New York Women in Philanthropic Work." *Municipal Affairs* 2, no. 3 (September 1898): 447-457.

372. Nagel, Thomas. *The Possibility of Altruism*. New York: Oxford Unversity Press, 1970.

373. Nason, John W. *Trustees and the Future of Foundations*. New York: Council on Foundations, 1977.

374. National Bureau of Economic Research, Inc. *Philanthropy and Public Policy*. New York: Columbia University Press, 1962.

375. National Catholic Development Conference. *Bibliography of Fund Raising and Philanthropy*. New York: National Catholic Development Conference, 1975.

376. National Center for Voluntary Action. "A Survey of the Voluntary Action Center Network." In *Research Papers of the Commission on Private Philanthropy and Public Needs*. Vol. 2. Washington, DC: Department of Treasury, 1977.

377. National Council of Jewish Women. "The Week the Volunteers Stayed Home." Program package designed by the Task Force on Voluntarism.

378. *The National Neighborhood Platform*. Washington, DC: National Association of Neighborhoods, 1979.

379. Naylor, Harriet H. *Volunteers Today: Finding, Training and Working with Them*. New York: Association Press, 1967.

380. Nazarene, Sr. Morando. *Characteristics of Charity*. Boston: Daughters of St. Paul, 1963.

381. Nelson, Ralph. "Private Giving in the American Economy." In *Research Papers of the Commission on Private Philanthropy and Public Needs*. Vol. 1. Washington, DC: Department of Treasury, 1977.

382. New York University. *Proceedings of New York University First through Tenth Biennial Conferences on Charitable Foundations*. New York: Matthew Bender, 1972.

383. Nielsen, Waldemar A. *The Big Foundations*. New York: Columbia University Press, 1972.

384. Nielsen, Waldemar A. "The Crisis of the Nonprofits." *Change*, January, 1980.

385. Nielsen, Waldemar A. *The Endangered Sector*. New York: Columbia University Press, 1979.

386. Nielsen, Waldemar A. "How Solid Are the Foundations?" *The New York Times Magazine*, October 21, 1962, Section 6, pp. 27.

387. Nielsen, Waldemar A. *The Third Sector: Keystone of a Caring Society*. Occasional Paper, no. 1. Washington, DC: Independent Sector, 1980.

388. Novak, Michael, ed. *Democracy and Mediating Structures: A Theological Inquiry.* Washington, DC: American Enterprise Institute, 1980.

389. Nye, Russel B. *William Lloyd Garrison and the Humanitarian Reformers.* Boston: Little, Brown, 1955.

390. O'Connell, Brian. *Effective Leadership in Voluntary Organizations.* New York: Association Press, 1976.

391. O'Connell, Brian. "From Service to Advocacy to Empowerment." *Social Casework* 59 (April 1978).

392. O'Connell, Brian. "Voluntary Agencies Must Ask: What Price Independence?" *Foundation News* 17, no. 4 (July/August 1976): 16-20.

393. Oleck, Howard L. *Non-Profit Corporations, Organizations, and Associations.* 2nd ed. Englewood Cliffs, NJ: Prentice-Hall, 1965.

394. Owen, David Edward. *English Philanthropy, 1660-1960.* Cambridge: Harvard University Press, Belknap Press, 1964.

395. Palmer, George H. *Altruism: Its Nature and Varieties.* 1919. Reprint. Westport, CT: Greenwood Press, Inc.

396. Park, Maud Wood. *Front Door Lobby.* Edited by Edna Lamprey Stantial. Boston: Beacon Press, 1960.

397. Parker, Franklin. "George Peabody, Founder of Modern Philanthropy." Ph.D. dissertation, Peabody College, 1956.

398. Parrish, Thomas. "The Foundation: A Special American Institution." In *The Future of Foundations,* edited by Fritz Heimann. Englewood Cliffs, NJ: Prentice-Hall, 1973.

399. Pearce, Jane L. "Apathy or Self-Interest? The Volunteer's Avoidance of Leadership Roles." *Journal of Voluntary Action Research* 9, no. 1-4 (1980): 85-94.

400. Penalosa, Fernando. "The Changing Mexican-American in Southern California." *Sociology and Social Research* 51, no. 4 (July 1967).

401. Penalosa, Fernando. "Recent Changes Among the Chicanos." *Sociology and Social Research,* October 1970.

402. Penfield, Wilder. *The Difficult Art of Giving: The Epic of Alan Gregg.* Boston: Little, Brown, 1967.

403. Pennock, J. Roland, and Chapman, John W., eds. *Voluntary Associations.* New York: Atherton Press, 1969.

404. Phelps, Edmund S., ed. *Altruism, Morality and Economic Theory.* New York: Russell Sage Foundation, 1975.

405. "Philanthropy in America and Europe." *The Nation* 4 (April 18, 1867).

406. Phillips, Michael H. "Motivation and Expectation in Successful Volunteerism." *Journal of Voluntary Action Research* 11, no. 2-3 (1982): 118-125.

407. Pickering, George W. *Voluntarism and the American Way*. Occasional Paper, no. 7. Washington, DC: Center for a Voluntary Society, 1970.

408. Pifer, Alan. *The Foundation in the Year 2000*. New York: The Foundation Library Center, 1968.

409. Pifer, Alan. "Foundations and Public Policy Formation." *Carnegie Corporation Annual Report*. New York: 1974.

410. Pifer, Alan. "Foundations and the Unity of Charitable Organizations." *Carnegie Corporation Annual Report*. New York: 1968.

411. Pifer, Alan. "The Jeopardy of Private Institutions." *Carnegie Corporation Annual Report*. New York: 1970.

412. Pifer, Alan. "The Nongovernmental Organization at Bay." *Carnegie Corporation Annual Report*. New York: 1966.

413. Pifer, Alan. "The Quasi Nongovernmental Organization." *Carnegie Corporation Annual Report*. New York: 1967.

414. Portenar, A.J. "Looking a Gift Horse in the Mouth." *The Independent* 68 (June 23, 1910): 1388.

415. Pray, Kenneth L. M. "Charity." *Encyclopedia of the Social Sciences*. Vol. 3. Edited by Edwin R. A. Seligman. pp. 340-345. New York: Macmillan Co., 1930.

416. Pumphrey, Ralph E. "Compassion and Protection: Dual Motives in Social Welfare." *Social Service Review* 33 (1959): 21-29.

417. Pumphrey, Ralph E., and Pumphrey, Muriel W., eds. *The Heritage of American Social Work*. New York: Columbia University Press, 1961.

418. Ratner, Sidney, ed. *New Light on the History of Great American Fortunes*. New York: Augustus M. Kelley, Inc., 1953.

419. Reeves, Richard. *American Journey*. New York: Simon & Schuster, 1982.

420. Reeves, Thomas C. *Freedom and the Foundation*. New York: Alfred A. Knopf, 1969.

421. Reeves, Thomas C., ed. *Foundations Under Fire*. Ithaca: Cornell University Press, 1970.

422. Remsen, Daniel S. *Postmortem Use of Wealth*. New York: G. P. Putnam's Sons, 1911.

423. Rendon, Armando B. *Chicano Manifesto*. New York: Macmillan Co., 1971.

424. Rice, Charles E. *Freedom of Association*. New York: New York University Press, 1962.

425. Rich, R. C. "The Dynamics of Leadership in Neighborhood Organizations." *Social Science Quarterly* 60 (March 1980): 570-587.

426. Rich, Wilmer Shields, ed. *American Foundations and Their Fields*. 7th ed. New York: American Foundation Information Service, 1955.

427. Riegel, Robert Edgar. *American Feminists*. Lawrence: University of Kansas Press, 1963.

428. Riesman, David. "Liberation and Stalemate." In *The Uses of Controversy in Sociology*, edited by Lewis A. Coser and Otto Larsen. New York: The Free Press, 1976.

429. Roberts, Ina Brevoort. "For Sweet Charity's Sake." *Lippincotts' Monthly* 77 (March 1906): 323-329.

430. Robertson, D. B. "Hobbes' Theory of Associations in the Seventeenth Century Milieu." In *Voluntary Associations: A Study of Groups in Free Societies*, edited by D. B. Robertson. Richmond, VA: John Knox Press, 1966.

431. Robertson, D. B., ed. *Voluntary Associations: A Study of Groups in Free Societies*. Richmond, VA: John Knox Press, 1966.

432. Rockefeller, John D. "The Difficult Art of Giving." *The World's Work*, 1908.

433. Rockefeller, John D., 3rd. "In Defense of Philanthropy." *Business and Society Review*, no. 25, Spring 1978.

434. Rockefeller, John D., 3rd. "The Third Sector." *Across the Board*, March 1978.

435. Rodriguez, Armando M. "Speak Up, Chicano." *American Education* 4, no. 5 (May 1968): 25-27.

436. Rosenbaum, Nelson. "Government Funding and the Voluntary Sector: Impacts and Options." In *Volunteerism in the Eighties*, edited by John D. Harman. pp. 249-259. Washington, DC: University Press of America, 1982.

437. Rosenbaum, Nelson. "New Approaches to Revenue Generation in the Voluntary Sector: An Entrepreneurial Perspective." In *Working Papers for Spring Research Forum: Since the Filer Commission*. Washington, DC: Independent Sector, 1983.

438. Rosenbaum, Nelson, and Smith, Bruce L. R. "Composition of Revenues and Expenditures in the Voluntary Sector." In *Working Papers for Spring Research Forum: Since the Filer Commission*. Washington, DC: Independent Sector, 1983.

439. Rosenthal, Joel T. *The Purchase of Paradise: The Social Function of Aristocratic Benevolence, 1307-1485*. Toronto: University of Toronto Press, 1972.

440. Rosenwald, Julius. "Principles of Public Giving." *Atlantic Monthly*, May 1929.

441. Ross, Robert J. "Primary Groups in Social Movements: A Memoir and Interpretation." *Journal of Voluntary Action Research* 6, no. 3-4 (1979): 139-152.

442. Rothschild-Whitt, Joyce. "Conditions for Democracy: Making Participatory Organizations Work." In *Co-ops, Communes and Collectives*, edited by John Case and Rosemary Taylor. New York: Pantheon, 1979.

443. Rousseau, Jean Jacques. *The Social Contract*. Translated by G. D. H. Cole. New York: Dutton, 1950.

444. Rudney, Gabriel G. "The Scope of the Private Voluntary Charitable Sector." In *Research Papers of the Commission on Private Philanthropy and Public Needs*. Vol. 1. Washington, DC: Department of Treasury, 1977.

445. Rudolph, Frederick. *The American College and University: A History*. New York: Vintage Books, 1962.

446. Russell, K., and Tooke, J. *Learning to Give*. Elmsford, NY: Pergamon Press, Inc., 1968.

447. Russell Sage Foundation. *Report of the Princeton Conference on the History of Philanthropy in the United States*. New York: Russell Sage Foundation, 1956.

448. Saccomandi, Pat, and Host, Bobette Reigel. *The Volunteer Skillsbank: An Innovative Way to Connect Individual Talents to Community Needs*. Boulder, CO: Volunteer: The National Center for Citizen Involvement, 1981.

449. Salem, Greta W. "Maintaining Participation in Community Organizations." *Journal of Voluntary Action Research* 7, no. 3-4 (1978): 18-27.

450. Samora, Julian, ed. *La Raza: Forgotten Americans*. South Bend, IN: University of Notre Dame Press, 1966.

451. Sanford, Terry. *Foundations: Their Role in Our American Pluralistic System*. Grass Roots Guides on Democracy and Practical Politics, Booklet No. 52. Washington, CT: The Center for Information on America, 1974.

452. Santiesteven, Henry. "A Perspective on Mexican-American Organizations." In *Mexican Americans Tomorrow*, edited by Gus Tyler. Albuquerque: University of New Mexico Press, 1975.

453. Savage, Howard J. *Fruit of an Impulse: Forty-five Years of the Carnegie Foundation, 1905-1950*. New York: Harcourt, Brace, 1953.

454. Scheier, Ivan H. *Exploring Volunteer Space: The Recruiting of a Nation*. Boulder, CO: Volunteer: The National Center for Citizen Involvement, 1980.

455. Scheitlin, George E., and Gillstrom, Eleanore L. *Recruiting and Developing Volunteer Leaders*. Philadelphia: Parish Life Press, 1979.

456. Schindler-Rainman, Eva, and Lippitt, Ronald. *Building the Collaborative Community: Mobilizing Citizens for Action*. Riverside: University of California Extension, 1980.

457. Schindler-Rainman, Eva, and Lippitt, Ronald. *The Volunteer Community*. Washington, DC: Center for a Voluntary Society, 1971.

458. Schlesinger, Arthur M., Sr. *The American as Reformer*. New York: Atheneum, 1971.

459. Schlesinger, Arthur M., Sr. "Biography of a Nation of Joiners." *American Historical Review* 50 (October 1944): 1-25.

460. Schlesinger, Arthur M., Sr. *Paths to the Present*. New York: Macmillan Co., 1949.

461. Schmidt, Alvin J., and Babchuk, Nicholas. "Formal Voluntary Organizations and Change Over Time: A Study of American Fraternal Organizations." *Journal of Voluntary Action Research* 1 (1972): 46-55.

462. Schmidt, Elizabeth; Blewett, Jane; and Henriot, Peter. *Religious Private Voluntary Organizations and the Question of Government Funding*. Maryknoll, NY: Orbis Books, 1981.

463. Schnaue, Fred. "Individual Giving, Then and Now." In *Working Papers for Spring Research Forum: Since the Filer Commission*. Washington, DC: Independent Sector, 1983.

464. Schwartz, Harold. *Samuel Gridley Howe: Social Reformer, 1801-1876*. Cambridge: Harvard University Press, 1956.

465. Selby, C. "Better Performance from Nonprofits." *Harvard Business Review* 56, no. 5 (September/October 1978): 92-98.

466. Selem, G. "Maintaining Participation in Community Organizations." *Journal of Voluntary Action Research* 3 (1978): 18-26.

467. Seymour, Harold James. *Design for Giving: The Story of the National War Fund, Inc., 1943-1947*. New York: Harper & Row, 1947.

468. Shapiro, Benson. "Marketing in Nonprofit Organizations." *Journal of Voluntary Action Research* 3, no. 3-4 (1974): 1-16.

469. Shaw, Albert. "American Millionaires and Their Public Gifts." *Review of Reviews* 7 (1893): 48-60.

470. Sheen, Fulton J. "The Philosophy of Charity." In *Old Errors and New Labels*, pp. 233-253. New York: The Century Co., 1931.

471. Sherry, Paul H. "Voluntary Associations and Public Policy." *Journal of Current Social Issues*, Autumn 1971.

472. Shryock, Richard Harrison. *National Tuberculosis Association, 1904-1954*. New York: National Tuberculosis Association, 1957.

473. Shultz, James, and Shultz, Margaret. *An Annotated Review of the Literature on Volunteering*. Occasional Paper, no. 9. Washington, DC: Center for a Voluntary Society, 1970.

474. Sieder, Violet M. "The Historical Origins of the American Volunteer." In *The Government of Associations*, edited by William A. Glaser and David L. Sills. Totowa, NJ: The Bedminster Press, 1966.

475. Sills, David. "Voluntary Associations: Instruments and Objects of Change." *Human Organization* 18 (Spring 1959): 17-21.

476. Sills, David. "Voluntary Associations: Sociological Aspects." *International Encyclopedia of the Social Sciences*. Vol. 16. New York: Macmillan and The Free Press: 1968.

477. Sills, David. *The Volunteers: Means and Ends in a National Association*. Glencoe, IL: The Free Press, 1957.

478. Silver, Morris. *Affluence, Altruism, and Atrophy: The Decline of Welfare States*. New York: New York University Press, 1980

479. Simmen, Edward, ed. *Pain and Promise: The Chicano Today*. New York: The New American Library, Inc., 1972.

480. Simon, John G. "Research on Philanthropy." Speech delivered at the 25th Anniversary Conference of the National Council on Philanthropy, Denver, Colorado, November 8, 1979. Reprinted as a Research Report for Independent Sector, July, 1980.

481. Simpson, Dick. "Neighborhood Empowerment and Neighborhood Government." *Neighborhood Organization Research Group News Bulletin* 4 (1981): 7-10.

482. Simpson, Dick. "The Philosophy of Neighborhood Empowerment." In *Volunteerism in the Eighties*, edited by John D. Harman. pp. 223-248. Washington, DC: University Press of America, 1982.

483. Smith, Bruce L. R. *The Rand Corporation*. Cambridge: Harvard University Press, 1968.

484. Smith, Bruce L. R., ed. *The New Political Economy: The Public Use of the Private Sector*. New York: John Wiley & Sons, Halsted Press, 1975.

485. Smith, Constance E., and Freedman, Anne. *Voluntary Associations: Perspectives on the Literature*. Cambridge: Harvard University Press, 1972.

486. Smith, David Horton. "Altruism, Volunteers and Volunteerism." *Volunteerism in the Eighties,* edited by John D. Harman. pp. 23-44. Washington, DC: University Press of America, 1982.

487. Smith, David Horton. "Dimensions and Categories of Voluntary Organizations/ NGO's." *Journal of Voluntary Action Research* 2, no. 2 (1973): 116-120.

488. Smith, David Horton. "The Impact of the Volunteer Sector on Society." In *Voluntary Action Research: 1973*. Lexington, MA: Lexington Books, D.C. Heath & Co., 1973.

489. Smith, David Horton. "The Importance of Formal Voluntary Organizations for Society." *Sociology and Social Research* 50, no. 4 (1966): 483-494.

490. Smith, David Horton. "Values, Voluntary Action and Philanthropy: The Appropriate Relationship of Private Philanthropy to Public Needs." In *Research Papers of the Commission on Private Philanthropy and Public Needs*. Vol. 2. Washington, DC: Department of Treasury, 1977.

491. Smith, David Horton. "Voluntary Action and Voluntary Groups." *Annual Review of Sociology*. Vol. 1. Edited by A. Inkles, J. Coleman and N. Smelser. Palo Alto: Annual Reviews, 1975.

492. Smith, David Horton. *Voluntary Sector: Policy Research Needs*. Washington, DC: The Center for a Voluntary Society, 1974.

493. Smith, David Horton, ed. *The Nature of Voluntary Action Around the World. Voluntary Action Research*. Lexington, MA: Lexington Books, 1974.

494. Smith, David Horton; Baldwin, B.; and Chittick, W. "U.S. National Voluntary Organizations, Transnational Orientations and Development." In *Volunteers, Voluntary Associations, and Development,* edited by D. H. Smith and F. Elkin. Leiden, Netherlands: Brill., 1981.

495. Smith, David Horton, and Dixon, John. "The Voluntary Society." In *Challenge to Leadership—Managing in a Changing World*. The Conference Board. New York: The Free Press, 1971.

496. Smith, David Horton, et al. "The Non-Profit Sector." In *The Non-Profit Organization Handbook,* edited by Tracy Conners. New York: McGraw-Hill, 1978.

497. Smith, David Horton, et al. "Types of Voluntary Action: A Definitional Essay." In *Voluntary Action Research, 1972*. Lexington, MA: Lexington Books, 1972.

498. Smith, Hayden. "Profile of Corporate Contributions Since the Filer Commiss .. In *Working Papers for Spring Research Forum: Since the Filer Commission.*" Washington, DC: Independent Sector, 1983.

499. Smith, T. V. "George Herbert Mead and the Philosophy of Philanthropy." *Social Service Review* 61 (1932).

500. Sommer, John G. *Beyond Charity: U.S. Voluntary Aid for a Changing Third World*. Washington, DC: Overseas Development Council, 1979.

501. Steele, Richard, and Addison, Joseph. "The Art of Conferring Benefits." In *Essays: English and American*, edited by Raymond MacDonald Alden. Chicago: Scott, Foresman & Co., Chicago, 1927. Originally published in *Spectator*, no. 248, Friday, December 14, 1711.

501. Steiner, G. A., and Steiner, J. F. *Business, Government and Society: A Managerial Perspective*. New York: Random House, 1980.

503. Stewart, William Rhinelander. *The Philanthropic Work of Josephine Shaw Lowell*. New York: Macmillan Co., 1911.

504. Stinson, Thomas F., and Stam, Jerome M. "Toward an Economic Model of Voluntarism: The Case of Participation in Local Government." *Journal of Voluntary Action Research* 5, no. 1 (1976): 52-60.

505. Stokes, Bruce. *Helping Ourselves: Local Solutions to Global Problems*. New York: W. W. Norton & Co., 1981.

506. Sugarman, Norman A. "Community Foundations." In *Research Papers of the Commission on Private Philanthropy and Public Needs*. Vol. 3. Washington, DC: Department of Treasury, 1977.

507. Suhrke, Henry. "Self-Regulation within the Philanthropic Sector." In *Working Papers for Spring Research Forum: Since the Filer Commission*. Washington, DC: Independent Sector, 1983.

508. Sullivan, Robert R. "The Politics of Altruism: An Introduction to the Food-For-Peace Partnership Between the United States Government and Voluntary Relief Agencies." *The Western Political Quarterly* 23, no. 4 (1970): 762.

509. Sumariwalla, Russy. "Preliminary Observations on Scope, Size and Classification of the Sector Since the Filer Commission." In *Working Papers for Spring Research Forum: Since the Filer Commission*. Washington, DC: Independent Sector, 1983.

510. Tebbel, John William. *The Inheritors: A Study of America's Great Fortunes and What Happened to Them*. New York: G. P. Putnam's Sons, 1962.

511. Thomas, Benjamin P. *Theodore Weld: Crusader for Freedom*. New Brunswick, NJ: Rutgers University Press, 1950.

512. Thomas, Lewis. "Altruism: Self-Sacrifice for Others." *The Saturday Evening Post*, May/June, 1982.

513. Thompson, Earl. "Charity and Nonprofit Organizations." In *The Economics of Nonproprietary Organizations*, edited by Kenneth Clarkson and Donald Martin. Greenwich, CT: JAI Press, Inc., 1980.

514. Thoreau, Henry David. "Civil Disobedience" (1848). In *Walden and Civil Disobedience,* edited by Owen Thomas. New York: W. W. Norton & Co., 1966.

515. Thoreau, Henry David. "Economy." *Walden,* Chapter 1. Columbus, OH: Charles E. Merrill Co., 1969.

516. Titmuss, Richard Morris. *The Gift Relationship.* London: George Allen & Unwin, Ltd., 1963.

517. Tjerandsen, Carl. *Education for Citizenship: A Foundation's Experience.* Santa Cruz, CA: Emil Schwarzhaupt Foundation, Inc., 1980.

518. Tomeh, A. K. "Formal Voluntary Organizations: Participation, Correlates, and Interrelationships." *Sociological Inquiry* 43 (1976): 89-122.

519. Toy, Kathryn. *Annual Survey of Corporate Contributions.* 1982 ed. New York: The Conference Board, Inc., 1982.

520. Trattner, Walter I. *From Poor Law to Welfare State: A History of Social Welfare in America.* New York: The Free Press, 1974.

521. "True and False Philanthropy." *Newly Revised Eclectic Reader,* edited by William W. McGuffey. Cincinnati, OH: 1844.

522. Tsu Yu-yue. *Spirit of Chinese Philanthropy: A Study in Mutual Aid.* 1912. Reprint. New York: AMS Press, 1978.

523. Turner, W. Homer. *Corporate Philanthropy in a Free Society: The First 25 Years of the U.S. Steel Foundation, 1978.* Unpublished.

524. Tyler, Alice Felt. *Freedom's Ferment.* 1944. Reprint. Freeport, NY: Books for Libraries Press, 1970.

525. Tyler, Gus, ed. *Mexican-Americans Tomorrow.* Albuquerque: University of New Mexico Press, 1975.

526. United Church of Christ, Office of Church Life and Leadership. *The Ministry of Volunteers: A Guidebook for Churches* (seven manuals). United Church of Christ, 1979.

527. U.S. Congress, House Select Committee to Investigate Foundations and Other Organizations. *Final Report,* 82nd Congress, 2nd session. House Report 2524. Washington, DC: Government Printing Office, 1953.

528. U.S. Department of Labor. *American Volunteer.* Washington, DC: U.S. Department of Labor, Manpower Administration, 1969.

529. U.S. Office of Education. *The Mexican American: Quest for Equality.* Washington, DC: Office of Education, 1968.

530. U.S. News and World Report. *People Helping People.* Washington, DC: U.S. News and World Report, Inc., 1971.

531. United Way of America. *People and Events: A History of the United Way.* Alexandria, VA: United Way of America, 1977.

532. United Way of America. *Youth and Voluntarism, highlights of the Report of the Critical Issue Subcommittee on Youth and Voluntarism.* Alexandria, VA: United Way of America, 1981.

533. Van Til, Jon. "Mixed Motives: Residues of Altruism in an Age of Narcissism." In *Working Papers for Spring Research Forum: Since the Filer Commission.* Washington, DC: Independent Sector, 1983.

534. Van Til, Jon. "Volunteering and Democratic Theory." In *Volunteerism in the Eighties,* edited by John D. Harman. pp. 199-220. Washington, DC: University Press of America, 1982.

535. Vandiver, Susan T. "A Herstory of Women in Social Work." *Women's Issues and Social Work Practice,* edited by Elaine Norman and Arlene Mancuso. Itasca, IL: F.E. Peacock Publishers, Inc., 1980.

536. Vasquez, Thomas. "Corporate Giving Measurements." In *Research Papers of the Commission on Private Philanthropy and Public Needs.* Vol. 3. Washington, DC: Department of Treasury, 1977.

537. Verba, Sidney, and Nie, Norman H. *Participation in America.* New York: Harper & Row, 1972.

538. Verity, C. William, Jr. "The Future is in Our Hands." Remarks delivered at the Midwest Governors' Conference, Milwaukee, Wisconsin, August 31, 1981. Pamphlet reprint by ARMCO.

539. Vermazen, Bruce. "General Beliefs and the Principle of Charity." *Philosophical Studies* 42 (June 1982): 111-118.

540. "Voluntary Health and Welfare Agencies in the United States," an exploratory study by an Ad Hoc Citizens Committee. Robert H. Hamlin, Study Director. New York: The Schoolmasters' Press, 1961.

541. *Voluntary Sector Policy Research Needs.* Washington, DC: Center for a Voluntary Society, 1974.

542. *Volunteer: A Weekly Magazine* 1, no. 1-5 (April 1869-May 1869). New York: Foley & Co., 1869.

543. *Volunteering in America, 1981-1982: A Status Report.* Arlington, VA: Volunteer: The National Center for Citizen Involvement, 1982.

544. Vonhoff, Heinz. *People Who Care, An Illustrated History of Human Compassion.* Philadelphia: Fortress Press, 1971.

545. Vosburgh, William W. "Client Rights, Advocacy and Volunteerism." In *Volunteerism in the Eighties,* edited by John D. Harman. pp. 75-93. Washington, DC: University Press of America, 1982.

546. Vosburgh, William W., and Hyman, Drew. "Advocacy and Bureaucracy: The Life and Times of a Decentralized Citizens' Advocacy Program." *Administrative Science Quarterly* 18, no. 4 (December 1973).

547. Waldhorn, Steven. "The Independent Sector Role in Government Reform." In *Working Papers for Spring Research Forum: Since the Filer Commission.* Washington, DC: Independent Sector, 1983.

548. Walker, Sydnor H. "Privately Supported Social Work." In *Recent Social Trends in the United States* (Report of the President's Research Committee on Social Trends), edited by Lewis A. Coser and Walter W. Powell. 1933. Reprint. Salem, NH: Arno, 1979.

549. Walzer, Michael. *Radical Principles: Reflections of an Unreconstructed Democrat.* New York: Basic Books, 1980.

550. Walzer, Michael. *Spheres of Justice, A Defense of Pluralism and Equality.* New York: Basic Books, 1983.

551. Warner, Amos G. *American Charities.* Revised by Mary Coolidge. New York: Russell Sage Foundation, 1971.

552. Warner, Amos G; Queen, Stuart A.; and Harper, Ernest B. *American Charities and Social Work.* New York: Thomas Y. Cromwell, 1930.

553. Washington, Booker T. "How to Help Men Most With Money." *The World's Work,* May 1910, pp. 13087-13088.

554. Washington, Booker T. "Raising Money." *Up from Slavery,* Chapter 12. Garden City, NY: Harper & Row, 1963.

555. Watson, Frank Dekker. *The Charity Organization Movement in the United States.* New York: Macmillan Co., 1922.

556. Weaver, Warren. *Alfred P. Sloan, Jr., Philanthropist.* Occasional Paper. New York: Alfred P. Sloan Foundation, 1975.

557. Weaver, Warren. *U.S. Philanthropic Foundations: Their History, Structure, Management, and Record.* New York: Harper & Row, 1967.

558. Webb, Ronald J. "Organizational Effectiveness and the Voluntary Organization." *Academy of Management Journal* 17 (December 1974): 663-677.

559. Weisberger, Bernard A. *They Gathered at the River: The Story of the Great Revivalists and Their Impact Upon Religion in America.* New York: Quadrangle/The New York Times Book Co., 1958.

560. Weisbrod, Burton A. "Toward a Theory of the Voluntary Non-Profit Sector in a Three-Sector Economy." In *Altruism, Morality, and Economic Theory*, edited by Edmund S. Phelps. New York: Russell Sage Foundation, 1974.

561. Weisbrod, Burton A. *The Voluntary Non-Profit Sector: An Economic Analysis*. Lexington, MA: D.C. Heath Co., 1977.

562. Weitzman, Murray S. "Measuring the Number, Hours Spent and Dollar Value of Volunteer Activity of Americans." In *Working Papers for Spring Research Forum: Since the Filer Commission*. Washington, DC: Independent Sector, 1983.

563. Whitaker, Ben. *The Philanthropoids: Foundations and Society*. New York: William Morrow & Co., Inc., 1974.

564. Wilhelm, Marion. "Voluntary Foreign Aid: 25 Years of Partnership." In *War on Hunger*. Washington, DC: Agency for International Development, 1971.

565. Williams, Peter, and Moyes, Adrian. *Not By Governments Alone: The Role of British Non-Governmental Organizations in the Development Decade*. London: Overseas Development Institute Ltd., 1964.

566. Wilson, Marlene. *The Effective Management of Volunteer Programs*. Boulder, CO: Volunteer Management Associates, 1976.

567. Winston, Ellen. "Some Aspects of Private Philanthropy in Relation to Social Welfare." In *Research Papers of the Commission on Private Philanthropy and Public Needs*. Vol. 2. Washington, DC: Department of Treasury, 1977.

568. Winthrop, John. "A Model of Christian Charity." In *The American Puritans*, edited by Perry Miller. Garden City, NY: Anchor Books, 1956.

569. Wolfe, Joan. *Making Things Happen: The Guide for Members of Volunteer Organizations*. Andover, MA: Brick House Pub. Co., 1981.

570. Wolfenden Committee Report. *The Future of Voluntary Organizations*. London: Croom Helm, 1978.

571. "Women and Charitable Work." *The Cornhill Magazine* 30 (July December 1874): 417-427.

572. Woodhouse, A. S. *Puritanism and Liberty*. Chicago: University of Chicago Press, 1957.

573. Woodhouse, Chase Going. "Volunteer Community Work." In *American Women: The Changing Image*, edited by Beverly Benner Cassara. Boston: Beacon Press, 1962.

574. Woodson, Robert. "Helping the Poor Help Themselves." *Policy Review*, no. 21, Summer 1982.

575. Woodson, Robert. *Turning Problems Into Opportunities*. Policy Dispatch No. 3. Washington, DC: National Center for Neighborhood Enterprise, 1983.

576. *Working Papers for Spring Research Forum: Since the Filer Commission*. Washington, DC: Independent Sector, 1983.

577. Wortman, Max S., Jr. "A Radical Shift from Bureaucracy to Strategic Management in Voluntary Organizations." In *Volunteerism in the Eighties*, edited by John D. Harman. pp. 161-191. Washington, DC: University Press of America, 1982.

578. Wycherley, R. E. *How the Greeks Built Cities*. New York: W. W. Norton & Co., 1976.

579. Wyllie, Irvin G. "The Reputation of the American Philanthropist." *Social Service Review* 32 (1958): 215-222.

580. Yarmolinsky, Adam. "The Foundation as an Expression of a Democratic Society." In *Proceedings of the Fifth Biennial Conference on Charitable Foundations*, edited by Henry Sellin. Albany, NY: Matthew Bender, 1961.

581. Yarmolinsky, Adam. "Philanthropic Activity in International Affairs." In *Research Papers of the Commission on Private Philanthropy and Public Needs*. Vol. 2. Washington, DC: Department of Treasury, 1977.

582. Yarmolinsky, Adam, and Fremont-Smith, Marion R. "Judicial Remedies and Related Topics." In *Research Papers of the Commission on Private Philanthropy and Public Needs*. Vol. 5. Washington, DC: Department of Treasury, 1977.

583. Young, Dennis. *If Not for Profit, for What?* Lexington, MA: D.C. Heath Co., 1983.

584. Young, Ruth C., and Larson, Olaf F. "The Contribution of Voluntary Organizations to Community Structure." *American Journal of Sociology* 71 (September 1965): 178-186.

585. Zablocki, Benjamin D. *The Joyful Community*. Baltimore: Penguin, 1971.

586. Zollman, Carl. *American Law of Charities*. Milwaukee: Bruce Publishing Co., 1924.

587. Zurcher, Arnold J. *Management of American Foundations: Administration, Policies, and Social Role*. New York: New York University Press, 1972.

588. Zurcher, Arnold J., and Dustan, Jane. *The Foundation Administrator: A Study of Those Who Manage America's Foundations*. New York: Russell Sage Foundation, 1972.

589. Zurcher, Louis A. "Ephemeral Roles, Voluntary Action and Voluntary Associations." *Journal of Voluntary Action Research* 7, no. 3-4 (1978): 65-74.

590. Zurcher, Louis A. *Poverty Warriors*. Austin: University of Texas Press, 1970.

Index

DATE DUE

OCT 22 '96			

DEMCO 38-297